M000247815

VSAM
Architecture, Theory, and Applications

VSAM

Architecture, Theory, and Applications

Larry Brumbaugh

McGraw-Hill, Inc.

New York St. Louis San Francisco Auckland Bogotá Caracas
Lisbon London Madrid Mexico City Milan Montreal New Delhi
Paris San Juan São Paulo Singapore Sydney Tokyo Toronto

Library of Congress Cataloging-in-Publication Data

Brumbaugh, Larry J. 1943-
  VSAM : architecture, theory, and applications / by Larry Brumbaugh.

  Includes index.
  1. Virtual computer systems.
I. Title.
QA76.9.V5B78 1992   005.4'3—dc20   92-6031
ISBN 0-07-008606-0 (h)

Copyright © 1993 by McGraw-Hill. Printed in the United
States of America. Except as permitted under the United States
Copyright Act of 1976, no part of this publication may be reproduced
or distributed in any form or by any means, or stored in a database
or retrieval system, without the prior written permission of the
publishers.

1 2 3 4 5 6 7 8 9 0 DOC/DOC 9 7 6 5 4 3 1

ISBN 0-07-008606-0

*The sponsoring editor for this book was Gerald T. Papke. The editor was Lori
Flaherty, and the production supervisor was Katherine G. Brown. This book
was set in CG Century.*

Printed and bound by R.R. Donnelly & Sons Company.

Information contained in this work has been obtained by McGraw-
Hill, Inc., from sources believed to be reliable. However, neither
McGraw-Hill nor its authors guarantees the accuracy or completeness of any information published herein and neither McGraw-Hill
nor its authors shall be responsible for any errors, omissions, or
damages arising out of use of this information. This work is published with the understanding that McGraw-Hill and its authors are
supplying information but are not attempting to render engineering
or other professional services. If such services are required, the
assistance of an appropriate professional should be sought.

*For more information about other McGraw-Hill materials,
call 1-800-2-MCGRAW in the United States. In other
countries, call your nearest McGraw-Hill office.*

To Diane, Susan, and Marie

Contents

Part 2

Part 3

Acknowledgments

I would like to thank all the following people for their help in developing this book. This help ranged from reviewing one or more chapters, contributing ideas and encouragement, to actually putting the book together: Kraig Angel, Patrica Bilan, Marie Brumbaugh, Susan Brumbaugh, Terri Early, Chris Elzer, Kevin Fahling, Brian Hartsock, Dave Kephart, Priscilla Krampitz, JoEllen Moore, Feng Oin li, Toni Obermeier, Roberta Pape, and Terry Plickbaum.

I would also like to thank Michael Wiese for a very thorough and detailed review of the entire manuscript. I am also grateful for the help provided by Lee Moulic and his staff at the Illinois State University Computer Center. Finally, I would like to thank Diane Brumbaugh for her support in all aspects of the development of this book.

Introduction

VSAM, or *Virtual Storage Access Method*, is composed of two parts: a group of data set organizations (often called types of files) and an accompanying collection of system software (called access methods and utilities) for programmers to process individual records in a data set and the complete data set itself. VSAM's software interface allows disk data to be processed and stored in a relatively "user friendly" way. VSAM is used on more than 95 percent of IBM mainframe computer systems.

Although VSAM was introduced in 1973, it did not gain widespread popularity until almost a decade later. Before VSAM was developed, IBM mainframe computer systems used an older group of data set organizations and software developed in the mid 1960s when the IBM 360 computer was introduced. These older types of files are called non-VSAM data set organizations. Throughout the 1970s and early 1980s, both non-VSAM and VSAM data sets co-existed on most computer systems. Today, however, IBM has instituted a long-range plan to replace non-VSAM data set organizations with their VSAM equivalents.

Because IBM mainframe computers are used by almost every organization that has a large data processing shop, including most of the *Fortune* 500 (1,000) companies, approximately 50 percent of all business application programming is done on IBM mainframe computer systems. In fact, many large and medium-sized data processing shops have completed their conversion to VSAM, and is now heavily used in the data processing environment. Therefore, even if it is not a present requirement, some knowledge of VSAM will eventually be essential for anyone who works on IBM mainframe computer systems.

Environments Where VSAM Is Used

Not only is VSAM very popular, it is an extremely versatile software product. There are four major processing environments where VSAM is used. First, VSAM can be employed as a stand-alone product. In this context, the various types of VSAM data sets can be created and processed by a powerful general-purpose utility program called IDCAMS, which is included with the VSAM system software. Second, when a (batch) application program written in COBOL, PL/I, assembler, etc., processes disk data, the records are commonly stored in VSAM data sets. These first two environments, VSAM data sets, IDCAMS and COBOL programs, are used to form the most popular complete application programming system in the world today.

The third VSAM environment is data set management. PDS (library) directories, catalogs, and Generation Data Groups are the three structures commonly used to manage groups of data sets. Catalogs and Generation Data Groups are themselves VSAM data sets, and there are specific IDCAMS commands to manipulate each of them, and PDS directories to a lesser extent. Furthermore, the IDCAMS utility can also process older, non-VSAM data set organizations in various ways. IDCAMS has become the most important utility on MVS systems supplanting the IEB/IEH family of utilities.

Fourth, many major IBM software products, including CICS, IMS, DB2, and TSO, either require that only VSAM data sets be used with them or use VSAM heavily. Sophisticated CICS and IMS processing requires substantial VSAM knowledge. Typically, significant work with many important software products on IBM systems requires some VSAM expertise. This includes teleprocessing (TP) monitors and database management systems (DMS) developed by both IBM and independent vendors.

VSAM: Architecture, Theory, and Applications is organized into four basic categories. Part 1 contains introductory and prerequisite information relevant to all four of VSAM's environments. The material in Part 1 is used throughout the rest of the book. The next two VSAM environments are encountered initially by most VSAM users. These topics are examined in Part 2 and Part 3. The third and fourth VSAM environments deal with more advanced concepts and are covered in Part 4.

VSAM can be learned by attending a seminar such as those offered by various independent vendors and taught in-house at some large data processing shops; independent self-study combined with hands-on, job-related experience; and a formal college course. *VSAM: Architecture, Theory, and Applications* can be used in conjunction with all three of these approaches. In fact, much of the material in this book has been used in my VSAM Personal Development Seminars, which I teach. It is an extremely effective teaching aid. It is an excellent self-study tool for many of the same reasons that it is a good textbook for a formal course and a reference—because of its order of presentation, choice of topics, and clarity.

Two and four-year colleges and universities with curriculum to train people for careers as programmers and analysts often teach VSAM-related material in one or more courses. The specific topics and the amount of time vary considerably among courses and schools. Some VSAM-related material can be studied in any of the following types of courses: COBOL (also PL/I and assembler language) programming, file design, CICS, database, data structures, operating systems, JCL, some combination of these, or perhaps other courses altogether.

VSAM Hardware and Software Environments

VSAM can be used with all three of the major IBM mainframe operating systems: MVS, VM, and VSE. Furthermore, VSAM data sets can be stored on almost all standard disk drives, including the 3390, 3380, 3350, 3370, etc. As mentioned before, most present and all foreseeable future IBM mainframe software products will be developed to process disk records stored in VSAM data sets.

There is no product on the immediate or even distant horizon that is discussed as the eventual successor for VSAM. Today's database management systems are too inflexible to replace VSAM in the same way that no existing fourth generation language has the same scope as the COBOL language. Hence, unlike many other major software products, VSAM is certain to enjoy a tremendously long lifetime, perhaps extending into the next century.

As IBM's Systems Application Architecture (SAA) becomes more thoroughly implemented, a VSAM compatible (either identical or merely equivalent) data set organization will be available on all IBM systems in the very near future, even those mini and micro computers where VSAM is not presently supported. Hence, it is quite likely that there will be many more VSAM users and VSAM applications. Furthermore, the power, flexibility, and range of VSAM processing will continue to increase. Most VSAM users today can provide a wish list of additional VSAM features that they would like to see available that should not be difficult to develop, but are not yet supported.

Finally, future VSAM software will almost certainly permit substantially more transparency than is currently available. The casual user and beginning programmer will welcome this transparency, but the true professional will still want to know the underlying details about how VSAM actually works and how best to use it.

How This Book Is Organized

VSAM: Architecture, Theory, and Applications is designed for use as a textbook. Topics are presented so that the book can be used both as a text for a course where VSAM is the major topic and a portion of a course where VSAM is one of the major topics. In the later case, the material in Parts 2, 3, and 1 are emphasized, in that order.

Because VSAM is usually studied as part of another course topic (COBOL, CICS, JCL, operating systems, etc.), some independence and overlap is built into the organization of the book. This small amount of repetition should not be confused with the heavy redundancy found in many IBM manuals, such as the IDCAMS manual. Rather, minimal repetition provides some additional independence for several topics.

Because it is meant to be used as a textbook, exercises are included with every chapter, ranging from straightforward short-answer questions to analyzing and developing theoretical concepts. Almost every chapter contains at least one sophisticated programming exercise and usually one or more exercises that require extensions to the material in the chapter. No other existing VSAM book is actually designed to be used as a text.

VSAM: Architecture, Theory, and Applications can be used as a reference. It is clearly preferable to IBM VSAM manuals as a source of specific, detailed information. Otherwise, the IBM manuals would be used as the reference source. This book is not as detailed as the manuals or discuss all aspects of a topic. Rather, for those topics in which the typical application programmer might have a strong or even moderate interest, the book is a superior source of information.

VSAM: Architecture, Theory, and Applications contains a more reader-friendly version of the concept/topic, information is easy to locate, and important concepts and topics are meaningfully illustrated in one or more relevant examples. By comparison, IBM manuals are infamous for containing numerous irrelevant and absurd examples. Furthermore, the written text in IBM manuals describing a topic or concept is often too brief or vague, or both.

For each major topic in the book, significant advantages or strengths and disadvantages or weaknesses associated with the topic are identified. Probable forthcoming changes in a specific area is also covered—the type of information most casual VSAM users are not aware of.

Various topics require prerequisite information discussed in earlier chapters. Significant interrelationships among topics are discussed in several places throughout the book. Every chapter begins with either an introductory paragraph containing a brief list of the topics and objectives to be covered in the chapter.

There are four types of computer listings that are important in this book: message data sets produced by IDCAMS, IDCAMS control statements, (COBOL) application program code, and JCL statements. Each of these important topics all has a role in the book.

IDCAMS message data sets are referenced in every chapter in Part 2 and chapters 10 and 11 in Part 3. Most of these message data sets are generated by DEFINE, PRINT, and LISTCAT commands. IDCAMS control statement listings are found in every chapter in Part 2 and also throughout Parts 3 and 4. COBOL code is found only in Part 3 and Part 4 (with CICS and Linear Data Sets). Several JCL listings are also included throughout the book.

Part 1 contains a general introduction to VSAM, discusses its scope, and describes its underlying internal structure. Much of the material in chapter 2 is probably not known to someone who learned VSAM haphazardly or uses VSAM sparingly. However, some knowledge of the material in chapter 2 (VSAM's internal organization) is absolutely essential in order to use VSAM efficiently in any setting. Likewise, chapter 1 contains an extremely important "big picture" discussion of VSAM's role in modern data processing.

A thorough understanding of the topics in Parts 2 through 4 of the book requires some knowledge of VSAM's internal structure and the role of the topic in a larger setting. However, various parts of the book require either a superficial knowledge or no knowledge of VSAM's internal structure. The only chapters that require almost no knowledge of internal structure are chapters 3, 13, and 14. Chapters 4, 5, 6, 7, and 17 require a very detailed knowledge.

Part 2 discusses the IDCAMS utility program and several closely related topics. The five chapters describe how IDCAMS is used to create and process, in a wide variety of settings, every type of VSAM-related object, except for catalogs, non-VSAM data sets, and Generation Data Groups. Much of the material in chapters 3, 6, and 7 is either not known or is only superficially understood. Part 2 of the book, along with chapter 8 in Part 3, can be used to teach a short course that concentrates on the mechanical aspects of creating and processing VSAM data sets.

The four chapters in Part 3 emphasize the processing of VSAM data sets in an application program. Chapters 10 and 11 provide additional information related specifically to the ESDS and RRDS. COBOL programming is emphasized throughout Part 3, and chapter 9 is one of the lengthiest chapters in the book. Various (short) segments of actual COBOL code are used throughout chapters 9, 10, and 11 to illustrate the concepts being discussed. For each of the three types of VSAM data sets, one complete meaningful COBOL program illustrating a wide range of processing is examined in detail.

A dynamic (both random and sequential) master file update program is examined with both a KSDS and an RRDS. An alternate index is used with the KSDS. With an ESDS, a sequential update program is illustrated. Material not specifically related to processing VSAM data sets is omitted or deemphasized in the COBOL programs.

Part 4 of the book discusses VSAM's relationship with a variety of components found on large computer systems: catalogs, Generation Data Groups, optimization techniques, and Job Control Language (JCL). While a subset of the topics in Parts 1, 2, and 3 comprise the VSAM material known by an experienced application programmer, Part 4 contains more advanced and sophisticated material. Part 4 also focuses on VSAM's role with some of the most important software products commonly used in the IBM mainframe environment, specifically CICS, IMS, DBII, and TSO. Individual chapters examine the use of VSAM with a TP-monitor (CICS) and with a Data Base Management System (IMS and DBII).

VSAM: Architecture, Applications and Theory is intended for people with some basic knowledge of both data processing and programming on IBM systems. The following table identifies chapters in the book categorized as to whether they would be of interest to a particular audience. Each of the various audience groups apply to both self-study and to formal course study. An asterisk (*) indicates that just part of the chapter (50 percent or less) would be of interest.

Specific Reader Interest   **Relevant Chapters**

Learning VSAM from scratch   1,3*, 4, 5, 9

VSAM application programmer (COBOL)	1, 3*, 4, 6, 8, 9*, 10*, 11*, 16*
True VSAM expert application programmer	1 – 11, 13, 16
True VSAM expert All aspects of VSAM	All chapters, 1 – 17

Part

1

Chapter

1

Introduction to VSAM

During the early 1970s, IBM introduced a collection of three new data set organizations—sequential, indexed, and relative—along with their accompanying access methods and utilities to be used on their large mainframe computer systems. Access methods are system software that supply low-level technical details to programmers so they can perform I/O operations. These new access methods are collectively called *Virtual Storage Access Method (VSAM)*. The three new types of VSAM data sets—KSDS, ESDS, and RRDS—were initially developed to supplement existing non-VSAM data set organizations: sequential (QSAM), indexed (ISAM), direct (BDAM), and partitioned (PDS). VSAM data sets can only be stored on direct access storage devices. The VSAM access method itself, however, can be used with non-VSAM data sets and with non-DASD devices.

The three VSAM data set organizations are a substantial improvement over the older ones, which were developed almost a decade earlier. Moreover, there is no candidate for eventually replacing VSAM data sets and access method. This implies that an increasing number of people will be using VSAM data sets, and VSAM will remain a significant data processing vehicle for at least the next decade. Although this book emphasizes VSAM with a MVS operating system on a large mainframe computer, VSAM is available in other IBM hardware and software environments.

The word *virtual* means only that VSAM was introduced at approximately the same time as the initial IBM virtual storage operating systems: OS/VS1 and OS/VS2. Analogously, a similar access method, the Virtual Telecommunications Access Method (VTAM), is used to perform I/O operations with terminal devices. VTAM was introduced at approximately the same time, and the virtual portion of its name was selected for the same reason. There is nothing inherently virtual about either VSAM or VTAM.

3

In almost every comparison, VSAM is clearly superior to older data set organizations, yet initial acceptance of VSAM was neither swift nor widespread. There was, at that time, and to an extent still remains, a substantial personal, financial, and intellectual investment in the older data set organizations.

Many programmers were very familiar with existing data set types and did not want to convert to VSAM. Many data processing shops thought that the cost of converting to VSAM was too great for the benefits provided. Primarily because not all of the major VSAM components were initially released. In fact, it was several more years before important additional components became available and still several more years before major design shortcomings were corrected. For this reason, terms like *Original* VSAM, *Old* VSAM, *Enhanced* VSAM, and *New* VSAM are given to identify the various releases. These terms are defined and discussed in chapter 12. It was not until the early 1980s that VSAM finally became firmly entrenched on computers that used the MVS, VM, or VSE operating systems. The new and improved features of VSAM have helped speed acceptance and popularity.

Since the introduction of VSAM, IBM has gradually and successfully deemphasized older, non-VSAM data set organizations. A good example is the various COBOL and PL/I language reference manuals released during the years following the introduction of VSAM. Almost all the disk I/O material now discusses processing VSAM data sets. In recent COBOL manuals, much of the non-VSAM data set information has been relegated to an appendix, an exact opposite of mid-1970s manuals.

There is no doubt that the conversion to VSAM will continue as more new features and improvements are added and as new products are introduced that require VSAM data sets. In fact, some truly dramatic additions and changes have recently occurred. These include using VSAM to support DB2; using JCL to create and delete VSAM data sets, data encryption, and decryption; allocating VSAM data sets with TSO and several new diagnostic tools. DB2 is a relatively new and extremely popular database management system that uses VSAM data sets and is discussed in chapter 15. DB2 uses a fourth type of VSAM data set organization. Chapter 12 contains additional historic information on VSAM including a summary identifying how VSAM has changed over the years.

Why is it necessary to learn VSAM? Can the non-VSAM data sets suffice for most programming applications? Ten years ago, non-VSAM data sets were still being used for many programming applications. Today, it is absolutely essential that application programmers working in IBM data processing shops have a good, working knowledge of VSAM. VSAM concepts have also become important with IBM minicomputers and microcomputers. Since IBM has almost completely shifted away from most non-VSAM data set types, a prudent user must do likewise.

In addition to DB2, many popular IBM software products, including Customer Information Control Systems (CICS) and Information Management Systems (IMS), use VSAM data sets. It is difficult to thoroughly understand or even work productively with either CICS or IMS without some knowledge of VSAM. Most relatively new IBM system software products, such as DB2, use only VSAM data sets. The same is true for recent releases of existing products. For example, beginning with release 1.6 of CICS in 1985, only VSAM and BDAM data sets can be used with CICS. ISAM data sets are no longer supported, and BDAM is on the endangered data set organization list. Comparable changes from non-VSAM to VSAM data sets have also occurred with IMS.

The role of VSAM with a TP monitor, such as CICS and Data Base Management Systems, IMS and DB2, is described in two separate chapters in the final part of this book. There is also a strong connection between the Time Sharing Option (TSO) program and VSAM. In addition, with MVS, the system catalog structure consists of a master catalog, which must be a VSAM data set, and a number of user catalogs, which are also VSAM data sets.

Chronologically related data sets, called *Generation Data Sets*, are created, managed, and deleted with VSAM. Catalogs and Generation Data Sets are discussed in Part 4. As with any sophisticated software product, VSAM can be merely used or used effectively and efficiently. The final chapter in Part 4 examine methods for optimizing VSAM's performance.

Fundamental Advantages of VSAM

Many significant advantages result when a VSAM data set is used in a programming application, of which the most important advantages are summarized in Table 1.1, each of which is briefly discussed in this section. Here, these advantages are presented in an overview format and expanded upon in great detail throughout the book. These are the primary reasons for using VSAM:

- Very little JCL is needed to process a VSAM data set. Ordinarily, only the DSNAME and DISP parameters are coded on the DD statement for a VSAM data set. IBM justifiably claims this is a significant advantage of VSAM, because considerably more JCL is required with non-VSAM data sets. My philosophy, always code as little JCL as possible, agrees. Although I am the

TABLE 1.1   Major Advantages of Using VSAM Versus Earlier Types of Data Sets.

VSAM Advantage	Chapters
Processing VSAM data sets requires very little JCL.	3,12,13,14
VSAM builds and maintains alternate index data sets.	8
Up to 256 record fields can easily be used as keys.	8-11,16,17
Dynamic allocation identifies the data set in the source code.	3,5
Dynamic access simplifies high-level language coding.	9,11
Status codes are provided following every I/O operation.	3,9
VSAM automatically blocks records.	1,2
VSAM utility functions employ user-friendly commands.	3-8
The individual bytes in a data set can be addressed.	2,5,10
Useful information is maintained for each data set in its catalog entry and labels.	7,12

author of a moderately successful MVS JCL book, writing JCL is difficult. On the other hand, the lack of JCL can also create problems. It is necessary to learn how the types of information provided by JCL can be specified in some other way for a VSAM data set. Furthermore, at present, some features provided through JCL cannot easily be obtained in any other way. The role of JCL with VSAM data sets is discussed in chapters 3, 12, 13, and 14. Chapter 13 explains how JCL can, for the first time, be used to create and delete VSAM data sets.

- Records can be accessed through one or more secondary keys using alternate indexes constructed and maintained by VSAM. Chapter 8 discusses VSAM's alternate indexes.

- With two of the VSAM data set organizations, the KSDS and ESDS, any field within a logical record can be easily used as a key to sequentially or randomly process the records. Comparable processing is more complicated, but also possible with a third type of VSAM data set, the RRDS. Using alternate key fields is discussed in chapters 8, 9, 10, 11, with CICS (chapter 16), and with Optimization (chapter 17).

- VSAM data sets can be dynamically allocated. This means that a data set can be identified by name directly in the application program source code as an alternative to using the DSNAME parameter on a JCL DD statement. Dynamic allocation completely eliminates the need for JCL with a VSAM data set. Dynamic allocation is defined and discussed in chapter 3. It is heavily used throughout chapter 5.

- Two types of VSAM data sets, the KSDS and RRDS, allow dynamic access. This means that the records in a KSDS or RRDS can be processed both sequentially and randomly in the same COBOL program using just one SELECT and one FD statement. Chapters 9 and 11 examine dynamic access.

- After every VSAM I/O operation, a status code is returned that specifies the outcome of the operation. In addition, a VSAM I/O operation almost never causes a program to abend. Rather, VSAM allows subsequent operations regardless of the outcome of earlier I/O operations. Each IDCAMS command returns a condition code. Chapters 3 and 9 discuss codes returned by VSAM.

- The importance of user-defined blocking is greatly minimized because VSAM selects default blocking factors. Although not foolproof, disk (track) utilization is greatly improved with VSAM. Chapters 1 and 2 describe how VSAM data sets are stored on disk.

- VSAM utility functions employ user-friendly control statements, or at least as user-friendly as can be found in an IBM mainframe environment. The IDCAMS Utility is introduced in chapter 3 and is the major topic in Part 2.

- Individual bytes in a VSAM (disk) data set can be accessed using their address on the disk. Consequently, with a KSDS and ESDS, records can be randomly processed using their Relative Byte Address (RBA). This is an alternative to using keys or relative record numbers to identify records during random processing. Byte addressing imparts a structure to a disk data set that is usually associated only with main memory. It also greatly extends the processing capabilities of a VSAM data set. Relative Byte Addressing is discussed in some detail throughout the book, including chapters 2, 5, and 10.

- Both the catalog entry and the "labels" for a data set contain a great deal of important information about a VSAM data set that is not available with a non-VSAM data set. Much of this information is examined in chapters 7 and 12.

Three Major Types of VSAM Data Sets

Three VSAM data set organizations were initially introduced: Entry Sequenced Data Set (ESDS), Key Sequenced Data Set (KSDS), and Relative Record Data Set (RRDS). All three data set organizations were initially developed to improve processing capabilities and correct deficiencies found in older, non-VSAM data set organizations. Collectively, the three VSAM data set organizations are designed as alternatives to all of the non-VSAM data set organizations except for partitioned. This suggests that future enhancements might possibly include a VSAM partitioned data set. A VSAM user catalog provides a way to group together a collection of data sets. This is functionally similar to managing member data sets with a partitioned data set. However, current software doesn't thoroughly exploit this. Table 14.1 and Exercise 4 in chapter 14 examines the similarities between a user catalog and a PDS library.

Unlike non-VSAM data set organizations and their multiple access methods, the type of data set and the access method is identified together in VSAM. With all three types of VSAM data sets, the access method is simply identified as VSAM. The relationship between VSAM and non-VSAM data sets and access methods is shown in Table 1.2.

The next section describes the data set organizations that were available prior to VSAM. The following three sections then give a brief overview of the fundamental properties for the three types of VSAM data sets. Chapters 2 and 9 con-

TABLE 1.2   Relationship between VSAM and Non-VSAM Data Sets.

Types of Non-VSAM Data Set Organizations	Corresponding Non-VSAM Access Methods	Equivalent VSAM Data Set Organizations
Sequential	QSAM and BSAM	ESDS
Indexed(ISAM)	QISAM and BISAM	KSDS
Direct(relative, direct, REGIONAL (PL/I) and absolute)	BDAM and BSAM	RRDS (similar to non-VSAM relative) (REGIONAL I-PL/I)
Partitioned	BPAM (and also QSAM and BSAM for processing the individual members)	nothing comparable, but the user catalog notion shares some similarities

tain a detailed examination of the KSDS structure and the methods for processing it. Chapters 10 and 11 describe the ESDS and RRDS from several points of view, including comparing and contrasting each of them with a KSDS, with each other, and also with their equivalent non-VSAM data set organization.

Pre (Non) VSAM Data Set Organizations

In order to appreciate VSAM, it is necessary to know a little about its predecessors. Prior to the release of VSAM, there were four major data set organizations: sequential, indexed, direct access, and partitioned. Indexed and direct access have been almost completely replaced by their VSAM equivalent.

Records in sequential data sets can only be processed in order, one record after another, beginning with either the first or last record. No random processing is possible and no overheads, such as keys or indexes, are present. A sequential data set is often loosely referred to as a QSAM data set after one of the access methods used to process it. If only sequential processing is to be performed, a sequential data set is an excellent choice for storing records. The primary reason for its superiority is that it does not use indexes or keys. Furthermore, large blocking factors can be used to efficiently use disk storage. Sequential data sets need not be stored on disk. All in-stream, print, and tape data sets are sequential.

The pre-VSAM indexed data set is called *ISAM*. An indexed data set allows a mixture of both sequential and random processing. Because of this flexibility, an indexed data set can be used when a sequential data set is inappropriate. In order to support both random and sequential processing, each record has to contain a key field that uniquely identifies it and approximates its location on disk. Unfortunately, the index and keys are also required for sequential processing. There are major processing overheads with ISAM data sets:

- Records can only be logically, not physically, deleted.
- Record additions require an overflow area where existing records are bumped.
- Constant reorganization is necessary.
- Records are stored on disk in COUNT-KEY-DATA format.
- Storage is allocated only in cylinders.
- The KSDS is a dramatic improvement over an ISAM data set.

Direct access data sets process records based on their relative location on disk. The disk is divided into slots and a given record is assigned to a certain slot. The size of the slot can range from an area sufficient to hold just one record to an entire track. When multiple records are stored in a slot, they can be identified by a leading disk KEY field. Direct access data sets are the most flexible choice among non-VSAM data set organizations. They also require the most programmer work. Specifically, some of the data within the records must be used to identify the slot in which to store the record. Direct access data sets are used when most or all processing is random. Random processing can be performed fastest with a direct data set organization.

A partitioned data set (PDS), commonly called a library, consists of a directory and a member area. The members area in a library can contain one or more sequential data sets. Indexed and direct access data sets cannot be members. Libraries provide a convenient way to group and process multiple data sets. When the name of the library is specified, every data set within it is available for processing. Individual members can be identified in a variety of ways, most often by coding libraryname(membername). Every data set in the library should have the same basic characteristics.

Various comparisons between VSAM and non-VSAM data sets are made throughout the book, which can be safely ignored if you have absolutely no interest in non-VSAM data sets. At the other extreme, if you want more information on non-VSAM data set organizations and access methods, see chapters 9, 12, 13, and 14 in MVS JCL and Utilities. The advantages of VSAM are most fully appreciated by studying older, non-VSAM data set organizations.

Keyed Sequenced Data Set

A key sequenced data set, or KSDS, is an indexed data set with each KSDS record containing a unique key field value. The KSDS contains an index (or directory) that can be used to locate a specific record without having to sequentially search the entire data set. The index contains pairs that consist of a key value and the approximate location of the record with the associated key. All the pairs in the index are stored in order by ascending key value. However, only certain records have their keys stored in the index. All the types of I/O operations permitted with earlier indexed data set organizations, such as ISAM, are also allowed with a KSDS. In addition, a KSDS allows several operations not commonly supported by earlier indexed data sets. Variable length records are permitted with a KSDS, and a record can have its length changed during a rewrite operation.

Records in a KSDS can be processed sequentially and randomly. Sequential processing can begin with any record in the data set and proceed in either direction—forward or backward. Sequential processing in either direction is always performed in order based on the record's key values. During sequential processing, records can be rewritten or physically deleted. After a record is deleted, the space it formerly occupied is reclaimed for future use. A KSDS can be sequentially extended by adding records to the end of the data set. Records can be randomly retrieved in a variety of ways. During random processing, records can be inserted, modified, and physically deleted.

Both sequential and random processing can also be done using a VSAM secondary or alternate key. Alternate key values can be changed during a rewrite operation and do not need to be unique. Thus, records in a KSDS can be accessed in a variety of ways:

- Sequentially, both in order by record key value and reverse sequential.
- Randomly, using the primary key value.
- Sequentially and randomly with an alternate key value.
- Sequentially and randomly based on a record's location or address (RBA) in the data set.

Entry Sequenced Data Set

An entry sequenced data set, or ESDS, is used when records are ordinarily processed in the same order in which they were written to the data set, i.e., chronological order. Processing must begin with either the first or last record in the data set. An existing ESDS can be modified in two ways: it can be sequentially extended by adding records after the last record in the data set or existing records can be read and rewritten. Although variable length records are permitted, a record's length cannot be changed during a rewrite operation. Random record insertion and physical deletion are not possible, but logical deletion is allowed.

Unlike a non-VSAM sequential data set, individual ESDS records can be randomly processed in several ways, including using a relative byte address and alternate keys. These techniques are described in detail in chapter 10. In all cases, random processing operations with an ESDS requires a substantial amount of either system or programmer overhead.

Relative Record Data Set

A relative record data set, or RRDS, is the VSAM equivalent of a non-VSAM direct access data set organization, of which there are several types. An RRDS most closely resembles a non-VSAM relative data set. The disk storage allocated to the data set is divided into fixed length slots that are numbered consecutively beginning with 1. Records in an RRDS are stored in slots on the disk the same way data is stored in a table or array in memory. The slot number is used in the same way as a subscript or index is with an array. Because the slots in an RRDS are fixed length, the disk location of a specific record can be quickly calculated. Once initially created, an RRDS cannot ordinarily be extended. Unlike the KSDS and ESDS, VSAM will not directly support alternate key processing with an RRDS. Furthermore, RRDS records cannot be processed using their relative byte address.

An RRDS allows almost every other type of I/O operation permitted with a KSDS. Records in an RRDS can be processed both sequentially and randomly. However, with random processing, logical records are identified by their slot number rather than a key field value. Because no index is present, records in an RRDS can be randomly processed much faster than records in a comparable KSDS. Because random RRDS I/O operations can be performed so rapidly, considerable effort is often made to organize a collection of records into an

RRDS structure. However, most groups of records do not contain a field whose values can be used to determine a unique slot number for each record in the data set. When multiple records are assigned to the same slot number, substantial processing complications can occur. Chapter 11 covers some of the methods used to resolve these complications.

Comparing VSAM Data Set Organizations

Table 1.3 summarizes several significant properties for each of the three types of VSAM data sets. These properties are expanded upon throughout the rest of the book. Exercise 7 at the end of the chapter suggests developing a comparable table for non-VSAM data set organizations. The distinction of how records are stored in the three types of VSAM data sets is illustrated in Fig. 1.1.

Assume that there are five records to be stored, each of which is 150 bytes. Two disk blocks, or *control intervals* (the VSAM term), are needed to hold the records in an ESDS, while three control intervals are used with a KSDS and RRDS. As many records that will fit are placed in an ESDS control interval. With an RRDS and a KSDS, unused space can be reserved to subsequently

TABLE 1.3 Comparative Properties for the KSDS, ESDS, and RRDS.

Property	KSDS	ESDS	RRDS
Number of Components	3	2	2
Record Formats	Fixed and variable; also spanned	Fixed and variable; also spanned	Fixed Only
Change Record Size Allowed	Yes	No	No
Physical Deletion	Yes	No	Yes
Reclaim Deleted Records Space	Yes	No	Yes
VSAM/IDCAMS Alternate Index	Yes; uses primary key	Yes; uses RBA value	No; but can use a KSDS
Key Index	Yes	No	No
Random Retrieval Methods	Primary key Alternate keys RBA value	Alternate keys RBA value	Relative record number
Speed of Random Processing	Middle (3 step)	Slowest Requires alternate key	Fastest (1 step)
Speed of Sequential Processing	Middle	Fastest	Rarely used in applications
Sequential Retrieval Methods	Forwards and backwards by all keys and RBA	Forwards and backwards by RBA only	Forwards and backwards by relative record number

ESDS—Five Contiguous Records

REC 1	REC 2	REC 3		REC 4	REC 5			

0000   0512   1024

KSDS—Five Records Separated by Free space

REC 1 ALPHA	REC 2 BETA			REC 3 DELTA	REC 4 GAMMA			REC 5 RHO	

0000   0512   1024

RRDS—Five Active Records and Four Dummy Slots

DUMMY	REC 3 SLOT2	DUMMY		REC 1 SLOT4	REC 4 SLOT5	DUMMY		REC 5 SLOT7	DUMMY	REC 2 SLOT9

0000   0512   1024

Figure 1.1   The five records stored in three different VSAM data sets.

store additional records at a later time. In a KSDS, the 5-byte key field is contained within each record, and in an RRDS, some field in each record determines the slot number.

Processing Records

The standard types of record processing in a VSAM data set are done to modify the three data sets. For example, suppose a new record with a key field of CCCCC is added to each of the three data sets, written in slot 3 with the RRDS. Record number 2 is deleted from the three data sets. It is physically deleted from the KSDS and RRDS and logically deleted from the ESDS. Record number 5 is modified in all three data sets, and its length is increased in the KSDS. Figure 1.2 shows the three data sets after the processing is completed. Notice that the ESDS contains 6 records because the deleted one still exists. The records in the KSDS are in order by key field value. The fact that the record with a key of CCCCC is placed in the second control interval should be accepted. Exercise 11 contains more I/O operations that the three data sets can perform.

VSAM Alternate Indexes

To illustrate the structure of a data set with an alternate index over it, an alternate index will be built over both the KSDS and ESDS depicted in Fig. 1.1. An ID number is used as the (alternate) key field in each case. It should be noted that other than a 5-byte header field, the two values shown in the rectangles in Fig. 1.3 comprise the entire alternate index record. The same three types of changes previously discussed with the base KSDS and ESDS are performed again. These changes cause significant modifications in the alternate index structures. See Fig. 1.4.

Exercise 12 suggests a group of additional I/O operations that can be performed to the two base data sets with an emphasis on the changes that occur in the alternate indexes.

IBM Reference Manuals

There are several IBM manuals that are strongly recommended as excellent reference sources when studying VSAM, which I have identified as Manual (I) through Manual (VI) throughout this book. No book, including this one, contains the vast volume of VSAM information contained in these manuals. Along with the many releases of VSAM, the various manual titles have changed substantially over the years. Basically, there are five or six categories of manuals:

Transaction	Record Number	KSDS Details	RRDS Details	ESDS Details
Add	6	Key=CCCCC	Slot Number=3	Last record
Delete	2	Physical	Physical	Logical
Modify	5	Length	Length	Length
		Changed	the Same	the Same
		Random	Random	Sequential
		Rewrite	Rewrite	Rewrite

ESDS—Six Contiguous Records

REC 1	REC 2 Delet	REC 3		REC 4	REC 5 Mod	REC 6 New		

0000   0512   1024

KSDS—Five Variable Length Records and Free space

REC 1 ALPHA			REC 6 CCCCC	REC 3 DELTA	REC 4 GAMMA		REC 5 RHO	

0000   0512   1024

RRDS—Five Active Records and Four Dummy Slots

DUMMY	REC 3 SLOT2	REC 6 SLOT3		REC 1 SLOT4	REC 4 SLOT5	DUMMY		REC 5 SLOT7	DUMMY	DUMMY

0000   0512   1024

Figure 1.2 The three data sets following update processing.

Record Number	RBA ESDS	RBA KSDS	KSDS Key Field	ID Number in each record
1	0000	0000	ALPHA	111
2	0150	0150	BETA	999
3	0300	0512	DELTA	222
4	0512	0662	GAMMA	600
5	0662	1024	RHO	567

Alternate Index Over the KSDS

| 111 ALPHA | 222 DELTA | 567 RHO | 600 GAMMA | | | 999 BETA | UNUSED |

Alternate Index Over the ESDS

| 111 0000 | 222 0300 | 567 0662 | 600 0512 | 999 0150 | | | EMPTY |

Figure 1.3   Records stored in a VSAM alternate index.

(I)   Using the IDCAMS utility
(II)   How VSAM data sets are put together and work.
(III)   VSAM technical details.
(IV)   VSAM catalog structure.
(V and VI) Using VSAM within a (COBOL) application program. Here, both the "old" COBOL and the COBOL2 manuals are listed.

- Add a sixth record with an ID number of 575 and a key field of CCCCC.
- Physically delete record 3 from the KSDS, and logically delete record 3 from the ESDS.
- Modify record 5 in the process, changing its ID number from 567 to 167. Whether its length changes in the base data set is irrelevant in the alternate index structure.

Updated Alternate Index Over the KSDS

| 111 ALPHA | 167 RHO | 575 CCCCC | 600 GAMMA | | | 999 BETA | UNUSED |

Updated Alternate Index Over The ESDS

| 111 0000 | 167 0662 | 575 0812 | 600 0512 | 899 0150 | | | EMPTY |

Figure 1.4   Alternate index records following update processing.

**(I)   MVS/XA Integrated Catalog Administration
AMS Reference GC26-4135 or OS/VS2 Access
Method Services—IBM Manual GC26-3841**

Manual I describes the IDCAMS utility program and provides a good overview of many VSAM features. It is an easy manual to read, and the material in the manual is language-independent. It is also easy to quickly locate specific information because it contains a considerable amount of redundancy.

(II)   OS/VS VSAM Programmer's Guide—IBM Manual GC26-3838

Manual II contains a detailed technical description of many important VSAM features. The first 100 pages of the manual is language-independent and should be required reading for any application programmer using VSAM. The second part of the manual describes the VSAM macro commands in great detail and requires some knowledge of assembler language.

**(III)   OS/VS VSAM Options for Advanced Applications—
IBM Manual GC26-3819**

Manual III explains the internal structure of a VSAM data set. It also includes a detailed discussion of the RDF and CIDF control fields and the structure of an index control interval, including index entries, section entries, key compression, and free control interval pointers. The entire manual (approximately 80 pages) is required reading for the serious VSAM student. Some sections require a knowledge of assembler language.

**(IV)   IBM VS COBOL for OS/VS—
IBM Manual GC26-3857 or IBM COBOL2**

The syntax required to use VSAM in a COBOL application program is included in manual IV. There is also a comparable PL/I manual. Chapters 9, 10, and 11 reference this material as well as manual V.

**(V)   IBM OS/VS COBOL Programmer's Guide—
IBM Manual SC28-6483 IBM COBOL2 Manual**

The relevant material in V and VI manuals concentrates on the interface between an application program and VSAM. Topics other than just syntax are discussed. There is a comparable PL/I manual.

The IDCAMS Utility Program

A powerful, general-purpose utility program called IDCAMS is used to create VSAM data sets. IDCAMS can also be used to perform a wide range of processing on VSAM data sets. IDCAMS is pronounced either I-D-cams or id-CAMS. In addition to numerous VSAM unique functions, IDCAMS can also

perform many of the same basic types of processing that the non-VSAM utilities (IEBxxx and IEHxxx) perform with non-VSAM data sets. There are
approximately 15 IEB/IEH utilities, each of which can perform a limited range
of functions. IDCAMS, on the other hand, consist of more than 20 commands,
each of which performs a specific type of processing. Hence, the IDCAMS
commands are capable of duplicating most of the processing functions performed by IEB/IEH utilities.

IDCAMS is one of the two important "VSAM-type" DF/DS utilities. The
other is the data management program, formerly known as ADRDSSU, that is
used to perform such functions as backing up and restoring entire disk volumes.
It is not commonly used by application programmers.

Whether working with a VSAM or a non-VSAM data set, care must be taken
to use the appropriate type of utility. Several basic guidelines should be followed
when selecting the appropriate type of utility:

- Non-VSAM utilities should be used only with non-VSAM data sets.

- IDCAMS utilities should always be used to process VSAM data sets.

- IEB/IEH utilities should not be used with VSAM data sets. In fact most IEB/
  IEH utilities will not work with VSAM data sets. However, some IDCAMS
  commands can be used to process non-VSAM data sets. These commands
  are identified in chapters 3, 4, and 5.

Because there is a gradual trend to replace IEB/IEH utilities with IDCAMS
commands, the number of functions performed by IDCAMS will continue to
grow during the next few years. IBM Manual (I) identifies the complete range
of functions that IDCAMS can perform with both VSAM and non-VSAM data
sets. However, the information is fragmented throughout the manual, and a
more useful summary is provided in chapter 3.

The IDCAMS utility is discussed in detail throughout all of Part 2. Using
IDCAMS with non-VSAM data sets is discussed in chapters 3 and 13. Comparable IDCAMS processing functions with VSAM data sets is described in chap-

TABLE 1.4   IDCAMS versus IEB and IEH Utilities.

Utility Category	Data Set Organization	
	VSAM Data Sets	Non-VSAM Data Sets
IDCAMS	Always correct.	Can occasionally be used. For details, consult the IDCAMS manual. Functions will be added in coming years in this category.
IEB and IEH Utilities	Should not be used; very few exceptions.	Always correct

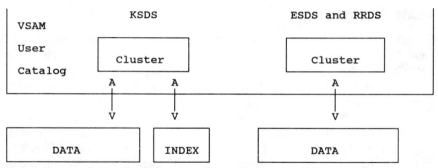

Figure 1.5 VSAM data set components and relationships.

ters 5 and 6. The guidelines for selecting the type of utility for a specific function are summarized in Table 1.4.

Along with standard utilities, there are a variety of sort programs available for processing VSAM and non-VSAM data sets. One such program, the IBM Sort/ Merge Program (DFSORT), is briefly discussed in chapter 13.

VSAM Data Set Components

The Key Sequenced Data Set (KSDS) is the most widely used of the three VSAM data set organizations. It also possesses the most complex structure. A KSDS consists of three distinct components: the cluster, data, and index. ISAM data sets also consist of three components: data, index, and overflow areas. On the other hand, Entry Sequenced and Relative Record Data Sets contain just the cluster and the data components. Analogously, the non-VSAM sequential and relative data sets are stored on disk in an identical manner. In chapter 2, the structure of a KSDS is examined in detail. Much of the control information and the structure of the data and cluster components of a KSDS remain the same for the data and cluster components of an ESDS. The data component of an RRDS, on the other hand, is significantly different from either a KSDS or ESDS. The essential differences between a KSDS and an ESDS are discussed in chapter 10. The difference between a KSDS and an RRDS are examined in chapter 11.

Figure 1.5 illustrates the relationships between the components of a VSAM data set. With each of the three VSAM data set organizations, the individual components within it are always considered separate entities with their own names and distinct catalog entries. In fact, the data and index components might reside on different volumes with their own entries in the Volume Table of Contents (VTOC) on those volumes. When the cluster name is used with an IDCAMS command or on a DD statement, the other components are also usually included for processing. On the other hand, when the data or index component is used in a command or on a DD statement, the other components are not included in the processing. Note in Fig. 1.5 that there is no direct relationship between the data and index components in a KSDS.

VSAM Catalogs

The cluster component of a data set is an entry or set of entries in a VSAM catalog. The purpose of the entries is to thoroughly describe the complete data set. Catalogs are used by the operating system in a variety of ways, one of which is to reduce the amount of information that a programmer must provide to process the data set. This includes locating existing data sets and providing descriptive information for processing the data sets. When a request is made to catalog a data set, a new cluster entry is placed in a catalog. There are several ways to request that a data set be cataloged. These include coding CATLG with the DISP parameter on the accompanying DD statement or specifying one of the various IDCAMS commands whose primary or secondary function is to create a catalog entry. Whenever a VSAM data set is created, an entry is placed in a catalog. There are five basic methods by which a specific catalog can be identified, two of which use JCL: the JOBCAT and STEPCAT DD statements.

The structure of a catalog has changed considerably with the different releases of VSAM. A common type of catalog structure contains two sections, a high-address portion and a low-address portion. The high-address area consists of 47-byte logical records that contain two fields. The first field contains the name of a cataloged object. Every object stored in a catalog is a data set of some type. Data set names can be up to 44 characters in length. Shorter names are left justified and padded with spaces. The second field is a 3-byte pointer to a record in the low-address section that contains information describing the cataloged object. If an object requires multiple records, the necessary records in the low-address portion are linked together.

The complete catalog entry (cluster component) for a VSAM data set can be intuitively thought of as shown in Fig. 1.6. The high-address section is ordinarily much smaller than the low-address section. It also has an index component. Other catalog structures are also possible and are described in chapter 12. In fact, Fig. 1.6 can be thought of as a generic catalog entry for a data set.

Once a specific catalog is selected for searching, information concerning an object is found by first locating the object's true name in the high-address por-

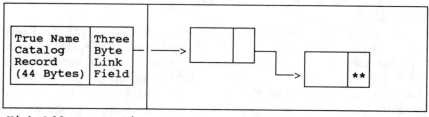

High-Address Section   Low-Address Section
(Stored as a KSDS with   (Stored as an ESDS with
Data and Index components.)   Data Component Only.)

Figure 1.6   The two sections in a "generic" VSAM catalog.

tion of the catalog. The high-address section is a small KSDS, which can be searched very quickly. The corresponding link field contains the address of a physical record in the low-address portion, which is an ESDS. This illustrates using the RBA value for random processing.

As many physical records required to describe an object are linked together in the low-address section. Low-address section information includes where the cataloged object is stored, describes the type of object it is, identifies all objects related to it, provides "DCB-type" values, and maintains processing statistics for the object.

All VSAM data sets must be cataloged. There are no temporary or kept (permanent uncataloged) VSAM data sets. Therefore, it is usually sufficient to code only DSN = data set name and DISP = SHR or OLD in order to identify an existing VSAM data set with a DD statement. VSAM data sets cannot be passed. Thus, they are almost always located through their catalog entry or, in very rare instances, by identifying the volume where they reside. Standard DD parameters such as UNIT, VOLUME, SPACE, and DCB are almost never coded with a VSAM data set.

There are two types of VSAM catalogs: a system master catalog and user catalogs. A system contains exactly one master catalog and any number of user catalogs. At one time, some installations kept all catalog entries in the master catalog. Today, most systems have a catalog structure that consists of the master catalog and numerous user catalogs. In this environment, the only entries permitted in the master catalog are frequently for the user catalogs and important system data sets (DSN = SYS1.---). Related groups of data sets have their entries stored in the same user catalog. Hence, most of the catalogs in the system are relatively small. This type of catalog structure provides rapid access to a specific entry and minimizes recovery problems if a single catalog is damaged or destroyed.

In addition to VSAM data sets, other types of objects can also be cataloged in a VSAM catalog. In particular, user catalogs have entries in the system's master catalog. Both VSAM and non-VSAM data sets, including Generation Data Groups, might be cataloged in either type of VSAM catalog. Alias names for VSAM and non-VSAM data sets along with user catalog aliases might also be stored in a catalog.

Some computer systems might still contain non-VSAM catalogs, which are called CVOLs. A data set entry in a CVOL consists only of the unit and volume values, and for tape data sets, the file sequence number. This is considerably less information about a data set than is contained in a VSAM catalog entry.

VSAM catalogs are an important topic in their own right, and all of chapter 12 is devoted to catalogs and related topics. The most current VSAM catalog structure is called the Integrated Catalog Facility (ICF), which is substantially different from that shown in Fig. 1.6. ICF catalogs are also discussed in depth in chapter 12.

VSAM Data Set Structure

The fundamental building block of every component of a VSAM data set is the control interval (CI). A control interval is the VSAM equivalent of a non-VSAM physical record or block. A data set placed on a 3380 or 3390 disk is stored using one of two formats: COUNT-DATA or COUNT-KEY-DATA. See chapter 15 in MVS JCL and Utilities for a detailed discussion on storing data on disk. The disk representation of a control interval is indistinguishable from that of an equivalent size non-VSAM block written in COUNT-DATA format. A VSAM control interval is never stored in COUNT-KEY-DATA format. Specific disk representation details are provided in the next section, including numeric results. The basic structure of a control interval remains the same for all of the components with all types of VSAM data sets. This consistency is sometimes of questionable merit.

Unlike non-VSAM data sets, a specific number of control intervals in a data component of a VSAM data set are grouped into a higher level structure called a *control area* (CA). The number of control intervals in a control area is determined implicitly when a VSAM data set is created. The final section in this chapter discusses how control area size is determined. Control area size remains constant for the life of the data set. The relationship between control intervals and control areas is pictured in the upper portion of Fig. 1.7. Several points should be carefully noted. Here, each control area consists of three control intervals. However, a control area will ordinarily be comprised of considerably more than three control intervals. VSAM numbers both control intervals and control areas starting with 0, as reflected in Fig. 1.7. The portion of Fig.

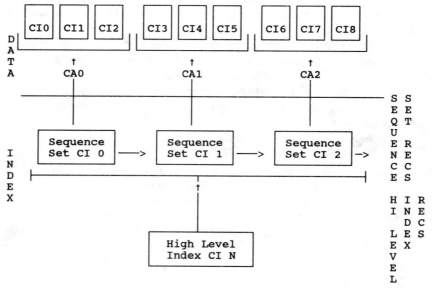

Figure 1.7 Relationship between control intervals and control areas.

TABLE 1.5   KSDS versus ISAM Data Sets.

KSDS Data Component	ISAM Data Area
Record Field	Record Field
Complete Logical Record	Complete Logical Record
Control Interval	Block or Physical Record
Control Area	Track
Multiple Control Areas	Cylinder
Data Set	Multiple Cylinders
	Data Set

Index Structure

Sequence Set	Track Index
(One Record Key Per CI)	(Two Record Keys Per Track)
High Level Index CI	Master Index

1.7 below the line is meaningful only for a KSDS. However, the concept of a control area applies to all three types of VSAM data sets.

At this point, a careful comparison should be made between VSAM and the non-VSAM data set organizations, especially ISAM. The data blocks in a non-VSAM data set are grouped together physically (and also logically with ISAM and Direct data sets) into tracks. All of the tracks on one cylinder are grouped together physically (and also logically with ISAM) into a higher level structure. Non-VSAM data sets permit no flexibility in these groupings; only tracks and cylinders are possible. With a VSAM data set, a specific number of physical records are grouped together to form a control area. However, the number of control intervals in a control area depends on several factors, including the number of blocks that will fit on one track and the number of tracks that comprise a cylinder. Hence, a VSAM data set is a structure with considerably more device independence than the comparable non-VSAM data set.

VSAM disk utilization is better than with ISAM and some Direct data sets because VSAM avoids the COUNT-KEY-DATA representation, which requires substantial additional overhead. Table 1.5 summarizes the relationship between the building blocks of a KSDS and a corresponding ISAM data set.

The actual logical records read and written by a utility or application program are stored in the data component. In addition to logical records, the data component also contains control information. A KSDS also contains an index component, whose primary function is to help locate a specific logical record in the data component as quickly as possible. It also permits logical records to be retrieved in order of ascending key value, regardless of how they are actually physically stored.

As Fig. 1.7 illustrates, the index component of every KSDS contains a sequence set, which is a collection of control intervals logically connected to the data component and to each other. If the data component consists of a single control area, no high-level index control intervals are present. In all other cases, the index component contains one or more high-level (index) control intervals.

The exact structure of the index component is dependent on the size and make-up of the data component and the logical records it contains.

Notice in Fig. 1.7 that one sequence set control interval is paired with an entire data control area, which, in effect, it manages. Hence, the index and data components are linked together using pointers that contain RBA values. Recall that the data and index components are physically distinct objects. Chapter 2 thoroughly describes the connections between the data and index components. Examine Fig. 1.7 carefully before continuing.

The control intervals in each VSAM component contains logical records. It will be explained later that a control interval in the index (in either the sequence set or the high-level index) contains exactly one logical record. Hence, one index control interval (one physical record) is composed of one logical record plus some additional control information. While each sequence set control interval monitors an entire data control area, a high-level index control interval monitors a group of index control intervals on the level immediately below it.

A comparison can be made between a KSDS and an ISAM data set, where the first track of every cylinder contains the index records (the sequence set record equivalent) for the cylinder. Each ISAM index record manages exactly one track of data or the overflow from one track. Whenever an ISAM data set becomes bigger than a single cylinder, a higher level index is created. Likewise, whenever a KSDS contains two or more data control areas, the index structure occupies two or more levels. During random I/O operations, the high-level index records determine where to begin searching in the sequence set.

ISAM allows three levels of master indexes. The number of levels in the KSDS index component is theoretically unlimited, although three or more levels ordinarily denotes an extremely large data set. In fact, more than 1 million logical records in a data component can be managed by a two-level index component structure consisting of a single, high-level index record and hundreds of sequence set records.

Finally, for a theoretic discussion of the internal structure of a KSDS, consult a thorough Data Structures textbook and read the material on B-trees. This is a concept that was developed earlier than VSAM, which can be used to formalize the properties of an indexed data set organization such as a KSDS. B-trees are not used with ISAM.

Storing VSAM Control Intervals on Disk

In order to understand many of the important details of creating and using VSAM data sets and to optimize the processing of VSAM data sets, it is necessary to understand the way in which control intervals are stored on disk. The same method is used with each of the three types of disk drives on which VSAM data sets are usually stored—3390, 3380, and 3350 disks.

The 3390 is the newest of the three disk drives and is replacing the 3380 and 3350. The 3380 is still the most widely used and, consequently, is emphasized throughout this book.

TABLE 1.6   Significant 3350, 3380, and 3390 Numeric Constants.

```
Property                                           3350        3380      3390

Number of bytes on each track                     19254   (1499)47968   56664
Number of tracks per cylinder                        30           15      15
Cylinders per volume                                555          888     ---
COUNT overhead bytes per block                      185     (15) 480     608
Additional overhead bytes per block                   0     (01) 32*     ---
Total overhead bytes per Control Interval           185     (16) 512     ---
KEY Overhead Bytes (non-VSAM) per block              82     (07) 224     288



_____

* Amount might be greater for non-VSAM data sets.
```

During the following discussion, it is important to remember that all of the numeric results apply to control intervals in any of the data sets components, provided that the control interval size is permitted with a specific type of component. Some size restrictions may hold for control intervals in the index and cluster components.

The most important numeric properties associated with both types of disks are summarized in Table 1.6. The 32 bytes of additional overhead required with each block on a 3380 (denoted by an asterisk in Table 1.6) is valid with any VSAM data set. However, values smaller than 32 are possible with non-VSAM data sets. The values in parentheses in the 3380 column is equal to the accompanying number of bytes divided by 32. The final row in Table 1.6 is irrelevant with VSAM data sets, but crucial with ISAM and Direct data sets.

The 3350, 3380, and 3390 disk drives store control intervals in the COUNT-DATA format. When a data set is stored as COUNT-DATA, the usable portion of each track where control intervals are written is formatted as shown in Fig. 1.8. Every control interval is preceded by a COUNT field that contains information on the size of the control interval and its location on the disk. Specifically, it identifies the cylinder and track where the control interval is stored along with its relative position on the track. For every type of data set organization, physical records on a track are numbered starting with 1.

The COUNT field also contains the number of bytes in the control interval (block), which is a constant value for each control interval in a component. Non-VSAM data sets might contain variable-length blocks. Some portions of the track that precede the first GAP cannot be accessed or processed by an application program, and this area is not shown in Fig. 1.8 and not discussed in this book.

```
G| COUNT |G|  Control   |G| COUNT |G|  Control   |G| COUNT |G|  Control
A| Field |A|  Interval  |A| Field |A|  Interval  |A| Field |A|  Interval
P|       |P|  (Block 1) |P|       |P|  (Block 2) |P|       |P|  (Block 3)
```

Figure 1.8   Control intervals stored in COUNT-DATA format.

The relative size of the rectangles in Fig. 1.8 is not accurate. The COUNT field contains 13 bytes of actual data. The two gaps that surround the COUNT field data occupy 467 bytes on a 3380 disk and 172 bytes on a 3350 disk. Hence, the TOTAL overhead space associated with each COUNT field is 480 bytes on an 3380 disk and 185 bytes on a 3350 disk.

It is often imprecisely stated that the COUNT field occupies either 480 or 185 bytes, depending on the type of disk drive. In any case, the meaning is clear. Overhead is an accepted part of disk storage and should be considered. Up to a point, larger control intervals result in a greater percentage of the track containing actual data because the number of COUNT fields is reduced. The crucial size can be determined using the information in Table 1.6 and the techniques employed in Examples 1, 2, and 3 at the end of the chapter.

Once a person understands the format used to store a control interval on disk, knows the size of the COUNT field and its gaps, and determines the number of bytes on a track that are available to hold data, it is very easy to calculate the number of control intervals that can be placed on one disk track. The number of control intervals that fit on a single track is always an integer. The unused portion of a track that is smaller than a control interval and its accompanying COUNT field is wasted space. Therefore, a large blocksize can waste more of a track than a smaller blocksize.

The following three examples illustrate how to determine the number of control intervals, of a specific size, that are written on a track:

Example 1. Determine the number of 512-byte control intervals that can fit on 1 track of a 3380 disk. Find the comparable value for a 3350 disk. With a 3380 disk, 1,024 is divided into 47,968, giving 46.84. Thus, exactly 46 control intervals fit on one track of a 3380 disk. Note that:

1,024 = 480 (COUNT field) + 512 (control interval) + 32 (additional overhead)

The function of the additional 32 bytes of overhead required for each control interval on a 3380 disk is not described in this book. The 512 total bytes of overhead is a constant and must be included for each control interval. With non-VSAM data sets, the rules for determining the additional overhead associated with a data set on a 3380 disk are more complex.

Note that on a 3350 disk 697 (512 + 185) is the total number of bytes required for each 512-byte control interval. It is then necessary to divide 697 into 19,254, which gives 27.62. Because fractions of a physical record cannot be put on a track, the .62 and its overhead are discarded, and the associated part of the track is unused.

It is interesting that, although approximately 2.5 (47,968/19,254 = 2.49) times as much data can theoretically fit on a 3380 track as fits on a 3350 track, in this situation, the 3380 actually holds considerably less than twice as many 512-byte control intervals (46/27 = 1.70). Essentially, this means that bad blocking choices have a much more dramatic impact on a 3380 (and even more so on a 3390; see Table 1.7) than on a 3350.

TABLE 1.7 Number of Control Intervals on a 3390 Track.

Control Interval Size	Complete Range		Number of CIs/Track
512	487	520	49
1024	1019	1086	33
1536	1483	1550	26
2048	1947	2082	21
2560	2547	2710	17
3072	2943	3174	15
3584	3441	3768	13
4096	3769	4136	12
4608	4567	5064	10
5120	5065	5726	9
5632	5065	5726	9
6144	5727	6518	8
6656	6519	7548	7
7168	6519	7548	7
7690	7549	8906	6
8192	7549	8906	6
10240	8907	10796	5
12288	10797	13682	4
14336	13683	18452	3
16384	13683	18452	3
18432	13683	18452	3
20480	18452	27998	2
22528	18452	27998	2
24576	18452	27998	2
26624	18452	27998	2
28672	27999	56664	1
30720	27999	56664	1
32768	27999	56664	1

Example 2. Determine the number of 8,192-byte control intervals that can fit on 1 track of a 3380 disk and on 1 track of a 3350 disk. Because $8,192 + 480 + 32 = 8,704$, and 8,704 divided into 47,968 gives a quotient of 5.51, exactly 5 control intervals will fit on a 3380 disk track. Because $8,192 + 185 = 8,377$ and 8,377 divided into 19,254 gives a quotient of 2.29, exactly 2 control intervals will fit on a 3350 disk track.

Notice that for an 8,192-byte control interval 2.5 times as many physical records fit on a 3380 track as on a 3350 track. This is the expected result. The reason the 3380 behaves as expected is that the COUNT field overhead is a relatively small percentage of the control interval size. In the previous example, the control interval and the accompanying overhead were the same size on a 3380 disk. Hence, approximately half of the track consists of overhead. Because a control interval cannot be smaller than 512 bytes, this control interval size requires the greatest amount of storage for COUNT fields. However,

512 is not the control interval size that uses the smallest percentage of the track for records.

It is possible to use a very mechanical formula to compute the number of control intervals that fit on 1 track of a 3380 disk. There are two fixed overheads associated with every control interval—480 and 32 bytes respectively. Therefore, divide 47,968 by 512 plus the control interval size. This formula is valid whenever the physical record size is a multiple of 32 bytes. This is, however, always the case with a VSAM data set, because the control interval size must be a multiple of 512.

In Example 2, a large number of bytes at the end of the track are wasted on both the 3380 and on the 3350. The exact values can be calculated as follows:

Wasted Bytes = (Total bytes per track) – (number of control intervals * (control interval size + overhead))

For the 3380 and 3350 disks, the calculation gives the values shown as follows, confirming that 8,192 is a more ''efficient'' control interval size on a 3380 than on a 3350.

- 3380 disk: $47,968 - (5 * (8,192 + 512)) = 4448$
  3350 disk: $19,254 - (2 * (8,192 + 185)) = 2500$

- Some large control interval sizes can waste a substantial percentage of a track. If a control interval size of 10,240 bytes is used with a 3350 disk, there are 8,829 bytes on the end of each track that do not hold logical records. Notice that 10,425 divided into 19,254 gives a quotient of 1.8.

A control interval size of 16K or 32K wastes even more storage on a 3380 disk. Table 1.8 contains the number of control intervals that will fit on 1 track of a 3350, 3380, and 3390 disks for the most common control interval sizes. The four entries denoted by an asterisk are the only valid control interval sizes for the index component of a KSDS.

With the 3380, disk storage is actually allocated in 32-byte increments. Hence, each track consists of 1,499 of these increments, and the COUNT and KEY fields are composed of 15 and 7 32-byte increments respectively. All numeric calculations can be done using 32-byte increments rather than the actual number of bytes. Thus, in Example 2: $8,192 = 32 * 256$ and $480 = 32 * 15$. Dividing 1,499 by 271 $(256 + 15 + 1)$ gives 5.5, again showing that a track can hold five 8,192-byte control intervals.

There is one other common approach for determining the number of control intervals that will fit on one track of a disk. This consists of consulting the appropriate green (or yellow) card provided with the disk drive. It specifies the range of values that will result in N-control intervals fitting on a track. It is sufficient to locate the multiples of 512 and 2,048 within these ranges using VSAM data sets.

This section is a small but very significant part of processing data sets on 3350, 3380, and 3390 disks. For a more complete discussion, see chapter 15 in MVS JCL and Utilities. In particular, it should be noted that the second technique used to store data sets on disk, COUNT-KEY-DATA, is not used with VSAM data sets. The next section discusses the substantial advantages that result from not using the COUNT-KEY-DATA format.

Disk-Specific Advantages of VSAM Data Sets

VSAM data sets have two significant advantages over several types of non-VSAM data sets that are related specifically to how data is stored on disk. Some non-VSAM data set organizations are stored using the COUNT-KEY-DATA format. This is a wasteful use of disk storage. In addition, actual processing is more complex or inefficient, or both because of the disk KEY fields.

When a data set is stored using the COUNT-KEY-DATA format, it appears as shown in Fig. 1.9. Unlike the COUNT-DATA format, three separate fields and their associated GAPs are used. The COUNT field and its gap overhead are used with both formats. However, COUNT-KEY-DATA also contains a KEY field and an additional gap that follows the KEY field. As with Fig. 1.8, the fields in Fig. 1.9 are not drawn to scale.

The additional space overhead associated with a disk KEY field is 224 bytes for a 3380 disk and 82 bytes for a 3350 disk. This is in addition to the size of the KEY field itself, which can be from 1 to 255 bytes. The COUNT-KEY-DATA format increases the track overhead associated with a physical record by approximately 50 percent. This results in fewer physical records per track, and hence, larger data sets, which take more time to process. If the amount of overhead is a substantial percentage of the size of the physical record or a greater value, very little actual data is stored on the track.

The disk KEY fields are essential to the logic used in processing three types of data sets: ISAM, Direct, and Partitioned. In each case, the KEY field results in more cumbersome processing. Further details can be found in chapters 12, 13, and 14 of MVS JCL and Utilities. More specific comparisons between ISAM, which uses KEY fields, and a VSAM KSDS can be found in chapters 1 and 2. Virtually every disadvantage of the ISAM key field is replaced by a comparable advantage using the KSDS where the key values used to manage the data set are stored in COUNT-DATA format.

Direct data sets are difficult to process. Much of this difficulty is related to the disk KEY fields. VSAM does not have a Direct data set equivalent. Disk KEY fields are most effectively used with Partitioned data sets because their use is confined to the directory. Even here, they are used sparingly compared to ISAM and Direct data sets. It is interesting that there are no VSAM equivalents to a non-VSAM Direct data set or a Partitioned data set.

G A P	COUNT Field	G A P	KEY Field	G A P	Physical Record (Block 1)	G A P	COUNT Field	G A P	KEY Field	G A P	Physical Record (Block 2)

Figure 1.9 A non-VSAM data set stored in COUNT-KEY-DATA format.

Determining Control Area Size

Because the control area is the second most important structure from which a VSAM data set is constructed after the control interval, it is important to know how to specify its size. The size of a control area depends on several factors. A control area always occupies an integral number of tracks. A track is never split between two control areas. Parts of a control area can be placed on different cylinders. A control area cannot exceed one cylinder. When creating a VSAM data set, the size of a control area cannot be explicitly requested. That is, VSAM does not presently support a statement such as control area size = N tracks or M control intervals. Rather, it is the relationship between the primary and secondary disk storage allocations that determines the control area size. This is a well-thought-out technique, because the need for additional control areas requires that VSAM obtain additional storage. A control area can be split between two cylinders, but this is not recommended. When the data set is created and the amount of space requested on the primary and secondary allocations differ, the smaller of the two values determines the size of a control area. If the two values are the same or only the primary value is specified, that value determines the size of the control area.

At one time, every VSAM data set was classified as either unique or suballocated when it was created. This is still true on VSE systems and with non-ICF catalog data sets. A suballocated VSAM data set is created as a subset of a previously defined data space. With suballocation, an attempt is made to give the data set the exact control area size it requests.

This same statement now holds if the VSAM data set is cataloged in an ICF catalog and is called a pseudo-unique data set. Formerly, a unique data set had its control area size rounded up to one cylinder if a smaller value was requested. With an ICF catalog structure and newer releases of VSAM, suballocation and true unique are no longer supported.

Example 3. Suppose a VSAM data set is to be created on a 3380 disk. If the same value is coded for both the primary and secondary allocations and the requested space is less than or equal to one cylinder, the requested value will be used as the control area size. With a control interval size of 2,048, 18 control intervals will fit on one track. Suppose the space request is one cylinder for both the primary and secondary allocations. Hence, 270 control intervals comprise a control area. With a control interval size of 4,096, 150 control intervals equal one control area. With 1,024 as the control interval size, 465 control intervals equal one control area on a 3380. The comparable values should be determined for a 3350 disk as an exercise.

Example 4. Suppose six tracks are requested for the primary and three for the secondary allocation. The control area occupies three tracks on any disk. With a control interval size of 2,048, one control area on a 3380 disk consists of 54 control intervals. Furthermore, two control areas are created during the primary allocation. If the primary and secondary values are switched, the size of the control area remains the same. In this case, however, only three tracks are initially allocated when the data set is created.

A control area structure is usually associated only with the data component of a VSAM data set. As discussed later in chapter 7, there are some instances when the term control area is extended to the index component. Note that control area and space allocation are considered somewhat synonymous terms. Finally, some IDCAMS options, such as IMBED, which can be coded when a VSAM data set is created, modify the rules for determining Control Area size.

Exercises

The results from Exercise 1 are used in a number of the following exercises in this chapter and also in chapter 2. Exercise 1 requests confirming that the specified values shown in Table 1.8 are actually the correct values.

1. Various control interval sizes are listed on the left-hand side in Table 1.8. Verify that for a specific control interval size the three values on the right identify the number of control intervals that will fit on one track of a 3350, 3380, and 3390 disk. Minimally perform these calculations to verify the values for the four control interval sizes denoted by an asterisk, except 512, which is thoroughly discussed in Example 1.

2. Examine the control interval sizes listed in Table 1.8. What additional control interval sizes are possible with a VSAM data set? Are any of the additional values restricted to just the data or index component?

3. A VSAM data set is to be created and stored on an IBM 3380 disk. For each of the pairs of values shown in Table 1.9, determine if it is possible to construct a data set that allows such a control area structure. Assume that only the criteria described in this chapter are relevant to the construction. For each pair, explain why the construction is or is not possible. For each

TABLE 1.8 Number of Control Intervals per Disk Track.

Control Interval Size (in Bytes and K)		Number of Control Intervals per Track		
		3350 Disk	3380 Disk	3390 Disk
512*	.5K	27	46	49
1024*	1K	15	31	33
1536	1.5K	9	15	26
2048*	2K	8	18	21
3072	3K	5	13	15
4096*	4K	4	10	12
6144	6K	3	7	8
8192	8K	2	5	6
10240	10K	1	4	5
12288	12K	1	3	4
16384	16K	1	2	3
32768	32K	0	1	1

TABLE 1.9 Analyzing Possible VSAM Data Set Structures.

Number of Control Intervals in a Control Area	Control Interval Size	Possible Structure (Yes or No) Yes-->Space Request
a. 40	4096	
b. 25	512	
c. 160	4096	
d. 30	2048	
e. 3	16384	
f. 1	32768	
g. 644	512	

possible structure, specify how disk storage can be requested in terms of primary and secondary allocations to create such a data set.

4. Under what conditions will an index component contain only sequence set records and no higher-level index records? What is the maximum number of sequence set records in this situation? Can an index component of a KSDS ever contain exactly two control intervals or logical records? Recall that the two terms are "equivalent" in the index components. The two records can be any combination of sequence set and high-level index records.

5. Fill in the entries in Table 1.10 with the number of logical records that will fit on one track of an IBM 3380 disk given each of the four control interval size values. All of the logical records alternate in size between 50 and 150 bytes in length. Assume a KSDS. Do any of the answers change if the KSDS is replaced by an ESDS or RRDS? Note: this exercise is continued in chapter 2.

6. What is the minimum number of control intervals that can comprise a control area? Identify the control interval and control area sizes where the minimum value occurs. What is the maximum number of control intervals that can comprise a control area? Identify the control interval and control area sizes where the maximum values occur.

7. Develop a table similar to Table 1.3 for the three equivalent non-VSAM data set organizations—indexed, sequential, and relative (direct access).

TABLE 1.10 Logical Records Contained on One Track of a 3380 Disk.

Control Interval Size	Logical Record Size	Number of Records per Track
a. 513	100	
b. 1024	50,100,50,...	
c. 1024	500	
d. 2048	2	
e. 2560	3000	
f. 8192	4096	

Use the same categories specified on the left-hand side in Table 1.3. Compare the entries for each VSAM data set with its non-VSAM equivalent.

8. For each of the categories listed, identify the advantages of a KSDS over an ISAM data set containing comparable records.

9. Design a VSAM data set structure that is basically equivalent to a non-VSAM partitioned data set. Specifically, how will the directory and member areas be represented as VSAM data sets? How will the two be connected?

10. Determine the control interval sizes that use the greatest and least percentage of available storage on a 3380 disk track. Determine the comparable values for a 3390 and 3350 disk.

11. Attempt various processing with the three VSAM data sets shown in Fig. 1.1 and Fig. 1.2. Assume the status in Fig. 1.2 prior to any processing. Not all of the operations are possible with some of the three data sets.
   Additions—Add a seventh record. It should have a key of DDDDD in the KSDS. Place it in slot 4 in the RRDS, and make it the second record in the ESDS.
   Deletions—Physically delete record 4 from the ESDS. Logically delete record 4 from the KSDS and RRDS.
   Modifications—Rewrite record 6, doubling its length in all data sets that allow a record size to be modified. For the other data sets, rewrite a record of exactly the same length.

12. Attempt various processing with the KSDS and ESDS shown in Fig. 1.2, where the emphasis is on determining the changes in the alternate indexes shown in Fig. 1.4.

Internal Structure
of VSAM Data Sets

Four distinct but related topics are discussed in this chapter. Generally, they can be grouped together and described as *the internal structure of VSAM data sets*, with emphasis on the KSDS. Control interval structure and record formats for all VSAM data sets are examined in detail. The index component of a KSDS is also thoroughly examined. Following this, the standard details of KSDS processing is given. Then, printed information in an index component is examined. Some comparable ESDS and RRDS material is presented in chapters 10 and 11.

The Structure of a Control Interval

The control interval is the fundamental building block for each component of each type of VSAM data set. The basic structure of a control interval is the same no matter in which of the three components the control interval is located. A control interval contains, at most, three types of fields: data (logical records), unused space, and control information. These fields are shown in Fig. 2.1. The Control Interval Descriptor Field (CIDF) and the Record Definition Field (RDF) are control fields VSAM uses to manage the control interval. A single CIDF is always present. If there are one or more logical records in the control interval, at least one RDF is present. Under certain conditions, either the data or unused space portion could be missing. Thus, two types of fields are always present. Unused space can be subsequently used with a KSDS and, under extremely restrictive circumstances, with an ESDS. Otherwise, unused space is wasted with an ESDS, and it is always wasted with an RRDS.

The Control Interval Descriptor Field

Each control interval contains a Control Interval Descriptor Field (CIDF), which occupies the four right-most bytes in the control interval. In some ways, the CIDF is the VSAM equivalent of a non-VSAM block description word (BDW) or field (BDF) used with variable length records. CIDFs and BDFs are four bytes in length, but the CIDF contains more information. The BDF identifies the total number of bytes in the block. This is irrelevant with a VSAM data set because every control interval in a component is the same size and the size is stored in the catalog entry for the component. With a KSDS and ESDS, however, the amount of logical record data and free space in the control interval are both variables.

The non-VSAM BDF uses just two of its four bytes. With VSAM, all four bytes are used. Using fixed-length control intervals, which contain a variable amount of data, allows VSAM data sets to be efficiently processed, similar to a non-VSAM data set with a fixed blocked standard (FBS) record format. The disk drive does not have to check the physical record (block) size value in the COUNT field before reading a block of data. There are no "short" blocks, embedded or otherwise, in any component of a VSAM data set.

The CIDF consists of two binary fields, each two bytes in length. These fields identify the size of the data area (the logical records) and the amount of unused space in the control interval. The two left-most bytes in the CIDF give the displacement from the beginning of the control interval to the beginning of the unused space or the control fields when there is no unused space. This value is equivalent to the number of bytes in the logical records contained in the control interval. If a control interval contains no data, the value is zero.

The right-most two bytes in the CIDF contain the amount of unused space in the control interval. This is equal to the size of the control interval, minus the length of the data portion + 4 + (3 * number of RDFs)—because each RDF occupies three bytes. The RDF's describe logical records. If there are no records in the control interval, the second CIDF value will be four less than the number of bytes in the entire control interval. The software end of file for a VSAM data set is identified by a CIDF consisting entirely of binary zeroes.

The maximum size of a control interval is 32,768 bytes (32K, or 2 raised to the power 15). Hence, one bit in each of the two CIDF fields is free to be used for other purposes. VSAM uses the first bit in the right-most field as a busy

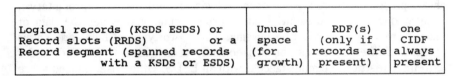

Logical records (KSDS ESDS) or Record slots (RRDS) or a Record segment (spanned records with a KSDS or ESDS)	Unused space (for growth)	RDF(s) (only if records are present)	one CIDF always present

<----------Data Portion---------->|<Unused>|<----Control Fields---->

Figure 2.1   The three field types in a VSAM control interval.

TABLE 2.1   The Two Fields Contained in the CIDF.

Offset	Length	Field Description
0	2 bytes	The displacement from the beginning of the control interval to the beginning of the free space or to the control fields if there is no free space (i.e. the number of bytes in the logical records).
2	2 bytes	The number of bytes of free space
bit 0	1 bit	A busy flag that is set for the duration of a control interval split.

flag. The flag is set when the control interval is being "split," and reset when the "split" is completed. A description of a control interval split is covered later in the chapter.

Once the busy flag is set, it prohibits other programs from accessing the data in the control interval. Amazingly, the first bit in the CIDF currently appears not to be used for any purpose. This seems to be one of the few places where the developers of VSAM were extravagant. The two fields contained in the CIDF are summarized in Table 2.1.

Example 1.   Suppose a data control interval in an ESDS or KSDS is 512 bytes long. It contains 5 logical records with byte lengths of 100, 80, 90, 10, and 70. In this case, the left-most 2 bytes of the CIDF contain the value 350. The right-most 2 bytes of the CIDF contain 143 because there are five RDF fields (one for each record) and $512 - (350 + (5*3) + 4) = 143$.

There are several common programming situations where the values contained in the CIDF determine if a requested operation, which will modify the CIDF values, can actually be performed. Two cases apply to random processing with a KSDS. When a new record is inserted into a control interval, the right-most field in the CIDF is examined to see if the control interval contains sufficient free space to hold the record. Second, when the size of a variable-length record must be increased during a rewrite operation, the CIDF is checked to see if there is sufficient free space in the control interval for the additional bytes. Finally, when writing records sequentially to the end of a KSDS or ESDS, the CIDF values are also accessed and modified. With an RRDS, CIDF values are of little significance. An unused control interval is identified by a CIDF that consists of binary zeroes.

The Record Definition Field

Each record definition field (RDF) is 3 bytes long. All RDFs are located together immediately to the left of the CIDF. In some ways, the RDF is the VSAM equivalent of a non-VSAM record description field, which is also abbreviated RDF. As with the CIDF, the VSAM RDF contains more information than its non-VSAM counterpart. The RDF consists of two values, a leading control byte and a 2-byte numeric value.

Logical Record 1	Logical Record 2	Logical Record 3	FREE SPACE	RDF for Rec3	RDF for Rec2	RDF for Rec1	CIDF

Figure 2.2   Three logical records and their control fields (RDF).

A VSAM RDF can be used to describe one specific logical record or a group of contiguous records, all of which are the same size. It can also identify spanned record segments. When each RDF is used to describe a single logical record, the control fields and records are located as shown in Fig. 2.2. Note the symmetric ordering of each record and its corresponding RDF on the unused space contained in the control interval.

The first byte of an RDF contains several types of information. With a KSDS and an ESDS, it specifies whether the associated record(s) is non-spanned or spanned. For a spanned record, 2 bits identify the relative location of the segment within the complete logical record. Also, with a KSDS and ESDS, one bit specifies whether a group of adjacent records are all the same size. With an RRDS, 1 bit specifies whether the associated logical record slot contains an active or dummy record. The final 2 bytes in an RDF contain one of three values: either a record or segment length, the number of adjacent contiguous

TABLE 2.2   The Information Contained in a Record Descriptor Field.

Offset	Length	Field Description
0	1 Byte	Control information.
bit 0	1 bit	Reserved.
bit 1	1 bit	0—No RDF "pair"; 1—the other member of an RDF "pair" is located to the left of this RDF.
bit 2	2 bits	Used to identify segments in a spanned record: 00—non-spanned, 01—first segment, 10—last segment, 11—an intermediate segment.
bit 4	1 bit	0—Final two RDF bytes contain the record length; 1—Final two RDF bytes contain the number of consecutive records with the same length (non—spanned) or the update number (spanned).
bit 5	1 bit	Used only with an RRDS: 0—denotes an active record; 1—a dummy or deleted record.
bit 6	1 bit	Reserved.
bit 7	1 bit	Reserved.
1	2 Bytes	There are three basic situations to consider. When bit 4 of the first byte in the RDF is 0, these two bytes contain the length of the record or record segment. When bit 4 of the first byte in the RDF is 1. When bits 2—3 of the first byte contain 00, these bytes contain the number of consecutive records of the same length. When bits 2—3 of the first byte contain a value other than 00, these bytes contain the segment update number for part of a spanned record.

Logical Record 1	Logical Record 2	Logical Record 3	FREE SPACE	RDF2 y003 recs	RDF1 x100 bytes	CIDF 0300 data	0202 free

Figure 2.3 Three adjacent 100-byte logical records.

records that are the same size, or the update number for a spanned record or record segment.

An RRDS contains fixed-length records. A KSDS and ESDS allow two record formats—variable and spanned. With a KSDS and ESDS, fixed-length records are treated as a special case of variable-length records. Each segment of a spanned record is described by a pair of RDFs. All VSAM control intervals are fixed length. This results in more efficient I/O operations than with non-VSAM variable-length records. In non-VSAM terminology, a VSAM data set appears to the disk drive as having RECFM = FBS (Fixed Blocked Standard). Furthermore, there is no "short" block at the end of the data set. Rather, the logical record length within a control interval is variable. The fields contained in the RDF, along with their length and location, are identified in Table 2.2.

Non-Spanned KSDS and ESDS Records

The default record format for both a KSDS and an ESDS is variable length. There is no difference in the way fixed and variable-length records are stored other than in the RDFs describing the records. Suppose a record is surrounded by two records in a control interval with lengths that differ from its own. If it is the first or last record in the control interval, the one adjacent record has a different length. In these cases, the record is described by its own individual RDF. When two or more adjacent records in a KSDS or an ESDS control interval are the same length, the entire group of adjacent records is described by a pair of RDFs. This is illustrated in Figs. 2.3 and 2.4.

If every record in a control interval has the same length, there will be one pair of RDFs associated with them. When every record has a different length, then each record has its own RDF. RDF information is relevant to a single control interval, except for spanned records, where a different set of rules apply. Likewise, with an RRDS, one RDF always describes exactly one logical record or an empty slot.

Example 2. Suppose the only three records in a 512-byte control interval are all 100 bytes long. In this case, the left-most RDF contains the value 003 in its final two bytes, and the right-most RDF contains the value 100 in its final two

RDF3 c002 recs	RDF2 b100 bytes	RDF1 a200 bytes	CIDF 0400 data	0099 free

Figure 2.4 Modified control information.

Left-most RDF		Right-most RDF	
Control Byte	The Segment Update Number	Control Byte	The Segment Length

Figure 2.5 Two RDFs describe a spanned record or a segment.

bytes. The control information in the first RDF byte describes the function of the final two bytes. The numeric values shown in Fig. 2.3 are the contents of the final two RDF bytes and both CIDF values. The first byte of the RDFs are denoted by x and y. The bit representation for x is ?1000???; for y, it is ?0001???. A ? denotes either a reserved or irrelevant bit.

Suppose that the preceding control interval is modified. The first record is rewritten and lengthened to 200 bytes. The new control information is shown in Fig. 2.4. The binary representations for a, b, and c are ?0000???, ?1000???, and ?0001??? respectively.

An RDF whose first byte contains a 0 in bit 1 might be describing exactly one record or specifying the number of consecutive records with the same length. It is necessary to examine the RDF on the right to determine which is the case. Both situations are illustrated in Fig. 2.4. An RDF has the identical structure and role with both an ESDS and a KSDS. In an RRDS, however, each record has its own RDF. This wastes disk storage because every record in an RRDS is exactly the same size. Furthermore, it is inconsistent with the RDF structure used with a KSDS and an ESDS.

Each RDF in an RRDS uses the sixth bit in its left-most byte to specify whether the record is an active record or a dummy record. VSAM uses this bit for the same purpose as the programmer-supplied delete byte in an ISAM, relative, or direct data set. VSAM maintains the RRDS delete bit, and it cannot routinely be accessed by an application programmer. Consequently, every RRDS delete is logical. However, the records cannot be subsequently accessed. The other seven RDF control bits are reserved or irrelevant with an RRDS.

Spanned Records (KSDS and ESDS)

A spanned blocked record format (RECFM = VBS) with non-VSAM data sets permits a logical record to be broken into segments and placed into adjacent physi-

Control Interval N				Control Interval N+1				
Data Portion	RDF2	RDF1	CIDF	Data	Unused	RDF2	RDF1	CIDF
First Segment (502 Bytes)	U: 0 p: 1 d: 3 t:	F: 5 r: 0 s: 2 t:	5 0 2	Last Segment (198 bytes)	Free Space (304 bytes)	U: 0 p: 1 d: 3 t:	L: 1 a: 9 s: 8 t:	1 9 8	3 0 4

Figure 2.6 A single record which spans two control intervals.

cal records. For example, the beginning of a logical record can be in one block, the middle segments in the second and third blocks, and the final segment in a fourth block. A block that contains the last segment of one record can also contain the beginning or all of a second logical record or multiple additional records.

Less flexibility is permitted with VSAM spanned records. Each control interval can hold one segment or one complete record. Thus, a control interval can never contain segments from two or more different logical records. This is comparable to the spanned, unblocked (RECFM = VS) non-VSAM record format. A spanned record must be entirely contained in one control area. Furthermore, spanned records are not permitted with a data set in which VSAM constructs an alternate index. Spanned records are also not allowed with an RRDS.

Two RDFs are used to describe each spanned record or record segment, as illustrated in Fig. 2.5. With spanned records, the first byte in each RDF classifies each segment as the first, middle, or last, or as a complete logical record (non-segmented). Refer to Table 2.2, where the left-most RDF in the pair contains the segment update number, and the right-most contains the length. The update number is incremented by one every time the segment is modified. If the update numbers for two or more segments in the same logical record are different, problems might have occurred while the record was processed. This rarely happens when a high-level language application program or utility is used to update the record. This can occur with "control interval" processing.

"Control interval" processing means that the complete control interval is processed as a single (logical and physical) record separate from the other control intervals in the VSAM data set. In this context, even CIDF and RDF values can be treated as data by the application program. Assembler language is commonly used to perform control interval processing, including updating a single segment within a logical record. With a little work, such processing can also be performed with COBOL.

An RDF whose first byte contains a 1 in bit 1 might be identifying the length of a group of consecutive records or the update number for a spanned record or segment. It is necessary to examine the following two bits to determine if the associated record has a spanned format. However, this is not always enough! It is a good exercise to determine how many of the 16 possible bit patterns for bits 1, 2, 3, and 4 are actually valid.

Example 3.   A 700-byte logical record is stored in a spanned VSAM data set where the data control intervals are 512 bytes. Figure 2.6 shows the values contained in the CIDF and RDFs for each of the two control intervals containing segments of the record. The update number is 13 for each segment.

Notice that the control fields always occupy 10 bytes in a control interval that holds a spanned record or segment. Furthermore, every record segment except the last is in a control interval with no free space. The first control interval illustrates both points.

Control Interval Summary

To summarize the most significant control interval features, three points should be reemphasized. A control interval contains logical records. A control interval is to a VSAM data set what a block is to a non-VSAM data set. A control interval in a KSDS is also analogous to a track in an ISAM data set in that one index entry is maintained for each data control interval. Data control intervals are further grouped together into a logical structure called a control area. With non-VSAM data sets, blocks can only be grouped together by tracks and tracks within cylinders. Finally, a KSDS or ESDS must have either a variable or spanned record format, while an RRDS always contains fixed-length records. It might be worthwhile to reexamine the properties for each of the three types of VSAM data sets given in Table 1.3 in chapter 1.

Internal Structure of the KSDS
Index Component

Each KSDS data control area has one control interval in the index component paired with it. The index control interval functions in the same manner usually associated with the index in any indexed data set. It helps locate a particular record in the data component quicker than if a sequential search is used. This is possible because every logical record in the data component has a unique key embedded within it, and the records are ordered by ascending key value.

This unique key must be in the same relative location within each record. Some of the record keys, or a portion of them, are stored in the index component along with the identification of the data control interval that contains the record with the specific key values. VSAM uses the key values stored in the index component to locate the corresponding record in the data component. Not all record keys are stored in the index, only those VSAM needs to quickly locate records. This type of index is called *non-dense*. Each index record occupies an entire control interval.

Randomly accessing a specific logical record in an indexed VSAM (KSDS) data set is a three-step process. The search for the record begins in the index component. First, the information within the index component determines the particular control interval in the data component in which to search for the record. Second, the address of the data control interval is determined and then read into memory. Finally, the data control interval is sequentially searched for the specific record. Thus, approximately half of the search process uses only

Control Information (24 bytes)	Pointers to 'Free' Data Control Intervals	Unused Space but not Free Space	Index Entries for Data Control Intervals	RDF 3 bytes	CIDF 4 bytes

<-----------------------one data record----------------->|<control fields>

Figure 2.7 The structure of a sequence set control interval.

the index component. Furthermore, it is this half that allows the most design creativity and opportunities for optimization.

Recall that the index component consists of sequence set and non-sequence set control intervals (Fig. 1.5). The differences between the two are minimal. A sequence set control interval contains one logical record, no control interval free space, and seven bytes of control information, which consists of the CIDF and one RDF. A sequence set record is pictured in Fig. 2.7.

The first 24 bytes of each record in the index component describes the record itself and identifies the control area in the data component that it controls or monitors. The values stored within the 24 bytes of control information are described as follows and apply to both types of index control intervals, the sequence set records and the high-level index records:

- The logical record length is included. This value is always seven less than the number of bytes in the control interval. The same value is also stored in the left-most two bytes of the CIDF and in the right-most two bytes of the RDF. There are historic reasons for why it is stored in a third location within the control interval.

- If there are index entry fields, they consist of a fixed and a variable portion. The length of the fixed portion is stored in the control information. The length is either 3, 4, or 5 bytes. The value coded will depend on the size of a subfield in the index entry field, which is used as a pointer. The subfield is 1, 2, or 3 bytes long, and the other two bytes are always required for certain functions. The variable portion of each index entry field contains a part of the highest key value in a data control interval. This allows quick reference to the appropriate data control interval.

  A horizontal pointer identifies the next index record on the same logical level as the present one. VSAM uses these pointers for two types of processing: standard sequential and skip sequential. Both techniques avoid having to continually begin record retrieval operations with the highest-level index record. These horizontal pointers are illustrated in Fig. 1.5 in the previous chapter.

- The level of the index record is stored in the record header. The values coded are: 1 for a sequence set record and 2 or more for higher-level index records.

- The displacement to the unused space within the logical record is maintained in the record header. Unlike a data control interval, the unused space is considered part of the logical record and is not treated as control interval free space. Hence, the CIDF contains the value 0 in its two right-most bytes.

- Several other displacements related to the index entry fields are also stored. Their function is to optimize the search of the index for a particular key value during the first step of record retrieval. These displacements are discussed in the "Section Entries" section later in the chapter.

- The base relative byte address (RBA) of the first control interval in the control area associated with the index record is included. Every component of a VSAM data set has its bytes numbered starting with 0. For example, if there are 10 control intervals in each control area on a 3380, and each data control interval occupies 4,096 bytes (Table 1.6), then the RBA values stored in the sequence set records are 0, 40K, and 80K . . . respectively.

Generally, an individual byte in a VSAM data set can be located through its relative byte address. Thus, a VSAM data set is far more flexible than a non-VSAM data set, which has no comparable addressing scheme. It is the RBA that allows VSAM to perform a wide range of data set accessing techniques that are either very difficult or impossible with non-VSAM data sets.

The most important of these techniques are thoroughly examined in chapters 10 and 11 with ESDSs and RRDSs. A complete list of all of the fields contained in the index record header, along with their length and displacement from the beginning of the record, and a summary of their function, is given in Table 2.3. In examining these values, refer back to Fig. 2.7 and recall that the index control interval consists of a single record—its RDF and the CIDF.

The sequence set record performs several important functions during an

TABLE 2.3   24-Byte Index Record Header Fields.

Offset	Length (Bytes)	Description
0	2	Logical record length; control interval size—7.
2	1	The length of the fixed portion of the index entry fields. The possible values are 3, 4, or 5 bytes.
3	1	The length of the field within the fixed portion of the index entry field that identifies a specific data control interval within the control area. The possible values are 1, 2 or 3 bytes. This field can be calculated by subtracting 2 from the previous field value. It is included for historic reasons and future changes.
4	4	The RBA of the first control interval in the control area managed by this index record.
8	4	A horizontal pointer; the RBA of the next (right-most) index record on the same level as this one.
12	4	Reserved.
16	1	Level number: 1—sequence set; 2 through N identify high-level index control intervals.
17	1	Reserved.
18	2	Displacement to the unused space that follows the free CI pointer field.
20	2	Displacement to control information in the left-most index entry, which contains the highest key value in the CA. This value identifies the beginning of the index entries.
22	2	Displacement to control information in the left-most index entry in the right-most section. This is where the search for a record begins.

24 Byte Header	EF	EE	ED	EC	.....	05	04	03	Unused Space	Index Entries for 3 Data CIs	RDF	CIDF

Figure 2.8   The free CI pointer list in a sequence set record.

update operation. It identifies unused data control intervals and non-empty data control intervals that contain a particular key value. Each data control interval in the control area associated with an individual index record is placed into one of two disjoint categories within the index record. The category is determined by the location in the index record of the pointer to the data control interval.

The pointer is placed in an index entry field if the corresponding data control interval contains one or more records. If a control interval does not contain records, its pointer is stored in the free control interval pointer section. When the KSDS is initially created, every control interval is identified as free. A non-sequence set index record does not contain a list of free control interval pointers. This is the most significant difference between sequence set and high-level index records.

A new index entry is created in a level two index record each time the first records are placed in a control area. A third level index record is needed only when the available space in a single, second-level index record is exhausted by the index entries.

Example 4.   Suppose that a control area consists of 240 control intervals. VSAM will assign the control intervals relative numbers from 0 to 239 (or 00 to EF in hex). Now suppose that exactly three data control intervals have records loaded into them. In this case, the free CI pointer section contains an entry for each of the remaining 237 control intervals. These values are stored in the sequence set control interval from left to right, as shown in Fig. 2.8.

The index entry section will contain pointers to the three control intervals that contain data records. Each index entry contains part or all of a key value and the relative number of the control interval associated with the key. In this example, the three index entries are stored from right to left following an initial load operation, as shown in Fig. 2.9. Recall that the key field information contains the variable portion of the record key and a fixed, 2-byte field. An additional field of 1, 2, or 3 bytes identifies the data control interval. VSAM selects the size of this field.

When a fourth data control interval is needed, the right-most value (03 in this case) is located in the free control interval pointer list and moved to the index

Index Entry CI02	Index Entry CI01	Index Entry CI00
key :data field : CI information:−02−	key :data field : CI information :−01−	key :data field : CI information :−00−

Figure 2.9   General overview of the index entries.

Control Header	Free Data CIs	Unused Space	Index Entries	Control Fields
24 bytes of control information	shrinks to left	expand's to left, shrinks from right	expands to left	7 bytes control info
fixed	<————<————————————<—————			fixed

Figure 2.10 Common field changes in an index record.

entry field. Records are written to the new data control interval. Following this, the key information for the index entry is written. As data sets are processed, it is possible that existing index entries will need to be rewritten also. This simple example illustrates the most common way in which the field entries change. The free CI pointer field contracts to the left. The right-most entry is removed and the space it occupied is added to the unused space. The index entries expand to the left using the unused space to store new entries, as shown in Fig. 2.10. Other changes in a sequence set control interval are also possible.

It is possible that a sequence set record can be too small to contain all of the index entries and free CI pointers required by a control area. A free CI pointer occupies at least 1 byte (actual size), and an index entry requires a minimum of 3 bytes, and 3 bytes is possible only for the very rare circumstance that no portion of the key is stored. For most control intervals, a variable portion of the key field is present. If a sequence set control interval is 512 bytes long, an absolute maximum of 481 ($512 - (24 + 7)$) bytes can be used to manage the associated control area. However, only 256 values can be represented with a 1-byte field. If there are more than 256 data control intervals in a control area, all the pointer field values must be at least 2 bytes long. Even if none of the control intervals contain data, this number is far too large with a 512-byte sequence set control interval.

Example 5.   How many data control intervals can be managed by a sequence set control inverval 512 bytes long? When the initial records are written to a data control interval, its reference within the index is moved from the free CI pointer field to the index entry field. Eventually, the index entries will consume all the unused space and reach the free CI pointer field. This occurs because every index entry except for the last one must be at least 3 bytes long. In addi-

0 to 255 bytes	1 byte	1 byte	1–3 bytes
Actual compressed key value	The number of characters stripped from the front of the key	The number of characters from the key that are stored in the entry	A vertical pointer identifying the data CI
<–variable–>	<————fixed portion of the index entry————>		

Figure 2.11 The four fields in each index entry.

tion, most index entries contain key field information that occupies more than 1 byte.

Assuming 1 byte for each key, a maximum of 120 control intervals can be managed by a 512-byte sequence set record. Assuming 2 bytes average for each key, a maximum of 96 control intervals can have index entries in the sequence set. Hence, if a control area consists of many data control intervals, 512 is a questionable control interval size for the index component of the KSDS.

Index entry fields

Index entries contain four fields. The left-most is variable in length and the other three are fixed length, as identified in Fig. 2.11. The size of each field is given above the field description. VSAM is able to conserve space in the index records by compressing key values. This is a major reason why a very small index component can monitor a large number of data control intervals. Key compression should be contrasted with the way ISAM stores complete key values in the index records. In addition, with a KSDS, only one key value is stored for each data control interval while two index records are needed for every track in the prime data area of an ISAM data set. One fewer value is needed because VSAM does not contain an overflow area.

The compressed key value stored in the index entry is constructed primarily from the highest key value of the logical records in the corresponding data control interval. Other factors can also influence the compressed value. VSAM allows keys up to 255 bytes long. Characters that VSAM determines are unnecessary when locating a record are stripped from both the front and rear of a key. In particular, an actual key value of 000123456 might be stored as 12 in the index entry. VSAM will also note that three characters were stripped from the front of the record and that two characters have been retained. Hence, VSAM can determine that four characters were stripped from the rear of this record. The key length value is stored in the cluster component. Hence, key length – (bytes from front + bytes stored) indicates the number of bytes stripped from the rear of the key.

It is possible that no characters from the actual key value are stored in the index entry. This commonly occurs in the data control interval that contains the highest key value in the entire data set. This is illustrated in the examples at the end of the chapter. When VSAM searches the index entries when locating a particular data record, it reconstructs all or part of the original key, starting with the compressed key value. This reconstruction reverses the logic used in the compression process.

During key compression and reconstruction, VSAM examines the key values stored in the adjacent index entries. VSAM might reconstruct the key value 000123456 and get 000123 X'FFFFFF' as the result. The reconstructed key might differ from the actual key value stored in the data control interval. The differences are insignificant for identification. The bytes stripped from the rear of the key are replaced by binary ones. Key compression saves space in the index control interval. VSAM uses other techniques to save time when searching for a specific logical record. For those interested in a more detailed discussion of key compression, a lengthy discussion and example is presented in the next section.

The random search of an indexed data set is a three-step process. The three steps are the same with both ISAM and a KSDS. The first step consists of searching the index for the initial key value that is greater than or equal to the key of the record being processed. The second step consists of locating the data portion of the data set that contains the record whose key was found in the index component. With a KSDS this is a specific control interval, with ISAM, it is a track in the Prime Data Area or its associated overflow area. Finally, the data portion is sequentially searched. Of these three steps, the first one, searching the index, can be optimized in several ways. Steps two and three cannot readily be optimized. With ISAM, they are especially inflexible because of the presence of an overflow area.

To facilitate the search for a specific key value, an additional field is coded within the index entries during the first step. In particular, if a control area consists of N control intervals, then this additional field occurs the square root of N times among the index entries. This subdivides the index entries, allowing an even quicker search for a given value.

For example, if there are 16 control intervals in a control area, then every fourth index entry is followed by an extra field pointing to the index entry four locations away. This means that the fourth, eighth, twelfth, etc., index entries will initially be examined while trying to locate a key value. Once these values are used to localize the search, the remaining four index entries can be examined. With 16 index entries in a sequence set record, this technique reduces the maximum number of index comparisons by approximately 50 percent.

If a control area contains 240 control intervals, then the maximum number of index entries that must be searched drops from 240 to approximately 30. This is also a significant improvement over ISAM, where every index record must always be examined in order.

The number of bytes needed to hold a vertical pointer for a free control interval or index entry varies depending on the number of control intervals in a control area. Obviously, only 256 distinct values can be represented with a 1-byte pointer. Hence, for more than 256 control intervals in a control area, a 2 or 3-byte pointer is used. VSAM selects the actual value. Index entries in a non-sequence set record contain a 3-byte pointer field.

The pointer value is multiplied by the size of a control interval in the data component to determine the RBA where the control interval is actually located. Recall that the actual address where the control area begins is stored in the first 24 bytes of the index record. Specific control intervals can be located as a displacement from this address. This is illustrated in the second part of the chapter when the details of actual I/O operations are discussed.

Key compression in the index entries

It is rarely necessary for VSAM to store a complete key field value in an index entry. Instead, both leading and trailing characters can be truncated from the actual key field value. This technique is called key compression. In fact, there are situations where none of the key is stored. Key compression is a sufficiently significant topic that a separate section is devoted to it. Understanding key compression allows a person to better understand how a KSDS functions.

VSAM performs key compression only in the index component of a KSDS and an alternate index. By storing fewer key field bytes, more index entries can be placed in an index control interval. This reduces the size of the index component and fewer I/O operations are required to process the KSDS. It is more efficient for VSAM to completely or partially reconstruct the key than to store the full key values in the index entries. Key field characters might be truncated for two reasons: they are redundant or they are irrelevant in locating data records.

The basic principles of key compression consist of two comparisons using the highest key value in a control interval. Leading characters are truncated based on a comparison with the key value in the previous (right-most) index entry. Leading truncated characters are redundant. Trailing characters are truncated based on a comparison with the first data record key in the next data control interval in ascending order. This is the control interval whose index entry is to the left of the present one. Trailing truncated characters are insignificant.

Front-end key compression is used to remove the leading characters that are identical to those in the previous (right-most) index entry key field. For example, if 356,721 and 356,975 are the greatest key values in two consecutive data control intervals, the second key field will be truncated and 975 is kept for the index entry. This is done because either the three leading bytes (356) have been stored in the previous index entry or can be determined from an even earlier index entry. VSAM notes that the first three bytes were truncated. If the high key value for the next control interval is 358,295, then 35 is truncated and 8,295 is kept for the index entry. When searching for a record, all truncated leading bytes can be determined by examining the previous index entries. The initial index entry does not have any leading bytes truncated.

There is one exception to how front-end compression is done. The left-most (first) index entry associated with a section contains the highest key value. This high key value is essential in determining if the individual entries in the section should be examined.

Back-end key compression is performed based on a comparison between the index entry key value and the key field in the next logical record in the data set. The next record is the first record in the control interval associated with the next index entry. The two key field values are compared on a character basis, starting with the most significant (left-most) byte. When a difference is found,

Index Entry	8	02	01	N+1	97	03	02	N	35672	00	05	N−1
High key value in control interval		358295				356975				356721		
Low key value in control interval		356987				356740				350008		

Figure 2.12 Front and rear key compression.

all of the remaining characters in the key field are truncated.

For example, suppose that 356,975 is the highest key value in a control interval and the next logical record has a key value of 356,987. Following rear-key compression, the value 35,697 will be saved for the index entry. Both types of key compression are illustrated in Fig. 2.12. The low key value in control interval N + 2 is 359,240.

Values that are removed during back-end key compression cannot be determined during subsequent processing by examining only index entries. The truncated values are replaced by hexadecimal F's (binary 1's) for comparison operations with the index entry. Thus, the truncated digits are irrelevant during subsequent index searching.

The final index entry in each level of the index has the same format as shown in Fig. 2.13. This means that no characters are stored in the index entry and none are truncated from the front. This implies that every character is truncated during back-end compression because the first digit in the entry is different than the next record (nonexistent) in the data set.

Key compression with spanned records

Spanned records result in one significant modification to the preceding description. No key is stored in the index entry except for the last segment in a record and a complete (unsegmented) record. Clearly, the high key value is the same for each segment in a spanned record and there is no reason to repeatedly store it.

Section entries

Two-byte section entry fields divide index entries into groups called *sections*. Sections reduce the number of index entry comparison operations required to locate a specific data set control interval. If sections or something comparable were not used, the index entries would have to be sequentially searched. Using differential calculus, the optimal location for a section entry can be determined. If a sequential search of N index entries is made, then, on the average, N/2 comparisons will be performed. In the worst case, N comparisons will be required.

00	00	CI—Number

Figure 2.13 The final index entry in the sequence set.

The number of index entries in a section and the number of sections are approximately equal to the square root of the number of control intervals in a control area. Suppose that a control area contains 150 control intervals. A section would then contain $12\sqrt{150}$ index entries. Each section would contain a two-byte pointer field specifying the displacement from the left-most index entry in the section to the left-most index entry in the next section to the right.

Defining the KSDS Used to Illustrate I/O Operations

This section contains a wide variety of samples in order to thoroughly illustrate the processing in both the data and index components in a KSDS as records are retrieved, added, deleted, and updated. Both random and sequential processing are examined. Once the actual details associated with a given I/O operation are understood, it is easy to master the specific syntax used to perform the processing with a given programming language or utility. Shorter collections of examples are provided in chapters 10 and 11 to illustrate processing an ESDS and RRDS.

For most of the examples in this section, assume that all logical records in the data component are 2,500 bytes long. Assume also that data component control intervals are 10,240 (10K) bytes long. A control area consists of 10 control intervals. As an historic footnote, this example was developed and tested several years ago on a 3350 disk, where a control area consists of four, 4,096 control intervals. See chapter 1 for the relevant numeric details. A 3380 disk provides unnecessary overhead but no additional educational benefits. However, all aspects of these examples are absolutely and numerically correct—these are the actual values.

The size of the index control intervals is not significant for these examples because the data set is small and there are few control intervals in a control area. Six records have been loaded into the data set. The only existing control area contains two control intervals which hold data while the remaining two are free.

Within each logical record, the top value in each data record is the 3-byte record key; the bottom value is the length of the record. CI2 and CI3 are identified as empty in the sequence set record. Because the highest key value in CI0 is 015 and 030 in CI1, compressed versions of both keys are stored in the sequence set index entries. More specific index entry details are provided in the final topic in this chapter following examples A through M.

It is assumed that the ensuing I/O operations are to be performed by an application program written in COBOL (or PL/I or assembler). The actual syntax needed to perform these operations in COBOL are not detailed here but are discussed in chapter 9. A very limited number of operations that process an individual record can be performed using just the IDCAMS utility. Chapter 5 identifies those I/O operations. The data set described here is also referenced in several later chapters. In particular, most of chapter 7 examines the status of the data set following the initial processing described here.

Before the first I/O operation can be performed, the data set must be located and opened. With an application program, an accompanying JCL statement identifies the name of the cluster component as DSN = cluster name. The master catalog and/or one or more user catalogs are searched until the name of the data set is found in the name portion of a VSAM catalog or the Basic Catalog Structure of an ICF catalog. The corresponding entries in the low-order part of the VSAM catalog or the VVDS contain the names and locations of the data and index components.

In order to reference them, I/O operations are identified by the letters A through M. The operations build upon each other, and if they are performed in a different order, different results might occur.

A. Update the record with a key value of 025.   When a KSDS is processed randomly, attempting to locate a logical record is a three-step process:

1. The index component is searched.

2. The search moves to the appropriate control interval in the data component.

3. The data component is sequentially searched.

In step 1, the relevant index entry in the sequence set control interval must be determined. This consists of evaluating that the comparison 025 < = 015 is false, but 025< = 03X'FF' (FOF2F5< = FOF3FF) is true. Hence, the second index entry contains the relative number of the data control interval (here 01), which might contain the record.

In step 2, the location of the data control interval is calculated using the formula:

CI address = RBA of CI0 + (relative CI number * data CI size)

Recall that the RBA of CI0 is stored in the first 24 bytes of control information in the sequence set record. Here, the relative byte address of CI1 is calculated as:

0 + (1 * 10240) = 10240

Similarly, if the relevant index entry had contained a pointer to CI3, the formula computes the relative byte address of CI3 as:

0 + (3 * 10240) = 30720

Finally, in step 3, the data control interval is sequentially searched. The RDF values are used to determine the location of the individual logical records and each key field is at the same relative location within the records. The first comparison of 025 is not equal to 020, but the second comparison gives 025 = 025.

Thus, the record to be rewritten is the second one in the second data control interval.

Rewriting a logical record results in the complete copy of the control interval in the buffer being rewritten. For a variable-length record whose length is changed, every record following the modified record must be shifted. Here, only the 2,500 bytes in the middle logical record are changed. Once the contents of the buffer are modified, the buffer is ready to be copied back to disk.

Initially, the KSDS contains only one index record. At the beginning of the first I/O operation, the index control interval is read from disk. It remains in memory as long as there is sufficient buffer space to hold its contents. Minimally, it remains until a second index control interval must be processed. Two data buffers and one index buffer are provided by default to process a KSDS. Following the retrieval operation, one of the data buffers holds CI1. In a COBOL program, the contents of the specific logical record are available in the 01 level associated with the FD for the data set following the READ operation.

For this initial I/O operation, the index search in step 1 is now described in greater detail. The key value of 025 is compared to the compressed key values stored in the index entries. The index entries are always processed from right to left. The compressed key values are expanded prior to the comparison. All comparisons are hexadecimal, which is based on the EBCDIC collating sequence values. Because $025 > 015$, the desired record is not in the control interval associated with the right-most index entry—CI0. Because $025 < = 03X'FF'$ (i.e., $F0F2F5 < = F0F3FF$), if the record is actually in the data set, it must be in the second control interval.

In reality, no digits are stored in the index entry for CI1, and the value X'FF-FFFF' is used for all comparison operations. Thus, even though the highest key value in the second control interval is 30, a record with a higher key value can be added, and the value stored in the index entry will remain unchanged. Consequently, the index control interval will not have to be rewritten. This improves VSAM's efficiency.

This approach should be contrasted with the initial processing in the search to locate a record in an ISAM data set. Note that this is an actual illustration of how key compression is performed (Fig. 2.13).

The sequential search operation in step 3 examines CI1, because of the value stored in its index entry (CI1). CI1 is read into memory, and the values in the RDF are used to determine the beginning of each logical record. By knowing where records begin and where the key is located in each record, records can be examined for a key value of 25. The desired record is found on the second compare.

If a COBOL READ statement is used, the logical record can be processed in the buffer. Alternatively, a READ...INTO allows access in a WORKING-STORAGE location. After fields in the record are modified and the record rewritten, the contents of the buffer are written to disk, replacing the old copy of CI1. If the length of the record is modified, all logical records that follow are also rewritten, along with the RDF and the two values in the CIDF. When the length of a record is increased, the CIDF is checked to ensure that there is sufficient free space in the control interval to allow the larger record. Note that after the operation completes, the program's buffers still contains both the index record and the modified data control interval.

The rest of the KSDS remains unchanged except for the cluster component where the data set's I/O and utilization statistics are updated. The sequence set record and data CI1 will remain in the buffer area until the space they occupy is needed for other control intervals. During subsequent I/O requests, VSAM will examine the records in the buffer area before it retrieves the same data control interval again from disk. This look-aside buffer processing is another significant advantage of VSAM.

B. Delete the record with a key value of 015.   In step 1, the index entry is searched to locate the appropriate data control interval. The first comparison in the sequence set is: 015 < = 015, which is true. Hence, if the record to be deleted is actually in the data set, it is in CI0. In step 2, the relative byte address of CI0 is computed as:

$$0 + (0 * 10240) = 0$$

The first data control interval is read into a second memory buffer. From this point through Example E, I/O operations are not needed to retrieve records. All the existing logical records are in memory along with the index record. During the sequential search in step 3, the records with keys of 005 and 010 are examined before the record with a key value of 015 is found. A delete operation is executed. This is implemented by rewriting the buffer that holds the control interval. The area formerly occupied by the deleted records is added to the free space. Unlike ISAM, all deletes with a KSDS are physical. After the CIDF and the left-most RDF are updated, the copy of control interval 0 in the buffer now looks as shown in Fig. 2.14. Note that the free space remains continuous. Subsequently, the buffer's contents are written back to disk, replacing the CI0 stored there.

The index entry for the control interval does not change. Thus, the disk sequence set record does not need to be rewritten. This technique improves processing efficiency. In fact, there are very few types of I/O operations that will cause the index entry for the control interval to change. The highest key value associated with the control interval remains F0F1F5(015).

Because VSAM works this way, there are some applications where considerable thought should be given to the highest key values in the data control inter-

005 2500	010 2500	Free space	2500	5000 5230

Figure 2.14 CI0 following the first delete operation.

vals when the KSDS is loaded. It could significantly affect future processing and can be completely controlled by the programmer by examining the record key values and selecting appropriate free space values. Examples A and B should be contrasted with updating and deleting records in an ISAM data set. See chapter 13 in MVS JCL and Utilities for a comparable discussion describing random processing with an ISAM data set.

C.   Add a record with a key value of 030.   Beginning with the add a record with a key value of 030 operation, the details of the three steps in the retrieval process will be described in less detail. Here,

    030 > = 015, and 030 < = 03 X'FF'

Hence, it is determined that CI1 will be used to hold the new record. A copy of CI1 is currently contained in a buffer. When the data control interval is sequentially searched, an existing record with a key value of 030 is found. The contents of the buffer that contains CI1 remains unchanged, and a non-zero status code is returned to the application program. The two-byte status code specifies that an attempt was made to add a record to the KSDS when it already contained a record with the same key. The status code value is classified as informatory information, and it is neither an error or an abend condition.

Whenever VSAM cannot successfully perform a requested I/O operation, it returns a non-zero status code to the application program that made the request. At this point, it becomes the responsibility of the application program to note the status code value and take any appropriate actions. Here, the appropriate action is usually to place an entry in the exception report that is generated in conjunction with the update. The value in the status code should be examined after every I/O operation, including opening and closing the data set. The status code value does not prohibit VSAM from attempting further operations with the data set. However, specific values might affect the outcome of subsequent operations.

D.   Delete the record with a key value of 005.   Comparing 005 with the index entries in the sequence set, VSAM determines that, if the record is in the data set, CI0 contains it. The record is found and then deleted by rewriting the control interval. Notice that exactly one disk I/O operation is performed—rewriting the control interval. This resulted because CI0 and the sequence set are both contained in the buffer area prior to the I/O request and each contained the correct data values. Following the delete, free space in the data control interval looks as shown in Fig. 2.15. Free space in the data control interval remains contiguous. Hence, the record with a key of 010 occupies the space that formerly held the deleted record. Just as in Operation/Example B, the index entry for CI0 does not change.

There are three special delete situations: removing the first record in the control interval, removing the last record, and removing the only record. If, for our

010 2500	010	Free space	2500	2500 7733

Figure 2.15   CIO following the second delete operation.

example, the single remaining record in the control interval is deleted here, the control interval is empty. When a control interval becomes empty, its index entry is removed, and an entry for it is placed at the right-most end of the free control interval pointer list in the sequence set record. An exception occurs with the control interval in the control area containing the highest key value. It does not have its index entry removed even if all its records are deleted. An empty control interval can be reused whenever the next control interval split occurs or under some conditions when the data set is extended. It should be noted that, with earlier versions of VSAM, when every record was deleted from a control interval, it was not returned to the free control interval pointer list. The key range remained fixed for each control interval.

E.   Add a record with a key value of 024.   From examining the index entries, VSAM determines that the new record belongs in CI1. The CIDF entry is checked to confirm that there is sufficient free space to hold the new record. In order to add the new record to the control interval, the records with keys of 025 and 030 are shifted to the right when the control interval is rewritten. Within a control interval, records are always stored in logical order by ascending key value. CI1 now appears as shown in Fig. 2.16.

F.   Add a record with a key value of 021.   The index entries in the sequence set record determine that the new record be added to CI1. The CIDF shows there is no space for it. In order to add the record, VSAM must perform a "control interval split." This is a technique that allows VSAM to avoid using an overflow area, much as the one ISAM employs in a comparable situation. There are two basic control interval split algorithms: direct and sequential.

With a direct insert strategy (DIS), approximately half the records in the control interval that will split get moved to a new control interval. The sequential insertion strategy (SIS) is discussed in the next section. With both strategies, the new control interval used for the split is identified by the right-most entry in the free CI pointers section of the sequence set record, here CI2. In this case, the records with the two highest keys get moved to the new control interval. Following the split, both CI1 and CI2 have their records in order control interval by key value. If there are N records in the existing control interval, the N/2

020 2500	024 2500	025 2500	030 2500	Free space	4	2500	10,000 0230

Figure 2.16   CI1 Contains 4 Logical Records—10,000 bytes.

Sequence Set Record

CI 0 is Unchanged

Control Information	03	Unused Space	3—1—1—02	24—1—2—01	15—1—3—00	RDF	CIDF

CI 1

020	021	024	Free space		3	2500	7500
2500	2500	2500					2730

CI 2

25	30	Free space		2	2500	5000
2500	2500					5230

Figure 2.17 The KSDS following a control interval split.

(rounded down) with the highest key values are moved to the new control interval and the new record is then added to the control interval where it belongs. Following a control interval split, it is possible that the physical order of the control intervals no longer reflects the logical order of the records. This is not the case here, however, and for this reason, this is referred to as a *simple split*. The data and index components now appear as shown in Fig. 2.17.

In order to avoid needless processing, VSAM first checks the records in CI1 to see that there is no existing record with a key of 024. If a duplicate key is found, there is no reason to perform a control interval split.

With a sequential insertion strategy, the control interval is split at the point where the new record is to be added. All records with higher key values are moved to the new control interval, and the new record becomes the last one in the existing control interval. Here, this would result in records with keys of 20 and 21 in CI1 and the others in CI2.

G. Add records with key values of 023 and 022, in that order. The first record will be added to CI1. Following the addition, CI1 will contain 10,000 bytes of data and 230 bytes of free space. The second record to be added also belongs in CI1, but there is insufficient space to hold it. Hence, a second control interval split is performed. This time, the records with keys 23 and 24 are moved to the new control interval, which is CI3. Notice that 03 was the last entry in the free control interval pointer section in the sequence set record.

Unlike before the previous control interval split, this split causes the logical records in the data set to no longer be stored in order based on their relative

3-1-1-02	24-1-2-03	22-1-2-01	015-1-2-00

Figure 2.18   The four index entry fields in the sequence set.

byte address values. Hence, this is classified as a *complex split*. However, they can still be processed in logical order because the sequence set index entries are rewritten following the control interval split. Figure 2.18 illustrates the four index entries values.

Notice that, at this point, because the key values are stored in the index entries, it appears that additional records cannot be added to CI1 and CI3. There are several processing situations that will allow additional records to eventually be added to these control intervals, however. If the records are processed without using the index entries, they will not be retrieved in logical order. Rather, following the record with a key of 022, records will be retrieved in order with keys of 025, 030, 023, and 024.

If a sequential insertion strategy is used, different results will occur depending on the order in which the records with keys of 022 and 023 are added to the data set. If the record with a key of 022 is added first, the records with keys of 020, 021, 022, and 023 will be placed in CI1 and the record with a key of 024 will be placed in CI3. If the record with a key of 023 is added first, that record will also be in CI3 following the split. This discussion ignores the freespace parameters in effect with the data set.

H.   Add records with key values of 026, 027, and 028, in that order.   The first two records are added to CI2. When an attempt is made to add the third record, VSAM notes that the new logical record clearly belongs in CI2 as well and there is no existing record in the data set with the same key. Thus, the add is a legitimate I/O request. The values in the CIDF determined that there was no room for the new record and a control interval split must be performed. When VSAM examines the free CI pointers list, however, it determines that there are no remaining empty control intervals in the control area. In this situation, VSAM performs a *control area split*.

In MVS JCL terminology, the data set receives a secondary space allocation. Sufficient storage is allocated to create a new control area. This assumes that secondary allocations were requested when the data set was created with the IDCAMS DEFINE CLUSTER or ALTER command and that not all of them have been used. As with control interval splits, there are two types of control area splits—direct and sequential—and they are functionally analogous to their control interval namesakes. The direct is most common with true random processing and is described next.

Whenever a new control area is allocated, an additional sequence set control interval must also be placed in the index component. When the second sequence set control interval for a KSDS is created, a high-level index control interval is also created to manage the multiple sequence set records. After additional space is allocated to the data and index components, the first part of a control area split is complete.

During the next phase of a direct insert control area split, about half the data control intervals in the original control area will be copied to control intervals in the new control area. The moved control intervals will then have pointers placed in the free CI pointer list in the old sequence set. Also, their index entries in the same sequence set will be removed.

Ordinarily, the control intervals containing records with the highest key values will be copied. If the copied control intervals do not contain records in logical order, the control intervals will be reordered during the copy operation. Hence, the former CI3 becomes CI0 and the former CI2 becomes CI1 in the new control area. Index entries in the high-level index record specify that the highest key value in CA0 is 022, and CA1 contains the highest key value found in the data set. This completes the second part of a control area split.

Recall that the control area split resulted while trying to add the record with a 028 key. This record will be added during the third part of the split. At this point, the one index buffer is now too small to hold the entire index component in memory. Hence, random processing becomes more time-consuming unless additional storage is available for index buffers. Buffer space can be specified in several ways, including using the IDCAMS ALTER command, which specifys a new, permanent buffer space value for the index. The AMP DD parameter can also specify a buffer space value for just the present job step.

If multiple index buffers are available, the high-level index record can be kept in memory for the duration of the processing. In any case, the high-level index record is examined, and then determined that the new record should be written in CA1—the new control area. The index entries in sequence set one are examined, and it is determined that the new record belongs in data CI1. Because CI1 does not contain sufficient free space to hold the record, a control interval split occurs. The entry for CI2 is taken off the free CI pointers list, and the records with keys of 28 and 30 are written to CI2. Figure 2.19 illustrates the data component and Fig. 2.20 shows the index component.

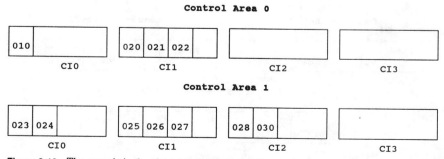

Figure 2.19   The records in the eight data dontrol intervals.

Because of the key values of the records, and the order in which the records were added to the data set, CI1 in CA0, along with CI0 and CI1 in CA1, cannot have additional records readily added to them. CI2 and CI3 in CA0 will probably remain unused unless a control interval split is performed with CI0. Hence, 5 of the 8 data control intervals will probably not play a significant role in subsequent modifications to the data set. To avoid situations such as this, the six initial records could have been loaded into the data set with a larger amount of free space specified for each control interval. This way, only one or two logical records would be placed in a control interval during the initial load process rather than three records.

I.   Delete the record with a key value of 010.   Because deleting is a random processing operation, the search for the record begins by examining index entries in the high-level index record. Since 010 < = 022, if the record is in the data set, it must be in CA0. The record is located in CI0 and deleted by rewriting the control interval.

Following the deletion, the first field in the CIDF will contain 0 because there are no logical records remaining in the data set. Thus, VSAM removes the index entry for CI0 from the sequence set record and adds an entry to the free CI pointers section. This is so CI0 can be identified as empty. This is one of the few situations other than control interval and control area splits where an I/O operation can cause a sequence set to be rewritten.

J.   Read 5 records sequentially beginning with one with a key value of 021.   Examine Figs. 2.19 and 2.20 to clarify processing. The first of the five records is located using random processing that begins by examining the high-level index record and the first sequence set record. Once the data control interval that holds the record is determined, the first record and any additional records in the control interval can be read without requiring any further information from the index component.

After the record with a key value of 022 is read, the sequence set record is checked for whether there is a record in the control area with a higher key value. The remaining three records to be read are in CA1. Recall that there is a

Sequence Set CI0   Sequence Set CI1

24 BYTES	03	02	Unused Space	CI1 022	CI0 010		24 BYTES	03	Unused Space	CI2 030	CI1 027	CI0 024

High-Level Index Record

24 BYTES		CA1 030	CA0 022

Figure 2.20   The index component following the control area split.

horizontal pointer in CA0 that contains the RBA of the second sequence set record. Because of this pointer, it is unnecessary to examine the high-level index record in order to extend the sequential processing from CA0 to CA1. The index entries in the second sequence set record specifies that the records in CA1 with the lowest key values are in the first data control interval. The next two records, with key values of 023 and 024, are read from CI0. The final record is retrieved from CI1.

K.   Randomly read the record with a key value of 027.   If only one index buffer is available, two I/O operations are required to determine whether the record exists in CI1 in CA1. In order to locate the data control interval, the second step of the random search process uses the following calculation:

address of CI1 in CA1 = 40960 + 1 * (10240)

Here, 40,960 is the RBA of CI0 in CA1 and is stored in the sequence set control information. Because CI1 is the second control interval in the control area, a displacement of 10,240 is added to the base value.

L.   Read the first record with the key value 02 in the left-most digits. VSAM can retrieve a record using a partial key value as long as they are the left-most characters or high-order portion characters of the key value. In this case, 02 > = 02 in the comparison using the first index entry in the high-level index record. Because 02 > = 02, the first record with the key value 020 is located first in CI1. Partial key values can be used to randomly read a record or to establish positioning within the data set preliminary to sequential processing.

M.   Rewrite the record with a key value of 025, increasing its length to 7500 bytes.   Again, three I/O operations are required to locate a record in CI1 in CA1. By examining the value in the CIDF, it is clear that the rewritten record won't fit in the control area. Hence, a control interval split is performed and records with key values of 26 and 27 are moved to CI3 in CA1. In order to increase the record length to 7,500, the maximum logical record length in the cluster component must be at least as large as 7,500.

Experimental Verification

In order to verify that the preceding 13 I/O operations are correct, each single operation should be performed in a separate job step. The complete contents of the KSDS is then printed and examined. This is done for the data, index, and cluster components. Although this is time-consuming, it can be used to determine the actual processing performed by VSAM in any situation. In fact, this technique was used to verify all of the preceding processing details. It is also an excellent way to answer any questions on how VSAM actually works.

Analyzing an Index Record

IDCAMS index records

Recall that there are four major sections in a sequence set record and only three in a high-level index record because it does not contain free CI pointers. There are five major components in a high-level index control interval. The two extra fields are the CIDF and a single RDF. Of the four fields in a sequence set record, three are moderately easy to examine and understand.

The first 24 bytes of each index record contains the basic control information. This is followed by the list of the free CI pointers, which identifies empty data control intervals in the control area associated with the sequence set record. The third field is a growth area of binary zeros used for new index entries. The fourth field consists of index entries for the non-empty control intervals in the control area managed by the sequence set record.

Figure 2.21 shows the index record associated with the control area described in this chapter prior to the update operations. This is the status prior to Operaton A. The left-most column in the figure contains RBA values. Every byte is represented by two hexadecimal characters in the middle columns. Printable characters are shown on the right. The RDF and CIDF are not

```
RBA OF RECORD - 0
000000    01F90301 00000000 00000000 00000000  *....  ....  ....  ....*
000010    0100001F 01EC01EC 03020000 00000000  *....  ....  ....  ....*
000020    00000000 00000000 00000000 00000000  *....  ....  ....  ....*
000030    00000000 00000000 00000000 00000000  *....  ....  ....  ....*
000040    00000000 00000000 00000000 00000000  *....  ....  ....  ....*
000050    00000000 00000000 00000000 00000000  *....  ....  ....  ....*
000060    00000000 00000000 00000000 00000000  *....  ....  ....  ....*
000070    00000000 00000000 00000000 00000000  *....  ....  ....  ....*
000080    00000000 00000000 00000000 00000000  *....  ....  ....  ....*
000090    00000000 00000000 00000000 00000000  *....  ....  ....  ....*
0000A0    00000000 00000000 00000000 00000000  *....  ....  ....  ....*
0000B0    00000000 00000000 00000000 00000000  *....  ....  ....  ....*
0000C0    00000000 00000000 00000000 00000000  *....  ....  ....  ....*
0000D0    00000000 00000000 00000000 00000000  *....  ....  ....  ....*
0000E0    00000000 00000000 00000000 00000000  *....  ....  ....  ....*
0000F0    00000000 00000000 00000000 00000000  *....  ....  ....  ....*
000100    00000000 00000000 00000000 00000000  *....  ....  ....  ....*
000110    00000000 00000000 00000000 00000000  *....  ....  ....  ....*
000120    00000000 00000000 00000000 00000000  *....  ....  ....  ....*
000130    00000000 00000000 00000000 00000000  *....  ....  ....  ....*
000140    00000000 00000000 00000000 00000000  *....  ....  ....  ....*
000150    00000000 00000000 00000000 00000000  *....  ....  ....  ....*
000160    00000000 00000000 00000000 00000000  *....  ....  ....  ....*
000170    00000000 00000000 00000000 00000000  *....  ....  ....  ....*
000180    00000000 00000000 00000000 00000000  *....  ....  ....  ....*
000190    00000000 00000000 00000000 00000000  *....  ....  ....  ....*
0001A0    00000000 00000000 00000000 00000000  *....  ....  ....  ....*
0001B0    00000000 00000000 00000000 00000000  *....  ....  ....  ....*
0001C0    00000000 00000000 00000000 00000000  *....  ....  ....  ....*
0001D0    00000000 00000000 00000000 00000000  *....  ....  ....  ....*
0001E0    00000000 00000000 00000000 000002F3  *....  ....  ....  ....*
0001F0    F0010201 F0F10002 00                 *0...  01..  .         *
```

Figure 2.21 The index record for a KSDS.

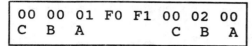

Figure 2.22 The two index entries.

shown, however, their values are 01F9 and 01F90000. Figure 2.21 was generated with the IDCAMS utility program. A control statement specified:

PRINT INDATASET(index-component-name)

Contrast this statement with either of these:

PRINT INDATASET(cluster-component-name)
PRINT INDATASET(data-component-name)

Both of these statements produce a printed list of the logical records in the data set. The PRINT command is described in detail in chapter 5.

The final two entries reference addresses in the index entries. Here, hexadecimal 01F1 translates to decimal 497, which is the beginning address of the highest value on the index entries—the left-most value. The fact that this address is repeated twice means that no sections have been created in the index. If sections had been created in the index entries, the two values would be different.

Immediately following the 24 bytes of control information is the free CI pointer list. There are two free control intervals in the control area, CI2 and CI3. Because this sequence set record was printed after data set loading, the free CI pointers are still in order. Subsequent update processing can cause them to get out of sequence, however. In this example, the index entries are also in order by control interval number.

Different processing situations during updating can also cause index entries to get out of order. On the other hand, certain values in a sequence set record never change. Which fields? In particular, the values in five of the control information fields never change.

The two index entries are shown in Fig. 2.22 and are read from right to left. Here, the A values identify the relative number of the data control interval associated with the index entry. The B values denote the number of characters from the key actually stored in the index entry. Finally, C denotes the number of characters stripped from the front of the key. The key field is 3 bytes long. Hence, $3 - (B + C)$ determines the number of characters stripped from the back of the key field.

For data $CI0(A = 00)$, two characters are included in the index entry—the first two characters within the key. Because $3 - (2 + 0) = 1$, the final character has not been stored. During subsequent processing, the key field value associated with the data control interval is F0F1FF in hexadecimal. Any record added to the data set that has a key beginning with 00 or 01 will be assigned to CI0.

For data CI1(B = 01), no characters have been stored in the index entry. Hence $3 - (0 + 0) = 3$ characters have been stripped from the back of the key. Because none of the key is stored, the key value associated with CI1 during subsequent processing is FFFFFF in hexadecimal. Thus, every record to be processed that is not associated with CI0 is associated with CI1.

Now, suppose the cluster is created with the identical parameters specified, but this time, 12 records are loaded into the data set. Because of the way the free space was defined, the additional six records are placed in a second control area. Hence, the resulting index structure contains three CIs, two sequence set records, and one high-level index record. There is only one change in the first sequence set record. The values in the sequence set records are so similar that no additional discussion is needed.

Exercises

1. Suppose that a VSAM KSDS data set has been created with a control area size of 1 cylinder, a control interval size of 2048 bytes in the data component, and 1024 bytes in the index component. Either a 3380 or 3350 disk can be used to hold the control area. No records have been loaded into the data set. After the data set is created, how many free CI pointers are there in the sequence set record and how much total space do the pointers occupy? How many index entries are there in the sequence set record, and how much space do these index entries occupy? Recall that one cylinder contains 15 tracks with a 3380 and 30 tracks with a 3350 disk.

   Suppose that a single record of 100 bytes is written in 200 of the data control intervals in the control area. After this, how many free CI pointers are there and how much space do they occupy? Now, how many index entries are there and approximately how much space do they occupy? Assume exactly two characters from the key are stored with each index entry. Include the section pointers when determining the length of the index entries. Describe the conditions in which the index record will run out of space and be unable to manage a complete control area in this data set.

2. Work through the questions in the previous exercise after making one change in the initial conditions. Assume a control area occupies three cylinders.

3. What is the relationship between the size of a vertical CI pointer field in an index entry and the size of a free CI pointer field in the same index record? What is the criteria used to select this size? What are the possible values for these sizes?

4. Draw a sketch that illustrates each of the control intervals described in Fig. 2.23. For each control interval, determine the values contained in the CIDF and in every RDF. Show the relative location of each record and its corresponding RDF along with the freespace in the control interval. Assume that

Control Interval Size	Number of Logical Records
1024 — KSDS	
512 — KSDS	
512 — RRDS	
2048 — ESDS	

Figure 2.23 Logical records contained in a control interval.

each control interval is in the data component unless otherwise specified. The control interval contains two, 100-byte records.

5. Describe several processing situations where spanned records would be appropriate.

6. Under what conditions must a vertical pointer in an index entry be stored in a field that is at least 2 bytes in length? Under what conditions must a 3-byte field be used to store the vertical pointers?

7. Describe conditions under which a vertical pointer in an index entry can be returned to the free CI pointer list. Can a control area in the data component ever be returned to the equivalent status in a higher-level index record?

8. Consider a VSAM KSDS where the control interval size in the data component is 4096 bytes, there are 10 control intervals in a control area, and every logical record is 1,000 bytes in length. How many logical records can be stored in a single control area? Derive an experiment to determine when VSAM actually switches from 1- to 2-byte vertical pointer fields. Also, determine when VSAM actually switches from 2- to 3-byte vertical pointers.

   Suppose the index control interval size is 512 bytes. How many records must be placed in the data set to construct an index component with three levels? Assume that all index entry keys are compressed to 2 bytes and that every index entry contains a vertical pointer stored in a 3-byte field.

   How many records must be placed in the data component so that the index component contains four levels? At this point, how many records will there be in the index component? How many of the index component records will be sequence set records?

9. For each of the following pair of objects, describe the similarities and differences between them. The first object in each pair is a VSAM control field, and the other is a non-VSAM control field. For more information on BDW, RDW, and SDW see chapter 11, ''Non-VSAM record formats in MVS JCL and utilities.''

   Determine, if possible, whether a CI split has occurred by examining the index entries in this sequence set record. Formulate some specific tests for determining if a control interval split has occurred in this control area. The tests need not be all-inclusive.

What is the value in the horizontal pointers in the other sequence set records? What conclusion can you draw from these values? In particular, has a control area split taken place? Formulate some specific tests for determining if a control area split has occurred in this data set.

10. Why are no characters stored in the key field in the index entry associated with the control area that holds the highest key values in the data set? How is this consistent with the way key values are stored in other index entries?

11. Will a compressed key value in an index entry ever be changed? If so, under what conditions will the index entry that holds the key value be physically rewritten?

12. Under some conditions, VSAM allows a generic delete operation. All records whose left-most key field values match a specified value are deleted. Describe how this generic delete could be done in terms of the I/O operations described in this chapter—START, random READ, sequential READ, WRITE, REWRITE, and DELETE.

3

The IDCAMS Utility

The material in this chapter is essential in order to thoroughly understand how to use the IDCAMS utility, which is so crucial for much VSAM processing. You'll learn all about the IDCAMS utility and how to use it, including the fundamental syntax of the utility control statements. Modal statements and processing commands are also discussed, followed by comments and continuation. Dynamic and static data set allocation are defined and contrasted. Finally, catalog identification methods are discussed.

Introduction to IDCAMS

IDCAMS is a powerful, general-purpose utility program used for processing VSAM data sets. Many utilities cannot be used with VSAM data sets, although there are two other utilities that can process VSAM data sets—the Sort/Merge programs (DFSORT and SYNCSORT) and ADRDSSU. Most of the older IEB/IEH utility programs cannot process VSAM data sets. The IEHLIST command LISTVTOC is an exception. If a data or index component is incorrectly identified as a non-VSAM physical sequential data set with an undefined record format, its control intervals (blocks) can be "processed" by some of the IEB/IEH utilities.

IDCAMS supports an extremely wide range of processing options. The entities that are processed can be divided into two general categories: data sets and control objects. Data sets contain records, while control objects manage one or more other objects or provide an alternate name for a data set or an entity of some type.

IDCAMS was introduced in the early seventies in conjunction with the original release of VSAM. Some of these original concepts are now out of date, but much of the basic processing notions and IDCAMS syntax remain intact. IDCAMS has not been improved as much over the years as it could have been.

A potential wish list of improvements in the syntax and functionality of IDCAMS can easily be developed.

IDCAMS can also be used to process non-VSAM data sets. Several IDCAMS commands that perform this function are REPRO, PRINT, LISTCAT, DELETE, ALTER, DEFINE NONVSAM, and DEFINE ALIAS. Details are provided with the various commands throughout chapters 5, 6, and 13.

IDCAMS was formerly required for creating a VSAM data set and is still the overwhelming choice for creating VSAM data sets today. However, data sets can now be created with JCL on a DD statement. The TSO ALLOCATE command, which could not be used for VSAM data set creation, can now do so. IDCAMS can also directly (DEFINE NONVSAM) or indirectly create (REPRO ... OFILE(DD1))—a variety of non-VSAM objects.

CICS can process records in a VSAM data set but cannot create the data set. Likewise, IMS, DB2, etc., can process records in existing VSAM data sets. As noted before, a VSAM data set can now be created on a DD statement. This holds with all types of VSAM data sets. Catalogs and alternate indexes are the next types of data sets that could also eventually be created and deleted with JCL.

IDCAMS performs various functions related to specific commands. Not all IDCAMS commands are discussed in this book. Specifically, the catalog management commands—DEFINE USERCATALOG, CNVTCAT, IMPORT CONNECT, and EXPORT DISCONNECT—are only briefly mentioned. Some commands allow a wide range of options, which are identified by coding specific parameters. Most existing parameters are discussed with each command and exceptions are noted. The group of available IDCAMS commands has changed and evolved over the years.

By contrast, VSE IDCAMS has limited capabilities compared to MVS IDCAMS. Major features not available with VSE include dynamic allocation, generic data set processing, and fewer parameters with some commands.

There are several standard methods for processing VSAM data sets, including the following three:

1. IDCAMS Utility Program. A wide range of processing is possible. If IDCAMS will perform the desired function, there is no reason to reinvent the wheel by writing an application program.

2. Batch Application Programs written in COBOL, PL/I, and Assembler. This approach requires more programmer effort than IDCAMS but allows much greater processing flexibility.

3. On-Line Application Programs (CICS), Data Base Management Systems (DB2 and IMS), and Interactive Systems (TSO). These allow additional features to be used.

Because the IDCAMS Utility program is the major topic throughout Part 2, it should be emphasized how important utility programs are. Reasons for studying utilities in general and IDCAMS in particular are given in Table 3.1.

TABLE 3.1   Reasons for Studying Utilities.

Why Study Utilities in General?	Why Study IDCAMS?
Avoid writing applications. Learn which functions are available. Practice with JCL and System Components.	Avoid writing applications. Practice and gain VSAM expertise. Absolutely essential for some types of processing.

The IDCAMS Program Structure

IDCAMS can be executed in a batch job as a stand-alone program (EXEC PGM = IDCAMS) or a cataloged procedure (EXEC IDCAMS) can be used. IDCAMS can also be called from an application program. The *Access Method Services* manual contains more information on this topic.

IDCAMS commands can also be interactively executed through native TSO. This topic is further discussed in chapter 13 on JCL. TSO provides a very convenient way to learn IDCAMS processing by practicing and experimenting with the various commands without the need to submit a batch job. Some additional related features not supported with batch IDCAMS are provided with TSO.

IDCAMS uses two required data sets: SYSIN and SYSPRINT. SYSPRINT identifies a message data set for printed information. SYSIN identifies the data set where commands and modal statements are placed. No other names can be used for either. SYSIN contains blocked or unblocked card images (80-byte records) that identify the specific processing to be performed. All SYSIN data set records are placed into one of two categories: (1) Commands—the specific fundamental functions to perform, usually with various optional parameters to choose among; and (2) Modal Statements—IF-THEN-ELSE structures, DO groups, and Assignment statements. SYSPRINT records are variable length and blocked:

$$DCB = (RECFM = VB, LRECL = 125, BLKSIZE = 629)$$

The message data set contains a listing of all the control statements, the results of each command's execution and summary information. SYSPRINT is also the primary output data set with some commands. In fact, with VSE, the LISTCAT and PRINT commands can use no other output data sets. Numerous examples of SYSPRINT output are included throughout the book.

If any additional DD (DLBL with VSE) statements are required, they are identified by their DDname with the various individual commands and classified as input, output, work data sets, etc. Ordinarily, DDnames are selected by the programmer. A few data sets have specific IDCAMS names, such as IDCUT1 and IDCUT2 with the BLDINDEX command, and AMSDUMP if an IDCAMS dump is to be taken. STEPCAT and JOBCAT are reserved DDnames used to identify VSAM catalogs.

Example 1. In Fig. 3.1, IDCAMS is executed as a stand-alone program. The processing requires several additional DD statements in addition to SYSIN and

```
//STEP1     EXEC PGM=IDCAMS
//STEPCAT   DD   DSN=VSAM-User-Catalog,DISP=SHR
//SYSPRINT  DD   SYSOUT=A
//INPUTREC  DD   parameters for data set to copy
//OUTPUT    DD   parameters for new data set
//REPORT    DD   parameters for printed report
//SYSIN     DD   *
   REPRO    copying an existing data set
   PRINT    the copied records
   LISTCAT  print the catalog information for the new data set
/*
```

Figure 3.1 IDCAMS commands and accompanying JCL.

SYSPRINT. There is no required order among the DD statements, although SYSPRINT is usually coded first and SYSIN last. If STEPCAT is coded, it usually precedes SYSPRINT. The REPRO and PRINT commands specify INPUT-REC, OUTPUT, and REPORT DDnames. All three names are programmer chosen.

During IDCAMS processing, it is necessary to identify a specific catalog or multiple catalogs to search in order to locate the data sets referenced on the commands. VSAM data sets are not located through a pass table entry and rarely located by coding UNIT and VOL on a DD statement. Catalog searching is discussed in the final section in this chapter.

Supplemental processing options can be specified with an IDCAMS PARM control statement. This is distinct from an EXEC statement PARM parameter. MARGINS(x y) determines the left and right margins on the control statements. For example, MARGINS(10 70) causes all data to the left of column 10 and to the right of column 70 to be ignored. MARGINS(2 72) is the default. Two other PARM statement values are GRAPHICS and TEST. GRAPHICS is used to produce fancy output. Various character sets can be specified. TEST is used to specify various diagnostic features. See the IDCAMS manual for more details.

Multiple IDCAMS commands can be executed in the same job step. Historically, many people have coded a single command per step. There are only a handful of situations where more than one step is specifically required to execute multiple commands. The author can only recall coming across two or three, and these could probably have been compressed into a single step with a real effort.

Syntax Fundamentals

IDCAMS control statements in the SYSIN data set are free format, meaning they can begin in any column and one or more separators can be used together:

- There is no specific column in which information must begin or be contained within.

- An arbitrary number of bytes (greater than or equal to 1) can be used to separate adjacent components in a statement.

- Almost all parameters are key words, and can be coded in any order. They use the format keyword (value) rather than keyword = value, as with JCL.

- Redundant parentheses are generally acceptable.

- A continued statement can resume anywhere, and the statement being continued can be interrupted at any point.

An IDCAMS command consists of four basic parts:

1. The command name itself must be coded first in each statement, and it can begin in any column within the specified MARGINS values.

2. The command is followed by the relevant parameters. These can range from none with some commands (LISTCAT) to dozens with other commands (DEFINE CLUSTER and DEFINE ALTERNATEINDEX). Several major commands require a minimum of one (DELETE and VERIFY) or two (ALTER) parameters for processing.

3. Optional comments can be interspersed before, between, and after the parameters and the command name.

4. In general, a space, comma, or comment can be used interchangeably as a separator.

IDCAMS control statements syntax contains two noteworthy omissions from programming languages and JCL. First, there is no statement label field. This rules out looping operations and unconditional transfer within control statements (PERFORM or GOTO...). Both of these features could be included on an IDCAMS wish list. Second, there is no continuation column.

All commands and parameters with six or more letters can be abbreviated, although some five-letter commands and parameters also have abbreviations. Abbreviation rules are basically the same as with PL/I and consist of two to five letters per word. Some commands and parameters allow multiple abbreviations. In particular, singular (abbrev) and plural (abbrevs) are equivalent. Abbreviation rules and patterns could be made clearer. For example, why is INDEXED abbreviated IXD rather than IDX? Complete parameter names are often quite

TABLE 3.2 Critiquing IDCAMS Abbreviations.

Complete Command or Parameter Name	Abbreviation	Comment
DEFINE GENERATIONDATAGROUP	DEF GDG	Good
CONTROLINTERVALSIZE	CISZ	Good
INFILE	IFILE	Silly
INDEXED	IXD	Confusing
VOLUME	VOL or VOLS	Multiples

lengthy and, hence, very descriptive. On the other hand, the abbreviations are very convenient during repetitive coding. There are also silly abbreviations such as IFILE. The best and worst of IDCAMS abbreviations are summarized in Table 3.2.

Most parameters that require a value be coded with them have a default value if the parameter itself is not coded. For example, if records contain keys but the KEYS parameter is not coded, then the first 64 bytes are used as the key. Many parameters are YES or NO choices. Generally, default values are the defensive choices (NOREUSE rather than REUSE) or capable of generating some additional information or benefits (often to IBM) (RECOVERY rather than SPEED). Some defaults are generated based on the values associated with several other parameters.

Some parameter values need to be enclosed in quotes. Quotes are usually required if special characters are coded. Special characters are symbols other than letters, numbers, and nationals. A quote within the parameter should be coded as two quotes. With specific parameters, some individual characters can be coded without using quotes. An example of this is periods with a data set name. IDCAMS is more flexible and user friendly than JCL in regard to special characters.

Numeric values can often be specified in any of three distinct representations: decimal, hexadecimal (X'hhhh'), or binary (B'bbbbbbbb'). For example, RECSZ(50 75), RECSZ(X'F3F2' X'F4C2'), and RECSZ(B'110010' B'1001011') are equivalent. Hexadecimal uses two characters for each data byte:

```
RECSZ(50 75)
RECSZ(X'F3F2' X'F4C2')
RECSZ(B'110010' B'1001011')
```

Command Condition Codes

A theoretically unlimited number of commands can be coded within a single IDCAMS job step. There is no legitimate reason to code exactly one command per job step. However, many programmers commonly do this, and it is uncertain whether historic precedence or bad advice accounts for this bizarre practice.

Combining multiple commands into one job step is much more efficient than executing isolated commands separately. The IDCAMS commands in a step might execute independently of one another, and each can be thought of as a semiautonomous entity. When multiple commands process the same data set, their effects can overlap. Tests can be made to control logic flow. In particular, a single command or a group of commands can be skipped and not executed.

Each IDCAMS command returns a condition code that reflects the degree of success or failure of the command. There are five standard IBM condition code

TABLE 3.3   Condition Code Values for IDCAMS Commands.

Value	Condition
0	Successful Execution.
4	Warning. Execution might possibly be successful, however.
8	Severe Error. Execution is unlikely to be successful. For example, a data set cannot be deleted because it cannot be found.
12	Non-recoverable Error. For example, a data set cannot be created because of conflicting parameters.
16	Disaster. With a disaster, IDCAMS processing terminates. For example, this occurs when a SYSPRINT DD statement is not coded or there is a major syntax error with a modal statement.

values used and which are defined in Table 3.3. Note that a condition code refers to a single command, not the entire job step. IDCAMS execution continues with the next command within the control statements except when a condition code of 16 occurs. Among all of the condition codes returned by the commands executed in the step, the greatest condition code value is printed in the JCL listing for the job step.

The condition codes returned by the command can be used to control the flow of execution within the job step. This is analogous to the JCL COND parameter that controls the flow of execution among job steps within a job. However, rather than using the cumbersome COND parameter, which was used for the past 25 years, the most recent releases of JCL use IF-THEN-ELSE logic, which is very similar to IDCAMS. The greatest condition code can be used to control the flow of execution within the job step. The condition code of the most recently executed command can also be used to control the flow of execution within the job step. This information is summarized in Table 3.4.

Example 2.   Three IDCAMS commands are executed in the same job step, and may or may not perform interrelated processing:

REPRO	Load records into a data set	Condition Code = 4
PRINT	The loaded records are displayed	Condition Code = 0
LISTCAT	Display catalog information	Condition Code = 8

The overall condition code for the step is an 8. If the LISTCAT command is skipped because of an earlier code, the overall condition code is a 4.

If the REPRO command returned a code of 12 or 16, any following dependant-related commands should probably be skipped. There are also situations where a code of 4 or 8 could also require skipping subsequent commands.

TABLE 3.4   IDCAMS and JCL Conditions.

Function	IDCAMS Command	JCL Job Step
Scope of the test	Command condition code	Step condition code
Interrogation method	Modal IF-THEN-ELSE statement	COND Parm-formerly JCL IF statement-Now
Storage location	MAXCC and LASTCC	Register 15

Modal commands

IF-THEN-ELSE logic can be used to control the flow of command execution during an IDCAMS job step. Note the similarity to PL/I syntax in the code throughout this chapter. When the IF "condition" evaluates to true, the command following THEN is to be executed; when the condition is false, the command associated with the ELSE is to be executed. The THEN can be coded without ELSE but not vice versa. A null THEN can be coded to specify no processing when the condition is true. A null ELSE can be coded, but it is unnecessary with a simple IF. A semicolon can be coded only with the last line in the IF-THEN-ELSE structure.

Example 3. Four versions of an IF-THEN-ELSE structure are shown in Fig. 3.2. If Condition 1 is true, Command 1 is to be executed, while Command 2 is to be executed if it is false. Versions I, II, III, and IV are all the same. In fact, I and III are exactly the same except for the semicolon. Notice that no continuation is coded anywhere except after the THEN and ELSE.

In an IF structure, DO GROUPS can be coded with either the THEN or ELSE clause or with both of them. Both DO and END should be coded on lines by themselves. Note that no semicolons are coded within the DO group structure. Notice also the continuation standards required with DO groups. Nesting is permitted, although rarely needed. This is illustrated on the right-hand side in Fig. 3.3. With nesting, it might be necessary to code null ELSE statements. As with COBOL and PL/I, an ELSE is paired with the nearest preceeding IF that is not already paired off. A nesting depth of 10 is allowed, but in practice, this number is rarely approached.

Once the IF-THEN-ELSE and DO GROUP syntax is mastered, the basic notion remaining is the IF condition. Only simple conditions are allowed. No 'OR' or 'AND' is permitted. Because of the limitation of only two registers to test, this is not a great restriction. If necessary, two consecutive IF statements can be used to implement an AND or OR test.

The format register operator condition-code-value is used for every condition. As noted earlier, condition-code-values can be 0, 4, 8, 12, or 16. The six

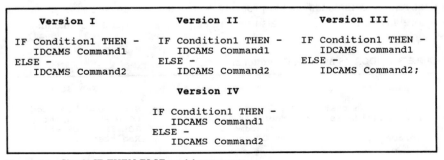

Figure 3.2 Simple IF-THEN-ELSE modal statements.

```
    Simple IF                      Nested IF

IF condition THEN    -        IF condition1 THEN        -
   DO                            IDCAMS Commands
      IDCAMS Command1         ELSE                       -
      . . .                       IF condition2 THEN     -
      IDCAMS CommandM             DO
   END                              IDCAMS CommandN
ELSE                 -             . . .
   DO                                IDCAMS CommandN+M
      IDCAMS CommandM+1           END
      . . .                    ELSE  /* Possibly Null */ -
      IDCAMS CommandN             IDCAMS CommandX
   END
```

Figure 3.3 IF-THEN-ELSE structures with DO groups.

standard operators can be identified by their abbreviation or numeric symbol:
1. EQ(=)
2. NE(not equal)
3. GT(>)
4. LT(<)
5. GE(> =)
6. LE(< =)

There are two IDCAMS registers: LASTCC and MAXCC. MAXCC contains the highest condition code returned by any command executed in the step up to this point or an initialized value provided by the SET command as discussed in the next section. LASTCC contains the condition code from the most recently executed command in the step or an initialized value provided by the SET command.

Note that every executed command supplies a value to LASTCC and possibly to MAXCC. Any command that is skipped because of an IF test, does not return a code.

Example 3. Figure 3.4 contains code that illustrates using the two IDCAMS registers. If the previous command executed correctly, execute a PRINT command. If at worst warnings were generated by all prior commands executed, then execute a REPRO command.

In addition to receiving values from the previously executed commands, the SET statement can be used to assign a value to either the LASTCC or MAXCC

```
previous commands
IF  LASTCC = 0 THEN    -
    PRINT . . .
IF  MAXCC <= 4 THEN    -
    REPRO . . .
```

Figure 3.4 Using condition to control command execution.

registers. LASTCC and MAXCC are initialized to 0 at the beginning of the step. The SET statement on the left is equivalent to MOVE 8 to LASTCC in COBOL, and the right-most SET statement is comparable to MOVE 12 to MAXCC.

SET LASTCC = 8 and SET MAXCC = 12

The IDCAMS Commands

In Table 3.5 the IDCAMS commands are grouped into five basic categories. For each command, the value in parentheses following the command denotes the chapter where it is discussed.

More IDCAMS syntax details

Studying IDCAMS is like learning to use any software package or programming language. Before any productive work can be accomplished, the syntax details must be mastered. For the serious VSAM student, this will be a well-spent investment in time and effort.

IDCAMS control statements can be coded between columns 2 and 72 inclusive. Column 1 identifies the beginning of a JCL statement. Columns 73 – 80 are ignored and are commonly used for sequence numbers.

IDCAMS control statements employ free format syntax, with both commands and modal statements. The command is the operator and must come first, however. The commands include all of the 20 or so listed in Table 3.5. Actual command syntax is as follows:

Command Separator Parameter Separator Parameter ... Continuation
Parameter Separator ...

Separators can be commas, spaces, comments, or almost any combination of all three, either interchangeable or collectively. Separators are unnecessary, however, when parentheses are available to specify the end of a parameter or subparameter value.

Parameter Syntax

Most parameters are keyword, which can be coded alone, require a single value, or require multiple values. Examples are REPLICATE (no value), CISZ(2048) (one value), and FREESPACE(20 25) (multiple values).

There are several positional parameters that must be coded first with some commands. With other commands, there are also a few required parameters, most commonly one parameter. There is a very strong overlap between positional and required parameters. One noticeable omission with IDCAMS control statements is the lack of symbolic parameters.

Keyword parameters can consist of multiple subparameters: KEYWORD(Va-

TABLE 3.5   The IDCAMS Commands.

Command	Category Function
	Data Set Creation
DEFINE CLUSTER(4)	Creates a VSAM data set. This is still the standard method for creating a VSAM data set
DEFINE(8) ALTERNATEINDEX	Creates a VSAM alternate index. This is required for IDCAMS secondary key processing
DEFINE PATH(8)	Primary function is to create a logical interface to a VSAM data set via an alternate index.
DEFINE NONVSAM(13)	Creates a Non-VSAM data set. This is more commonly done with a JCL DD statement.
DEFINE ALIAS(13)	Creates an alias for a catalog or Non-VSAM data set
DEFINE GDG(14)	Creates a Generation Data Group Base Table
DEFINE USERCATALOG(12)	Creates a VSAM usercatalog, all environments (or) a Master catalog, except for MVS
DEFINE PAGESPACE(12)	Creates a page space
	Printing Information
PRINT(5)	List the records contained in any type of VSAM data set or component. Non-VSAM data set records can also be printed.
LISTCAT(6)	Print catalog information.
	Modifying System Properties
ALTER(6)	Change catalog information for a data set. VSAM and Non-VSAM data sets may be processed.
DELETE(6)	Scratch (delete) a data set. If it is cataloged, the data set is also uncataloged. VSAM and Non-VSAM data sets may be processed.
VERIFY(6)	Synchronize the catalog entry for a VSAM data set with actual status of the records in the data set.
	Copying Records
REPRO(5)	Copy records from one data set to a sec data set. It can be used in a wide variety of settings with almost every type of data set.
BLDINDEX(8)	Load records into an alternate index.
EXPORT(5)	Unload a VSAM data set to tape.
IMPORT(5)	Reload an unloaded VSAM data set.
	Catalog Management Functions
CNVTCAT(12)	Converts VSAM catalogs to ICF catalogs.
EXPORT DISCONNECT	Disconnects a user catalog from the master catalog.
DIAGNOSE	Detect catalog structure errors
IMPORT CONNECT	Connects a user catalog to the master catalog.

```
REPRO  INFILE(SYSUT1)  OUTFILE(SYSUT2)  SKIP(500)

REPRO  OUTFILE(SYSUT2),  INFILE(SYSUT1),  SKIP(500)

REPRO  SKIP(500)  IFILE(SYSUT1) /*COMMENT*/ OFILE(SYSUT2)

REPRO  INFILE(SYSUT1)OUTFILE(SYSUT2)SKIP(500)
```

Figure 3.5 Illustrating basic command syntax.

lue1 Value2 . . . ValueN). Sub-subparameters are rare but do occur. Several examples are included to illustrate the variation available. TRACKS(10 2) has two positional values. This corresponds to SPACE = (TRK,(10,2)) on a DD statement. VOLUMES(SYS001 SYS002 SYS003) contains three positional values and corresponds to coding VOL = (,,3,,SER = (SYS001,SYS002,SYS003)) on a DD statement. KEYRANGE ((A D)(E H))(I N) (O T) (U Z)) has five parameters, each of which contain two subparameter values.

Keyword subparameters are much rarer than positional subparameters. Both the DEFINE CLUSTER and DEFINE ALTERNATEINDEX commands are confusing exceptions to this statement. This is because most values coded are actually subparameters, although they are described and discussed as parameters throughout this book and the IDCAMS manual. With both commands, the only true parameters are CLUSTER, DATA, INDEX, and CATALOG.

Example 4.   The four versions of the REPRO command in Fig. 3.5 are equivalent. Note that all of the four parameters are keywords and can be coded in any order. A specific coding style should be selected for consistency and to reduce the chance of error. Note that INFILE and OUTFILE are abbreviated as IFILE and OFILE in the third version of the REPRO command. Note also the comment in the middle of the third version. In the last version, the closing parenthesis serves as a separator. Probably the most popular coding style consists of putting the command and each parameter on a separate line. This is illustrated in Fig. 3.6. Parentheses must be balanced.

Control Statement Comments and Blank Lines

Comments are used to provide documentation and improve readability. An IDCAMS comment uses the same syntax as PL/I: /*COMMENT*/. Failure to code /* or */ correctly will result in the same problems as with other MVS data sets or with PL/I. If /* is coded in column 1, it is interpreted as the JCL delim-

```
REPRO              -
   INFILE(SYSUT1)  -
   OUTFILE(SYSUT2) -
   SKIP(500)
```

Figure 3.6 Most common IDCAMS command coding style.

```
      REPRO  IFILE(DD1)  ODS(A.B.C)               -
/*            REPLACE                             - */
/*            FROMKEY(QQQ)  Comments  TOKEY(XXX)    */
```

Figure 3.7 Turning comments into control statements.

iter, which ends an in-stream data set. Consequently, all subsequent commands are included as part of a second-GENERATED SYSIN data set, which is then ignored because of its duplicate DDname. If */ is omitted, everything following /* is treated as a comment until an */ is eventually encountered. Commands and modal statements are then processed as part of the comment. A comment might occupy the entire statement:

/*THIS COMPLETE STATEMENT IS A COMMENT */

Within a DO GROUP, a record that contains just a comment must also contain a continuation character. The MARGINS PARM option can be used to turn comments into executable commands by changing the portion of the control statement that is scanned. This is illustrated in Fig. 3.7. If the /* and */ are considered outside the text scanned, there are three lines and five parameters. It is also possible to turn executable commands into comments.

Blank statements can also be used to improve readability and the appearance of the source code. Blank statements are an alternative to comments in some regards. Use both comment lines and blank lines with care within DO GROUPS. Blank lines and statements that are entirely comments within DO GROUPS must be followed with continuation marks or they might terminate the THEN or ELSE clause.

Continuing IDCAMS Commands

IDCAMS commands can be continued. DO and END statements cannot be continued. A hyphen should be the right-most, non-blank character on a continued statement. The hyphen should follow a complete parameter, subparameter, command name, or comment. If a statement is to be continued in the midst of a value, use a plus instead of a hyphen. One or more spaces can be coded on each side of the hyphen or plus. Consecutive hyphens or plus signs should not be coded. A non-continued statement should not end in a continuation character, although it can optionally end with a semicolon.

Example 5. The REPRO command and three parameters are first coded without continuation as:

REPRO__INFILE(DD1)__OUTFILE(DD2)__COUNT(100)

```
Method 1              Method 2              Method 3

REPRO              - REPRO-              REPRO INFILE(DD1)-
   INFILE(DD1)     -   INFILE(DD1)  -          OUTFILE(DD2)-
   OUTFILE(DD2)    -   OUTFILE(D+             SKIP(500);
   SKIP(500)           D2)-              PRINT INFILE(DD2)
PRINT              -   SKIP(500)
                   - PRINT-
   INFILE(DD2)     /*COMMENT*/   -
                      INFILE(DD2)

                      Method 4

REPRO INFILE(DD1) OUTIFLE(DD2) SKIP(500); PRINT INFILE(DD2)
```

Figure 3.8 Various continuation methods.

The same command can be continued in any of the three ways shown in Fig. 3.8. A subsequent PRINT command is also included for further clarification. The preferred method for continuation is the REPRO command in Method 1, where all hyphens are aligned, because omissions are easy to detect. This standard is used throughout the rest of this book. Note the embedded blank line in Method 1. There is a problem with Method 4. The semicolon causes the PRINT command not to execute.

Example 7. Figure 3.9 illustrates the two classic examples of potential problems that can occur when DO Groups, Comments, and blank lines are combined. On the left-hand side, the comment statement in the DO group is not followed by a continuation mark. This is interpreted as the end of the THEN processing. The LISTCAT is unconditionally executed, and the following END statement generates a syntax error. IDCAMS control statements are interpreted and not compiled. Hence, the unbalanced END is not detected until it is executed. On the right-hand side, a blank line is inserted in the midst of the ELSE DO group, terminating the ELSE and causing the final LISTCAT to be unconditionally executed.

Detailed IDCAMS Syntax Example

In the detailed IDCAMS syntax example in Fig. 3.10, a KSDS called SECOND-.DATASET is to be created. It is to be assigned the same properties and char-

```
IF MAXCC LE 4 THEN   -        IF LASTCC = 0 THEN        -
   DO                              LISTCAT ENT(X.Y.Z)
      PRINT IDS(X.Y.Z)         ELSE                      -
/*ENTIRELY A COMMENT STATEMENT*/   DO
      LISTCAT ENT(X.Y.Z)  -           PRINT IFILE(DD1)
      ALL
   END                                LISTCAT LEVEL(A.B)  -
                                      ALL
                                   END
```

Figure 3.9 Special DO group syntax problems.

```
//A          EXEC PGM=IDCAMS
//SYSPRINT DD   SYSOUT=A
//SYSIN     DD  *
  DEFINE  CLUSTER(NAME(SECOND.DATASET)                     -
                 MODEL(FIRST.DATASET)                      -
                 (numerous remaining parameters follow))
  IF LASTCC = 0 THEN                                       -
     DO
        REPRO to copy records to the second data set
        PRINT to list the records in the second data set
        IF MAXCC LE 4 THEN                                 -
           DO
              DEFINE  CLUSTER(NAME(THIRD.DATASET)          -
                      . . .                                -
                      (rest of the parameters))
              REPRO to copy records to the third data set
                      . . .                                -
              PRINT to list the records in the third data set
           END
        ELSE                                               -
           /* ONLY ONE NEW DATASET WAS CREATED*/           -
           DO
              LISTCAT ENT(FIRST.DATASET) ALL
              LISTCAT ENT(SECOND.DATASET) ALL
           END
     END
  ELSE          /* NO NEW DATA SETS WERE CREATED */        -
     LISTCAT ENT(FIRST.DATASET) ALL
  /* THE STRUCTURE BEGUN BY 'IF LASTCC=0' IS ENDED */
  Other unrelated commands may be coded here
  /*   End of the Control Statements   */
```

Figure 3.10 Detailed example of commands and modal statements.

acteristics as the existing KSDS, FIRST.DATASET. If SECOND.DATASET is created successfully, the records in the original KSDS are to be loaded into it and the records printed. If the second data set is both created and loaded successfully, a third data set called THIRD.DATASET is created. If either of the data set creations fail, a list of catalog information for the existing data sets up to this point is provided. The IDCAMS comments included in Fig. 3.10 describe the processing being performed.

Static and Dynamic Data Set Allocation Concepts

Prior to the introduction of IDCAMS, data sets on large IBM systems were always statically allocated. Static allocation means that it is necessary to code a DD statement in the JCL for each data set to be processed. The DD statement provides the actual name of the data set and identifies its location. Furthermore, the name of the data set cannot be specified in non-JCL source code. Rather, an indirect reference is made to the data set by specifying the DDname of the JCL statement that actually contained the name. As shown in Fig. 3.11, static allocation is implemented with various software environments.

In all cases, a DD statement must be coded with the job step, and it contains the actual name of the data set:

//DDname DD DSN = Actual Data Set Name,Other DD Parameters

Software	Method of Identifying the Actual Data Set
COBOL Program	SELECT FILENAME ... ASSIGN TO UT-S-DDname
PL/I Program	DECLARE DDname FILE ...
Assembler Program	DCB DDNAME=DDname,...
Linkage Editor	INCLUDE DDname(Module),...
Command Level CICS	EXEC CICS VSAM Command DATASET(DDname) ...

Figure 3.11 Methods for identifying disk data sets.

There are two great advantages of static allocation. First, is its historic "consistency" and efficiency. It has been used for almost 30 years, and all IBM mainframe programmers are familiar with it. Second, it guarantees the existence and availability of the data set prior to step execution. Because static allocation requires JCL, however, numerous pitfalls associated with JCL can occur. These include a JCL syntax error on a DD statement (it causes the entire job to be scratched); coding a syntactically correct but nonexistent data set name (the job terminates prior to executing the step containing the DD statement); coding the name of an existing data set while trying to create a new data set (the wrong data set is identified); and numerous other problems, most of which have a very negative impact on processing.

IDCAMS provides an alternative approach to static data set allocation. It permits the name of the data set to be specified directly in the source code, eliminating the need for an accompanying JCL statement. When dynamic allocation is used, many of the problems and hazards associated with JCL are removed and others reduced. IDCAMS contains a much more flexible, user-friendly syntax than JCL. IDCAMS syntax errors are usually localized to a specific command. They rarely cause a job step to be scratched, let alone an entire job. Missing and duplicate data set names are identified as such and processing continues with the next statement or command. Dynamic allocation offers many substantial improvements over static allocation. Hence, dynamic allocation should be used whenever there is an equal choice between static and dynamic. Figure 3.12 illustrates how much simpler it is to use dynamic allocation with a PRINT statement than static allocation with a DD statement. IDS is the abbreviation for INDATASET, which is the parameter specifying dynamic allocation.

Dynamic allocation limitations

Unfortunately, there are some types of data sets and some processing situations that rule out or severely restrict the use of dynamic allocation. In particu-

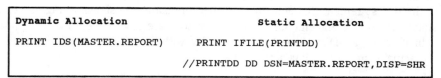

Dynamic Allocation	Static Allocation
PRINT IDS(MASTER.REPORT)	PRINT IFILE(PRINTDD)
	//PRINTDD DD DSN=MASTER.REPORT,DISP=SHR

Figure 3.12 Amount of code with static and dynamic allocation.

lar, programming language applications and most non-IDCAMS utilities do not yet support dynamic allocation syntax. Thus, it is currently restricted to use with IDCAMS or an interactive environment such as TSO/ISPF.

By its very nature, the coding of the data set name in source code replaces the information provided by the JCL DD statement. One crucial function of the DD statement is to identify the location of the data set. The UNIT and VOL-UME DD parameters, catalogs, and the pass mechanism are used for this purpose. Because UNIT and VOLUME values are not part of the dynamic allocation and passed VSAM data sets are not supported, dynamic allocation uses only system catalogs to locate a data set. Consequently, only cataloged data sets can be dynamically allocated. This is no hindrance with VSAM data sets but can cause exclusions with non-VSAM data sets. It is anticipated that the percentage of data sets that are cataloged will increase.

JCL also provides a method of determining the degree of data set sharing allowed during processing. Coding DISP = SHR allows other jobs to process a data set concurrently, while DISP = OLD locks all other jobs out of the data set. Ordinarily, DISP = OLD is needed only when modifying a data set or library. Dynamic allocation generates a DISP = OLD level of sharing no matter how the records in the data set are to be processed. Clearly, this is inappropriate with many important heavily used system data sets. This would seem to suggest the need for an additional IDCAMS parameter to specify sharing with dynamic allocation.

Dynamic allocation does not allow any additional JCL features to be associated with a data set. These include convenient features with which many programmers have become familiar with over the years. It is occasionally upsetting for a person with a great deal of JCL expertise to lose access to these features.

JCL allows a group of data sets to be linked together and processed as input one after the other. This technique is called concatenation and is identified by specifying the DDname on the first DD statement and then omitting the DDname on all the rest of the statements.

```
//INPUTETC DD DSN = FIRST.DATASET,DISP = SHR
//         DD DSN = SECOND.DATASET,DISP = SHR
//         DD DSN = THIRD.DATASET,DISP = SHR
```

The dynamic allocation equivalent would seem to be allowing a user to code INDATASET(FIRST.DATASET SECOND.DATASET THIRD.DATASET). However, this is not presently supported by IDCAMS.

Two widely used types of data sets cannot be dynamically allocated. These are in-stream data sets denoted by DD * and print data sets denoted by the SYSOUT parameter. Strengths and weaknesses associated with dynamic allocation are summarized in Table 3.6.

TABLE 3.6 Advantages and Disadvantages of Dynamic Allocation.

Advantages	Disadvantages
No JCL Needed Friendlier Syntax Less Overall Code	DISP=OLD processing occurs Only cataloged data sets may be allocated No concatenation with input data sets No supplemental JCL features are available In-stream data sets are not permitted SYSOUT data sets are not permitted Requires the IDCAMS utility (at present)

Generic Data Set Names—LISTCAT, ALTER, and DELETE Commands

Records in a KSDS are identified by primary record keys. Records in a KSDS or ESDS can be processed through an alternate index. Some IDCAMS commands permit just a portion of the key to be specified. If there are N bytes in the key field, a generic key is identified by coding from 1 to N-1 bytes. These bytes are assumed to be the high-order (left-most) bytes in the key. The data set is searched during an input operation for a match just on the bytes in the generic key, not the complete key. Both exact matches and the first record with a key greater than or equal to the search value are permitted with generic keys. Generic keys are also supported in batch application programs and with CICS.

When using IDCAMS, the word *generic* occurs in a second context. Here, the partial name of a data set is specified rather than a partial key. Data set names consist of one or more levels of qualification. A generic data set name can have two meanings. Like generic keys, one or more left-most qualifiers are coded. Rather than locating just the first data set, however, every data set that matches the specified leading qualifiers is processed. If only a first-level qualifier is specified, a tremendous number of data sets can be processed.

The second format of a generic data set name is even more common. All but one of the qualifiers in a data set name are coded. The missing qualifier is identified by an asterisk. Suppose N levels of qualification are coded, one of which is the asterisk. Any data set that has exactly N qualifiers (no more), where the N-1 matches the generic value, are processed.

Both versions of generic data set names require that values be specified in terms of complete qualifiers. Some systems allow a combination of generic data set names where one or more qualifiers are treated the same as generic keys. Then values such as ABCDEF.GH*, ABC.DE*.FGH, and ABC.*.E*, etc., are allowed. These are not supported with IDCAMS.

Data Set Identification via Catalog Entry

Identifying specific catalogs to search for data set entries is a major component of VSAM processing. VSAM objects of all types are cataloged. This includes catalog entries for the cluster components and the data and index component. There are a wide variety of non-VSAM data set objects that can be processed by VSAM and have entries placed in VSAM catalogs. When identifying an object to process, it is the responsibility of the programmer to somehow identify the catalog that contains the descriptive information for the object to be processed. There are four fundamental methods for identifying the appropriate catalog to be used:

1. CATALOG (catalog name) parameter.
2. JOBCAT and STEPCAT DD statements in JCL.
3. First level of qualification in data set name.
4. Default—system master catalog.

There are several additional restrictions in effect with some of the IDCAMS commands. See the *Access Methods Services* manual for additional details. With some commands, the other locations will not be checked if CATALOG is coded.

The CATALOG Parameter

One of the four methods for identifying the appropriate catalog is only available with IDCAMS commands. In fact, almost every IDCAMS command allows a CATALOG parameter to be coded with it. The value specified with CATALOG should identify either a VSAM or ICF catalog. As with all four methods of catalog identification, the appropriate catalog has an entry placed in it if an object is being created. If an existing object is to be processed, the catalog is searched for information used to describe and locate the object. For example:

```
DEFINE   CLUSTER(NAME(. . .))   CATALOG(USERCAT5)
PRINT   INDATASET(data set name)   CATALOG(VSAM123)
```

For the DEFINE CLUSTER command, the VSAM data set and its components have their catalog entries placed in USERCAT5, assuming the DEFINE CLUSTER executes successfully. For the DELETE command, the user catalog VSAM123 is searched for an entry for the input data set.

JOBCAT and STEPCAT DD Statements

The DDnames JOBCAT and STEPCAT are reserved for a specific type of processing. They are coded to identify specific catalogs to be used for the duration of the job(JOBCAT) or just the jobstep(STEPCAT). With both statements, requests to catalog a data set or retrieve a cataloged data set are directed to the data set coded on the DD statement.

The two data sets shown in Fig. 3.13 in step A will use USERCAT1 for processing if no CATALOG parameter is included in the source code. Hence, the catalog entry for the NEW.DATASET1 will be placed in USERCAT1. Likewise, USERCAT1 will be searched for an entry for OLD.DATASET. For the processing in step B, the JOBCAT catalog is completely ignored because a STEPCAT DD statement is coded. Here, the catalog entry for NEW.DATASET2 is placed in USERCAT2. Likewise, USERCAT2 will be initially searched for an entry for

```
//          JOB  Statement
//JOBCAT    DD   DSN=USERCAT1,DISP=SHR
//A         EXEC PGM=FIRST
//DD1       DD   DSN=NEW.DATASET1,DISP=(NEW,CATLG),
//               UNIT=SYSDA,SPACE=(CYL,1)
//DD2       DD   DSN=OLD.DATASET,DISP=SHR
  . . .
//B         EXEC PGM=SECOND
//STEPCAT   DD   DSN=USERCAT2,DISP=SHR
//DD3       DD   DSN=NEW.DATASET2,DISP=(NEW,CATLG),
//               UNIT=SYSDA,SPACE=(TRK,1)
//DD4       DD   DSN=OTHER.OLD.DATASET,DISP=SHR
//C         EXEC PGM=IDCAMS
//STEPCAT   DD   DSN=USERCAT3,DISP=SHR
//SYSIN     DD   *
   references to data sets
   CATALOG parameters
/*
```

Figure 3.13   Using JOBCAT and STEPCAT to identify catalogs.

OTHER.OLD.DATASET. USERCAT3 is in effect with the IDCAMS utility in the third step.

In summary, if STEPCAT is coded, it is used for catalog processing functions and JOBCAT is ignored. For each step where STEPCAT is not coded, JOBCAT is in effect and searched. Both JOBCAT and STEPCAT allow multiple catalogs to be linked together. For input processing, the concatenated data sets are searched in the order in which they are coded.

First Level of Data Set Name Qualification

The first level of qualification in a data set name might identify either the actual name of a catalog, or an alias for it. It is the fundamental alternative to using JOBCAT and STEPCAT DD statements. As always, any approach that minimizes the amount of JCL coded has some advantages. Some installations have used this approach and prohibit altogether coding JOBCAT and STEPCAT DD statements.

System Master Catalog

If the three preceding methods described fail to locate a data set or are not used, then the system master catalog can be used. The system master catalog should only be used as a last approach to catalog a new data set or attempt to locate an existing data set when all other approaches are exhausted. As discussed in chapter 1, the use of the master catalog is commonly restricted to "important" data sets.

Data Set Backup

In any data processing environment, it is important to periodically back up important system data sets. There are two IDCAMS commands that perform this function with VSAM data sets—REPRO and EXPORT. The trade-offs between the two are discussed in chapters 5 and 6. There are also non-IDCAMS programs that can perform backup operations, often on entire disk volume rather than a data set. REPRO creates a copy of the records within a data set. EXPORT copies the records and also control information.

IDCAMS Error and Diagnostic Messages

The *MVS Systems Messages* manual contains approximately 140 pages of messages ranging from informatory to serious errors. The manual provides some additional information for many of the messages. The IDC3009I error message should also be noted because it actually identifies hundreds of error conditions—30 pages. Not surprisingly, it has a very confusing syntax that must be carefully examined to avoid erroneous conclusions. It would probably have been better to divide this one error message into dozens of different categories.

Exercises

1. A variety of classic IDCAMS syntax errors are included in the control statements listed in Fig. 3.14. Find the syntax errors in the following segments of IDCAMS control statements. Some statements contain multiple errors. Don't worry about the actual functions performed; this is strictly a syntax drill. Each statement is meant to be a complete command.

2. Try to identify one or more processing situations involving IDCAMS commands that require multiple job steps be used because the correct results cannot be achieved in a single jobstep.

```
a)  PRINT IFILE=DDNAME1,OFILE=DDNAME2
b)  REPRO IFILE(DDNAME1) OFILE(DDNAME2)
c)  IFILE E(ALPHA.BETA) REPRO OFILE(GAMMA.DELTA)
d)  LISTCAT E(ALPHA.BETA)
e)  DEFINE CLUSTER(NAME(ALPHA(BETA)) VOL=SER=DISK01)
f)  DELETE ALL.DATASETS.*.WITH.*
g)  DELETE A.B.C; PRINT IDS(E.F.G)
h)  IF MAXCC <= 8 THEN
        DELETE A.B.C
        PRINT IDS(E.F.G)
i)  REPRO IFILE(DDABCD)
        OFILE(DDPQRS)
```

Figure 3.14 Determining IDCAMS syntax errors.

3. This can actually be an ongoing exercise throughout Part 2 of this book. Construct an IDCAMS wish list of features not provided by IDCAMS, items that would be nice to have available. Candidates include improved syntax, more flexibility with existing commands and modal statements, and new commands.

4. Try to identify several syntax similarities between IDCAMS and PL/I. What is the reason for this strange relationship between the two?

5. Seven significant disadvantages of dynamic allocation are listed in Table 3.6. Which of the seven are candidates to be "fixed," in the sense that they can be removed from the disadvantages list?

6. Why is the IDCAMS control statement data set translated and executed one statement at a time rather than compiled as a high-level language program would be? What are the advantages and disadvantages of the translation approach?

The DEFINE CLUSTER Command

This chapter discusses DEFINE CLUSTER, the most important and complicated of all the IDCAMS commands. DEFINE CLUSTER is used to create VSAM data sets. The first part of the chapter compares the role of DEFINE CLUSTER with the JCL DD statement to create non-VSAM data sets. This is followed by rules and conventions for naming clusters and their components. Next, the parameters that give a cluster its structure are discussed. These include, among others:

- Type of data set.
- The key field.
- Freespace.
- Control interval size.
- Record size.
- Control area size.
- Disk volume.

The non-structural parameters are examined next, including ownership identification, security techniques, and recovery methods. Various other types of properties, such as modeling, optimization, and purely unclassified optional are discussed. Finally, four complete DEFINE CLUSTER examples are presented.

The DEFINE CLUSTER Command and JCL

Since the introduction of VSAM, the DEFINE CLUSTER command (abbreviated DEF CL) has been the standard method for creating a VSAM data set.

Prior to the release of DFSMS with MVS/ESA, VSAM data sets could not be created by coding a JCL DD statement, which contained or implied DISP = NEW.

Using JCL to create VSAM data sets is supported with DFSMS and is discussed as a separate topic in chapter 13. Cluster creation and deletion with JCL is not yet widely implemented but promises to be a convenient viable alternative to IDCAMS. Hence, this chapter should be thought of as just the major portion of the general topic of VSAM data set creation, half of the entire subject. Prior to 1992, an overwhelming majority of VSAM users had probably not created or deleted a VSAM data set with JCL.

DEFINE CLUSTER (and its companion command DEFINE ALTERNA-TEINDEX) is the IDCAMS command with the largest number of parameters available, approximately 40. The reason for such a wide variety of required and optional parameters is that DEFINE CLUSTER performs the same basic creation function for a VSAM data set as the MVS JCL DD statement with DISP = (NEW,CATLG) coded does for a non-VSAM data set. Consequently, most of the DD parameters used during data set creation have an IDCAMS equivalent. Likewise, most IDCAM parameters have a JCL equivalent. To illustrate the relationship between DD parameters and DEFINE CLUSTER parameters, consider the following JCL statement, which creates a cataloged, non-VSAM sequential (QSAM) data set:

```
//DD1 DD DSNAME = XYZ,DISP = (NEW,CATLG),UNIT = DASD,
//    VOL = SER = WORK01,SPACE = (TRK,(2,1)),DCB = (LRECL = 100,
//    BLKSIZE = 1000,RECFM = FB),LABEL = RETPD = 14
```

DEFINE CLUSTER parameters that do not have a DD statement equivalent are the parameters used to optimize processing and a large group of security features.

The IDCAMS code to create an "equivalent" VSAM ESDS is shown in Fig. 4.1. Each line in the IDCAMS code has a functionally similar JCL parameter or subparameter, which is shown on the right side of Fig. 4.1. Note that these are similar but not identical. There are significant differences among the SHA-REOPTIONS, TRACKS, and CONTROLINTERVALSIZE parameters and their DD statement companion. There is no required order with any of the DD parameters or IDCAMS parameters except for NAME, which must immediately follow DEFINE CLUSTER.

```
VSAM DEFINE CLUSTER            The DD Parameter Equivalents to
Command and Parameters            the DEFINE CLUSTER Parameter

DEFINE CLUSTER(              -   DD statement operator
NAME(XYZ)                    -   DSNAME=XYZ,
SHAREOPTIONS(2 3)            -   DISP=(NEW,CATLG),
VOLUME(WORK01)               -   VOL=SER=WORK01,(UNIT=DASD also)
TRACKS(2 1)                  -   SPACE=(TRK,(2,1)),
RECORDSIZE(100 100)          -   DCB=LRECL=100 and RECFM=FB,
CONTROLINTERVALSIZE(1000)    -   DCB=BLKSIZE=1000,
FOR(14) or TO(92366)         -   LABEL=RETPD=14 or LABEL=EXPDT=92366,
 additional parameters)         other DD parameters
```

Figure 4.1 DD parameters and equivalent DEFINE CLUSTER code.

IDCAMS—An Alternative to JCL

IBM claims that a major advantage of using VSAM is that the amount of JCL that must be coded is greatly minimized. This is certainly true for a variety of reasons. To perform many of the equivalent JCL functions with VSAM data sets, however, it is necessary to use the IDCAMS utility. The IDCAMS utility requires a significant effort to learn the required material—approximately 400 pages in the IBM manual—to adequately use VSAM data sets. Creating a data set requires more JCL than processing an existing data set. The same relationship also holds among DEFINE CLUSTER and other IDCAMS commands to process data sets.

As stated in chapter 1, the effort required to master IDCAMS is worthwhile for someone planning to work in an IBM environment. There is no doubt that the importance of VSAM and IDCAMS will continue to grow over the next decade. VSAM is a candidate to be a Systems Application Architecture (SAA) product in that it is supported across all hardware platforms and portable in the sense that it can be moved from one operating system to another. The same is not true for JCL, however, which is operating system unique.

There are many significant advantages of using IDCAMS to create or reference a data set versus using JCL for the same purpose. Some of the reasons were discussed in more general terms in chapter 3. First, because IDCAMS is free format, allows abbreviations, and uses an Englishlike syntax, it is syntactically easier and safer to successfully create a data set with IDCAMS.

If errors do occur when creating or referencing a data set with IDCAMS, the results are not nearly as dramatic as with JCL. In particular, when JCL is used to reference a data set in any way (creation or deletion included), a syntax error causes the entire job to be scratched. If a data set is to be created and there is already a data set with the same name, the job is scratched. Third, if a data set is referenced that doesn't exist, the job ends before step execution with the message: DATA SET NOT FOUND.

In all three of these situations, syntax errors, duplicate names, and referencing a data set that cannot be found, IDCAMS merely return a non-zero code and goes onto the next command within the step or onto the next step. This is an aspect of user friendliness that is not available with JCL. In all fairness, JCL has moved more from its original syntax over the years toward user friendliness than IDCAMS has moved from its original base.

The approach followed in this chapter with the DEFINE CLUSTER command is to describe most of the parameters that can be coded when creating a VSAM data set. Many of these parameters have default values that can be frequently used and need not be coded. In fact, it is rare when most of the parameters need to be explicitly coded. Defaults can be applied to the most common processing situations. As with all IDCAMS commands, to invoke a DEFINE CLUSTER command, code PGM = IDCAMS or use the IDCAMS cataloged procedure. Both approaches are illustrated in Fig. 4.2. Practically every installation has a cataloged procedure very similar to the one shown on the right in Fig. 4.2.

```
    Stand-Alone Program                Cataloged Procedure
//A  EXEC  PGM=IDCAMS    or      //A  EXEC  IDCAMS
//SYSPRINT  DD  SYSOUT=A         //SYSIN      DD  *
//SYSIN    DD  *                    other IDCAMS commands
   other IDCAMS commands           . . .
   . . .                           DEFINE CLUSTER(parameters)
   DEFINE CLUSTER(parameters)      . . .
   . . .                           other IDCAMS commands
   other IDCAMS commands        /*
/*
```

Figure 4.2 JCL for using the IDCAMS utility.

Notice that a DEFINE CLUSTER command can be coded in the control statement data set along with any other IDCAMS commands. Hence, it is possible to precede the DEFINE CLUSTER command with a DELETE command to remove an existing data set with the same name from the system. After a cluster has been defined, it is possible to load records into it and then begin processing the records in the same IDCAMS job step.

Recall that IDCAMS is like PL/I in that any name containing six (occasionally five) or more characters can usually be abbreviated. Most of the parameters described in this chapter have an abbreviation. Whenever a parameter or command is first discussed, the abbreviation is identified.

DEFINE CLUSTER Parameters

Throughout this chapter and in chapters 5, 6, and 8, each parameter is classified with which of the three portions of the DEFINE CLUSTER command it can be coded and to which it applies. Many of the parameters can be coded with all three components. In this case, nothing is specifically stated. For each parameter, all of the possible default values are identified. After the parameters are described, four complete examples are presented to illustrate many of the parameters. Additional DEFINE CLUSTER examples are discussed throughout the book, including chapters 10 (ESDS), 11 (RRDS), 13 (Using JCL with VSAM), and 15 (Linear Data Sets).

The NAME(Data Set Name) Parameter

The NAME parameter must be coded with the cluster component. It is optional with the data and index components. Along with the VOLUME and Space Allocation parameters, NAME is one of only three required parameters. Furthermore, MODEL can be used to specify volume and space allocation information. It is not necessary to code a name on a DD statement with a non-VSAM data set. A VSAM data set always contains a data (and index for a KSDS) component, which can be given a name with this parameter.

If NAME is not coded for the data and index components, default values will be supplied by IDCAMS. It was formerly a bad programming practice to use the default names. With most VSAM releases, the generated names were an unwieldy combination of 44 characters, which included the job name along with the date and time the job was run. It is a good practice to specify names that show the relationships among components, as in the examples throughout this book. Recent releases of VSAM generate reasonable choices for data and index component names. These are discussed in more detail further in the chapter.

The actual syntax rules for coding a data set name with IDCAMS are practically identical to those used when coding a DSNAME value on an MVS JCL DD statement. Up to 44 alphanumeric and national (@, #, $) characters can be coded. The complete name is decomposed by periods into levels of qualification. Anywhere from one to eight characters form a level of qualification, with the first character in each level being alphabetic (not alphanumeric) or national. Temporary data set names (beginning with & or &&) are not permitted with VSAM.

The first level of qualification in the data set name can be used to identify the user catalog that the data set will be cataloged in when a VSAM data set is created or to search for a catalog entry for an existing data set. In order to utilize these features, the first level of qualification must be the name of a user catalog or an alias for its name. Security packages such as RACF can be used to specify which qualifier is valid and the processing limitations allowed with each. For example, a specific user might be able to read or update any data set whose first level qualifier is ALPHA, but only read data sets whose first level qualifier is BETA. Processing restrictions can be set up so that only specific qualifiers are valid when a data set is created.

Example 1. A variety of both valid and invalid names are identified in this example and in Example 2. Here, all of the names in Fig. 4.3 are valid cluster and data component names. Notice that the letters FML are used as a qualifier in several of the names. These represent the programmer's initials. Coding this or some other comparable value as part of the cluster name is a good defensive programming practice for several reasons. It contributes to generating a unique name, it provides an identification scheme, and it supports generic processing with various other IDCAMS commands. The type of data set is not specified, but if it is a KSDS, the index component should have the same name as the data component except for a final qualifier of INDEX rather than DATA. It is assumed that ACSSTU and ACSFAC are true names or aliases for a user catalog. A variety of interrelational naming conventions are illustrated here. The

Cluster Component Name	Data Component Name
NAME(ACSSTU.FML.VSAM.STUFF)	NAME(ACCSTU.FML.VSAM.DATA)
NAME(ACSSTU.TEMP.DATASET)	NAME(ACSSTU.TEMP.DATASET.DATA)
NAME(ACSFAC.KSDS.MASTER.CLUSTER)	NAME(ACSFAC.KSDS.MASTER.DATA)
NAME(ACSFAC.FML.TEST.CL)	NAME(ACSFAC.FML.TEST.DATA)

Figure 4.3 Naming data set components.

TABLE 4.1 Common Naming Errors.

Cluster Name	Reasons Why Name is Invalid or Valid
&&TEMP	Invalid VSAM name, (begins with &), but valid for a non-VSAM data set.
nothing coded	Invalid, since the Cluster name is required. Valid for data and index components.
ACSTU.FML	ACSSTU is misspelled.It does not identify a user catalog.
A.B.C.5D	Invalid first (A) (not first qualifer and) fourth (5D) qualifiers (starts with number).
ACSSTU.	Invalid since name cannot end with a period.
ACSSTU.FMLSSSS03	Invalid, Nine characters in second qualifier.
ACSSTU.DATA	Valid, but a poor choice for cluster name.
ACSSTU.FML.MASTER	Valid, and a good choice for several reasons.

final two are the preferred because of the wide range of generic processing capabilities they provide and the component identification.

Example 2. Several of the cluster names shown in Table 4.1 are valid, however, most of the names are invalid for the reason given on the right-hand side. The cluster is to be cataloged in either the ACSSTU or ACSFAC usercatalog.

Because both the data and index components have their own catalog entries, each can be individually referenced. This allows either of them to be processed as a separate entity, independent from the rest of the VSAM structure. This is discussed further with the PRINT, LISTCAT, DELETE, and ALTER commands in chapters 5 and 6. Individual components are not ordinarily processed with the REPRO, EXPORT, IMPORT, and VERIFY commands.

Whether the cluster name or the name of one of the components is identified determines the degree of processing performed with most IDCAMS commands, other utilities, or even application programs. In general, whenever the cluster name is specified, all of the other related components are also allocated and processed. If just the data or index component is identified, then only that component is processed without the benefit of related information in the other components.

Example 3. A VSAM KSDS is created and the name ALPHA.TAX.CLUSTER is given. A portion of the IDCAMS code needed to accomplish this is shown in Fig. 4.4. Note that the names for the data and index components contain the same first two qualifiers as the cluster names. Very carefully note how the continuation is handled. A continuation mark (hyphen) is required on every line, including the final lines of the CLUSTER and DATA component parameters. If a continuation mark is not included on the line immediately before the DATA component, IDCAMS interprets the word DATA as a nonexistent command name and generates an error message. The same holds for the line before the INDEX parameter.

The command ends following the CATALOG parameter in Fig. 4.4 and after the index component is defined in Fig. 4.5. The order of the DATA and INDEX parameters in the DEFINE CLUSTER command can be reversed and their associated subparameters and values reordered. The CATALOG parameter can be coded to identify the specific catalog in which to place an entry for each component in the data set. In this case, the last line in the INDEX parameter in Fig. 4.4 must be continued also. CATALOG cannot be coded as part of either the DATA or INDEX parameter. If there is a user catalog named ALPHA, the data set will be cataloged in it (Fig. 4.5). Otherwise, the JOBCAT, STEPCAT, or system master catalog will be used to determine the specific catalog.

When creating a data set, the IDC3009 DUPLICATE DATASET NAME error message might print. The message might be referring to any one of the two or three names coded with DEFINE CLUSTER. Unfortunately, it does not specify which.

Structural Parameters

The parameters that actually describe the data set itself and the logical records it contains are examined in this section. These parameters are responsible for the physical structure of the data set:

Type of VSAM Data Set		
INDEXED(KSDS)	or	IXD (KSDS)
NONINDEXED(ESDS)	or	NIXD (ESDS)
NUMBERED(RRDS)	or	NUMD (RRDS)
LINEAR(LDS)	or	LIN (LDS)

These four mutually exclusive parameters are used to specify the type of VSAM data set being created. The type of data set must be coded with the cluster component. INDEXED is the default value and need not be coded. The default value is underlined throughout the text. For the other three

```
DEFINE  CLUSTER(NAME(ALPHA.TAX.CLUSTER)            -
        other Cluster parameters                   -
            . . .                          )       -
        DATA(NAME(ALPHA.TAX.DATA)                  -
        other parameters for the Data Component    -
            . . .                          )       -
        INDEX(NAME(ALPHA.TAX.INDEX)                -
        other parameters for the Index Component   -
            . . .                          )       -
        CATALOG(catalog name)
```

Figure 4.4 Overview of the DEFINE CLUSTER command.

```
DEFINE CLUSTER(NAME(ALPHA.TAX.CLUSTER)      -
       other Cluster parameters             -
          . . .                         )   -
       DATA(NAME(ALPHA.TAX.DATA)            
       other parameters for the Data Component  -
          . . .                         )   -
       INDEX(NAME(ALPHA.TAX.INDEX)          
       other parameters for the Index Component -
          . . .                             -
       last Index Component Parameter    )
```

Figure 4.5 DEFINE CLUSTER command without the CATALOG parameter.

types, the appropriate entry must be coded because IDCAMS can't always determine the data set organization by examining the other values coded. In fact, it does not even try. Note that these parameters identify the data set organization, not how the records are to be processed. Access information such as sequential, random, or dynamic cannot be specified with the DEFINE CLUSTER command.

KEYS (length offset) coded only with a KSDS

KEYS is coded only by KSDS. KEYS cannot be abbreviated, and KEYS can be coded with the cluster or data component. The KEYS parameter contains the same two types of information coded in the KEYLEN and RKP DCB subparameters when an ISAM data set is created. With SMS, the KEYLEN and KEYOFF JCL parameters supply the same information as the KEYS parameter. As with many of the IDCAMS parameters where a numeric value must be supplied, the values can be coded in three formats: decimal (n), hexadecimal (X'hh'), or binary (B'bbbb'). When an existing KSDS is to be processed in an application program, the same two values are specified again and the values compared. If the values don't match, the data set is not processed.

The KEYS parameter is associated with the primary key field, and it is necessary to qualify key field because alternate key fields are allowed. Alternate keys cannot be specified within the DEFINE CLUSTER command, however. The default value for KEYS is (64 0). After more than 12 years of working with VSAM, I've never encountered a situation where the default was appropriate. The primary key can be from 1 to 255 bytes in length, and must be an embedded key. It must also occur within the first 32,760 bytes of each logical record. The data type of the key field is irrelevant to IDCAMS, which processes it as hexadecimal.

Example 4. To specify that bytes 2 through 10 are to serve as the primary key, code KEYS(9 1). Note that KEYS(X'F9' X'F1') and KEYS(B'1001' B'1') will also give the correct results. The single most common error that occurs when coding the

KEYS parameter is specifying the offset relative to 1 rather than 0. In this example, such an error would be to code KEYS(9 2). This is incorrect.

The FREESPACE(%-of-data-per-CI %-of-CIs-per-CA) parameter

The FREESPACE(%-of-data-per-CI %-of-CIs-per-CA) parameter, abbreviated as FSPC, can only be coded with a KSDS. FREESPACE can be coded with the cluster or data component. There is no ISAM equivalent to this parameter, because ISAM uses an overflow area rather than FREESPACE to handle record insertions. The two values coded represent percentages from 0 to 100. However, the percent sign should not be coded. The two values coded are used to determine the amount of freespace that is to be reserved in the data component control intervals during the initial load operation. The default value is 0 for each subparameter. However, there is no real way to let just the first value default to zero. If you only specify one value, it will assume it to be the first value and, hence, the second parameter is the one that defaults to 0. When the default is used, as many records as possible are placed in each control interval during the load operation.

The major function of the FREESPACE parameter is to help reduce the initial frequency of performing control interval and control area splits. The first subparameter determines the approximate number of bytes in each data control interval, which are to be left empty during the initial load into the control interval. For example, FREESPACE(50) means that approximately half of each data control interval that contains logical records will consist of free space. Some imprecision might result from rounding down. The second subparameter specifies the number of control intervals in each control area that will be left completely empty during the initial load operation. For example, FREESPACE(0 20) means that approximately 1/5 of all control intervals in a control area are to remain empty during the initial load operation and, hence, available for use during subsequent control interval splits. The first value (0) specifies that the other 80 percent of the control intervals are to be completely filled during the load operation.

When values close to zero are coded for these parameters, control interval and control area splits can occur immediately after the data set is loaded. Add and update operations quickly exhaust the little, if any, free space available. FREESPACE parameter values close to 100 are usually wasteful of disk space. In particular, coding FREESPACE(100 100) allows one logical record to be written in the first control interval in each control area. The rest of the control area becomes free space. Loading 1,000 records into a data set with FREESPACE(100 100) coded and a control area size of 1 cylinder, creates a 1,000-cylinder data set, a tremendous waste of disk storage.

Example 5. Suppose a KSDS exists where each control area consists of 16 control intervals and each is 4,096 bytes in length. If FREESPACE(25 33) is coded, then 11 control intervals in each control area will contain data after the

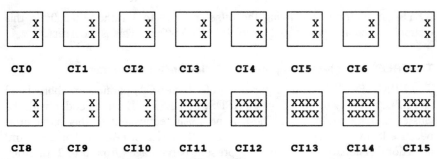

Figure 4.6   A CA consists of 16 CIs and FREESPACE(25 33).

load operation, and 5 will be completely empty. The control intervals where logical records are written will each contain approximately 1,000 bytes of free space. These figures assume that there are sufficient data records to fill the 11 control intervals. This is shown in Fig. 4.6. Note that X represents the empty space left during the initial load. The final control area loaded might contain less than 11 control intervals with data records.

Example 6.   It is possible to code a FREESPACE value that does not accomplish its purpose. For example, for a CISZ of 2,048 and a maximum logical record size of 250, coding FSPC(10) results in 204 bytes of free space being reserved in each control interval. This is insufficient to hold a single, logical record requiring 250 bytes. Hence, the FREESPACE value does not prevent a CI split from occurring when a 250-byte record must be added.

CONTROLINTERVALSIZE(size)

The CONTROLINTERVALSIZE(size) parameter is abbreviated as CISZ, which is used extensively throughout the rest of the book. With a KSDS, it can be coded with multiple components; it can be coded with any component. When CISZ is coded with the data component, the value must be a multiple of 512 or 2,048. This confusing statement calls for some additional explanation. Any multiple of 512 is permitted up to 8,192. For values greater than 8,192, only multiples of 2048 are allowed. With earlier releases of VSAM, the only values that could be coded with the Index Component CISZ were: 512, 1,024, 2,048, and 4,096. Recent releases allow the same values as the data component. Whenever an invalid value is coded with CISZ, IDCAMS automatically ''rounds up'' to the next valid value. No message is issued.

   CISZ is frequently coded only with the data component with a KSDS. This allows IDCAMS to supply a default CISZ value for the index component. Likewise, if CISZ is coded with a KSDS cluster component, the size value is associated just with the data component and the index component gets a default value. There is an interesting interrelationship between the control interval sizes in the data and the index components of a KSDS. As a general rule, as the

CISZ value of the data component increases, the CISZ value of the index component decreases, and vice versa. This assumes a fixed data control area size (see chapter 2).

It is important to remember that a VSAM control interval is equivalent to a non-VSAM physical record or block. Hence, disk utilization efficiency is related to the value specified. Recall from chapter 1 that the COUNT field occupies 480 bytes and the DATA field contains 32 bytes of overhead for each VSAM control interval on a 3380 disk. Clearly, CISZ(512) uses the smallest percentage of each track. The accompanying overhead is 512 bytes for each control interval, which wastes half the track. Buffer utilization is probably also poorer with sequential processing and a small CISZ value.

Another problem with a small CISZ value applies only to the index component. For a data set with "many" control intervals in a control area, the index control interval must be large enough to hold an index entry for each data control interval. CISZ(512) is a poor choice with such a KSDS. VSAM uses a straightforward algorithm to select an index CISZ if none is coded. The maximum number of control intervals in a control area is identified in Table 4.2. Note that there are only four possible default CISZ values for the index component. Furthermore, these selections are based on an average index entry of 8 bytes long.

RECORDSIZE(average maximum)

The RECORDSIZE(average maximum) parameter is abbreviated as RECSZ, which is used extensively throughout the rest of this book. RECSZ should be coded with either the cluster or data component. For a KSDS, the RECSZ values apply only to the data component. For the index component, the RECORDSIZE is always equal to 7 bytes less than the index CISZ. The CIDF and a single RDF occupy 7 bytes in each index control interval. RECORDSIZE is the VSAM equivalent of LRECL with non-VSAM data sets. RECORDSIZE should be specified with all three types of VSAM data sets. The default values are extremely large (4,089 4,089) for non-spanned records and (32,760 32,760) for spanned records.

The two RECORDSIZE values coded each have a significant but distinct role with the data set. Note that the first RECORDSIZE subparameter is the aver-

TABLE 4.2 Number of Entries in a Sequence Set Record.

# of CIs/CA	Index Component CISZ
1 - 58	512
59 - 120	1024
121 - 248	2048
249 - 502	4096

age value, not the minimum. The average value is used in conjunction with the RECORDS parameter to allocate space for the data set. If RECORDS is not coded, the importance of the first subparameter greatly diminishes, and an accurate value does not need to be provided except for documentation.

The maximum RECORDSIZE value is in effect for the lifetime of the data set unless ALTER is used to change it while the data set is empty. Attempting to write a larger record is prohibited by VSAM. When variable-length records are used, some thought should be given as to how large a logical record in the data set might eventually become the data set.

Record formats and SPANNED

Record Formats and SPANNED CISZ and RECSZ correspond to two of the three most important DCB subparameters—BLKSIZE and LRECL. What is the VSAM equivalent of the third major DCB subparameter, RECFM? There is no real equivalent because one is not necessary. The records in an RRDS are always fixed length. The records in a KSDS or ESDS are always treated as variable length. There are no logical records in a linear data set. Hence, the data set organization determines the record format.

To specify that all records are the same size in a KSDS or ESDS, code the same value for both average and maximum in the RECSZ parameter. With fixed-length records, an "optimal" relationship exists between CISZ and RECSZ when $CISZ = (n*RECSZ) + 10$, where n is the number of records that fit in a control interval. In this situation, there is no wasted space in the control interval. In every other case, the control interval contains unused space (free space with a KSDS) that is never used with an ESDS or RRDS.

With SPANNED, or SPND, no parameter value is coded. SPANNED can be coded with either the data or cluster component, although it applies only to the data component. As mentioned before, VSAM assumes a variable-length format for every KSDS and ESDS. The only possible variation involves coding SPANNED. Spanned records are variable length and can cross control interval boundaries. If SPANNED is coded, a default value of RECSZ(4086 32760) is generated.

A spanned VSAM data set is equivalent to a spanned, unblocked non-VSAM data set (RECFM = VS). Hence, only one record or record segment can be placed in a given control interval. Chapter 2 contains a complete description of the format of the RDFs for a spanned data set. SPANNED should be coded whenever a data set contains some variable length records that exceed what otherwise would be a "good" control interval size. A logical record cannot span multiple control areas. Hence, the largest possible spanned record must contain fewer bytes than a control area, and a logical record cannot contain more than 32K bytes.

Example 7. A data set consists of logical records, some as large as 10,000 bytes. Most of the records are between 2,000 and 4,000 bytes. A CI size of

4,096 and spanned records are used to process the data set. The relevant values included in the DEFINE CLUSTER command are:

- CISZ(4096)
- RECSZ(3000 10000)
- SPANNED

If a CISZ of 8,192 had been selected, most data control intervals would contain 50 to 75 percent free space, and this is usually not desirable. Do any other CISZ values also seem like a reasonable choice?

Example 8. This example is meant to illustrate the interplay and interrelationships among the FREESPACE, RECORDSIZE, and CISZ values. A KSDS is to be created and loaded that contains at least two control areas. At least one of the control areas should contain multiple control intervals with data. Twenty records are then to be loaded into the data set, and all are 100 bytes in length. Hence, RECSZ(100 100) must be coded.

There are four factors that determine the number of control intervals and control areas containing or holding records after a REPRO operation. These are the CISZ of the data component, the number of control intervals in one control area, the two FREESPACE values, and the size of the logical records. Suppose a CISZ of 2,048 is selected on a 3380 disk, and TRACKS(1 1) is used to allocate space. Thus, 18 control intervals equal one control area. To use two control intervals in the first control area, code FSPC(?? 87). The result is 87 percent of 18 gives 16 free control intervals.

It remains to determine an appropriate first parameter value. Make certain that not all of the records are placed in the first control area. By coding FSPC(60 87), eight logical records are placed in Control Interval0 and Control Interval1. Four records are placed in Control Interval0 in the second control area.

Buffers

There are three parameters that can be used to specify the number of buffers to assign to the data set for subsequent processing:

BUFFERSPACE(size) or
BUFND(Number of Data Component Buffers) or
BUFNI(Number of Index Component Buffers)

BUFFERSPACE, abbreviated BUFSP, can be specified with the cluster or data component. BUFND and BUFNI do not have abbreviations and cannot be specified with DEFINE CLUSTER. They must be added with ALTER. These three parameters are the VSAM equivalent of the DCB subparameter BUFNO. The size value specifies the total number of bytes in the application program's address space reserved for buffers. The default value is two buffers for the data component, and with a KSDS, one buffer for the index component. A smaller

BUFFERSPACE value should never be coded, but if it is, it is ignored and the default is used. This is one of the very few IDCAMS parameters that can be explicitly coded on a DD statement, where even more flexibility is available. This is described with the AMP parameter in chapter 13.

The BUFFERSPACE parameter values are very important, especially with a KSDS. Situations can arise when processing a KSDS randomly where efficiency is almost directly proportional to the amount of buffer space available. Buffer utilization is discussed in more depth in chapter 17. If you are uncertain of the values to code with BUFFERSPACE, accept the default values.

Example 9.   There are several methods available for requesting buffer storage. Suppose that for efficient processing, the data component requires 6 buffers, and 3 buffers are "optimal" for the index component. Assume a data CISZ of 2,048 and an index CISZ of 4,096. There are three coding methods that could be used:

1. BUFND(12288) BUFNI(12288) with ALTER

2. BUFFERSPACE(24576) with DEFINE CLUSTER or ALTER

3. ACB = (BUFND = 6,BUFNI = 3) with a JCL DD statement

The first two methods use IDCAMS to identify the actual number of bytes to reserve for buffers. The last method uses a DD statement to specify the number of buffers for the data and index components. Note that the specific desired results cannot be guaranteed using the second method. Rather, VSAM will decide how best to use the designated 24K bytes.

Unique Cluster Space and Suballocated Clusters

Whenever non-VSAM data sets are stored on a disk volume, an entry is made in the Volume Table of Contents (VTOC). The data management routines initially check the VTOC when attempting to locate a data set on the volume. Every non-VSAM data set has a VTOC entry. The VTOC serves as a directory to the data set objects stored on the volume along with available space on the volume.

Early versions of VSAM provided two distinct methods for allocation of disk storage to a VSAM data set. The first method consists of creating a general storage area, which was often quite large, on a disk volume. In theory, this area could be as small as a track or occupy the entire volume. Multiple VSAM storage areas can be created on the same volume. A pool of storage such as this is not assigned to any specific data set, but rather is managed by VSAM and available for subsequent requests for VSAM storage on that volume.

This first method uses the DEFINE SPACE command to allocate a storage pool. Subsequent DEFINE CLUSTER and DEFINE ALTERNATEINDEX commands might specifically request a portion of this storage pool. DEFINE commands cannot identify the storage pool by name, only the volume on which the data set is to be placed. In fact, the DEFINE SPACE command does not have a NAME parameter.

Example 10.   DISK23 is a 3380 disk volume consisting of 888 cylinders. All of them are initially managed by the disk management routines component of the operating system. These routines are often referred to as DADSM. Hence, DADSM initially manages all 888 cylinders. A DEFINE SPACE command is executed to create a 200-cylinder storage pool. For simplicity, this is identified as SPACEA. Once this is done, subsequent DEFINE CLUSTER and DEFINE ALTERNATEINDEX commands can request a portion of SPACEA by specifying VOLUME(DISK23) and the SUBALLOCATION parameter with either command.

Example 11.   A second DEFINE SPACE command is executed that identifies DISK23 as the same volume as the one in Example 10. For identification, this area is called *SPACEB*. Volume DISK23 now contains two storage pools, which may or may not be contiguous. The next DEFINE CLUSTER with the SUBALLOCATION parameter will allocate storage from one of the two areas. Assuming each contains sufficient storage, VSAM uses an algorithm to select the specific storage area to use, either from SPACEA or SPACEB. Subsequent secondary allocations do not have to come from the same pool, or even from the same volume for that matter. Only clusters and alternate indexes will be placed in suballocated storage.

Although there is an entry in the VTOC of the volume for each of the two data spaces, individual clusters within the data spaces do not have entries in the VTOC of the volume. Instead, all information concerning them is provided and managed by VSAM. In a sense, the disk storage management DADSM routines do not know of their existence.

The second general method for allocating storage for VSAM data sets is to code UNIQUE with the DEFINE CLUSTER command. In this case, the exact amount of storage requested by the command is allocated and all of the storage is available just to this data set. No storage excesses are permitted in either direction unless less than a cylinder is requested on the primary or secondary allocation. In this case, the storage request is rounded up to 1 cylinder. Every unique VSAM data set has an entry in the VTOC of the volume for the data component and for the index component for a KSDS.

UNIQUE data sets allow a certain amount of flexibility not found in suballocated data sets. All UNIQUE data sets are somewhat jointly managed by VSAM and the operating system. VSAM is responsible for all I/O operations with the data set; but there is an entry in the VTOC of the disk volume.

Both UNIQUE and SUBALLOCATED data sets permit exactly one primary allocation. UNIQUE allows a maximum of 15 secondary allocations, the same number allowed with a non-VSAM data set with the SPACE parameter. SUBALLOCATION allows a maximum of 122 secondary allocations.

Example 12. The space allocation for a DEFINE CLUSTER command is coded as CYL(10 5). A maximum of 85 cylinders (10 + (5*15)) are allocated for a UNIQUE data set, while a maximum of 620 cylinders (10 + (5*122)) could be allocated with a SUBALLOCATED data set.

Example 13. The space allocation for a DEFINE CLUSTER command is coded as TRACKS(6 2). A maximum of 36 tracks (6 + (15*2)) are allocated for a UNIQUE data set, while a maximum of 250 tracks (6 + (122*2)) are allocated for a SUBALLOCATED data set. This is incorrect for a UNIQUE data set, because storage must be rounded up to a control area size of 1 cylinder.

Requesting Disk Space for a VSAM Data Set		
RECORD(primary)	or	RECORD(primary secondary) (REC)
TRACK(primary)	or	TRACK(primary secondary) (TRK)
CYLINDER(primary)	or	CYLINDER(primary secondary) (CYL)
KILOBYTES(primary)	or	KILOBYTES (primary secondary) (KB)
MILLEBYTES(primary)	or	MILLEBYTES(primary secondary) (MB)

Just as with the JCL SPACE parameter, there are many possible ways to request disk space: by allocating space in cylinders, tracks, (logical) records or bytes. The first two are comparable to coding CYL or TRK with the SPACE parameter in JCL. The third replaces the "blocksize" format used with the SPACE parameter. The fourth and fifth identify the actual number of bytes of disk storage rounded up to tracks. These final two methods are relatively new and add additional flexibility to space allocation. With SMS, if AVGREC is coded, logical records can be specified with the JCL SPACE parameter. The actual format for the five DEFINE CLUSTER space allocation parameters is: allocation unit (primary-allocation secondary-allocation).

The following space allocation parameters illustrate the five possible keywords that can be coded for unit:

1. RECORDS(1000 200)

2. TRACKS(1 1)

3. CYLINDERS(5)

4. KILOBYTES (50000 10000)

5. MILLEBYTES (50 10)

Up to 122 secondary allocations can be made no matter which of the five methods for space is requested. UNIQUE and SUBALLOCATION must also be considered in this regard. Furthermore, all space will actually be allocated in tracks, no matter which of the five methods is coded.

Case I-Tracks	Case II-Cylinders	Case III-Records
TRACK(5 3)	CYL(2 2)	RECORD(5000 1)
SUBALLOCATION	UNIQUE	UNIQUE
RECORDSIZE(100 100)	RECORDSIZE(200 200)	RECORDSIZE(500 500)
CISZ(4096)	CISZ(4096)	CISZ(4096)

Figure 4.7 Various space allocations.

The first parameter requests space for 1,000 logical records. In this instance, VSAM uses the first RECORDSIZE subparameter (average size) in order to determine how many tracks this will require. It does not take the FREESPACE values into account when performing this calculation. However, the CISZ value will also determine the actual values selected. One primary allocation is made. The secondary allocation amount is also converted to tracks and is provided whenever the primary space is exhausted.

IDCAMS has nothing equivalent to the SPACE parameter values: CONTIG, ROUND, ALX, MXIG, RLSE, ABSTR, the pds directory sub-subparameter, etc. If an amount of space less than 1 cylinder is requested, the tracks might be allocated on different cylinders. In this case, disk processing is considerably slower.

Example 14. For each of the three partial groups of DEFINE CLUSTER parameters shown in Fig. 4.7, calculate the maximum amount of space allocated if all primary and secondary allocations are used. Assume 3380 disks are used. In Case I, five primary tracks are allocated and 366(3*122) secondary tracks are also provided. In case II, two primary and 30(2*15) secondary cylinders are allocated. In both cases I and II, the RECORDSIZE and CISZ values are irrelevant to the amount of disk storage allocated. In case III, the values coded with these two parameters are crucial. In particular, note that 8 records fit in each control interval—4096/500 = 8.2. Because 10 control intervals occupy 1 track, 80 records fit on a track. Hence, 5000/80 = 63 tracks are requested as the primary allocation and 115 tracks as the total secondary allocations. Note that requesting 1 record rounds up to a 1-track allocation. Note also the control area size is 1 track.

Specifying Control Area Size

With all types of VSAM data sets, requests for disk storage produce a very significant side effect. The smaller of the primary and secondary allocation values determine the control area size. Hence, if TRACKS(6 2) is coded, the control area will occupy 2 tracks. Likewise, if RECORDS(500 100) is coded, the number of tracks needed to hold 100 logical records will comprise a control area. One exception is if the smaller of the two allocation values is larger than a cylinder. In this case, a control area occupies 1 cylinder. Hence, a control area is always greater than or equal to 1 track and less than or equal to 1 cylinder in size. With a KSDS, a control area split results in one or more secondary allocations being made. When either an ESDS or RRDS is extended by adding additional records, a secondary allocation might occur. This is not the same as a true control area split.

One additional space allocation anomoly should be mentioned. Because a records size is not permitted to exceed the size of the control area with spanned records, the minimum of the primary and secondary allocations must contain sufficient bytes to store any size record along with all of its RDF and CIDF overheads. For example, suppose that TRACKS(1 1), CISZ(512), and RECSZ > 23K are coded. Because there are less than 23K data bytes in a 1-track control area, not even spanned records will permit a record of maximum size to be stored.

Example 15.   Determine the number of control intervals that comprise a control area. CYL(1 1) and CISZ(2048) are coded for the data component, which is to reside on a 3380 disk. Here, 18 control intervals fit on 1 track. Thus:

A control area = one cylinder = 15 tracks/cylinder * 18 CIs/track = 270 control intervals.

Suppose a 3390 disk is used:

A control area = one cylinder = 15 tracks = 15 * 21 = 315 control intervals.

In summary, the three primary factors that determine the number of control intervals in a control area are:

1. The primary and secondary allocation amounts.
2. The size of the data control intervals.
3. The type of disk.

The REPLICATE and IMBED parameters, which are discussed in the next section, can be used to modify the number of control intervals in a control area.

With a KSDS, disk storage can also be requested for the index component. Any of the three keyword parameters can be coded with INDEX. Alternatively, KSDS space can be requested with just the cluster component. The value specified is used by VSAM to determine the actual amount of space allocated to both the data and index components.

Disk Timing Considerations—REPLICATE and IMBED

Unlike computer memory, a disk drive is an electromechanical device—it has moving parts; it starts and stops. There are several physical factors that significantly effect the speed at which a disk drive performs I/O operations. These include rotational delay, the time required for access arm movement, and the rate at which data is transferred. The DEFINE CLUSTER command contains parameters that theoretically explicitly reduce the time required for rotational delay and access arm movement. Ordinarily, timing delays associated with these are measured in thousandths of a second. Computers execute potentially (hundreds of) millions of instructions per second. Hence, disk timing considerations are significant objects of optimization. There are also several parameters that directly effect the data transfer rate.

REPLICATE Coded Only with a KSDS

REPLICATE, which can be abbreviated REPL, can be coded with the cluster or index component. The time required for the disk to revolve until the desired control interval is under the read/write head is called rotational delay. In the slowest situation, a complete revolution must take place. If the desired physical record is about to pass under the read/write head, minimal rotational delay occurs. Under certain conditions, the minimal delay will occur whenever I/O is performed. REPLICATE does this by filling a track with as many copies of a single control interval (physical record) as will fit. Note that every control interval on the track contains exactly the same data. The desired record is then always the next one to be read, and the absolute minimum value of rotational delay occurs.

The efficiency of REPLICATE must be balanced against the overhead necessary to support the replicating. Only index control intervals are affected by REPLICATE. Searching the index component is a very time-consuming portion of KSDS processing. With REPLICATE, every index control interval now occupies an entire track. Furthermore, if an index record is modified, every control interval on the track must be rewritten. Recall that changes to index records are avoided by VSAM during ordinary processing. This concerns record additions and deletions. However, the REPLICATE parameter is usually coded with a KSDS whose index records are to be read only.

IMBED Coded Only with a KSDS

IMBED, which can be abbreviated IMBD, can be coded with the cluster or index component. The IMBED parameter reduces the time required for access arm movement. Theoretically, IMBED guarantees that the absolute minimum amount of time needed for access arm movement will occur when moving back and forth between the data and index components. This results only if no access arm movement is required. Suppose the data and index components are on the same volume. In this case, IMBED causes the sequence set record to be included in the same cylinder as the data control area that it monitors. When IMBED is coded, a track is subtracted from the storage ordinarily allocated to the data control area. Hence, if TRACKS(5) and IMBED are coded, a control area occupies four tracks. Coding TRACKS(1) and IMBED generates an exception to this rule. In this case, the control area and the sequence set record each occupy 1 track.

TABLE 4.3   Using REPLICATE, IMBED, or Both.

	Neither Coded	REPLICATE only	IMBED only	REPLICATE and IMBED
Data component	TRK(8 4)	TRK(8 4)	TRK(7 3)	TRK(7 3)
Index component	TRK(2 1)	TRK(12 2)	REC(2 1)	TRK(12 2)
Data control area size	4 Tracks	4 Tracks	3 Tracks	3 Tracks

Notice that both REPLICATE and IMBED affect only the index component. Either or both can be coded with the cluster component parameters, however. REPLICATE results in every index control interval being replicated over an entire track, although the index and the data components can be physically disjoint. IMBED causes each sequence set record to be replicated and placed in the disk storage (same cylinder) associated with the data control area. High-level index records are not replicated with IMBED. REPLICATE requires additional index component space. This space is disjoint from the data component. On the other hand, IMBED acquires its additional space from the data component. Both REPLICATE and IMBED are discussed further in chapters 7 and 17.

Example 16.   Suppose TRACK(8 4) and RECORD(12 2) are coded as the space allocation requests for the data and index components, respectively, of a KSDS. Assume 10 index control intervals will fit on one track. Table 4.3 shows the actual amount of space allocated depending on whether REPLICATE or IMBED is also coded. The two values are the primary and secondary allocations, in that order.

The ERASE Parameter

The ERASE parameter provides some low-level security for a data set. When space is requested for a data set, the logical records formerly contained in the location allocated to the data set are not erased. Rather, the former data remains on the disk until it is overwritten when new records are added to the data set. Hence, if the contents of the acquired disk storage is printed before any records are written, the previous information can be examined. IDCAMS commands can be used. DEFINE CLUSTER should be used to create a VSAM data set, but not load records into the data set. Rather, use a PRINT command coded as: PRINT IFILE(DD1), where DD1 identifies a data set as:

    //DD1 DD DSN = DATA.XYZ,DISP = SHR,DCB = (RECFM = U,BLKSIZE = 32760)

This is undesirable with important, confidential information. Numerous computer crimes have been built around accessing the information in a ''deleted'' data set. If the ERASE parameter is coded, the contents of the data component can be automatically overwritten with binary zeroes when the data set is deleted. If it is important to protect the information in a data set, then ERASE should be coded. When the data set is actually to be deleted, the ERASE option can also be requested with the DELETE command. This is a property ERASE shares with the REUSE parameter discussed later in the chapter. Both ERASE and REUSE can be coded with the cluster component. Their actual effect takes place when a second IDCAMS command, DELETE and REPRO respectively, is executed.

VOLUME(volser1) or VOLUME(volser1 volser2...volserN)

VOLUME, which can be abbreviated VOL, is the third and final required DEFINE CLUSTER parameter in conjunction with the cluster name and space allocation. One or more specific volumes must be identified when a VSAM data set is created. IDCAMS does not permit a non-specific volume request when defining a cluster. This is primarily because of historic reasons and, in particular, the notion of specific volumes being owned by a certain catalog. Non-specific volume requests should be allowed, and have always been available with JCL and are allowed with SMS. Multiple volume names must be separated using standard IDCAMS delimiters. The IDCAMS VOLUME parameter is equivalent to coding:

$$VOL = SER = (volser1, volser2, ..., volserN) \text{ on a DD statement}$$

The other four VOL subparameters—PRIVATE, RETAIN, volume sequence number, and total number of volumes—are not meaningful with VSAM data sets and have no DEFINE CLUSTER equivalent. There is, however, some overlap with the KEYRANGES parameter discussed later in the chapter.

VOLUME, which determines the volume that will hold the data component, can be coded with either the cluster or data component for an ESDS and a RRDS. The volume used to hold the cluster is not identified by the VOLUME parameter. Rather, it is the volume where the user catalog with an entry for the cluster is stored. VOLUME can be coded with both the data and index components with a KSDS. This allows the two components to be placed on different volumes, which can be different device types. This is an optimization feature that is further discussed in chapter 17.

REUSE

All VSAM data sets are cataloged and do not support the equivalent of a non-VSAM temporary or work data set. The closest thing to a temporary data set is a cluster defined with the REUSE parameter. A data set created with REUSE can be treated as a new data set at any subsequent time. The cluster value HI-USED-RBA identifies the end of the logical records in the data component. If this value is set to zero, the data set is interpreted as containing no logical records, or empty. When records are loaded into a cluster where REUSE is specified, the HI-USED-RBA for the data set can be reset to zero. Hence, the records loaded into the data set are placed at the beginning of the data set and become the only records in the data set.

Clearly, REUSE is rarely coded with important, permanent data sets. However, temporary and work data sets are frequently created with REUSE. The REUSE parameter must also be coded on the REPRO command when records are loaded into the data set. Like ERASE, REUSE can be specified with two commands. REUSE cannot be specified with a cluster that will have an alternate index constructed over it. REUSE and KEYRANGE cannot be used together. These are two of several reasons why NOREUSE is the default value with DEFINE CLUSTER. However, the most important reason to use REUSE is to delete all records from a data set.

Data Set Security

There are five data set security features, of these, passwords are the most complicated of the group. ATTEMPTS and CODE are extensions of passwords, and AUTHORIZATION identifies a user verification routine. Finally, TO and FOR are unrelated to passwords. They specify expiration dates and retention periods respectively.

Passwords

VSAM data sets can be password protected. This provides a low level of protection that, unfortunately, is not always worth the trouble it takes to implement it. There are several negative aspects to using passwords. Each component can have its own individual passwords. If a programmer or operator cannot supply the correct password, the data set cannot be processed. Passwords can be provided within an application program or with IDCAMS. With IDCAMS, the required syntax is to follow the name of the object or the DDname with a slash (/) and then the password value. For example:

INDATASET(ACCSTU.MASTER/SECRET) and INFILE(MASTDD/TOPSECRT)

This value illustrates specifying the passwords SECRET and TOPSECRT respectively. With COBOL, only one password can be specified with a SELECT statement. On the other hand, coding the password in the WORKING-STORAGE of a COBOL program or on an IDCAMS control statement, seriously threatens the integrity of the password. Anyone who can browse the libraries where either of these are stored can then learn the password. Dynamically or interactively supplying the passwords would be better. JCL has no provision for passwords. Historically, it was probably thought that this was an even more visible location than the other types of source code.

TABLE 4.4 Four Levels of Password Protection.

Parameter	Level of Access Permitted
MASTERPW	All I/O operations are allowed including deletion of the data set. The master password is by far the most important password.
CONTROLPW	Access to any information in a control interval in the data set is permitted.
UPDATEPW	Records can be read, added, deleted, or updated.
READPW	Records in the data set may be read only.

Four different types of passwords can be supplied, with each level limiting the types of processing that can be performed with the data set. The four levels of password protection are listed in Table 4.4. MASTERPW implies CONTROLPW, which implies UPDATEPW, which implies READPW.

A KSDS can have 12 different passwords associated with it. The four levels of access that are available with VSAM data sets are the standard levels. Security packages such as RACF, ACF2, and Top Secret allow the same basic levels of access. Password protection is rarely used with non-VSAM data sets. However, by using IEHPROGM, such data sets can be password protected.

Example 17. A KSDS is to be created with three levels of password protection: read only, update, and master. Some applications will only need to read the records in the data set. Still others will update the data set and only one person should have the capability to delete the data set. The three password values are MARIE, SUSAN, and DIANE. The partial DEFINE CLUSTER code to implement this is:

```
. . .
MASTERPW(DIANE) –
UPDATEPW(SUSAN) –
READPW(MARIE) –
. . .
```

Passwords are more complex than they might initially appear. One complication associated with passwords is their "upward propogation" property. This is potentially a significant problem in the sense that VSAM users who password-protect their data sets are often unaware of this property. This can lead to serious security breeches. To illustrate upward propogation, suppose that a READPW of ALPHA is assigned to a data set. If the other three levels of passwords are not assigned, ALPHA automatically becomes the value for each of the other three higher levels of passwords. If BETA is assigned as the CONTROLPW for a data set and no master password is assigned, BETA becomes the master password also. If ALPHA and BETA are both assigned to the same data set, then ALPHA becomes just the read only and not the update password.

In Example 9, SUSAN does not become the CONTROLPW value. Thus, upward propogation can be summarized by saying that a password at level N, propogates upwards to levels N-1, N-2, etc., until a password coded at a higher level is encountered to block it. Here, N can be 2, 3, or 4. Note that coding MASTERPW prohibits upward propogation. It is necessary to code MASTERPW to use ATTEMPTS, CODE, and AUTHORIZATION.

A higher blocking password can lead to a "password gap," a second concer of passwords. If there is a password between the highest and lowest values specified that is not assigned a value, then it does not have a password value.

Finally, a password assigned to one component of a data set does not provide security for the other components. In fact, an unprotected component often negates any passwords with the other components.

Preventing accidental data set deletion

Another low level of data set security results by coding either the TO or FOR parameters. Both parameters are meant to prevent the accidental deletion of a data set, with each specifying a certain period of time in which the data set cannot be accidentally or easily deleted. TO and FOR provide the same information as coding RETPD and EXPDT with the fifth LABEL subparameter on a DD statement with a non-VSAM data set. In both cases, it is necessary to code the PURGE operator when deleting the data set before the expiration data. Expiration dates and retention periods are illustrated with both IDCAMS and JCL in Example 18. Either To (yyddd) or To (yyyyddd) may be coded, although FOR(9999) is allowed.

Example 18. A data set is not to be accidentally deleted until the end of 1997. A second data set is not to be accidentally deleted during the next 10 days. Two approaches for protecting these data sets are:

Using IDCAMS	Using JCL
TO(97365)	LABEL = EXPDT = 97365
FOR(10)	LABEL = RETPD = 10

ATTEMPTS(Value)

ATTEMPTS, abbreviated ATT, can be coded with any component. One major weakness of passwords is that their values are often stored in source code from which they are eventually submitted for execution. A more secure approach would be to provide the password interactively when a request to process the data set is issued. A value from 0 to 7 can be coded to specify the number of attempts an operator can make to interactively enter a password value. The default value is

2, presumably to allow for one possible careless error. ATTEMPTS(0) can be specified to prohibit any attempts at providing the password by an operator other than a user.

CODE(character-string)

CODE has no abbreviation. CODE, which provides the next step in security sophistication after both passwords and ATTEMPTS, can be specified with any component. Following the reasoning described earlier, ATTEMPTS can be coded to allow an operator to supply the password when the data set is to be processed. However, it requires that the operator know the specific passwords of a data set. The CODE parameter reduces this security breach somewhat by replacing the name of the data set with an arbitrary alias value. It is with this alias name that the operator will be prompted and must supply the password. The alias name can be any character string from 1 to 8 bytes.

The MASTERPW is required to use CODE. The DEFINE CLUSTER command in Fig. 4.8 illustrates these concepts. When the code in Fig. 4.8 is executed, a message is sent to the operator specifying that the password for SECRETXX must be provided. Here, that password is AARDVARK. No reference will be made to the data set name ALPHA.BETA.GAMMA. Realistically, with a general awareness of which data sets are being processed, an operator could probably determine the actual name of the data set associated with the CODE value.

AUTHORIZATION(program string)

The AUTHORIZATION(program string) parameter, abbreviated AUTH, can be coded with any component. This parameter allows a User Security Verification Routine (USRV), identified by program, to receive control when a cluster is accessed without specifying the master password value. String information passed to the program can consist of substantial information or logic.

EXCEPTIONEXIT(program)

EXCEPTIONEXIT, abbreviated EEXT, can be coded with any component. EXCEPTIONEXIT identifies a user-written program that is to receive control if various I/O errors occur while moving data back and forth from disk and the

```
DEFINE  CLUSTER(NAME(ALPHA.BETA.GAMMA)  -
                CODE(SECRETXX)           -
                UPDATEPW(AARDVARK)       -
                MASTERPW(BIZARRE)        -
                . . .
```

Figure 4.8 Parameters to protect a data set.

application program area. In assembler terminology, any SYNAD exit causes the program to be invoked.

WRITECHECK

The disk drives two decades ago were extremely prone to errors when compared with the technology available today. The WRITECHECK parameter was provided with DEFINE CLUSTER to double check that an I/O operation was performed correctly, and there was some rationale for using it during the seventies. Today, however, there is no reason to routinely code it. The 3380 and 3390 disk drives have outmoded the WRITECHECK parameter.

FILE(DDname)

The parameter FILE, which has no abbreviation, can be coded with any component. FILE is coded to identify the disk volume(s) coded with the VOLUME parameter. Separate FILE parameters can then be coded for the data and index component. If FILE is not coded, an attempt is made to dynamically allocate the volumes. Today, most volumes are resident and can be dynamically allocated.

OWNER(owner + id)

The OWNER parameter, which should be routinely coded when creating a VSAM data set, is coded to identify the owner of an entire data set or a component.

OWNER(LARRY)

Anywhere from one to eight characters can be coded for owner-id. If special characters are used, the owner-id value should be enclosed in apostrophes. The code usually contains the programmer's last name or a specific project name. This is important because there are numerous situations where it is necessary to locate the "owner" of a data set.

RECATALOG

RECATALOG, abbreviated RCTLG, can only be coded with the cluster component. NORECATALOG (NRCTLG) is the default. When RECATALOG is in effect, a catalog entry is reconstructed using data set label information in the VSAM Volume Data Set (VVDS). If valid VVDS values do not exist, the command terminates. Old security information is not valid.

SHAREOPTIONS(value1 value2)

The SHAREOPTIONS parameter, abbreviated SHR, is used extensively throughout the rest of the book. SHR is one of the more complex and sophisticated of the DEFINE CLUSTER parameters. It has numerous short-term and long-range side effects. The two positional subparameters must be assigned the value 1, 2, 3, or 4. The values coded control the number of jobs and degree of sharing access among users wanting to process the records in a data set. Thus, SHR is similar to coding DISP = SHR, or OLD with a non-VSAM data set.

Notice that some traditional DISP values—NEW, DELETE, CATLG, UNCATLG, and PASS—have always been irrelevant with VSAM data sets. There is also some additional interaction between SHR and the first DISP subparameter value in that DISP = SHR must be coded on a DD statement in order for the IDCAMS SHR values to be in effect. If DISP = OLD is coded, the SHR values are ignored.

The first group of subparameter values describe the degree of sharing within a single system. SHR(1) allows the most restrictive access to a VSAM data set. If one job is processing the data set for output, no other jobs can concurrently process it for any type of I/O. If no job is processing it for output, any number of jobs can concurrently access it for input processing. Hence, either one job can be output processing or multiple jobs can perform input processing, but not both. SHR(1) guarantees total data integrity.

SHR(2) replaces the OR in SHR(1) processing with AND. Any number of the jobs can be reading records from the data set, and one job can be concurrently modifying records in the data set. Without additional safeguards, another job could modify a record after it is read.

SHR(3) allows any combination of concurrent accesses (reading and writing) and VSAM attempts to ensure data set integrity. Separate copies of control intervals are given to distinct jobs.

SHR(4) also allows any combination of accesses, but the jobs must try to protect the integrity of the records themselves, without help from VSAM.

The second SHR subparameter values control cross-system accesses. Only 3 and 4 can be meaningfully coded. Additional details are discussed in chapter 17. In particular, using 3 and 4 are beyond the scope of the typical COBOL application programmer. Rather, system software and assembler language are required to fully exploit their values. The ENQ, DEQ, and RESERVE macros play a major role in this process.

MODEL

The MODEL parameter—the VSAM referback feature—is used to copy information from one or more components of an existing VSAM data set. Usually, MODEL is followed by the name of an existing VSAM data set, although a data or index component can also be identified with MODEL. The values associated with the existing object, which is used as the model, are then assigned to the cluster being defined in the present DEFINE CLUSTER. In some ways, this is similar to a referback in JCL, where information is retrieved from any of three parameters on earlier DD statements:

DSN = *.referback   referback = any earlier DDname or
DCB = *.referback   referback = any earlier DDname within Stepname
VOL = REF = *.referback

More accurately, the MODEL parameter is similar to coding DCB = (dsname) or VOL = REF = (dsname). This less-frequently used JCL feature identifies a specific data set and information is copied from the labels in each case. Notice that this is different from a true referback in JCL.

If two or more clusters are to be created with many of the same properties, MODEL can be used to reduce the amount of code needed with all except the first. MODEL shares one other property with DCB = (dsname). Suppose most of the values in the old cluster are appropriate for the new cluster but a few must be changed. With both DCB and MODEL, the different values can be coded that override the values associated with the existing data set. Figure 4.9 shows the three possible locations for coding MODEL parameters. MODEL is coded first here only for emphasis. The objects being used as models do not need to be related.

Example 19. A KSDS was created and named FIRST.X. using the code in Fig. 4.10. Approximately 20 parameters were coded. A second data set with almost identical properties must be created. The only differences will consist of the three component names, the CISZ value for the data component, and the ERASE parameter. The order of MODEL and ERASE could be switched, and the results would be the same. Notice that it is not necessarily to code a space allocation or VOLUME parameter because both values are provided by the MODEL cluster.

KEYRANGES((low1 high1) (low2 high2) ... (lowN highN))

KEYRANGES, coded only with a KSDS, is abbreviated as KRNG. This parameter is used in conjunction with the VOLUME parameter values and places specific portions of a KSDS on multiple, separate disk volumes. The division is

```
DEFINE  CLUSTER(NAME(ALPHA.TAX)                   -
           MODEL(EXISTING.CLUSTER)                 -
           other cluster parameters        )      -
        DATA(NAME(ALPHA.TAX.DATA)                  -
           MODEL(EXISTING.DATA)                    -
           parameters for the Data Component)      -
        INDEX(NAME(ALPHA.TAX.INDEX)                -
           MODEL(EXISTING.INDEX)                   -
           parameters for the INDEX Component)     -
        CATALOG(catalog name)
```

Figure 4.9   Overview of the DEFINE CLUSTER command with MODEL.

```
DEFINE  CLUSTER(NAME(SECOND.Y)              -
                MODEL(FIRST.X)              -
                ERASE)                      -
            DATA(NAME(SECOND.Y.DATA)        -
                CISZ(6144))                 -
            INDEX(NAME(SECOND.Y.INDEX)))
```

Figure 4.10   Coding the MODEL parameter.

based on the key field values. Thus, KEYRANGES can be used to divide a very large data set into more manageable components. The keyranges must be coded in ascending order and cannot overlap. There might be gaps between them, but records are not permitted with gap values. Different keyranges may be assigned to the same volume.

ORDERED

ORDERED is used in conjunction with the VOLUMES and KEYRANGES parameters. When ORDERED is coded, these parameters are paired off 1-1 in the order in which they are coded.

Example 20.   Social Security number is the key. All records with Social Security numbers beginning with 0, 1, and 2 are to be placed on disk volume VOL012; all those beginning with a 3 are to be stored on volumes VOL333; and all others are to be written to VOL459. In this situation, the number of keyranges and volumes is the same. Because ORDERED is coded, a 1-1 pairing will take place. The relevant parameters are shown in Fig. 4.11.

SPEED and RECOVERY

SPEED and RECOVERY parameters relate to initially loading records into the data set. They are available with every type of VSAM data set. RECOVERY is the default. When RECOVERY is used, VSAM notes the addition of each new record to the data set in such a way that if the loading operation is terminated, it can be resumed at the very next record. If RECOVERY is not in effect and the load operation terminates abnormally prior to processing the final input record, the load must be repeated from the beginning of the input data set.

```
VOLUMES(VOL012 VOL333 VOL459)                            -
KEYRANGES((00000000 299999999) (300000000  399999999)   -
(400000000  999999999))                                 -
ORDERED
```

Figure 4.11   Using key ranges with a multi-volume data set.

TABLE 4.5   DEFINE CLUSTER and DD Statement Comparison.

JCL DD Statement Parameter	DEFINE CLUSTER Parameter
DSNAME (only one)	NAME(CLUSTER, DATA, and INDEX)
SPACE	RECORDS, TRACKS, or CYLINDERS
VOL=SER	VOLUME
DISP=(NEW,CATLG)	DEFINE CLUSTER
DISP(=OLD or SHR)	SHAREOPTIONS
UNIT	FILE or VOLUME
LABEL	
EXPDT	TO
RETPD	FOR
DCB	
LRECL	RECORDSIZE
BLKSIZE	CISZ
RECFM	either nothing or SPANNED
BUFNO	BUFFERSPACE BUFND BUFNI
KEYLEN and RKP	KEYS
DSORG	INDEXED, NONINDEXED, NUMBERED, or LINEAR
OPTCD	REPLICATE, IMBED, and WRITECHECK
*.referback	MODEL (all other parameters)
(DSN, DCB, VOL)	

RECOVERY is a questionable choice for a default value. In order to allow successful recovery in the midst of a load operation, RECOVERY requires a substantial overhead. It is a rare application where RECOVERY should be specified. There should be an extremely large number of records to load along with a method to resume the load at the point of termination. Because of these limitations, SPEED is commonly coded instead.

Example 21.   The data set used throughout the earlier part of the book consisted of logical records between 500 and 2,000 bytes in length. The DEFINE CLUSTER command required to create this KSDS is shown in its entirety in chapter 7. It should be noted that defaults exist for most DEFINE CLUSTER parameters. Hence, considerably less code can be used to create the same data set.

A detailed comparison of the DEFINE CLUSTER parameters and their JCL DD statement counterparts is given in Table 4.5. Note that some latitude is taken in identifying some objects as counterparts.

Processing Existing VSAM Data Sets

The DEFINE CLUSTER command rather closely equates to a DD statement, which contains parameters to create a cataloged data set. This type of DD statement contains DISP = (NEW,CATLG). There is no specific IDCAMS command that equates to processing an existing data set with a DISP of OLD or SHR. Rather, a DD statement can be used to identify the cluster by coding the name of the cluster as the DSN value and one of the two DISP values. In addition, with most of the remaining IDCAMS commands, just the name of the cluster is coded. This equates to DISP = (OLD,KEEP) except with the DELETE command, where it is equivalent to DISP = (OLD,DELETE).

Complete DEFINE CLUSTER Examples

In this section, four complete programming situations that require a VSAM data set to be created are considered. Coding Example 1 could be called an "every bell and whistle" example because the intent is to code as many parameters as possible with a KSDS. This is for illustration purposes only and need not be considered the norm. Coding Example 2 is as near the other extreme as possible. A very simple KSDS is built, where simple applies to both the data structure and processing requirements. Example 3 illustrates distinctions between creating a KSDS and an ESDS. Other DEFINE CLUSTER ESDS examples are found in chapter 10. Finally, the fourth example uses the MODEL parameter.

Coding example 1

Write a DEFINE CLUSTER code to create a KSDS to process a data set with the following properties:

```
DEFINE CLUSTER(NAME(ACSSTU.MEDCAT.
              INDEXED                              -
              KEYS(24 81)                          -
              REPLICATE IMBED                      -
              SHAREOPTIONS(2 3)                    -
              UNIQUE                               -
              FREESPACE(20 20)                     -
              RECORDSIZE(350 5000)                 -
              OWNER('LARRY B')                     -
              MASTERPW(DOCTORL)                    -
              UPDATEPW(DOCTORJ)                    -
              READPW(DOCTORB)                      -
              TO(96186)                            -
              CODE(MDMDMDMD))                       -
         DATA(NAME(ACSSTU.MEDCAT.DATA)             -
              VOLUME(DISK23)                       -
              TRACK(6 3)                           -
              CISZ(2048))                          -
         INDEX(NAME(ACSSTU.MEDCAT.INDEX)           -
              VOLUME(DISK75)                       -
              TRACK(1 1)                           -
              CISZ(4096))
```

Figure 4.12   Creating a "complex" KSDS structure.

- Each record is that of an individual patient at a small medical facility.
- Most records are approximately 300 to 400 bytes in length, but a few reach almost 2,000 bytes.
- The key is a concatenation of last name and Social Security number.
- It is 24 bytes in length and starts in byte 82.

Confidentiality and rapid access are of the highest priority when working with this data set. Any parameters related to these two points should be coded. There are currently 5,000 patient records in the data set, and it is growing slowly. The DEFINE CLUSTER code is contained in Fig. 4.12. The data set described in this example is used in several other places. Specifically, two alternate indexes are built over it in chapter 8.

Coding example 2

Write the DEFINE CLUSTER code needed to create a KSDS that will hold 80-byte card images. There are 1,000 records in the data set. The records contain an 11-byte key field beginning in column 2. The data set is expected to remain essentially static. Practically no insertions, deletions, or modifications (which change the record size) will be made. Notice that the DEFINE CLUSTER code in Fig. 4.13 is at the opposite extreme from the previous example, and a bare minimum of DEFINE CLUSTER code is needed.

Coding example 3

How should the DEFINE CLUSTER code in example 2 be written if all future processing is to be sequential? If all future processing is to be sequential, a KSDS should not be used to hold the records. Here, an ESDS is created, and those parameters that have meaning only with a KSDS are not coded. The DEFINE CLUSTER code is contained in Fig. 4.14.

```
DEFINE  CLUSTER(NAME(ACSSTU.STATIC.CLUSTER)    -
               KEYS(11 1)                      -
               SHR(2 3)                        -
               UNIQUE                          -
               RECSZ(80 80)                    -
               FREESPACE(0 0)                  -
               VOLUME(DISK99)                  -
               CISZ(2048)                      -
               CYL(1 1))                       -
          DATA(NAME(ACSSTU.STATIC.DATA))       -
          INDEX(NAME(ACSSTU.STATIC.INDEX))
```

Figure 4.13 Building a "simple" KSDS.

```
DEFINE  CLUSTER(NAME(ACSSTU.STATIC.SEQ.CLUSTER)  -
               NONINDEXED                        -
               SHR(2 3)                          -
               UNIQUE                            -
               RECSZ(80 80)                      -
               VOLUME(DISK99)                    -
               RECORDS(1100 100))                -
            DATA(NAME(ACSSTU.STATIC.SEQ.DATA))
```

Figure 4.14 Creating an ESDS.

Coding example 4

Define a KSDS moderately similar to that created in example 1. Any suggestion of similarity means that the MODEL parameter should be considered within the DEFINE CLUSTER code for the new data set. The relevant code is contained in Fig. 4.15.

Exercises

1. Analyze in detail the differences among each of the DEFINE CLUSTER parameters on the left in Table 4.4 and the DD statement parameter paired with it on the right-hand size. Which pair is closest to being functionally identical? Which pairs are the most different? Which DEFINE CLUSTER parameters have no DD statement equivalent?

2. Which DEFINE CLUSTER parameters can only be coded with a KSDS? Which DEFINE CLUSTER parameters can only be coded with an RRDS? Which DEFINE CLUSTER parameters can only be coded with an ESDS?

3. Classify each of the parameters that can be coded with DEFINE CLUSTER into one of six basic categories:

   ▪ Describe logical records.

   ▪ Describe control intervals.

   ▪ Identification.

```
DEFINE  CLUSTER(NAME(ACSSTU.MEDCAT.ADDITION)           -
               MODEL(ACSSTU.MEDCAT.ADDITION/DOCTORL)  -
               KEYS(5 0)                              -
               SHR(1 3))                              -
            DATA(NAME(ACSSTU.MEDCAT.ADDITION.DATA)    -
              MODEL(ACSSTU.MEDCAT.DATA)               -
              VOLUME(DISK 24))                        -
            INDEX (NAME(ACSSTU.MEDCAT.ADDITION.INDEX))
```

Figure 4.15 Modeling the KSDS built-in.

- Security.

- Performance features.

- Others.

4. Create a cluster exactly like the one in the DEFINE CLUSTER coding example 2 except that it contains 10,000 records and the key is only 21 bytes in length starting at the same location. Decide whether a record in the input cluster or data set should replace a corresponding record in the output cluster. This replacement takes place depending on the values of the keys in the two clusters.

5. A VSAM data set has been created and loaded with records. How can the exact number of control intervals in the data component containing records be determined? Consider various IDCAMS commands, including LISTCAT, PRINT, etc., to determine this information. How can the number of control areas in the data component containing records be determined? Note that the methods for determining this value are different from those for control intervals.

6. What is the absolute minimum set of parameters that must be coded to successfully create a KSDS. What default values are provided or generated. What is the absolute minimum set of parameters that must be coded to successfully create an ESDS? An RRDS?

7. How big can the largest KSDS ever be in terms of disk storage? What factors are responsible for this maximum value?

8. What is the rationale for refusing to allow REUSE to be coded with a VSAM data set with an alternative index constructed over it?

9. Write the equivalent DEFINE CLUSTER command to create a KSDS with as many similar properties as possible with the ISAM data set described on the DD statement.

```
//DD1 DD DSN = ISAM.DATASET,DISP = (NEW,CATLG),UNIT = DASD
//    VOL = SER = (WORK01,WORK02),SPACE = (CYL,(5,1)),
//    DCB = (LRECL = 85,BLKSIZE = 425,RECFM = FB)
//    DSORG = IS,KEYLEN = 12,RKP = 0,OPTCD = ILYR),
//    LABEL = RETPD = 100
```

5

IDCAMS Commands
for Record Processing

This chapter is intrinsically connected with chapter 6. In fact, the two chapters form a pair, and this relationship is described in the first part of the chapter. Next, four record processing commands are discussed in approximate order of importance from most to least—REPRO, PRINT, EXPORT, and IMPORT. REPRO is most important in that it can duplicate much of the processing performed by the other three commands. Some of the processing performed by EXPORT and IMPORT would probably be classified as crucial, but the two commands would probably tie as least important from an application programmer's point of view.

Record Processing Commands

This chapter and the next examine the eight major IDCAMS commands used to process existing data sets. In various places throughout the book, they are called *The Big Eight IDCAMS Commands*. The first four commands discussed process the actual logical records in VSAM data sets. These are the REPRO, PRINT, EXPORT, and IMPORT commands. These commands copy, print, unload, and load individual records in a data set. For this reason, they are referred to as the IDCAMS record processing commands.

In addition, REPRO and PRINT can process records in most types of non-VSAM data sets. Furthermore, EXPORT and IMPORT process exactly one VSAM and one non-VSAM data set during each command execution. An unload operation copies a VSAM data set to a non-VSAM sequential data set on tape or disk. EXPORT performs an unload operation and IMPORT a load operation in which an unloaded data set is recreated as a VSAM data set. Functionally, the

TABLE 5.1   The "Big Eight" IDCAMS Commands.

Record Processing Commands	Basic Function Performed	Used with Non-VSM Data Sets
REPRO	Copy data sets	Yes
PRINT	Print reports	Yes
EXPORT	Unload VSAM data sets	No*
IMPORT	Reload unloaded data sets	No*

System Components Processing Commands	Basic Function Performed	Used with Non-VSAM Data Sets
LISTCAT	Print catalog information	Yes
ALTER	Modify catalog information	Yes
DELETE	Delete data sets	Yes
VERIFY	Synchronize catalogs entries	No

*The unloaded version of a VSAM data set is always a non-VSAM sequential data set

four commands discussed in this chapter are analogous to some of the IEB data set utilities used to process non-VSAM data sets.

The four commands discussed in the next chapter process system information related to the entire data set rather than the logical records contained in the data set. These are the LISTCAT, ALTER, DELETE, and VERIFY commands. They print and modify information in catalogs, data set labels, PDS directories, and other system components. They are collectively identified as *the system component commands*.

LISTCAT, ALTER, and DELETE can also be used to perform a more limited range of processing with certain non-VSAM data sets. Only cataloged objects can be processed with LISTCAT and ALTER. In addition, DELETE is very rarely used with non-cataloged objects. Functionally, the IDCAMS system component commands are analogous to some of the IEH system utilities available with non-VSAM data sets. A summary of the Big Eight IDCAMS Commands is shown in Table 5.1.

Although the VERIFY command is classified here with the system information commands, it has one very significant similarity with the record processing commands. REPRO, PRINT, EXPORT, IMPORT, and VERIFY all allow choices between dynamic and static data set allocation. An argument could be made to move VERIFY to chapter 5.

The concept of dynamic allocation is not a relevant issue with LISTCAT, ALTER, and DELETE, because none of these commands process individual logical records. There is one further similarity between VERIFY and the four record processing commands. In a sense, VERIFY can modify the contents of the data set.

REPRO, PRINT, EXPORT, and IMPORT all perform various types of copy operations where exactly one input and one output data set is ordinarily specified with each command. With these four commands, either one input data set or one DDname can be identified. With PRINT and REPRO, non-VSAM data sets can be processed as both input and output. For those familiar with the IEB utilities, REPRO is similar to IEBGENER; PRINT to IEBPTPCH; and EXPORT and IMPORT to IEBGENER, IEBCOPY, and IEBISAM, which unload and load sequential data sets, PDSs and ISAM data sets respectively.

By comparison, a single LISTCAT, ALTER, or DELETE command can process multiple data sets. All three commands allow generic data set processing where a qualifier in a data set name can be replaced by an asterisk, which functions as a wild card. In particular, every data set whose non-asterisk qualifiers match those specified in the command are processed together. In a sense, this could be called simple or standard *generic* processing. LISTCAT supports an even wider range of possible generic processing opportunities. LISTCAT and DELETE both allow a mixture of generic and complete data set names to be specified as input and processed together in a single command. Only one input parameter value, generic or otherwise, can be specified with each ALTER command.

The same basic order of presentation is followed with all eight commands in this chapter and in chapter 6. The primary functions performed by the command are first described. All possible parameters available with the command are identified and classified. Next, the input and output parameters—in that order—are discussed. Any additional parameters available with the command are then examined in detail. Finally, a lengthy group of coding examples are provided to illustrate the complete processing scope provided by the command. Similarities with other commands and utilities are mentioned along with the limitations or weaknesses and potential improvements.

The REPRO Command

The REPRO command is the standard IDCAMS command for copying data sets. The copy operations can be performed in a wide variety of ways. Both VSAM and non-VSAM data sets can be processed using REPRO. In fact, every type of VSAM and non-VSAM data set organization can be used as input. When paired with compatible input, every type of VSAM data set can be used as output. There are, however, several types of non-VSAM data sets that cannot be output.

REPRO performs ''copy'' operations, creating an additional copy of all or part of an existing data set. By contrast, a ''move'' operation creates a copy of an existing data set and then deletes the original input data set. By using DD statements that specify DISP = (OLD,DELETE) with the input data set, REPRO will perform a (somewhat risky) move operation in that after the output data set is created, and the input copied to the output, the input data set is deleted.

Unfortunately, because the DD statement cannot check on the status of the copy operation, the data set gets deleted even if the copy operation was unsuccessful. This is what makes it a ''risky'' move using JCL. With IDCAMS a

DELETE following the REPRO can be preceded by an IF statement, which interrogates the condition code returned by the REPRO. This way, the REPRO, IF, DELETE combination will safely perform move operations.

REPRO parameters

REPRO parameters are grouped into five general categories, which are shown in Table 5.2. Exactly one parameter must be specified in each of the first two categories. The third and fourth categories contain default values not among the four available parameters. All parameters in the fifth category are optional and nonoverlapping. Several parameters—MERGECAT, ENTRIES, and LEVEL—which can be coded only when copying VSAM catalogs, are included in the fifth column.

ENTRIES and LEVEL are also used with the LISTCAT command. Likewise, the complete group of encryption parameters is identified later in the chapter. Catalog copying and data encryption are not routinely performed by (COBOL) application programmers.

Input and Output Parameters					
INFILE(DDname)	or	INDATASET(Data Set Name)	IFILE	or	IDS
OUTFILE(DDname)	or	OUTDATASET(Data Set Name)	OFILE	or	ODS

The parameters are listed on the left and their abbreviations are shown on the right. With each REPRO command, exactly one data set name, or DDname, must be used for input and exactly one of the two for output. Multiple input data sets can be processed in a single command by concatenating their DD statements together. Various concatenation examples are illustrated with the PRINT command. The output data set can exist before the step or be created in the step prior to the REPRO command execution. The REPRO command does not create the data set, it loads records into it. If the objects being processed are password-protected, the password should be specified.

One optional parameter can be specified with either INFILE or INDATASET.

TABLE 5.2   REPRO Parameters and Processing Categories.

Input Parameters	Output Parameters	Initial Record Processed	Final Record Processed	Additional Parameters
1 Required	1 Required	1 Optional	1 Optional	All Optional
INDATASET	OUTDATASET	FROMADDRESS	TOADDRESS	REUSE or NOREUSE
INFILE	OUTFILE	FROMKEY	TOKEY	REPLACE or NOREPLACE
No Default	No Default	FROMNUMBER	TONUMBER	Encryption Parameters
Optional		SKIP	COUNT	MERGECAT(Catalogs)
ENVIRONMENT		Default(1st)	Default(Last)	ENTRIES(Catalogs)
				LEVEL(Catalogs)

Coding ENVIRONMENT(DUMMY) is relevant only with an ISAM input data set. When this parameter is coded, dummy (logically deleted) records are copied to the output data set. For example, to specify that dummy records are to be copied from the cataloged ISAM data set ALPHA.BETA, you would code:

```
INDATASET(ALPHA.BETA ENVIRONMENT(DUMMY))
```

The default is to omit the dummy records from the copy operation.

Static and dynamic data set allocation

The REPRO command allows data sets to be accessed either statically or dynamically, and you can choose either with both the input and output data sets. As discussed in chapter 3, the same advantages, disadvantages, and limitations are available with both source and target REPRO data sets.

Record order in the input data set

When records are loaded into a KSDS or RRDS, they must be in ascending order by key field value or slot number respectively. This holds for both the initial loading and later extending or sequential updating. Any records out of order or which duplicate existing records are rejected and processing continues with the following input record. This is somewhat similar to INVALID KEY processing in a COBOL program. Even if the input data set itself is not a KSDS, the input records must be in order by key field value in order for REPRO to copy them into a KSDS or RRDS.

Very restrictive copying operations are permitted with linear data sets. In particular, the complete data set must be copied, and both input and output data sets must be linear. Several examples involving processing linear data sets with IDCAMS are illustrated in chapter 15. Record order is irrelevant when adding to an ESDS.

Specifying the Initial Input Record to Copy with REPRO	
Keyword	*Abbreviation*
FROMKEY (Key Value)	(FKEY)
FROMADDRESS (RBA Value)	(FADDR)
FROMNUMBER (Relative Record Number)	(FNUM)
SKIP (Unsigned Integer)	(none)
Default – none of the above; the first input record is copied	

Exactly one of the four initial record parameters can be coded to identify the location in the input data set where the copy operation is to begin. The four parameters are mutually exclusive, and none of them need be coded. By default, the copy operation begins with the first record in the input data set, (and standard VSAM syntax is in effect). The integer coded with FROMAD-DRESS, FROMNUMBER, and SKIP can be specified in decimal, hexadecimal, or binary, as illustrated in Example 4. Quotes are not needed unless the Key Value contains special characters. See chapter 3.

SKIP can be coded with all three types of VSAM data sets as well as with every type of non-VSAM data set. FROMKEY can be used only with a KSDS, a path over a KSDS or ESDS, or an ISAM data set. FROMNUMBER can be used only with an RRDS, and FROMADDRESS can be used with either a KSDS, ESDS, or a path over a KSDS or ESDS. Only FROMADDRESS parameters are permitted with a linear data set. Using SKIP with a path carries a "results are unpredictable" warning. FROMADDRESS cannot be used with a path. If a REPRO parameter is explicitly coded to identify the final input record to be copied, the parameter terminating the copy operation must be compatible with the initial record parameter. This is further discussed in the next section.

FROMKEY allows generic processing. In this context, generic meaning a complete key field value need not be coded. Rather, for an N-byte key field from 1 to $N-1$ of the left-most leading bytes can be specified followed by an asterisk (*). The copy operation begins with the first record with the specified number of leading bytes that matches those coded with FROMKEY. If there is no record whose key field is an exact match, the record with the next higher (partial) key is the initial record copied.

With a COBOL program, this is similar to coding START filename GENERIC KEY IS NOT LESS THAN. Neither FROMNUMBER nor FROMADDRESS allow generic processing. The concept does not make sense with either, because there is no method for specifying it as a generic value. If FROMNUMBER specifies an empty slot, the copy operation begins with the first active record following the empty slot. If there are no slots following the designated slot that contains active records, no records are copied.

The value specified with FROMADDRESS must identify the first byte in a logical record or the command will terminate with no records copied. If SKIP(N) is coded, the $N+1$st record is the initial one copied to the output data set.

Specifying the Final
Input Record to Copy with REPRO

Keyword	Abbreviation
TOKEY (Key Value)	(none)
TOADDRESS (RBA Value)	(TADDR)
TONUMBER (Relative Record Number)	(TNUM)
COUNT (Unsigned Integer)	(none)
Default-none of the above; the last input record is copied	

TABLE 5.3   Initial and Final Processed Records.

Initial and Final REPRO Command Parameters	First Record Processed	Last Record Processed	Remarks
FROMKEY(BD*) COUNT(500)	3rd Record	Last record	Generic key
FROMKEY(B D) TOKEY(EE*)	2nd Record	4th record	Generic key
FROMKEY(ABC) TOKEY(ABC)	1st Record	1st record	
FROMKEY(CDE)	3rd Record	Last record	
FROMADDRESS(512)	6th Record	Last record	
FROMADDRESS(080)			Invalid address Not 0, 100, 200, etc
SKIP(30)			Beyond End of File Only 26 records
COUNT(5) SKIP(2)	3rd Record	7th Record	
FROMNUMBER(3)			Execution error Invalid with KSDS

These four parameters are the counterparts to the parameters identifying the initial record to copy and are mutually exclusive. None of them need be coded. By default, the copy operation terminates after the final record in the input data set is processed. The syntax of the parameter arguments is exactly the same as with the initial record parameters. TOKEY allows either a full or generic key. A generic value with these parameters means that the first record with an exact match or the previous record in collating sequence order is identified as the final record processed. TOADDRESS, TONUMBER, and COUNT require an unsigned positive integer that can be specified in decimal, hexadecimal, or binary.

Among the 16 possible initial and final record parameter combinations, only certain ones are not allowed. SKIP can be paired with any output parameter, and COUNT can be used with any input parameter. Other than this, FROM-NUMBER must be paired only with TONUMBER. TOKEY and TOADDRESS can be used with either FROMKEY or FROMADDRESS.

Example 1.   There are 26 100-byte records in a KSDS. The control intervals are 512 bytes, and no free space is specified. The records have three byte keys with specific values of ABC, BCD, CDE, ..., XYZ, YZA, and ZAB. Determine the initial and final record copied in each situation in Table 5.3. Note that some parameter combinations are invalid, and others are valid but will result in no records being copied.

REUSE parameter (Default NOREUSE)

Every cluster component contains a HI-USED-RBA field identifying the end of the used portion of the data component, which is the final control interval containing a logical record. There is also a somewhat comparable field that identifies the final byte in the last control area that contains records. There is also a HI-USED-KEYRBA for the index component of a KSDS. The only function of the REUSE parameter is to set the HI-USED-RBA (and HI-USED-KEYRBA

TABLE 5.4   Categorizing REUSE and NOREUSE Parameters.

DEFINE CLUSTER Parameter	REPRO Command Parameters	
	REUSE	*NOREUSE (Default)*
REUSE	The data set is opened as reusable. The HI-USED-RBA is set to 0. Any existing records are lost.	If the data set is empty, the records are added as usual. If the data set is non-empty:
NOREUSE (Default)	If the data set is empty, the records are added.	ESDS-records are added at the end of the data set; DISP processing is ignored.
	If the data set is not empty, the REPRO command terminates.	RRDS and KSDS—processing is controlled by the REPLACE and NOREPLACE parameter.

for a KSDS) to 0. The cluster component HI-USED-RBA will be reset to 0 when the output data set is opened by REPRO.

This cluster component parameter value has the effect of causing VSAM to determine that the data set is empty, and REPRO adds the records at the beginning of the data set. Any existing records in the data set are then overwritten and their contents lost. When NOREUSE is specified, new records are added to the end of the data set and existing records are not overwritten. The various possible categories to consider are shown in Table 5.4.

Suppose OUTFILE is specified, and the DISP parameter is coded on the accompanying DD statement. Ordinarily, DISP = MOD implies NOREUSE, and DISP = OLD implies REUSE. The particular value coded with REPRO, however, overrides the DISP value.

The REUSE parameter determines the mode of access for the copy operation. REUSE always specifies sequential processing. With NOREUSE, the output data set is accessed sequentially with an ESDS and randomly with an RRDS and a KSDS.

REPLACE and NOREPLACE (the default) parameters (REP and NREP)

The REPLACE and NOREPLACE parameters are meaningful only with a non-empty output KSDS or an RRDS containing records. If REPLACE is coded and a record in the input data set contains a key that matches a record key in the output indexed data set, the input record replaces the output record. With an output RRDS, an input relative record number must match the relative record number of an output record, assuming the input is an existing RRDS. For an output KSDS, the input can have almost any data set organization. With REPLACE, an input record with a key or relative record number not matching any output record is inserted into the output data set in its correct location. A duplicate record message is printed if NOREPLACE is specified and a source record with a key value or relative record number matches that of a destination record. The actual message is an IDC ACTION ERROR. After four such duplicate records are found, the REPRO command terminates. IDCAMS classifies this as an action error. As with REUSE, the REPLACE parameter overrides any value coded with DISP on an accompanying DD statement.

REPLACE and NOREPLACE are used to control random processing. Hence, they are meaningful only with a KSDS and an RRDS. REPLACE serves no purpose with an ESDS. When the output data set is empty, both REPLACE and REUSE are meaningless. If REPLACE is coded with an ESDS, it is ignored.

Example 2. An input KSDS contains records with keys of 02, 05, 10, 15, 20, 30, 40, etc. The output KSDS currently contains records with keys of 03, 05, 12, 15, and 25. If REPLACE is specified, the results shown in Fig. 5.1 occur as the input records are processed.

A REPRO command with a REPLACE parameter can be used to update a KSDS in a relatively easy fashion. This technique is often called *"Cheap" Master File Update*. Suppose there are three types of transaction records: add, delete, and change. The delete transactions are identified and separated into a second data set. The add and change transactions are sorted into ascending order based on key field value. The delete and sort can be done in a single step with most sort utilities. REPRO with REPLACE specified is then used to copy the sorted add and change transactions into the existing master file. A simple

Input Records	Existing Records	Output Records
02	03	02 New
05	05	03 Old
10	12	05 New
15	15	10 New
20	25	12 Old
30		15 New
40		20 New
		25 Old
		30 New

Input Record Key Field	Action Occurring with Associated Input Record
02	Record is added as first record in the data set
05	Record replaces the existing record with a key of 05
10	Record is added as the fourth record in the data set
15	Record replaces the existing record with a key of 15
20	Record is added as the seventh record in the data set
30, 40, ...	All remaining records are added to the end of the data set

Figure 5.1 Using the REPLACE parameter with a KSDS.

application program then reads the delete transactions and deletes the corresponding master records.

A "Cheap" Master File Update assumes that all transactions are valid, especially if the transactions do not specify whether they are to be added or updated. If invalid transactions are present and the transaction type is coded on the record, then two REPRO commands are needed. For the add transactions, NOREPLACE is used. For the change transactions, REPLACE is coded. A snapshot should be taken before and after the change. A "Cheap" Master File Update will also work with an RRDS, provided the transactions are loaded into their appropriate slots in an input RRDS before the REPRO.

Encryption and decryption

Sensitive data can be encrypted before it is copied to an output data set. Data encryption mathematically encodes the data into a format that safely conceals its actual meaning or contents. The data is then decrypted at a later time before it can be used. A comparable algorithm used for decryption and processing requires that appropriate IBM decryption software be available. The IBM software conforms to the National Bureau of Standards (NBS) specifications for encryption. Encryption and decryption require the availability of one of two programs: the IBM Programmed Cryptographic Facility or the IBM Cryptographic Unit Support.

There are a great many parameters used with encryption. Many are only briefly discussed here. See the *Access Method Services Reference* manual for more information. Either ENCIPHER or DECIPHER must be coded depending on the processing requested. All of the parameters coded with either ENCIPHER or DECIPHER must be enclosed within parentheses.

When ENCIPHER is specified, the output data set receives an enciphered (encrypted) copy of the input data set. Individual records are encrypted as they are copied. EXTERNALKEYNAME, INTERNALKEYNAME, and PRIVATEKEY identify how the encryption keys are to be managed. CIPHERUNIT identifies the number of logical units that will be encrypted together, probably improving data security even further.

For example, if CIPHERUNIT(12) is specified, each group of 12 consecutive logical records is encrypted as a unit. Either DATAKEYFILE or DATAKEYVALUE should be coded if a programmer-supplied encryption key is used. All of the remaining parameters except for USERDATA refer to information about the encryption keys. USERDATA identifies 1 to 32 bytes of strictly user data, which preceded the enciphered data generated from the INFILE or INDATASET data set records.

When DECIPHER is coded, the input data set is to be decrypted during the copy operation. DATAKEYFILE and DATAKEYVALUE have the same basic role as with ENCIPHER, while SYSTEMKEY is similar to PRIVATEKEY. SYSTEMDATAKEY and SYSTEMKEYNAME are analogous to the comparable CIPHER parameters.

TABLE 5.5   IDCAMS Functions Requiring Two Commands.

DEFINE CLUSTER Parameter	Basic Parameter Function	Corresponding IDCAMS Commands and Parameter	
REUSE	Logically delete all of the records. VSAM then considers the data set empty	REPRO	REUSE
TO	Establish an expiration date	DELETE	PURGE
FOR	Establish a retention period	DELETE	PURGE
ERASE	Allow the data component to be overwritten with binary zeroes	DELETE	ERASE

IDCAMS Processing and related DEFINE CLUSTER parameters

REPRO processing uses several DEFINE CLUSTER parameters that allow a corresponding parameter specified with a later IDCAMS command to either provide the same effect, or complete the processing initiated by the DEFINE CLUSTER command. These parameters, their basic function, and the corresponding IDCAMS command that performs the same function, or is used to complete their processing, are listed in Table 5.5. The parameters on the left must be initially coded with DEFINE CLUSTER or later added with ALTER. The second command can be executed in the same step or a later job step or job. Notice that REUSE involves REPRO, and the other three parameters involve DELETE.

Processing limitations

REPRO has several significant processing shortcomings that are uncommon with other utilities that perform copy operations. The most important of these limitations are discussed here. For the most part, if one of these features is desired, it is necessary to write an application program.

REPRO does not have the capability to readily process every Nth input record. This means skip over the first N-1 records, process a record, skip over N-1 additional records, process a record, etc., to generate a cross section of a data set. The IEBPTPCH utility supports such a feature.

REPRO does not allow individual fields within a record to be modified. It is also impossible to rearrange the order of fields, delete fields, or add new fields. The IEBGENER and IEBPTPCH utilities support these types of functions with input data set records.

REPRO processes the records in the input data set in sequential order. The input records cannot be presorted by REPRO prior to processing. If the input records must be reordered, it must be done in a separate step with a sort utility program (DFSORT, SYNCSORT, etc.) before using the REPRO command.

It is currently not possible to dynamically concatenate input data sets. Rather, concatenation requires the use of the INFILE parameter. There appears to be no valid reason at this point for not supporting dynamic concatenation other than historic precedence.

Unlike utilities such as IEBGENER and DFSORT, the attributes of the input data set (LRECL, BLKSIZE, RECFM) are not automatically assigned to an output data set, which is created during REPRO execution with none of these values provided in the JCL. With REPRO, until ESA, this situation could only occur with non-VSAM data sets because all VSAM data sets must have been created prior to the REPRO operation. The information describing a data set and the records it contains is provided from three different sources: within an application program (when present), on a DD statement in the JCL, or from stored system information such as catalog entries and data set labels. REPRO will not process a non-VSAM record with an LRECL greater than 32,760.

REPRO coding examples

Example 1.   All records in the existing VSAM data set OLD.MASTER are to be copied to the data set NEW.MASTER, which is created during the same step immediately prior to using REPRO to copy the records. NEW.MASTER is a non-VSAM data set. In a batch-processing environment, the EXEC statement and the SYSIN and SYSPRINT DD statements are required with each of the REPRO examples but are shown only with the first one in Fig. 5.2.

Example 2.   The records copied into NEW.MASTER in the previous example are now to be loaded into the existing KSDS ALPHA.BETA, replacing the existing records that it contains. This is accomplished by coding REUSE. Notice that both static and dynamic allocation are used in Fig. 5.3.

Example 3.   Two groups of records are to be copied from an existing KSDS to the ALPHA.BETA data set loaded in the previous example. The key field for both data sets is last name, and only those records where the last name begins with an A or E are to be copied. Because of the two key ranges, two separate REPRO commands are required in Fig. 5.4. Dynamic allocation is used for both the input and output data sets. Notice that the TOKEY parameters will identify the last record to copy as the final record beginning with an A and E respectively. Notice that a record with a key of AZZZSTRANGE will not be copied.

```
//A         EXEC  PGM=IDCAMS
//SYSPRINT  DD    SYSOUT=A
//SYSIN     DD    *
     REPRO  INFILE(INPUTDD)       -
            OUTFILE(OUTPUTDD)
/*
//INPUTDD   DD    DSN=OLD.MASTER,DISP=SHR
//OUTPUTDD  DD    DSN=NEW.MASTER,DISP=(NEW,CATLG),UNIT=3390,
//                VOL=SER=DISK23,SPACE=(CYL,(1,1)),
//                DCB=(LRECL=100,BLKSIZE=5000,RECFM=FB),
```

Figure 5.2 Using REPRO for a complete copy operation.

```
         REPRO  INFILE(DD1)                         -
                ODS(ALPHA.BETA)                     -
                REUSE

//DD1    DD    DSN=NEW.MASTER,DISP=SHR
```

Figure 5.3 Using dynamic and static allocation with REPRO.

Example 4.   A total of 50 records beginning with the third record are to be copied from one RRDS to a second RRDS. If relative numbers match, the input record should replace the corresponding output record. Note that numeric parameter values are specified in binary and hexadecimal in Fig. 5.5. This is for illustration purposes only. The application does not require it.

Example 5.   Three members of a cataloged partitioned data set library called SYS1.MASTER are to be copied to a second existing cataloged partitioned data set. Three separate REPRO commands and three separate DD statements are used in Fig. 5.6. The DD statements are used in order to specify DISP = SHR with the input data set, a heavily used library. Dynamic allocation generates DISP = OLD. Three separate REPRO commands are used because concatenation would generate only one output member. Dynamic allocation is appropriate with the output data set, which is a cataloged private library. Notice that individual member names can be specified either with a DD statement or dynamic allocation. If the private library currently contains one or more members named ALPHA, BETA, or GAMMA, the new members replace the existing members with the same name. This is a consequence of coding DISP = OLD (here implicitly) with an output PDS.

Example 6.   An entire ESDS is to be enciphered and stored on a cartridge tape, and 10 logical records are to be enciphered together. The IBM cryptography program will manage the keys, and the character string "SECRET" will be stored in the header of the output data set as user data. The relevant code is shown in Fig. 5.7.

Additional REPRO examples are found throughout the book. Examples using FROMADDRESS and TOADDRESS are found in chapter 10. Examples using FROMNUMBER and TONUMBER are found in chapter 11. Additional ENTRIES and LEVEL parameter examples are contained in the next chapter with LISTCAT.

```
REPRO  IDS(EXISTING.DATASET)  ODS(ALPHA.BETA)      -
       FROMKEY(A*)  TOKEY(AZZ*)
REPRO  IDS(EXISTING.DATASET)  ODS(ALPHA.BETA)      -
       FROMKEY(E*)  TOKEY(EZZ*)
```

Figure 5.4 Using generic keys to identify the first and last records.

```
REPRO  INDATASET(INPUT.RRDS)      -
       OUTDATASET(OUTPUT.RRDS)    -
       SKIP(B'10')                -
       COUNT(X'F5F0')             -
       REPLACE
```

Figure 5.5 Using binary and hexadecimal data values with REPRO.

Example 7. A linear data set (LDS) is to be copied from one disk volume to another. Very few parameters are permitted with an LDS.

```
REPRO IDS (OLD.LINEAR)  -
      ODS (NEW.LINEAR)
```

The PRINT Command

The PRINT command is used to generate printed reports. It is possible to route PRINT output to a non-printer destination such as disk or tape, although this is rarely done because REPRO is available for this type of processing. PRINT shares many syntax similarities with the REPRO command. The PRINT parameters can be classified into five basic categories, four of which are comparable to groups of REPRO parameters. PRINT parameters are identified and categorized in Table 5.6.

Each of these five categories is examined in detail in the next several sections and then many PRINT command examples are presented. Each category in Table 5.6 explicitly (user coded) or implicitly (default) supplies exactly one parameter value for each PRINT command.

Identifying PRINT command input INFILE(DDname)
IFILE or INDATASET(datasetname) IDS

Input data to be printed can be identified either statically through JCL with the INFILE parameter or dynamically with the INDATASET parameter. The advantages, disadvantages, and trade-offs between static and dynamic are the same with PRINT as with the REPRO command. Every possible type of VSAM and non-VSAM data set can be used as input with the PRINT command. Including such diverse objects as:

```
//DD1   DD   DSN=SYS1.MASTER(ALPHA),DISP=SHR
//DD2   DD   DSN=SYS1.MASTER(BETA),DISP=SHR
//DD3   DD   DSN=SYS1.MASTER(GAMMA),DISP=SHR

   REPRO IFILE(DD1)  ODS(NEW.MASTER.BACKUP(ALPHA))
   REPRO IFILE(DD2)  ODS(NEW.MASTER.BACKUP(BETA))
   REPRO IFILE(DD3)  ODS(NEW.MASTER.BACKUP(GAMMA))
```

Figure 5.6 Using REPRO to copy PDS library members.

```
REPRO IDS(SEQUTL.CLUSTER)                         -
      OFILE(ENCIPHER)                             -
      ENCIPHER(EXTERNALKEYNAME(KEY123)  -
      CIPHERUNIT(10)                              -
      USERDATA(SECRET))
//ENCIPHER DD DSN=TOP.SECRET,DISP=(NEW,CATLG),UNIT=CART,
//            VOL=SER=123987,DCB =(MASTER. DATA)
```

Figure 5.7 Enciphering data during a copy operation.

- The directory of a PDS.
- Individual members in a partitioned data set library.
- The individual data and index components of a KSDS.
- A linear data set.
- VSAM catalogs.

If the input object is password-protected, the password (any level) should be specified. Unlike the REPRO command, the ENVIRONMENT(DUMMY) parameter cannot be used with PRINT. If a printed listing including dummy records is desired, the REPRO command can be used with OUTFILE to identify a SYSOUT data set.

Identifying PRINT command output OUTFILE(DDname) OFILE

There are two possible methods for identifying the output destination. Note that, unlike REPRO, the PRINT command does not provide an OUTDATASET parameter. Also unlike REPRO, the PRINT output default is to code nothing. In this case, the printed listing is included in the message data set. If appearance is unimportant, this is the most convenient way to generate a printed report. As an alternative, the OUTFILE parameter can be coded. The DDname included with OUTFILE ordinarily identifies a SYSOUT data set. However, any possible output destination can be specified on the DD statement. Because the REPRO command is also available, non-SYSOUT output data sets are rare with PRINT.

TABLE 5.6   PRINT Parameters and Processing Categories.

Input Parameters	Output Parameters	Initial Record Printed	Final Record Printed	Format of the Printed Report
1 Required	No Required	1 Optional	1 Optional	No Required
INDATASET	OUTFILE	FROMADDRESS	TOADDRESS	DUMP-default
INFILE	Default -	FROMKEY	TOKEY	CHARACTER
No Default	SYSPRINT	FROMNUMBER	TONUMBER	HEXADECIMAL
		SKIP	COUNT	
		Default(1st)	Default(Last)	

OFILE allows any DD parameters available with SYSOUT data sets to be coded on the accompanying DD statement. Such parameters can be used to select a specific printer, print train, font, number of copies, OUTLIM value, etc. None of this information can be specified with the PRINT command. Coding the OUTPUT DD parameter allows most of this information to be specified on the OUTPUT JCL statement. This is illustrated in the final example (Example 6) at the end of this section.

Initial record and final record processed with PRINT

Initial record and final record processed with PRINT parameters are used to identify the first and last input data set records to process. The identical parameters are available, as with REPRO. For the initial record, FROMKEY, FROMADDRESS, FROMNUMBER, and SKIP can be coded. TOKEY, TOADDRESS, TONUMBER, and COUNT can be coded for the final record.

All the characteristics of the REPRO command also apply to these two groups of parameters. The default is to process every input record, i.e., no SKIP parameter coded (or SKIP(0)) and no COUNT parameter coded. SKIP and COUNT should not be used when printing records through a path. If a linear data set is to be printed, only FROMADDRESS and TOADDRESS can be used to qualify the records selected from the input data set. Furthermore, the RBA values are rounded to the nearest 4096 byte-control interval boundary.

Format of printed output

There are three possible formats of printed output to choose from: HEXADECIMAL (HEX), CHARACTER (CHAR), and DUMP, which is the default. If HEX is specified, the complete contents of each record is displayed and each byte value is printed as two hexadecimal characters. If CHAR is specified, each "printable" character is printed as exactly one position. Each nonprintable character is represented by a decimal point. DUMP produces a combination of HEX and CHAR. With DUMP, each record is printed in both hexadecimal and character using the rules in effect with both of those formats. The hexadecimal portion occupies the left-most $2/3$ of the listing page and the character portion the right-most $1/3$ of the listing page. DUMP is a good defensive choice when some of the data consists of nonprintable characters.

There are several examples of printer IDCAMS output throughout the text. Table 8.3 shows three records printed in dump format. If they were printed in hex format, only the left portion of the listing would appear. Likewise, character format consists of the portion of the listing.

Features not included with the PRINT command

There are several parameters available with REPRO that are not allowed with PRINT. These include REPLACE, REUSE, Encryption, and several catalog-processing commands. REPLACE is used with random access and is meaningless with an output data set, which is usually a printed report. REUSE is coded to empty all records out of the output data set preliminary to process the input records and is also meaningless with a printed report. Encryption is also not available for obvious reasons. What use is a printed copy of encrypted data? Finally, there is no real reason for PRINT command equivalents of the catalog-processing commands.

IEBPTPCH is the IEB/IEH utility that is comparable to PRINT. IEBPTPCH provides numerous features not supported by the PRINT command. These include processing every N-th record, carriage control, field editing, user page numbering, providing titles and subtitles, adding sequence numbers to each line or record, specifying the number of lines per page, and processing every member in a library.

Another potential improvement would be to allow the capability of processing every object within a specific category. This includes every member in a PDS (not supported), every data set in a catalog (not supported), or every data set in a GDG (supported!).

Coding examples

Example 1.   The records in the KSDS MASTER.ALPHA are to be printed in both CHARACTER format and HEX format. Two PRINT commands are required. Note that if two copies of the data set are to be printed in character format, only the first PRINT command is needed, and COPIES = 2 should be added to the DD statement. Just as with the REPRO coding examples, the EXEC statement and the SYSIN and SYSPRINT DD statement are needed with each of the PRINT examples but are shown only with the first one in Fig. 5.8.

Example 2.   Three listings of the records in the KSDS MASTER.ALPHA are produced by the coding in Fig. 5.9. All three listings should be in character format. The key field contains last name values. First, print the records in order by key value. Second, in order by RBA value. Finally, print all records with a key value starting with a letter in the second half of the alphabet. Note that either the first or last DD statement can be omitted by changing the corresponding INFILE parameter values on the corresponding PRINT command. It is almost always

```
//A          EXEC  PGM=IDCAMS
//SYSPRINT DD SYSOUT=A
//SYSIN     DD *
     PRINT INFILE(INPUT)  CHARACTER
     PRINT INFILE(INPUT)  HEX
/*
//INPUT DD DSN=MASTER.ALPHA,DISP=SHR
```

Figure 5.8 Standard PRINT processing.

```
//SYSIN   DD   *
    PRINT INFILE(KEYED)     CHARACTER
    PRINT INFILE(RBA)       CHARACTER
    PRINT INFILE(NTHRUZ)    CHARACTER FROMKEY(N*)
/*

//KEYED  DD   DSN=MASTER.ALPHA,DISP=SHR
//RBA    DD   DSN=MASTER.ALPHA.DATA,DISP=SHR
//NTHRUZ DD   DSN=MASTER.ALPHA,DISP=SHR
```

Figure 5.9 Printing three different reports with the same input.

the case with IDCAMS that the name of the data set needs to be coded on just one DD statement in the step, such as in the previous example.

Example 3.   There are situations where it is necessary to print out the information in a VSAM catalog. PRINT can be used to process a catalog in the same way that it is used with an ordinary data set. Unlike REPRO, there are no specific PRINT parameters used just with catalogs. The use of dynamic allocation is questionable in this context:

```
//CAT123 DD DSN = ACSSTU.VSAMCTLG,DISP = SHR
    PRINT IDS (ACSSTU.VSAMCTLG) or PRINT INFILE(CAT123)
```

Example 4.   Print the records in three members of the cataloged partitioned data set SYS1.PROCLIB. The members are IDCAMS, SORTD, and COBUCG. Several approaches can be used depending on whether or not dynamic allocation is used and the desired appearance of the output. Initially, dynamic allocation is used.

With the approach first used in Fig. 5.10, the records in each member begin on a separate page and the individual members are labeled. Unfortunately, the PRINT command does not allow multiple members to be specified in one dynamic allocation. Hence, IDS (SYS1.PROCLIB(IDCAMS, SORTD, COBUCG)) is not

```
    PRINT IDS(SYS1.PROCLIB(IDCAMS))
    PRINT IDS(SYS1.PROCLIB(SORTD))
    PRINT IDS(SYS1.PROCLIB(COBUCG))

//PDSMEMBR DD DSN=SYS1.PROCLIB(IDCAMS),DISP=SHR
//          DD DSN=SYS1.PROCLIB(SORTD),DISP=SHR
//          DD DSN=SYS1.PROCLIB(COBUCG),DISP=SHR
//SYSIN     DD *
    PRINT   IFILE(PDSMEMBR)  CHARACTER
/*
```

Figure 5.10 First and second techniques for printing multiple PDS members.

```
//PDSMEMB1 DD DSN=SYS1.PROCLIB(IDCAMS),DISP=SHR
//PDSMEMB2 DD DSN=SYS1.PROCLIB(SORTD),DISP=SHR
//PDSMEMB3 DD DSN=SYS1.PROCLIB(COBUCG),DISP=SHR
//SYSIN    DD *
    PRINT    IFILE(PDSMEMB1) CHARACTER
    PRINT    IFILE(PDSMEMB2) CHARACTER
    PRINT    IFILE(PDSMEMB3) CHARACTER
/*
```

Figure 5.11 Third method for printing multiple PDS members.

valid. Historic reasons account for this. It is almost unreasonable not to support it today.

The "same" report can be generated by identifying the three library members on individual DD statements. Here, the records in all three members are combined into one continuous listing. This is the bottom portion of code in Fig. 5.10.

A third approach uses static allocation and prints every member on a separate page, which will be individually titled. The code is shown in Fig. 5.11.

It is also possible to process every member in the PDS. Omitting the member name could specify that every member is to be printed. With REPRO, the same approach could cause every member to be copied. IEBPTPCH and IEB-COPY perform these respective features with every PDS member.

Example 5.   The code in Fig. 5.12 prints out the directory of the partitioned data set (library) SYS1.PROCLIB. Although the library is cataloged, dynamic allocation should not be used because SYS1.PROCLIB is constantly accessed by other jobs and would result in DISP=OLD. Either DUMP or HEX should be specified because most of the information in the directory is stored as noncharacter data. Here, the DCB information overrides the values in the labels for the library. Consequently, IDCAMS believes it is processing a sequential data set consisting of unblocked, 256-byte records. The EOF marker at the end of the directory halts processing before the member area is reached.

Example 6.   Various features that affect the appearance of printed output cannot be specified within the IDCAMS control statements, but can be identified using JCL. The values can be specified on the DD statement or on an OUTPUT

```
//DIRECTRY DD DSN=SYS1.PROCLIB,DISP=SHR,
//            DCB=(RECFM=U,BLKSIZE=256)
//SYSIN    DD *
      PRINT    IFILE(DIRECTRY) DUMP
/*
```

Figure 5.12 Printing the directory of a library.

```
//REPORT   OUTPUT   parameters to identify fonts, copies, etc.
    .    .    .
//PRINTETC DD  SYSOUT=A,OUTPUT=REPORT,additional parameters
//SYSIN    DD  *
   PRINT INFILE(PRINTETC)
/*
```

Figure 5.13 Using JCL for "fancy" printing options.

JCL statement identified on the DD statement. These techniques are illustrated in Fig. 5.13.

The EXPORT Command

For a variety of reasons, it might be necessary to back up or transport a VSAM data set. Usually, the backup copy or version of the data set to transport is placed on (cartridge) tape. When a VSAM data set is exported to tape, it loses its structure as a VSAM data set and becomes a sequential non-VSAM data set. When a data set is exported, the original can remain on the system or it can be deleted. Likewise, records in an exported data set that is retained can be locked from update processing until the data set is later imported. The parameters available with EXPORT are categorized and identified in Table 5.7. There are three types of objects that can be exported: clusters, alternate indexes, and catalogs.

Input and output parameters

Exactly one VSAM data set—of any type—must be identified as the input to be exported. The data set name must be listed first before any of the keyword parameters. If the data set is password-protected, the password must be specified. Only a cluster name should be specified. Specifying the name of the data set by itself does not cause it to be dynamically allocated. Rather, it makes it possible to use INFILE to identify the data set on a DD statement. If INFILE is not coded, the data set being exported will be dynamically allocated.

The exported copy of the VSAM data set is stored as a non-VSAM sequential

TABLE 5.7 EXPORT Parameters and Processing Categories.

Input Parameters	Output Parameters	Subsequent Processing Status	Additional Parameters
1 Required	1 Required	All Optional	All Optional
INFILE	OUTFILE	TEMPORARY or	INFILE
Data Set Name	OUTDATASET	PERMANENT	ERASE or NOERASE
No Default	No Default	INHIBITSOURCE or	PURGE or NOPURGE
		NOINHIBITSOURCE	CIMODE or RECORDMODE
		INHIBITTARGET or	
		NOINHIBITTARGET	

(QSAM) data set. The OUTFILE parameter can identify the DDname used to specify the name and location of the exported copy. In particular, DSN, UNIT, and VOL parameters are almost always coded. SPACE should be coded with a disk data set, and LABEL may be coded with a cartridge data set. It is unnecessary to code DCB values because IDCAMS generates the appropriate values for LRECL, BLKSIZE, and RECFM. Under most conditions, a DISP value of NEW will be coded or implied. The exported output can, however, be added to an existing data set. The OUTDATASET parameter can be used but must identify an existing data set, which is not usually the case during an export operation.

At this point, some thought should be given as to the format of the output data set created by EXPORT. For illustration purposes, assume that a KSDS is to be exported. For the other three types of VSAM data sets, there is no index component to export. The KSDS consists of three components and, intuitively, the basic contents of each is copied—in order—to the OUTFILE data set. The exported data set can be imagined as pictured in Fig. 5.14. The keyword here is "imagined."

Because all three components can contain logical and physical records of different sizes, the exported data set must consist of variable length records, which are most likely blocked and perhaps spanned. In fact, RECFM = VBS and BLKSIZE = 2048 are used unless overridden.

Although this scenario seems reasonable, it is not quite correct. Rather, only the "essential" data is exported, which consists of the logical records and some cluster component information. Other cluster information and the index component are ignored. VSAM believes that it is more efficient to recreate this information during an import operation than to store it. Hence, a more realistic representation of an exported KSDS is shown in Fig. 5.15, which might represent any type of exported VSAM data set (KSDS, ESDS, or RRDS).

Data set status following the EXPORT

Once the exported copy is created, should the original input data set continue to exist or be deleted? This major decision is made by coding TEMPORARY (the data set will not be deleted from the catalog after it is exported) or PERMANENT (the data set is deleted from the catalog after it is exported). Hence, TEMPORARY means that a permanent copy of the original data set is kept, while PERMANENT means that it ceases to exist! Clearly, the words TEMPORARY and PERMANENT are more descriptive of the exported copy than of the original data set.

Cluster Component	Index Component	Data Component
Data	Data	Records

Figure 5.14   Intuitive representation of exported KSDS.

Cluster Component	Data Component
Data	Records

Figure 5.15 More accurate representation of an exported KSDS.

The INHIBITSOURCE parameter applies to the data set that is being exported, the input data set. In particular, this data set is not to be modified or updated in any way following the export. Rather, only record retrieval is permitted. INHIBITSOURCE can only be coded with TEMPORARY. NOINHIBITSOURCE allows any type of modifications to the records in the input data set following the EXPORT.

INHIBITTARGET is related to the exported copy of the data set. Whenever it is imported into a subsequent target system, the imported copy cannot be updated or modified in any way. Rather, only record retrieval is permitted. NOINHIBITTARGET allows it to be updated. Both INHIBITSOURCE and INHIBITTARGET can be modified with the ALTER command.

Additional parameters

The ERASE and PURGE parameters, both of which can be coded with EXPORT, are discussed in more detail with the DELETE command. ERASE and PURGE can affect a delete operation to the source data set following the EXPORT operation where PERMANENT is specified. PERMANENT means delete the original object. ERASE and PURGE are both meaningless if TEMPORARY is coded. This is because the original data set is not deleted. PURGE overrides any retention period in effect as a result of a TO or FOR parameter. ERASE causes the data component to be overwritten with binary zeroes.

A choice can be made between processing each individual logical record or to ignore record boundaries and process entire control intervals. RECORDMODE processes individual records and is the default with a KSDS, ESDS, and RRDS. Unused space and deleted records are not exported. CIMODE copies the entire control interval, including deleted records in an RRDS, freespace in a KSDS, and unused space in an ESDS. CIMODE is the default with an LDS. Whether RECORDMODE or CIMODE is used, the IMPORT command can determine the status of the exported data set and process it accordingly. CIMODE cannot be used with an ESDS, which contains an alternate index over it.

Using EXPORT and IMPORT with alternate indexes

Care should be taken when exporting and importing a data set with one or more alternate indexes and accompanying paths over it. In particular, the alternate indexes should be exported before the base cluster. Otherwise, problems occur after the base KSDS or ESDS is exported. Specifically, there is no existing underlying data set for the alternate index to relate to.

This order should be reversed when importing a KSDS or ESDS, and the alternate indexes that were exported with it. The base cluster must be imported prior to the alternate indexes. This is necessary in order to have an existing cluster for the alternate index to relate to.

EXPORT vs. REPRO

Both EXPORT and REPRO can be used to copy logical records from an input to an output data set. REPRO copies just the logical records. EXPORT copies additional information along with the records. Only one type of output data set is produced by EXPORT. REPRO allows a wide variety of destination data sets. After the records have been copied, how can the original data set be recreated? With a VSAM data set built and traded by IDCAMS, DEFINE CLUSTER must be used to create a new data set and REPRO records from the copy to the newly defined data set. Once EXPORT creates a new data set, the original data set can be reconstructed and loaded with an IMPORT command. The information stored in the exported copy can be used by IDCAMS to create a new data set. Hence, in a sense, IMPORT = DEFINE CLUSTER + REPRO.

Coding examples

Example 1. The ESDS MASTER.ESDS is to be exported to cartridge. However, the MASTER.ESDS cluster is not to be deleted, and the original copy can be replaced at any later time by the exported copy. The original copy is not allowed to be modified, but the records in MASTER.ESDS can be read. Because FILE is coded, dynamic allocation is not used, and entire control intervals are processed. As with the REPRO and PRINT examples, the EXEC statement and SYSIN and SYSPRINT DD statements are required with each example, but are shown only with the first one in Fig. 5.16.

```
//A         EXEC    PGM=IDCAMS
//SYSPRINT  DD      SYSOUT=A
//SYSIN     DD      *
    EXPORT  MASTER.ESDS      -
            FILE(MAST)       -
            OUTFILE(CART)    -
            CIMODE           -
            TEMPORARY        -
            INHIBITSOURCE
/*
//MAST      DD  DSN=MASTER.ESDS,DISP=SHR
//CART      DD  DSN=EXPORTED.ESDS,DISP=(NEW,KEEP),LABEL=(1,SL),
//              UNIT=CART,VOL=SER=010103,DCB=(BLKSIZE=32000)
```

Figure 5.16 Exporting a KSDS to cartridge.

```
        EXPORT  MASTER.KSDS       -
                OUTFILE(TAPEDD)   -
                PERMANENT         -
                PURGE             -
                ERASE
        PRINT   INDATASET(EXPORTED.KSDS)  DUMP

//TAPEDD  DD DSN=EXPORTED.KSDS,DISP=(NEW,CATLG),
//             UNIT=TAPE,VOL=SER=123123
```

Figure 5.17   Additional EXPORT command options.

Example 2.   The KSDS MASTER.KSDS is to be exported to tape. Following the export, the original copy of the KSDS is to be deleted. The original data set has an expiration date that has not yet occurred. Furthermore, the data component of MASTER.KSDS contains confidential data and is to be overwritten with binary zeroes. Following EXPORT command execution, the newly created copy is printed in order to analyze the actual format of an exported copy of a KSDS. All processing details are coded in Fig. 5.17.

Example 3.   In Fig. 5.18, both a KSDS and an alternate index over it are to be exported. The original copy is not to be deleted and no changes are to be made to the original data set or the exported copy. Alternate indexes should be exported before the base clusters over which they are built, especially when both are being permanently exported.

The IMPORT Command

The IMPORT command is a companion to the EXPORT command and is used to recreate and reload exported data sets (cluster and alternate index) and cata-

```
        EXPORT  MASTER.KSDS.AIX        -
                OUTFILE(EXPAIX)        -
                TEMPORARY             -
                INHIBITSOURCE         -
                INHIBITTARGET
        EXPORT  MASTER.KSDS            -
                OUTFILE(BACKUP)        -
                TEMPORARY             -
                INHIBITSOURCE         -
                INHIBITTARGET

//BACKUP  DD DSN=MASTER.ALPHA,DISP=SHR
//EXPAIX  DD DSN=MASTER.ALPHA.AIX,DISP=SHR
```

Figure 5.18   Exporting a KSDS and an alternate index built over it.

TABLE 5.8   IMPORT Parameters and Processing Categories.

Input Parameters	Output Parameters	OBJECTS Modification Sub-Parameters	Other Parameters
1 Required	1 Required	All Optional	All Optional
INFILE	OUTFILE	data set name	ALIAS or NOALIAS
INDATASET	OUTDATASET	VOLUMES	ERASE or NOERASE
No Default	No Default	NEWNAME	INTOEMPTY
		KEYRANGES	LOCK or UNLOCK
		ORDERED	PURGE or NOPURGE
		FILE	SAVRAC or NOSAVRAC

logs. Hence, IMPORT uses as input an exported VSAM data set and uses it to construct a true VSAM data set. IMPORT is a more complex command than EXPORT and has substantially more parameters available than with EXPORT. The parameters available with IMPORT are identified and categorized in Table 5.8.

Input parameters

Any object to be imported must be a portable data set containing a ''copy'' of a VSAM cluster, an alternate index, or a catalog. Either INFILE or INDATASET must be coded to identify the object to import, and the usual trade-offs between static and dynamic allocation apply. It is important to note that this is the actual name (or altered) associated with the exported copy. Other names can be specified with the OBJECTS parameter.

Output parameters

Either OUTFILE or OUTDATASET must be coded to identify the data set after it is imported back to the system. Several restrictions are in effect with OUTFILE. It should not be used if the data and index component are on different volumes. If the data set is to be placed on a different volume, then VOLUME (volser) must also be coded with OBJECTS. Most commonly, the DD statement should contain the name of the data set, VOL = volser, UNIT = value, DISP = OLD, and AMP = 'AMORG'. AMP is needed to identify a VSAM data set.

Modifying parameters

Somewhat analogous to the MODEL parameter, it is possible to IMPORT an object and in the process override or change several of the major properties stored with it when it was exported. Three major properties can be changed during the IMPORT process:

1. The name of the object.

2. The volume on which it is to reside.

3. Partitioning a KSDS onto a group of volumes using the KEYRANGES parameter.

Other parameters

Multiple objects can be modified by a single OBJECTS parameter. For example, while importing an alternate index, the names of the data and index components, along with one or more of the paths, can be changed. The syntax with OBJECTS is somewhat more complex than most other IDCAMS parameters. Additional parameters available with IMPORT perform a variety of functions:

- ALIAS is used to retrieve aliases that were associated with a user catalog when it was exported.

- ERASE and PURGE have the same basic functions as when used with DELETE and EXPORT. If ERASE is specified with an object exported as TEMPORARY, the data component is overwritten with binary zeroes as part of the subsequent object exported as part of the IMPORT operation. If PURGE is specified with an object exported as TEMPORARY, the object will be deleted, even if its expiration date has not occurred.

- INTOEMPTY specifies that the exported data set is to be imported into an empty data set. INTOEMPTY is required if the data set into which the portable data set is to be imported is empty.

- LOCK is used only with ICF catalogs.

- SAVRAC and NOSAVRAC are meaningful only with RACF. If SAVRAC is coded, the RACF profile associated with the object being imported will be used following the operation.

- NOSAVRAC causes a new RACF profile to be generated for the object being imported.

Coding examples

Example 1. The KSDS MASTER.KSDS had previously been exported to cartridge and given the name EXPORTED.KSDS.COPY. It is now to be imported back to the original system where it is to again be known as MASTER.ALPHA. The

```
          IMPORT   INFILE(INPUT)                    -
                   OUTDATASET(MASTER.KSDS)

//INPUT  DD  DSN=EXPORTED.KSDS.COPY,DISP=(OLD,PASS),
//           UNIT=CART,VOL=SER=123123
```

Figure 5.19 Importing a KSDS from cartridge.

```
        IMPORT  INFILE(SOURCE)                      -
                OUTFILE(DESTINAT)                   -
                OBJECTS((EXPORTED.ESDS.COPY          -
                    NEWNAME(NEW.ESDS.NAME)           -
                    VOLUMES(WORK23)))

//SOURCE DD DSN=EXPORTED.ESDS.COPY,DISP=(OLD,KEEP),
//           UNIT=CART,VOL=SER=123321
//DESTINAT DD DSN=NEW.ESDS.NAME,DISP=OLD,AMP='AMORG'
//           VOL=SER=WORK23,UNIT=DASD
```

Figure 5.20 Importing an ESDS and modifying some of its properties.

EXPORT command had specified PERMANENT and there is presently no MASTER.KSDS data set on the system. The necessary IDCAMS code and JCL is shown in Fig. 5.19.

Example 2. The ESDS EXPORTED.ESDS.COPY had previously been exported. It is to be imported to the original system, defined in a different catalog, given a new name, and stored on a different volume. Notice that both OUTFILE and NEWNAME identify the new (changed) name of the data set. The current name is coded with OBJECTS as its first subparameter. Notice the syntax used with the objects parameters in Fig. 5.20, especially the parenthesis.

Example 3. In the last of the EXPORT command coding examples in Fig. 5.21, a base cluster KSDS and an alternate index were both exported. Here, the two objects are imported back to the original system where they are to replace the original copies. Base clusters should be imported prior to importing alternate indexes built over them.

Exercises

1. What is the absolute minimum number of parameters that can be coded with a REPRO command when copying a KSDS? What is the absolute maximum number of parameters that can be coded in the same situation? Hint: see Fig. 5.1. What are the actual parameters (not subparameters) in each of these cases? How does the answer change if a different type of object is to be copied? For example, a Non-VSAM data set or catalog.

```
        IMPORT  INFILE(BASEKSDS)                     -
                OUTDATASET(MASTER.KSDS)
        IMPORT  INFILE(AIXDD)                         -
                OUTDATASET(MASTER.KSDS.AIX)

//BASEKSDS DD  DSN=MASTER.ALPHA,DISP=SHR
//AIXDD    DD  DSN=MASTER.ALPHA.AIX,DISP=SHR
```

Figure 5.21 Importing a KSDS and an alternate index built over it.

```
REPRO IDS(PQR)  SKIP(5)  COUNT(5)
REPRO IDS(PQR)  FROMKEY(20*)  TOKEY(21*)
REPRO IDS(PQR)  REPLACE REUSE COUNT(10)
REPRO IDS(PQR)  TOKEY(01*)  SKIP(200)
REPRO IDS(PQR)  FROMADDRESS(0)  TOKEY(0248)
```

Figure 5.22 Identifying the first and last records copied.

2. A cataloged data set contains 5,000 records. Two copies of these records are to be created. The first copy should contain all 5,000 records. The second copy should contain 500 records that consist of a copy of every tenth record in the input, starting with the first record. Use IDCAMS to create the two copies.

3. Use dynamic allocation to print out the directory of SYS1.PROCLIB, a large system-procedure library.

4. The KSDS PQR consists of 1,000 records. The four-digit key fields contain the values 0005, 0010, 0015, 0020, etc. Identify the records that are processed in each of the situations coded in Fig. 5.22.

5. The records in a KSDS are to be printed. The minimum number of parameters required to identify the input is 1. What is the maximum number of parameters that can be coded? Give an example illustrating the use of the maximum number.

6. For the PRINT, EXPORT, and IMPORT parameters, categorize the functions they perform as: (a) can also be performed by REPRO, and (b) cannot be performed by REPRO.

Chapter

6

IDCAMS
System-Component Commands

This chapter on system-component commands completes the discussion of fundamental IDCAMS commands for processing data sets. Each of the four commands are covered in detail, including their basic processing functions and every important parameter. Input, output, and other parameters are discussed in detail, and a comprehensive group of coding examples is included to illustrate how the commands are used.

The REPRO, PRINT, EXPORT, and IMPORT commands discussed in chapter 5 all process the logical records contained in the data component of a VSAM data set. None of the commands examined in this chapter explicitly process individual logical records. The two commands initially discussed, LISTCAT and ALTER, process the control information contained in the cluster component. LISTCAT uses this information to generate printed reports, and ALTER is used to modify various values stored in the cluster component. Because of their functions, LISTCAT causes no structural changes to the data set, while the affect of ALTER can be used to impact subsequent processing.

The only potentially dramatic result associated with using LISTCAT is when it is accidentally or intentionally used to print an overwhelming amount of data. There are a number of ways in which this can easily happen. On the other hand, ALTER can dramatically modify the structure and processing environment for a data set.

The other two commands discussed in this chapter, DELETE and VERIFY, allow a much more limited range of processing options and associated parameters. For those familiar with IEH utilities, LISTCAT shares some similarities with IEHLIST; ALTER and DELETE both have functional similarities with IEHPROGM; and VERIFY has no IEH equivalent.

TABLE 6.1 Major IDCAMS Commands Hierarchy.

Significance	Commands	Substitute or Overlapping Commands
Most Crucial	REPRO LISTCAT DELETE	
Middle Crucial	VERIFY ALTER	Default Action DEFINE CLUSTER and REPRO
Least Crucial	PRINT EXPORT IMPORT	REPRO OFILE identifies SYSOUT REPRO REPRO DEFINE CLUSTER and REPRO

LISTCAT, ALTER, and DELETE allow generic data set names to be specified. This is distinct from using generic key field values with REPRO and PRINT. When a generic data set name is specified, a group of data sets with related names is processed with a single command. In order to take full advantage of generic processing, naming conventions should be developed for the first several levels of qualification in data set names. Even if installation standards for the data set names do not exist, individual programmer standards should be used.

LISTCAT allows a very wide range of generic processing options. The ALTER and DELETE commands also allow generic processing, but their generic processing scope is not as broad as with LISTCAT. VERIFY does not allow generic data set names. Each of the Big Eight IDCAM commands is crucial when performing a function. However, an absolutely crucial hierarchy among the commands is something like that shown in Table 6.1.

The LISTCAT Command

LISTCAT, which can be abbreviated LISTC, produces printed reports. The information displayed is retrieved from the cluster component, no matter which part(s) of a VSAM data set are identified. The IEHLIST utility performs a functionally comparable operation with non-VSAM catalogs, where the LISTCTLG command dumps out all of the information stored in the catalog for a non-VSAM data set. This fixed amount of information consists of the:

- Data set name.

- Volume where it resides.

- Device type (unit) file sequence number for a tape data set.

In addition, LISTCTLG can only be used with a CVOL catalog. LISTCAT allows the programmer considerable flexibility in selecting the amount of information to be printed. Furthermore, much more information is stored in a VSAM catalog to describe a VSAM data set than is stored in any type of catalog structure to describe a non-VSAM data set. This holds for ICF catalogs, VSAM catalogs, and CVOLS. Some of the information available with LISTCAT is also provided by the LISTVTOC command with IEHLIST.

LISTCAT is one of the major IDCAM commands. As evidence of its importance, it is a significant topic both in this chapter and also in chapter 7. In this chapter, the function of the command itself and the syntax employed to use it are emphasized. In chapter 7, the report produced by LISTCAT is examined.

Parameters

LISTCAT parameters can be grouped into five general categories. Exactly one parameter can be coded in the first three categories, while any multiple number of parameters can be coded with the final two. Because there is a default value in each category, it is possible to code just LISTCAT followed by no parameters. A summary of the parameters available with LISTCAT is given in Table 6.2. In addition, CATALOG and FILE can be coded in order to identify a specific catalog to search for the input data sets.

Unlike record-processing commands such as REPRO and PRINT, any number of objects can be identified with the input parameter. Both the Type of Object and Additional Qualifications parameters are used to determine which data sets from among those identified with the Input Parameter should actually be processed. Without using one or both of these categories of parameters, a tremendous number of data sets can be identified and a great amount of information generated and printed.

Input parameters

There are two input parameters, ENTRIES and LEVEL. ENTRIES can be followed by one or more data set names:

TABLE 6.2   LISTCAT Parameters and Processing Categories.

Input Parameter	Output Parameter	Amount of Information	Types of Objects	Additional Qualifications
No Required	No Required	No Required	All Optional	All Optional
ENTRIES	OUTFILE	NAME-default	ALIAS	CREATION
LEVEL	default-	HISTORY	ALTERNATEINDEX	EXPIRATION
default-	SYSPRINT	VOLUME	CLUSTER	default-none
all entries		ALLOCATION	DATA	
		ALL	GENERATIONDATAGROUP	
			INDEX	Other
			NONVSAM	Parameters
			PAGESPACE	Optional
			PATH	FILE
			SPACE	
			USERCATALOG	
			Default-none	

ENTRIES (dsname1, dsname2, ... dsnameN)

Furthermore, each occurrence of dsname can be replaced by a generic name. This consists of representing one level of qualification with an asterisk. Hence, if four levels of qualifications are coded, one of which is an asterisk, all data sets whose name contains exactly four qualifiers where the given three match are processed.

An asterisk cannot be coded as the first level of qualification, but it can be the last. Currently, multiple asterisks can now be coded within a data set name. It is not possible to include just a portion of a level of qualification. For example, ENT(X.ABC*.Y) is not supported. This convenient feature is possible with TSO/ISPF. Here again, the asterisk cannot be a part of the first qualifier.

The LEVEL parameter allows only one data set name to be coded. Although it can be a generic value, the final level of qualification coded cannot be an asterisk. Generic processing must be explicitly requested with ENTRIES, and it is always in effect with LEVEL. However, the format is different. If a data set name is coded with N levels of qualification, every date set name whose first N level of qualification matches the specified value is processed. Therefore, the final level of qualification coded cannot be an asterisk.

For example, if LEVEL(ALPHA.BETA) is coded, the data sets with the names of ALPHA.BETA, ALPHA.BETA.GAMMA, and ALPHA.BETA.A.B.C.D.E.F.G will all be processed. Thus, LEVEL allows generic processing in two different ways. Generic processing with ENTRIES is simple (one way), but double generic processing is possible with LEVEL. If LEVEL(*.BETA) is coded, all of these data sets will be processed along with data sets with the names BETA.BETA, GAMMA .BETA, etc. Example 1, which follows, categorizes and summarizes how data sets are identified by ENTRIES and LEVEL.

As mentioned before, if neither ENTRIES or LEVEL is coded, every cataloged data set will be processed depending on the catalogs identified. If neither

TABLE 6.3   Using ENTRIES and LEVEL Parameters to Identify Data Sets.

LISTCAT Parameter Coded	Data Sets Identified	Remark
ENTRIES(A.B, A.C, A.D)	A.B A.C A.D	Non generic
ENTRIES(A.*)	A.B A.C A.D	Simple generic
LEVEL(A.*)	none	Invalid syntax
LEVEL(A.*.C)	A.B.C A.B.C.D	Doubly generic
ENTRIES(A.*.C)	A.B.C.	Simple generic
LEVEL(A)	all data sets but A and B	Simple generic
ENTRIES(A)	A	
ENTRIES	none	Syntax error
no Input Parameter coded	every data set in catalog	Always
ENTRIES(A*.B)	none	Syntax error
LEVEL(A B)	none	Syntax error

ENTRIES or LEVEL is coded, every data set in the catalog is selected for processing by default. This could involve a tremendous number of data sets unless subsequent parameter qualifications reduce this number.

Security violations, both RACF and VSAM passwords, cause some data sets identified for processing to be skipped. Messages will be generated in each case, however.

Example 1.   A VSAM catalog contains data sets with name A, B, A.B, A.C, A.D, A.B.C, A.B.D, and A.B.C.D. For each of the LISTCAT input parameters on the left in Table 6.3, the data sets selected for processing are listed on the right.

Output parameter default

The output parameter default—the IDCAMS SYSPRINT message data set OUTFILE (DDname) OFILE is much like the PRINT command. LISTCAT allows two output options. The LISTCAT report is printed by default in the message data set identified by the SYSPRINT DD statement. Alternatively, the OUTFILE parameter can be coded to specify a DDname that identifies the DD statement where the report is to be printed.

The reasons for choosing between the message data set and OUTFILE are the same ones given with the PRINT command. OFILE can use DD parameters to control the destination, quality, and quantity of the printed output.

Amount of information printed

Five parameters are available to specify the amount of information printed for each entry: NAME, HISTORY(HIST), VOLUMES(VOL), ALLOCATION(AL-LOC), and ALL. NAME is the default value and produces the least information, little more than the name of the data set and the type of object it is. ALL produces the most information, nearly two full pages for a KSDS. ALL prints out almost every field (both useful and useless information) associated with the object. HISTORY, VOLUMES, and ALLOCATION are infrequently used because they are not the most reasonable choices to set up. However, this is merely just part of a more general complaint concerning the usefulness of much of the information provided by LISTCAT.

Among the three rarely used parameters, HISTORY provides the least amount of information. It supplies all the information provided by NAME and also includes the owner ID, creation date, and expiration date. VOLUMES supplies all the information provided by HISTORY and also volume and device information for the data and index components. ALLOCATION supplies all the information provided by VOLUMES, along with detailed allocation information for the data and index components.

For a KSDS, the basic appearance of the LISTCAT output is shown in Fig. 6.1. With the other types of VSAM data sets, there are three basic portions in the LISTCAT report because the index component information is not present.

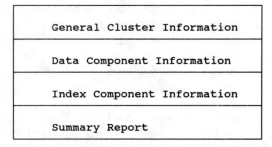

Figure 6.1   Four basic components of a LISTCAT report for a KSDS.

Types of objects processed

Among all the objects identified by the LEVEL or ENTRIES parameter (or the entire catalog), it is possible to qualify this input group in two ways. One method involves data set creation and expiration dates and is discussed in the following section. It is also possible to qualify the input entries based on the types of objects. For example, out of all possible entries satisfying a generic criteria or among every object in an entire catalog produce LISTCAT reports for only those which are index components, or only those which are non-VSAM data sets. The following is a list of the parameters, along with their abbreviations, that can be processed with the LEVEL or ENTRIES parameters:

- ALIAS
- ALTERNATEINDEX (AIX)
- CLUSTER (CL)
- DATA
- GENERATIONDATAGROUP (GDG)
- INDEX (IX)
- NONVSAM (NVSAM)
- PAGESPACE (PGSPC)
- PATH
- SPACE (SPC)
- USERCATALOG (UCAT)

Anywhere from 0 to 11 of these parameters can be specified. Coding all 11 parameters has the same effect as coding none of them. An object that satisfies the ENTRIES/LEVEL criteria must also match one of the type of objects parameters. This can be used as a check to determine that only the desired entities are printed. For example, suppose that a group of alternate indexes are to be processed. They all have names with the form at REPORT.*.AIX.

To ensure that only the correct objects are processed, code LISTCAT ENT (REPORT.*.AIX) AIX. Any object that is not an alternate index but has first and third qualifiers of REPORT and AIX will not be processed. If no parameters are specified to identify the type of objects, no qualification is performed and all ENTRIES/LEVEL objects are processed. If CLUSTER is specified but not DATA or INDEX, then information is provided only for the CLUSTER component but not the DATA or INDEX component. Likewise, if DATA or INDEX is specified but not CLUSTER, then no CLUSTER information is printed.

Qualification parameters

CREATION and EXPIRATION are two additional parameters that can be used to further qualify objects selected with ENTRIES or LEVEL. CREATION must reference an unsigned integer. CREATION(N) means that an object is to be processed only if it was created N days ago or earlier. CREATION(0) means all entries are to be listed, provided they meet all other qualifying criteria. The largest number that can be specified with CREATION is 9999. An unsigned integer must be supplied if the EXPIRATION parameter is coded.

EXPIRATION(N) means that entries are to be processed only if their expiration data will occur within: (1) N days from today or earlier or (2) they have no expiration date. EXPIRATION(0) means that entries are to be printed only if the expiration date has already occurred (or they have no expiration date).

NOTUSABLE is a third parameter that was formerly included in this group. Any data set marked as not usable in its catalog entry that met the other selection categories was processed.

Processing limitations

As an editorial comment, the LISTCAT command produces a marginally adequate report. Many installations have developed alternatives to using LISTCAT to provide comparable information. LISTCAT output is discussed in detail in subsequent chapters including especially chapter 7.

Several major LISTCAT report shortcomings are noted here. Each LISTCAT command always produces a summary page reflecting the processing performed. This occurs even when only one object has been processed (see chapter 7). It should be possible to suppress the summary report. In addition, some individual parameters are specified with objects with which they are meaningless (see chapter 7). A third possible improvement would be in the choice of the numeric values actually displayed. Some of the numerics are very un-intuitive,

```
//A          EXEC PGM=IDCAMS
//SYSPRINT DD   SYSOUT=A
//SYSIN     DD  *
   LISTCAT ENTRIES(ALPHA.BETA.GAMMA)    ALL
/*
```

Figure 6.2 Complete LISTCAT report for one KSDS.

to say the least, and more-or-less equivalent straightforward values could be calculated and displayed. See chapter 7 for further details.

In conclusion, the LISTCAT command needs a major revision to bring it into the 1980s. Maybe in about 10 years it will be updated to the 1990s. Note that this book was published in 1992.

Coding examples

Example 1.   Print all catalog information associated with the three components of the KSDS—ALPHA.BETA.GAMMA. The report should print in the message data set. The code in Fig. 6.2 is about as straightforward as a LISTCAT command can be.

Example 2.   Print information from the cluster component for both the data and index components for all data sets more than two weeks old whose expiration data will be reached within the next year and whose first level qualifier is BETA. Print the maximum amount of information for each object selected.

```
LISTCAT LEVEL(BETA) ALL  –
CREATION(14) EXPIRATION(365) –
DATA INDEX
```

ALL is used to print the maximum amount of information. If DATA and INDEX were not coded, general cluster information would also be printed for each data set.

Example 3.   Print the minimum amount of information found in the cluster components of all data sets whose names consist of exactly two levels of qualification and the first level is SYSTEM. For this same group of data sets, print the maximum amount of information for the data and index component of each KSDS. Naming conventions are: if X.Y is the cluster name, X.Y.DATA and X.Y.IN-DEX are the names of the data and index components respectively.

Notice that two separate LISTCAT commands are required because of the amount of information printed. Furthermore, CLUSTER must be coded with the first command or data and index component information will also be printed. Try to determine the objects processed by the third LISTCAT command. How does it overlap the first two groups of objects processed?

```
LISTCAT     ENT(FIRST.X    SECOND.Y    THIRD.Z)    -
            ALL                                     -
            CATALOG(ALPHA.USER.CATALOG)             -
            OUTFILE(DD1)

//DD1   DD   SYSOUT=A,COPIES=3,OUTPUT=LASER38
```

Figure 6.3   Producing multiple copies of multiple complete LISTCATs.

```
LISTCAT ENTRIES (SYSTEM.*) NAME CLUSTER
LISTCAT ENTRIES (SYSTEM.*.DATA SYSTEM.*.INDEX) ALL
LISTCAT LEVEL (SYSTEM.*) ALL
```

Example 4.   The maximum amount of catalog information for the three data sets—FIRST.X, SECOND.Y, and THIRD.Z—is printed by the code in Fig. 6.3. The three data sets are cataloged in ALPHA.USER.CATALOG. Three copies of the output should be produced on a 3800 laser printer, which is identified on an OUTPUT JCL statement.

Example 5.   One copy of the minimum amount of catalog information for just the data components of the three clusters identified in the previous example is produced by the code in Fig. 6.4. Any printer can be used. Notice that, in this situation, the OUTFILE parameter is unnecessary.

Example 6.   Print all of the catalog information for every data set with an entry in the user catalog ALPHA.USER.CATALOG and for every data set in the system master catalog. Notice that two separate commands are required. One or both of these commands could operate a substantial amount of output:

```
LISTCAT CATALOG (ALPHA.USER.CATALOG) ALL
LISTCAT ALL
```

The ALTER Command

The ALTER command is used to modify values for an object in the catalog entry. This information is stored in the cluster component for a VSAM data set. With an ICF catalog, the information might actually be stored in the catalog itself or in the VSAM Volume Data Set of the volume where the data set

```
LISTCAT     ENT(FIRST.X    SECOND.Y    THIRD.Z)    -
            NAME   /*THE DEFAULT */                 -
            CATALOG(ALPHA.USER.CATALOG)             -
            DATA
```

Figure 6.4   Additional LISTCAT processing options.

resides. In addition to VSAM data sets, ALTER can also be used with VSAM objects and with non-VSAM data sets.

When considering the ALTER command, it is reasonable to separate the properties associated with a data set or object into three basic categories:

1. Those properties that can always be altered.

TABLE 6.4   Parameters That ALTER Will Process.

Attributes that Can be Altered (Denoted by X)	ALTERNATEINDEX	AIX DATA	AIX INDEX	CLUSTER	CLUSTER DATA	CLUSTER INDEX	PAGESPACE	PATH	USERCAT DATA	USERCAT INDEX	NONVSAM	GDG	LINEAR
ADDVOLUMES		X	X		X	X							X
ATTEMPTS	X	X	X	X	X	X	X	X	X				X
AUTHORIZATION	X	X	X	X	X	X	X	X	X				X
BIND		X	X		X	X							X
BUFFERSPACE		X			X				X				X
BUFND									X				
BUFNI										X			
CODE	X	X	X	X	X	X	X	X	X				X
CONTROLPW	X	X	X	X	X	X	X	X	X				X
CYLINDERFAULT		X	X		X	X							X
DESTAGEWAIT		X	X		X	X							X
EMPTY												X	
ERASE		X			X								X
EXCEPTIONEXIT		X	X		X	X							X
FOR	X			X				X	X		X	X	X
FREESPACE		X			X				X				
INHIBIT		X	X		X	X							X
KEYS	X	X		X	X								
LOCK				X									
MASTERPW	X	X	X	X	X	X	X	X	X				X
NEWNAME	X	X	X	X	X	X	X	X			X		X

NODESTAGEWAIT		X	X		X	X							X
NOEMPTY												X	
NOERASE		X			X								X
NONUNIQUEKEY		X											
NOSCRATCH												X	
NOUPDATE								X					
NOUPGRADE	X												
NOWRITECHECK		X	X		X	X				X	X		X
NULLIFY	X	X	X	X	X	X	X	X	X		X	X	X
AUTHORIZATION	X	X	X	X	X	X	X	X	X				X
CODE	X	X	X	X	X	X	X	X	X				X
CONTROLPW	X	X	X	X	X	X	X	X	X				X
EXCEPTIONEXIT		X	X		X	X							X
MASTERPW	X	X	X	X	X	X	X	X	X				X
OWNER	X	X	X	X	X	X	X	X	X		X	X	X
READPW	X	X	X	X	X	X	X	X	X				X
RETENTION	X			X			X	X	X		X	X	X
UPDATEPW	X	X	X	X	X	X	X	X	X				X
OWNER	X	X	X	X	X	X	X	X	X		X	X	X
READPW	X	X	X	X	X	X	X	X	X				X
RECORDSIZE	X	X		X	X								
REMOVEVOLUMES		X	X		X	X							X
SCRATCH												X	
SHAREOPTIONS		X	X		X	X				X			X
STAGE		X	X		X	X							X
STRNO									X				
TO	X			X			X	X	X		X	X	X
TYPE				X									
UNINHIBIT		X	X		X	X							X
UNIQUEKEY		X											
UNLOCK				X									
UPDATE								X					
UPDATEPW	X	X	X	X	X	X	X	X	X		X	X	X
UPGRADE	X												
WRITECHECK		X	X		X	X				X	X		X

2. Properties that can occasionally be changed under specific restrictive conditions.

3. Properties that can never be changed.

Properties that can always be changed under any circumstances include object names, passwords, owner-ID, various security parameters, and free-space with a KSDS. Parameters that can be changed only under specific conditions include KEYS and RECORDSIZE. For example, both parameters can be changed only when the associated data set is empty. Parameter values such as control interval size, volumes actually in use, and space allocation, cannot be changed under any condition.

The first group contains a subcategory consisting of objects that can be modified even if the data set is not empty and will affect the physical structure of the data set. By examining Table 6.4, it is possible to identify those parameters that can be modified under some circumstances. Note that many physical and record-related properties are not contained in the table.

For purposes of this discussion, the parameters coded with ALTER are grouped into three general categories. An input parameter must be coded, existing parameters can be modified, and there are some parameters that can be nullified:

Input Parameter	Parameter to Modify Along with its new	Nullify Value

Input parameters

Only one entryname can be coded with each ALTER command. However, a generic name can be specified. Here, generic means that one level of qualification in the data set name can be replaced by an asterisk. If a data set name matches all the levels of qualification except for the asterisk, it is processed. The entryname is a positional parameter and should be coded immediately after ALTER and before any of the keyword parameters. When several objects are identified with the same generic name, some can be modified while others are ignored depending on the type of object.

Modifying parameter values

Some IDCAM parameters permit their value to be changed with ALTER. These include:

- Most of the security-related features (passwords, ATTEMPTS, AUTHORIZATION, CODE).
- Buffer information (BUFFERSPACE, BUFND, BUFNI).
- Expiration dates (TO, FOR).
- Record properties (KEYS, RECORDSIZE).

- Disk volumes (ADDVOLUME, REMOVEVOLUME).
- Names of objects (NEWNAME).
- Freespace.
- Share option parameters.

When renaming a cluster in a user catalog to a name that belongs in another catalog, it appears that the object is lost unless the CATALOG parameter is used.

Nullifying parameter values

There are nine parameters that can have their value/effect nullified rather than modified. This includes any of the four possible passwords, the owner, the retention period specified with TO or FOR, AUTHORIZATION, CODE, and EXCEPTIONEXIT values. As noted in the previous section, each of these parameters can also be assigned a new value. This is done in the standard way of coding a parameter (value).

Adding and removing volumes

Two parameters that can be coded with ALTER are used to modify the values coded with the VOLUME parameter. In particular, if additional volumes are required to hold a growing data set, the ADDVOLUMES parameter can be used to specify the additional volumes. At the other extreme, if volumes that were allocated have never been used or will no longer be needed, they can be released by specifying the REMOVEVOLUMES parameter. The code here shows two volumes initially identified, a third volume later added, and two volumes still later being removed:

```
DEFINE CLUSTER(NAME (ALPHA.BETA) VOLUMES(WORK01 WORK02)
. . .
ALTER ALPHA.BETA ADDVOLUMES (WORK03)
ALTER ALPHA.BETA REMOVEVOLUMES (WORK02 WORK03)
. . .
```

A complete list of parameters that can be modified with one or more type of IDCAMS object is shown in Table 6.4. Note the similarity between clusters and alternate indexes. Note that some important parameters can only be modified with the data or index component rather than the cluster component.

Coding examples

Example 1. Change the name of the KSDS ALPHA.X to BETA, remove its retention period, and change the freespace values. Because freespace can only be specified with the data component, it is necessary to code two ALTER commands in Fig. 6.5.

```
//A          EXEC PGM=IDCAMS
//SYSPRINT   DD   SYSOUT=A
//SYSIN      DD   *
   ALTER ALPHA.X                    -
         NEWNAME(BETA.Y)            -
         NULLIFY(RETENTION)
   ALTER ALPHA.X.DATA               -
         FREESPACE(50 25)
/*
```

Figure 6.5 Changing various properties of a KSDS.

Example 2. Change the names of several members in the cataloged partitioned data set library, SYS1.WHATEVER. Member ALPHA should become NEWALPHA, and BETA should be renamed NEWBETA:

```
ALTER SYS1.WHATEVER(ALPHA) NEWNAME(SYS1.WHATEVER(NEWALPHA))
ALTER SYS1.WHATEVER(BETA) NEWNAME(SYS1.WHATEVER(NEWBETA))
```

Example 3. This could be called the classical ALTER command example. Almost every VSAM book and IDCAM manual contains a variation of the coding shown in Fig. 6.6. A VSAM KSDS is initially created and must now be loaded. The nature of the records in the data set, along with projected future changes,

```
DEFINE  CLUSTER(NAME(NEW.KSDS)          -
        FREESPACE(25 33)                -
           . . .
     REPRO  IDS(INPUT.RECORDS)          -
            ODS(NEW.KSDS)               -
            COUNT(50000)
     ALTER  NEW.KSDS.DATA               -
            FREESPACE(10 10)
     REPRO  IDS(INPUT.RECORDS           -
            ODS(NEW.KSDS)               -
            SKIP(50000)                 -
            COUNT(30000) NOREUSE
     ALTER  NEW.KSDS.DATA               -
            FREESPACE(50 50)
     REPRO  IDS(NEW.KSDS)               -
            ODS(NEW.KSDS)               -
            SKIP(80000) NOREUSE
```

Figure 6.6 Altering FreeSpace values during an initial load operation.

suggests that different percentages of freespace be reserved within various portions of the data set.

The DEFINE CLUSTER FREESPACE values are appropriate for the initial 50,000 records loaded into the data set. Following these records, about 30,000 records are to be loaded where almost no subsequent changes seem likely to occur following the load. A tremendous amount of future activity including adds, deletes, and changes is anticipated in the last portion of the data set.

The second and third REPRO commands can be done more efficiently than shown here by initially dividing the input into three separate data sets. Here, the first 50,000 records are read three times, and the next 30,000 records are read twice. Note that, to alter the freespace values, the data component is specified.

Example 4.   The KSDS EXISTING.KSDS is currently protected with a master password. In Fig. 6.7, the value of the password is to be changed and a read-only password created. Furthermore, the number of default buffers for processing the data component is to be increased to 4. Two ALTER commands are required because of the nature of the changes. Furthermore, only a best approximation is possible with the four buffers. Assume that the CISZ for the data component is 2,048 and 1,024 for the index component.

Example 5.   A VSAM KSDS is being processed by a CICS application that continuously writes records to it. The disk storage on the only volume allocated to the data set has been used. Additional volume(s) should be specified for the data set. Because both the data and index components are different volumes, two ALTER commands are necessary:

```
ALTER LARGE.KSDA.DATA ADDVOLUME(DISK22)
ALTER LARGE.KSDA.INDEX ADDVOLUME(DISK28)
```

Example 6 (Generic Processing).   A large group of data sets are to have their names changed. All data sets whose first and third qualifiers are ALPHA and ZETA, including any middle qualifier, are to be changed so that the third qualifier is now NEWZETA. Only the data set ALPHA.BETA.ZETA is not to be changed:

```
ALTER ALPHA.*.ZETA NEWNAME(ALPHA.*.NEWZETA)
ALTER ALPHA.BETA.NEWZETA NEWNAME(ALPHA.BETA.ZETA)
```

```
ALTER  EXISTING.KSDS/'master password'  -
       MASTERPW(SECRET)                  -
       READPW(READONLY)
ALTER  EXISTING.KSDS.DATA                -
       BUFFERSPACE(10240)
```

Figure 6.7 Modifying passwords and bufferspace values.

The DELETE Command

The DELETE command is used to delete a variety of system entities, including every type of VSAM and non-VSAM data set, catalog, VSAM Volume Record in the VSAM Volume Data Set, generation data group, and partitioned data set member. Delete, scratch, and uncatalog are three closely related concepts that are occasionally confused.

Scratch means to physically delete a data set by freeing the storage used to hold the records in the data set and also removing the VTOC entry. A catalog entry is unaffected by the scratch. Uncatalog means to remove the catalog entry for an object. However, the object continues to exist and occupy space on the disk volume.

Delete can be used to mean scratch, uncatalog, or both together. For example, with VSAM data sets, the DELETE command scratches the data set and removes its catalog entry. Coding DISP = (OLD,DELETE) on a DD statement can have different effects depending on the other values coded on the statement.

The DELETE command uses a combination of various syntax properties, many of which are also available with LISTCAT or ALTER. Parameters that can be coded with DELETE can be grouped into three basic categories. The input parameter is required and must identify one or more objects. Like LISTCAT, it is possible to qualify the complete group of objects identified with the input parameter by specifying the types of objects to process.

Finally, there are several optional Parameters, each of which are used in a specific situation. Table 6.5 identifies and categorizes all the parameters available with DELETE except for CATALOG, which, as usual, identifies the catalog to initially search for entries.

Input parameters

Any number of entries can be processed with each DELETE command. The entries to be deleted should be listed immediately after DELETE and before

TABLE 6.5   DELETE Parameters and Processing Categories.

Input Parameter	Type of Object	Additional Property
Required	*All Optional*	*All Optional*
single entry	ALIAS	ERASE or NOERASE
multiple entries	ALTERNATEINDEX	FORCE or NOFORCE
simple or generic	CLUSTER	PURGE or NOPURGE
with each	GENERATIONDATAGROUP	RECOVERY or NORECOVERY
entry	NONVSAM	SCRATCH or NOSCRATCH
	PAGESPACE	FILE(DDname)
	PATH	
	SPACE	
	TRUENAME	
	USERCATALOG	
	VVR	

any of the keyword parameters. If multiple objects are to be listed, the complete group of names must be enclosed in parentheses. With one object, no parentheses are necessary. With every object in the input parameter list, generic processing can be specified.

Qualifying delete objects

Qualifying the type of objects to delete is done through using any one of the following parameters, which are comparable to their function with LISTCAT:

- ALIAS
- ALTERNATEINDEX (AIX)
- CLUSTER (CL)
- GENERATIONDATAGROUP (GDG)
- NONVSAM (NVSAM)
- PAGESPACE (PGSPC)
- PATH
- SPACE
- TRUENAME (TNAME)
- USERCATALOG (UCAT)
- VVR

Of all the entries identified by the input parameters, only those that are in this group are actually deleted. In theory, all 11 of these parameters could be coded together. However, this is equivalent to coding none of them. Four are actually required to delete the types of objects they identify. These are: USERCATALOG, SPACE, TRUENAME, and VVR. If one of these parameters is not coded, the corresponding entry is not deleted. At this point, only the USERCATALOG has been discussed in some detail, and it is further examined in chapter 12, where SPACE, TRUENAME, and VVR are also discussed.

When a user catalog is identified for deletion, its (catalog connection) entry, along with all of its aliases in the master catalog, are deleted. Merely coding DELETE with USERCATALOG will delete the catalog if it is empty. If it contains entries, then FORCE must also be coded. Application programmers do not routinely create or delete user catalogs.

When a VVR entry is identified for deletion, the VVR entry on the VSAM volume is deleted. The VVR is discussed in more detail in chapter 12, along with ICF catalogs.

TRUENAME is most commonly coded when it is necessary to delete just one component of a VSAM data set (a data or index component) or an alternate index where the base cluster cannot be processed. Hence, TRUENAME is used with the objects where processing problems have caused an important, related object to be deleted.

When a SPACE entry is identified for deletion, all empty VSAM data spaces on volume are deleted. To delete empty VSAM data spaces on a volume, code DELETE SPACE FILE(DD1). If the data space is not empty, then FORCE must also be coded.

Special processing properties

There are five, special-purpose parameters used with the DELETE command, of which two of the four are related to security and data set protection:

- ERASE or NOERASE (ERAS) (NERAS)
- FORCE or NOFORCE (FRC) (NFRC)
- PURGE or NOPURGE (PRG) (NPRG)
- RECOVERY or NORECOVERY (RCVRY) (NRCVRY)
- CRATCH or NOSCRATCH (SCR) (NSCR)

ERASE or NOERASE (ERAS) (NERAS).   The ERASE parameter 25 used to overwrite the data component of a deleted data set with binary zeroes. NOERASE is the default. A DELETE command results in a scratched data set, but the data in the logical records remains intact on the disk volume. Another job could request space on the same volume and then immediately dump out the contents of the space. ERASE prevents security breaches such as this. ERASE can be time-consuming when a large data set is deleted.

FORCE or NOFORCE (FRC) (NFRC).   The FORCE parameter is meaningful when deleting three types of objects: a user catalog, a data space, and a generation data group. Among the 11 types of objects that can be deleted, only these three can contain sub-objects within them. If an attempt is made to delete any of these three objects when they are not empty, the delete command will fail unless FORCE is coded. NOFORCE is the default and causes the delete to scratch the identified object only if it is empty.

PURGE or NOPURGE (PRG) (NPRG).   If an attempt is made to delete a data set whose retention date or expiration date has not yet occurred, the delete will fail. The TO or FOR parameter assigns an expiration date to the data set that has not yet occurred. Coding PURGE will cause the expiration date to be overridden and the data set deleted. If there is no retention period or expiration date, PURGE is meaningless and ignored.

RECOVERY or NORECOVERY (RCVRY) (NRCVRY).   RECOVERY is coded when a user catalog is deleted and replaced with an imported backup copy. RECOVERY results in the user catalog, the VVR, and the VTOC entry all being deleted.

```
//A          EXEC PGM=IDCAMS
//SYSPRINT DD   SYSOUT=A
//SYSIN    DD   *
   DELETE MASTER.ALPHA   -
          PURGE
/*
```

Figure 6.8 Deleting all components of a KSDS.

SCRATCH or NOSCRATCH (SCR) (NSCR).   SCRATCH allows a data set to be deleted without using or affecting its catalog entry. This is commonly used with a non-VSAM data set, which is not cataloged. In this case, the location of the data set must be identified, and the FILE parameter can be used for this purpose.

Limitations

DELETE provides practically every feature available with JCL or other utility programs, such as IEHPROGM or deletion via the DD statement. A comparison of IDCAMS and JCL after the interrelationship between VSAM and JCL is discussed is shown in Table 13.3.

Coding examples

Example 1.   Delete the KSDS MASTER.ALPHA, which has an unexpired expiration date. Because no qualification is specified, data, index, and cluster are all deleted. Three corresponding messages are printed in the IDCAMS SYSPRINT message data set. If CLUSTER was also coded, the delete would fail. The relevant code is shown in Fig. 6.8.

Example 2.   Delete the three VSAM data sets FIRST.X, SECOND.Y, and THIRD.Z. All three are cataloged in ALPHA.USER.CATALOG. The disk storage occupied by FIRST.X should be overwritten with binary zeroes. Because of the overwriting, two separate DELETE commands are used in Fig. 6.9. Other approaches to accomplish the same results are also possible. If the CATALOG parameter is

```
DELETE FIRST.X                -
       ERASE                  -
       CATALOG(ALPHA.USER.CATALOG)

DELETE (SECOND.Y.THIRD.Z)     -
```

Figure 6.9 Erasing and deleting data sets.

not coded, the standard order of catalog search described in chapter 3 would be used.

Example 3. Delete every data set that begins with a first-level qualifier of ALPHA and has a third-level qualifier of ANYTHING. All of the data sets to be deleted are cataloged in ALPHA.USER.CATALOG. Some of the data sets might have unexpired expiration dates. As discussed in chapter 14, this approach can be used to delete generation data groups and all of their generation data sets:

```
DELETE ALPHA.*.ANYTHING –
       PURGE           –
       CATALOG (ALPHA.USER.CATALOG)
```

Example 4. Delete two partitioned data set members, ALPHA and BETA, from the cataloged library SYS1.PDS. Note that separate delete commands are required for each member. Coding DELETE SYS1.PDS deletes the entire library. Coding DELETE SYS1.PDS(ALPHA,BETA) generates a syntax error. Both JCL and IDCAMS syntax allow only one member name to be coded as a qualifier to the library name:

```
DELETE SYS1.PDS(ALPHA)
DELETE SYS1.PDS(BETA)
```

Example 5. Delete every member of the Generation Data Group ALPHA .BETA, including the individual data sets and the Generation Group Base TABLE itself. Also, delete the model Data Set Control Block. Note that order is crucial with the first two DELETE commands. The issue is further explored in chapter 14. The first command deletes all of the Generation Data Sets. It uses the Generation Group Base Table, which is subsequently deleted in the second DELETE command. The model DSCB is an uncataloged data set, and for this reason, a DD statement is needed to scratch it. The three required DELETE commands are shown in Fig. 6.10.

The VERIFY Command

The VERIFY command is used to perform a single function. It is coded to correct or reset the catalog entry (entries for a KSDS) for a VSAM data set that was not

```
     DELETE  ALPHA.BETA.*
     DELETE  ALPHA.BETA
     DELETE  ALPHA.BETA    FILE(DD1)

//DD1   DD   UNIT=3390,VOL=SER=DISK95,DISP=OLD
```

Figure 6.10   Deleting a GDG base table, data sets, and DSCB.

TABLE 6.6   VERIFY Parameters and Processing Categories.

Input Parameter	Output Parameter
Required	*Cannot be coded*
DATASET(datasetname) FILE(DDname)	Implicitly the same data set as input

closed properly. This can occur as a result of the processing program itself or as a side effect of some other processing on the system. Whatever the cause, the cluster component information (in a catalog) disagrees with the actual physical status of the data set. VERIFY removes the discrepancy. The parameters available with VERIFY are identified and classified in Table 6.6.

Overlapping commands

The ALTER command can also be used to reset catalog values. However, with ALTER, the programmer must supply the new values. ALTER explicitly provides the new values while VERIFY supplies them implicitly.

Input and output parameters

A VERIFY command processes exactly one VSAM data set. No generic processing or non-VSAM data sets can be used as input. Either static allocation can be specified with the FILE parameter or the data set can be dynamically allocated with the DATASET parameter. Because VERIFY performs an output operation that changes the structure of the data set, it might be appropriate to lock other users out of the data set until processing is completed.

The data set, specified with DATASET or FILE, is both the input and output data set. No changes occur in the data or index component. No other data sets are involved in VERIFY processing, except for the catalog that contains an entry for locating the data set.

Coding Examples

Example 1. A VSAM KSDS must be verified because it was improperly closed because of some unrelated nebulous system problems. The KSDS is currently allocated to a production CICS system. Notice in Fig. 6.11 that the DATASET parameter cannot be used because the KSDS is always allocated to CICS.

Example 2. VERIFY and LISTCAT can be used together to determine if any previous additions to the data set have been lost because the KSDS was not

```
//A          EXEC PGM=IDCAMS
//SYSPRINT   DD   SYSOUT=A
//SYSIN      DD   *
  VERIFY FILE(TEST)
/*
//TEST   DD   DSN=TEST.KSDS,DISP=SHR
```

Figure 6.11 A KSDS is verified.

properly closed the last time it was processed. ALL should be coded with LISTCAT:

```
LISTCAT ENT(MASTER.KSDS) ALL
VERIFY DATASET(MASTER.KSDS)
LISTCAT ENT(MASTER.KSDS) ALL
```

Exercises

1. For the Big Eight IDCAMS commands, which commands can be used to process generic data set names? What are the limitations associated with each command? Which commands allow generic key values to be specified? Identify whether the generic keys are used with input or output data sets or both. Which commands allow a choice between static and dynamic allocation with the input data set? Which commands allow a choice between static and dynamic allocation with the output data set? With which commands is there a default output parameter value? With which commands is there a default?

2. Describe the interrelationship among the three commands in the situation described in Example 3 with LISTCAT.

3. Compare the possible operations that can be performed with the IEHPROGM utility with their comparable IDCAMS commands and corresponding JCL processing.

IDCAMS exercises for VSAM data sets

The comprehensive IDCAMS exercises in this section are used to develop or confirm a moderate level of expertise with the IDCAMS utility. There are four such comprehensive exercises included in this book: KSDS, ESDS, RRDS, and a non-VSAM data set respectively. All four comprehensive exercises use the DEFINE CLUSTER and the "Big 8" IDCAMS processing commands in a wide variety of settings. In fact, most commands are used more than once.

The comprehensive exercises for an ESDS and RRDS are found in chapters 10 and 11 respectively. Both are similar to the comprehensive KSDS exercises, but necessarily simpler. The exercises for the KSDS and non-VSAM data sets follow.

Reading about VSAM and IDCAMS imparts a superficial level of knowledge. The IDCAMS commands sound straightforward to use and understand, but to use them successfully, you must actually use them. I strongly encourage you to write the IDCAMS code and JCL even if you don't actually run them.

a. Create a KSDS and load it with card image (80 byte) records, where the record key is the final 5 bytes in each record and contains numeric character data. Load exactly 100 records into the KSDS. Define the KSDS in such a way that, after the load operation, the records occupy exactly three control areas and the first two of the control areas contain multiple control intervals with logical records.

In order to accomplish this, it is necessary to very carefully select the following DEFINE CLUSTER parameters: FREESPACE, RECORDSIZE, CI size, Space Allocation, and (type of disk) VOLUME. The KSDS should be created with a retention period and a master password. As will be seen later, the choice of the individual record key values is also significant.

b. Use the PRINT command to confirm that the output data set meets the control interval and control area specifications. Now, use the LISTCAT command to independently confirm the same information. There are several ways this can be done with both the PRINT and LISTCAT commands. In fact, with either command, the data or index component alone will suffice to confirm the status of the data set. Chapter 7 describes using the LISTCAT report to interpret the structure of an existing data set.

c. Change the name of the KSDS to NEW.KSDS.NAME; extend its retention period by 30 days; and allocate 5 buffers to just the data component. Confirm that these changes have been made correctly.

d. Export the KSDS to cartridge, storing it as a cataloged data set with a different name. Do not delete the original data set. Allow all processing with it to be permitted following the export operation.

e. Print out the complete, exported copy of the data set and analyze the information it contains.

f. REPRO additional records into the original KSDS while generating both a control interval and control area split. Try to use a minimum of records to accomplish the splits. This necessitates choosing the record key values very carefully both here and when the KSDS was initially loaded in a. Use LISTCAT to confirm that the splits occurred.

g. IMPORT the exported data set back to the original system. Give it a completely new name, and partition it onto 5 volumes, depending on whether the first byte in the key is 0-1, 2-3, 4-5, 6-7, or 8-9.

h. Verify the original KSDS and also the imported copy. Use both static and dynamic allocation. Finally, delete all of the objects. Of the original data set involved in this project. Use a generic delete to get rid of as many objects as possible with a single command. This might require reconsidering the names selected for all the objects.

IDCAMS exercises for non-VSAM data sets

Two existing data sets are used extensively throughout these exercises: TEMP.PROCLIB and TEMP.MACLIB, both card image libraries that contain multiple members. The members in TEMP.PROCLIB are named C, CL, and CG. Not every request will be possible with non-VSAM data sets.

a. Create a new card image library and copy the members from TEMP.PROCLIB into it using the same member names.

b. Rename the three members to FMLC, FMLCL, and FMLCG respectively. Rename the library itself to NEW.PROCLIB.FML. Put an expiration date and a password on the library.

c. Print out the directory of the new pds library. Print out the complete catalog entry for the library. Print out the data set (format-1 dscb) labels for the library.

d. Use concatenation to print out the three members in the library. Do not print out more than 25 total records. The records should be printed in the message data set.

e. Delete member C from TEMP.PROCLIB and CL from NEW.PROCLIB.FML. Use concatenation to print out the directories of all three libraries involved in processing.

f. Extend member CG by concatenating member C to it. Print two copies of the results. Delete every remaining object.

7

Understanding LISTCAT Reports

A VSAM KSDS was created for this chapter, and the complete DEFINE CLUS-TER command is shown in Fig. 7.1. Examine all of the parameters carefully because they are used throughout the rest of this chapter. In particular, note that a CI size of 4096 is specified for the data component, and FREESPACE values of 25 and 50 percent are coded.

After the VSAM KSDS was created, the REPRO command was used to load 12 records into the data component. Each record was 1,000 bytes in length. Hence, three logical records were loaded into a data control interval. The cluster, record, and key values were selected in order to ensure that significant results could be illustrated with a relatively small number of logical records.

Three additional points should be carefully noted. TRACK(1 1) was specified to request disk storage for the data component. RECORD(1 1) requests 1 track for the primary and secondary allocation for the index component because space is rounded up to the next track value. All three of the data set components are on a 3380 disk volume. The cluster is on ISU013, and the data and index components are on ACD000 and WORK01 respectively. The LISTCAT report shown in Fig. 5.2 was created by coding:

LISTCAT ENT(cluster name) ALL

By specifying ALL, the maximum amount of information is printed. The hierarchy among the three KSDS components determines the amount of indentation in the listing. The cluster is the primary entry and is described first. Its two major components are the data and index, which are described in that order. Four general categories of information are included at the beginning of the information for the cluster, data, and index components:

```
DEFINE  CLUSTER(NAME(cluster component name) -
           INDEXED                                -
           KEYS(3 0)                              -
           FREESPACE(25 50)                       -
           OWNER('LARRY B')                       -
           TO(92366)                              -
           MASTERPW(AARDVARK)                     -
           READPW(GENER)                          -
           BUFFERSPACE(10000)                     -
           SHAREOPTIONS(2 3))                     -
        DATA(NAME(data component name)            -
           CONTROLINTERVALSIZE(4096)              -
           RECORDSIZE(500 2000)                   -
           VOLUME(ACD000)                         -
           TRACK(1 1))                            -
        INDEX(NAME(index component name)          -
           CONTROLINTERVALSIZE(512)               -
           VOLUME(WORK01)                         -
           RECORD(1 1))
```

Figure 7.1   The DEFINE CLUSTER code to create a KSDS.

- In-cat
- History
- Protection
- Associations

Four additional information categories are included just with the data and index components:

- Attributes
- Statistics
- Allocation
- Volume information

The four general component categories

In-cat is one of the four general categories of information that is included at the beginning of the information for the cluster, data, and index components. In-cat identifies the VSAM catalog that contains the entry for the object being described. For all three components, the user catalog SYS1.ACSCTLG1 contains the entry for the object identified on the previous line. The In-cat entry does not specify whether SYS1.ACSCTLG1 is the system master catalog or a user catalog. In this case, it is a user catalog.

The History component identifies four values, and the value coded with each of the OWNER parameters is displayed. Here, OWNER was coded only with the cluster component, and the value LARRY B was specified. The same or different OWNER values can be coded with either of the other components. Release 2 of VSAM is used to process this IDCAMS job step. The creation and expiration date are printed in YY.DDD format. The expiration date is supplied by the TO parameter. From examining the printed value, it is clear that any TO value can be specified. The system supplies the creation date. The expiration date can also be coded with the FOR parameter.

Protection identifies the two types of data set security that is available. Any one of four levels of VSAM passwords can be specified with any of the components, but no passwords are used here. Even if passwords are coded with the DEFINE CLUSTER command, their values would not print in the LISTCAT report. The Resource Access Control Facility, an IBM security product (RACF), can also be used to protect a VSAM data set from illegal access, as is the case here. As a result of the RACF, passwords are ignored.

The Associations entry identifies and classifies related cataloged objects. The cluster is associated with both the data and index components, and the data and index component are also associated with the cluster. Note, however, that the data and index component are not directly associated with each other; either can be processed as an independent entity. For example, when just the data (and cluster) component is processed, the information in the index component is not available. In this case, data records are retrieved in physical rather than logical order. When this is the case, each record is identified by its RBA value rather than its primary key value.

ATTRIBUTES information

Almost all the attribute entries directly identify parameters or values coded in the DEFINE CLUSTER command or their default values. In fact, only one attribute value does not fall into this category, that is the number of CIs/CA.

KEYLEN and RKP identify the two values coded with KEYS in the DEFINE CLUSTER command. Notice that the two values are meaningful only with the data component even though they are printed with the index component. This type of "consistency" results in confusing and redundant information appearing throughout LISTCAT reports for a KSDS. Most LISTCAT users feel that a printed LISTCAT report suffers from several poor design problems, including inflexibility.

The two values AVGLRECL and MAXLRECL in the data component are coded with the RECORDSIZE parameter. The two values printed with the index component are always 0 and CISZ(index) − 7 respectively, here 505. In reality, for the index component: $RECSZ = average - lrecl = maximum - lrecl = CISZ - 7$. Recall that each index control interval contains 1 logical record, which completely fills the control interval except for the final 7 bytes of control information.

```
                    LISTCAT ENT(dsname)    OUTFILE(DD1)

//DD1   DD   DSN=&&LISTCAT,DISP=(MOD,PASS),
//           UNIT=SYSDA,SPACE=(TRK,(1,1)),
//           DCB=(LRECL=125,RECFM=VB,BLKSIZE=1024)
```

Figure 7.2 User-generated LISTCAT report.

The BUFSPACE value in the LISTCAT output is taken directly from the DEFINE CLUSTER code. If BUFFERSPACE is not coded, the value defaults to sufficient space for two data and one index control intervals. The total amount of buffer space is printed with the data component. The index entry always contains a 0 value. Thus, no matter how the buffers are actually used, the total amount is listed with the data component.

EXCPEXIT identifies user-written exit routines. In the listing in Fig. 7.2, no such routines are available. EXCPEXITs are ordinarily written in assembler to handle exceptional processing situations. With considerable care, they can be written in COBOL.

The CISIZE values are taken directly from the DEFINE CLUSTER code: 4,096 for the data component and 512 for the index component. If either value is omitted, a default value is supplied.

The CI/CA value is determined by several factors. Recall that all the KSDA components reside on 3380 disks. Note that $128*32 = 4,096$ and 15, 32-byte blocks comprise the COUNT field. The data component is considered first because the CISIZE is the block size and all VSAM data sets are represented on disk in COUNT – DATA format, $129 + 15 = 144$ is divided into 1,499. This gives a quotient of 1. Hence, 10 blocks fit on 1 track.

The DEFINE CLUSTER code specifies that a control area occupies 1 track. Hence, a control area consists of 10 data control intervals. For the index component, 32 is divided into 1,499 because $17 + 15 = 32$. This gives a quotient of 46. Hence, 46 index control intervals fit on 1 track. Because a control area is only defined in the data component, the index entry should more appropriately read: # of CIs/track = 46.

Eleven additional attributes are listed with the data component. These are meant to be read left to right, one line at a time. Nine of the same attributes are included with the index component. INDEXED and NONSPANNED, printed only with the data component, identify the data set organization (KSDS) and record format (variable length) respectively. With the index component, INDEX is redundant, and NONSPANNED is meaningless. The SHAREOPTIONS values are taken directly from the DEFINE CLUSTER code. The remaining eight entries reflect whether a specific keyword parameter was included with the DEFINE CLUSTER code. The parameters NOERASE, NOWRITECHK, NOIMBED, NOREPLICATE, UNORDERED, and NOREUSE imply that their respective counterparts, ERASE, WRITECHK, IMBED, REPLICATE, ORDERED, and REUSE were not coded. RECOVERY and UNIQUE were also not coded, but are the default values with the DEFINE CLUSTER command.

In particular, with an ICF catalog structure, SUBALLOCATION is not permitted, and a UNIQUE cluster is always created.

STATISTICS information

The Statistics section prints the running totals for 13 important categories. All 13 values are maintained for both the data and index components. Four additional entries are kept only for the index component. The four index entries are meaningless with the data component and, fortunately, are not printed with the data component.

Record counts are maintained for the four types of logical record processing that takes place with the data set. This consists of the four standard update operations with a data set: read or retrieve, write or add, delete, and update. VSAM uses some unusual criteria in deciding whether an operation is an update or an insert (add).

The fifth record total reflects the number of records presently in the data set. The listing shown in Fig. 7.2 specifies that there are 12 logical records in the data component and 1 sequence set record in the index component following the initial REPRO.

The next two entries contain the number of control interval and control area splits respectively that have occurred since the data set was created. Here, both values are 0 because no splits can occur during an initial REPRO operation. The notion of control interval and control area splits holds only for the data component even though both entries are also printed with the index component.

The two FREESPACE values are printed next. In the data component, these are the two values specified with the DEFINE CLUSTER command. Under certain circumstances, the ALTER command can be used to change the DEFINE CLUSTER values. FREESPACE is a meaningless notion with the index component, so 0 is coded for both values.

The FREESPC – BYTES entry requires some explanation. It does not specify the total number of unused bytes in the particular component. Rather, it is the number of bytes contained in all of the control intervals, which are completely empty. Because FSPC(25 50) was specified and 12, 1,000-byte records were loaded into the data component, three logical records are placed in each of the first six data control intervals in each control area. The remaining six data control intervals in the control area are empty. Hence, $4,096*6 = 24,576$.

In the index component, 46 control intervals occupy 1 track. Only one control interval is used after the data component is loaded because there is just one control area in the data component. Thus, the other 45 are empty. Note that $45*512 = 23,040$.

Example 1. To further illustrate how FREESPC – BYTES is calculated, suppose 16 records are loaded into the KSDS; five control intervals in CA0; and 1 control interval in CA1 will contain records. Here, $(5+9) = 14*4,096 = $ FREESPC –

BYTES(Data). Furthermore, three control intervals are required in the index component. Hence, FREESPC – BYTES(Index) = 43*512.

EXCPS identifies the number of actual I/O operations involving a control interval in the component. Here, five I/O operations were performed with the data component. Recall that four control intervals contain records. The fifth operation created an End of File Marker. Three I/O operations were performed with the 1 record in the index component. Also recall that two data control intervals can be held concurrently in buffers. Thus, the index entry does not need to be rewritten each time a data control interval is modified.

An extent is a contiguous area of space on the disk volume. Both the data and index occupy 1 track. Hence, each is contained within a single extent. Space is always rounded up to include an integral number of tracks. Thus, a request for one index record allocates a complete track.

Finally, the system-timestamp contains the date and time in which the component was last processed.

The four additional index entries are now described. The index level is 1 because there is only a single sequence set record. Usually, the index level is the height of the tree structure that contains the index. The number of entries per section is defined approximately as:

ENTRIES/SECT = SQRT(#CIs/CA)

In this example, SQRT(10) = 3. Recall that sections are used to quickly locate the specific index entry during random retrieval. The sequence set RBA begins with 0, and there is no high-level index. Hence, its value is also 0.

ALLOCATION information

There are three ways that space can be requested: cylinders, tracks, and records. Disk space is actually allocated in either cylinders or tracks. In Fig. 7.2, the space for the data component was coded as TRK(1 1). This gives a primary allocation and secondary allocation both of one track. Furthermore, because minimum {1,1} = 1, 1 control area = 1 track. The same primary and secondary values are used for the index component.

The HI-ALLOC-RBA is computed using the formula:

HI-ALLOC-RBA = CISZ*(#CIs/CA)*#CAs

The actual numeric values in the LISTCAT printout are then derived as follows:

HI-ALLOC-RBA(Data) = 4096*10*1 = 40,960 HI-ALLOC-RBA(Index) = 512*46*1 = 23,552

Whenever part of a control interval contains records, the entire control area is considered used. In the index, only the sequence set record is considered used.

Recall that the role of the REUSE parameter is to reset the HI-ALLOC-RBA value to 0.

Example 2. Suppose, as in Example 1, that 16 records are loaded into the KSDS:

HI-ALLOC-RBA(Data) = 0 4096*10*2 = 81,920

Because there are 16,000 bytes of logical records in the data set, approximately 80 percent of the data component is not being used:

HI-ALLOC-RBA(Index) = 512*46*1 = 23,552

VOLUME information

The LISTCAT report contains a section for each volume, which contains part of the component. Volume information for a component falls into two categories. For both the data and index components, overall information is printed indentifying the part of the component residing on the specific volume. This is followed by one or more entries that describe each extent on the volume. These two categories, overall information and extents, are printed for every volume in the exact order in which they are used, which also contains part of the component.

Because there is one extent on one volume in the report in Fig. 7.2, some of the VOLUME information duplicates values printed with ALLOCATION. This will not be the case with a data set that requires secondary allocations or occupies multiple volumes.

VOLSER identifies a specific disk volume. DEVTYPE identifies a particular type of disk. The specified value represents a 3380 disk. VOLFLAG identifies this as PRIME. The physical record size is the same as the control interval size. This is always true whenever the CISZ is 512 or a multiple of 1,024. Control intervals of other sizes frequently decompose into several, disjointed physical records. For example, a CI size of 1,536 bytes might be stored in three, 512-byte physical records.

The number of physical records that will fit on 1 track is explained with the CI/CA = 10 discussion in the preceding ATTRIBUTES section. This is also contingent on one control interval occupying exactly one physical record. The number of tracks in a control area is also described with the primary and secondary allocations in the ALLOCATION section.

HI-ALLOC-RBA and HI-USED-RBA maintain the same values as under ALLOCATION. As previously mentioned, this is not true in general. Likewise, the EXTENT-NUMBER value is the same as that printed under ALLOCATION. EXTENT-TYPE contains a code. The values X'40' and X'20' are used with the data and index component respectively.

Extent information consists of five values. The LOW-CCHH and HIGH-CCHH values specify the location of the extent on the disk volume. Because both of the extents in Fig. 7.2 occupy a single track, LOW-CCHH = HIGH-CCHH. The specific location is cylinder X'16' and head (or track) X'02'. The low and high RBA values specify byte addresses relative to the beginning of the cluster. Finally, the extent occupies 1 track in each case.

Modifying the standard LISTCAT report

Many people feel that a standard LISTCAT report suffers from several significant design problems. In particular, redundant, irrelevant, and confusing information is coded with the data and index components. Consequently, the overall format of the report makes it difficult to find information that is actually important. Much of the information printed is of no interest to the typical applications programmer. Furthermore, two pages are required and the summary is almost never needed except with a LISTCAT of a catalog or a generic LISTCAT.

A fundamental rule in on-line programming calls for displaying the most important information near the top of a terminal screen; the less important information further down the screen; and the unimportant information nowhere. The LISTCAT report completely violates this rule.

It is straightforward to write a short program that can be used to produce an edited LISTCAT report containing just the desired information in the cluster. To produce a LISTCAT report with the modified format, the IDCAMS control statement and accompanying DD statements should be coded as shown in Fig. 7.2.

The records in the &&LISTCAT data set are passed to an application program that processes them as input. Each LISTCAT command produces a one-page report that highlights the most important information and does not contain the irrelevant or redundant fields and no summary statements are produced.

The application program reads the lines in the original LISTCAT report into a table and then selects and reformats any desired information on a set of parameters passed to the program.

8

Alternate Indexes and Secondary Key Processing

This chapter consists of four major topics. The basic concept of using a secondary key to process the records in a data set is initially discussed, and most of this material is applicable to both VSAM and non-VSAM data set organizations, in fact, to any data set organization that allows random record access. Several general examples with indexed and relative data sets are used to illustrate the concepts.

The second part of the chapter describes the actual physical and logical data set structure used by VSAM to support alternate key processing. Following this, the three IDCAMS commands—DEFINE ALTERNATEINDEX, BLDINDEX, and DEFINE PATH—required to allow VSAM alternate key processing are examined. The functions, parameters, and accompanying JCL for each command are discussed.

Finally, several peripheral topics involving alternate keys are described and discussed. A very lengthy example that traces processing a KSDS in a COBOL application program through both primary and alternate keys is discussed at the end of the next chapter.

Secondary Key Processing Concepts

It is often desirable to either randomly and/or sequentially process a (nonsequential) data set using a field other than the key field, slot number, or disk address provided by the access method with the data set organization. Throughout chapters 8 and 9, a data set consisting of employee records is used to illustrate these concepts. Each record contains a Social Security number, a complete name (Last, First, M.), department number, and additional key and

TABLE 8.1 Employee Data Set Records Fields.

Relevant Key Fields	Type of Key	Uniqueness
Social Security number	Primary key	Unique values
Complete name	Alternate key	Nonunique values
Department number	Alternate key	Unique values

non-key fields. The records are stored as an indexed data set (KSDS or ISAM), and Social Security number is the key. The relevant information about this group of records is summarized in Table 8.1.

There are times when it would be more convenient to process the employee records using name and other times when the records should be processed in ascending order by department number. For example, when the data set is randomly processed with an on-line application, most records will be identified by the name field value because the terminal operator requesting the inquiry will not know the corresponding Social Security number.

On the other hand, most batch application programs will use Social Security number as the key. There are some batch and on-line applications that will use department number to identify records. To satisfy such a wide variety of processing needs, VSAM allows multiple fields to be used as key fields for both random and sequential processing. Comparable alternate key processing is possible with non-VSAM data sets. However, it requires substantially more work by the programmer. In addition, the final results are probably not achieved as efficiently as with VSAM.

When the employee data set described previously is created, the field designated as the key is called the *prime* or *primary* key. These terms are used to distinguish it from other key fields, called *alternate* or *secondary* key fields, which can also be used to process the records. In the case of the employee data set, the Social Security number is the prime key field and both the name and department number are alternate key fields. In a VSAM environment, the underlying collection of records is called *the base data set* or *the base cluster*.

Using VSAM's alternate keys provides increased processing flexibility and convenience. Unfortunately, they require a substantial amount of overhead. This is because, in addition to the original base cluster, a separate data set must be constructed and maintained for each alternate key. Generally though, the overhead is minimal when compared with keeping several copies of the same base data set, each with a different key field.

Maintaining duplicate copies of the same group of records is a tremendous waste of disk space. Furthermore, serious data integrity problems can occur if two of the data sets ever get out of synchronization. When physically separate data sets containing the same records are processed, it becomes extremely difficult to guarantee that all copies are identical. Furthermore, when two of the data sets contain different data, how can it be determined which is correct? User confidence in a computer system is severely shaken when the same field value in a record, such as a phone number or an address, is different in two copies of the "same" record in each group.

In the past, it was quite common in many universities for various administrative areas to maintain "their" own personal copy of the student records data set. Their reasons for doing this were twofold: (1) so that other areas would not have access to "their" (confidential) information and (2) other areas would make mistakes and cause problems with their data.

Hence, Registration, Student Housing, and Financial Aid, etc., each had a complete set of student records. Consequently, many college students had portions of their university mail sent to two, three, or more different addresses at the same time because there were two or more inconsistent copies of the student records.

It is virtually impossible to keep physically disjointed copies of the same data synchronized, and alternate keys are an excellent way to maintain multiple access to copies of the same records. Alternate keys are sometimes overused and employed in inappropriate situations, however. For example, suppose that a periodic report requires that the records in a data set be processed in a specific, non-prime key field order. If only one application requires this order, the records should be sorted prior to generating the report rather than maintaining them with an alternate key that will use them only once for the report.

Alternate indexes are expensive in terms of processing time and disk storage. Therefore, before you consider using alternate keys, the additional overhead they require should be carefully weighed against the conveniences. Only when the advantages outweigh the disadvantages should alternate keys be used.

Before the development of VSAM, nonsequential data sets were processed using multiple alternate keys. Alternate key processing could be performed using ISAM and BDAM as base data sets, but with the advent of VSAM, the process of constructing and maintaining an alternate key data set was greatly simplified. VSAM's alternate key processing services are difficult for the average programmer to easily duplicate although, in rare cases, a programmer might prefer to construct his own alternate key data set.

The "Using RBA values for random record retrieval" section in chapter 10 discusses such applications with an ESDS. However, a user-created alternate index structure should be built only when its construction provides a clear advantage. Determining the advantages of a user-built structure requires a detailed knowledge of how VSAM constructs and maintains alternate indexes.

Potential alternate key fields

Specific restrictions must be satisfied in order to use VSAM to create and process records in a KSDS or ESDS with an alternate key. Any collection from 1 to 255 contiguous bytes within a record can be used as an alternate key. Alternate keys can overlap one another or overlap the primary key. An alternate key can also be embedded entirely within another key, either alternate or primary. An alternate key cannot, however, completely overlap the primary key. VSAM will support a maximum of 255 alternate keys for a single data set. A VSAM alternate key field must be contained entirely within the first control interval of a spanned record. In theory, the bytes that comprise the alternate key field do not have to be contiguous or even be byte values for that matter. These two features are not presently available with VSAM.

Processing a data set with alternate keys

Records in a KSDS can be retrieved either randomly or sequentially using an alternate key in the same manner as when the primary key is used. In a COBOL program, the syntax of the statement requesting the record retrieval must somehow specify which key is to be used and whether the processing is to be sequential or random. Generic processing can also be performed with both primary and alternate keys. However, output operations (writing, rewriting, and deleting records) must actually be performed by VSAM using the primary key as the key of reference.

When a record is rewritten, the alternate key values can be changed. Primary key values in a KSDS can never be modified during a rewrite operation. Such a change requires the existing record to be deleted and a new record added. Likewise, the relative byte address of a record in an ESDS can never be changed.

Each record in the base data set must have a field that can provide a value that is used to identify a single record, even though this same alternate key value can occur in any number of records in the data set. Because of this, alternate key processing consists of two general categories: each record contains a unique alternate key value or duplicate alternate key values are allowed.

Usually, processing is considerably simplified if every alternate key value is unique. In the employee data set discussed previously, there might be several employees named John Q. Smith. By using the name field as an alternate key, the John Q. Smith records can be retrieved one at a time until all of them have been processed. If the department number is an alternate key and 100 people work in department 789, then 100 sequential read operations will supply the records to the application program. Furthermore, as each of the first 99 records are read, VSAM will indicate that additional records with the same alternate key remain to be processed. Then, when the final department 789 record is read, VSAM will indicate that there are no remaining records containing the same alternate key value as the record just read.

The syntax and logic in a COBOL program usually require that the first record be randomly located and the rest accessed sequentially. However, because of the way alternate indexes are constructed and processed, the retrieval of an individual record by its alternate key value always requires some random processing.

The actual John Q. Smith records are not stored in adjacent locations in the base cluster. Just as records in a KSDS cannot be sequentially processed in key

TABLE 8.2   Record-Key Pairs. (Maintained on Disk and Optionally in Memory).

Record Number	Primary Key (3 Byte Numeric Field)	Alternate Key (1 Byte Alphabetic Field)
1	005	A
2	010	B
3	015	A
4	020	B
5	025	C
6	030	A

field order without using the index component, it is impossible to sequentially access the records in a base cluster through an alternate index.

Performing Secondary Key Processing with Data Sets

Before examining VSAM's methods to construct and maintain alternate indexes, which is discussed in the next section, processing a comparable type of data set in general is first described. These basic techniques can be used with different data set organizations, including indexed, relative, and direct access. Although theoretically possible, an alternate index built over a partitioned data set would be difficult to implement and would have very limited use. An alternate index cannot be built over a non-VSAM sequential data set.

Throughout this chapter, the same group of records is used to illustrate alternate key processing with both non-VSAM and VSAM data sets. For simplicity, there are six records in the data set. The values in the two fields used as keys are shown in Table 8.2. The primary key is actually a logical record key only if the base data set is indexed. It is a relative record number for a relative data set and a disk KEY field for a direct access (non-VSAM) data set. In every case, it uniquely identifies a record.

The primary and alternate key values within a record are stored together as pairs in a second data set. These pairs can also be copied into memory during actual processing. At this point, the actual data set organization on disk of the group of pairs is not specified. Likewise, there are several ways in which the information in Table 8.2 can be stored in memory.

The Primary/Alternate Key pairs in the Record-Key table are used to perform alternate key processing. Suppose it is necessary to process the record having an alternate key value of C. In this case, a three-step procedure is required to locate the record in the base data set:

1. The Record-Key pairs in Table 8.2 are searched for a C entry. If a sequential search is used, five comparisons are necessary.

2. The (primary key) value paired with C, here 025, is moved to the primary key field (relative record number, disk KEY, etc.) in the application program.

TABLE 8.3 Fixed and Variable Length Table Entries.

Fixed-Length		Variable-Length				
Alternate Key	Primary Key	Alternate Key	Number	Primary Keys		
A	005	A	003	005	015	030
A	015	B	002	010	020	
A	030	C	001	025		
B	010					
B	020					
C	025					

3. A random retrieval operation is performed with the value in the primary key by the underlying access method used by the base data set.

When this approach is used, any record can be randomly retrieved based on its alternate key value. To sequentially process all of the records containing a specific alternate key value, the first record is located using this same three-step process. In addition, during the middle step, a pointer is set to the following entry in the Record-Key table, here 030-A. Depending on how the table of primary-alternate key pairs is organized, two or all three of the steps are then repeatedly executed to process all additional records that contain the same alternate key field value.

Example 1. Suppose that every record with an alternate key value of B is to be processed. The first B entry in the table is located, and the record with a primary key of 010 is retrieved. In addition, a pointer is set to the next entry in the table, the 015-A pair. To process the additional records with an alternate key of B, the table search resumes from the location of the pointer, and the record with a primary key of 020 is found and processed. The pointer is then set to the 025-C pair. This approach is used until the last entry in the table is examined. If it is known how many table entries are associated with a given alternate key value, this type of processing could be simplified. Such additional information could be maintained in a separate location or within the table entries as shown in the right-most alternate key table in Table 8.3.

Possible alternate key structure

Clearly, the existing format of the Record-Key pairs in Table 8.2 is not optimal for the steps required in the retrieval process. To determine that a specific alternate key value does not occur in the data set, every entry in the table must be searched. Processing duplicate alternate key values is especially cumbersome. Hence, to simplify record retrieval, the primary/alternate pairs should be organized so that a specific alternate key value can be quickly located. Furthermore, all primary keys associated with the same alternate key should be grouped together.

The information in Table 8.2 can be reorganized in several different ways depending on whether the table entries will be fixed or variable length. Two of the most common types of organizations are shown in Table 8.3. The second field in the variable-length entries table identifies the number of records in the base data set with the alternate key value. If the alternate key values are unique, the records in the two tables are identical except for this field. The spacing in Table 8.3 in both tables is only for readability; there would be no embedded blanks.

Both tables in Table 8.3 make certain aspects of alternate key processing easier. The fixed length table is a simpler structure, but the variable length requires less storage. A binary search can be used with the variable length table to locate the desired alternate key value. Both approaches make some aspects of record retrieval or table maintenance more difficult.

For each of the two approaches, some thought should be given as to how new table entries will be added and existing table entries modified or deleted. The Fixed Length Table is particularly ill suited for these types of operations. It is also usually not convenient to load either type of table in memory before processing. It is simpler to process an alternate primary key table as a separate disk data set that allows random access. There are several categories of alternate key processing. The simplest processing occurs when:

1. Only record retrieval is to be performed, and the alternate key values are unique. There are several major factors that complicate processing.

2. Multiple records contain the same alternate key value.

3. It is necessary to perform adds, deletes, and changes to the alternate key table itself.

4. Both the complications of items 2 and 3 might occur. VSAM automatically handles 2 and some parts of 3. However, some programmer effort might be required with 3 and, consequently, 4.

Using alternate keys with indexed and relative data sets

At this point, several actual approaches for processing the six records identified in Table 8.2 through an alternate key are examined. Example 2 is very similar to the VSAM implementation with a KSDS. Example 3 does not have a straightforward VSAM equivalent. However, there are some similarities with a VSAM alternate index over an ESDS and Example 3.

Example 2.   Suppose that the six base records referenced in Table 8.2 are stored as an indexed (KSDS or ISAM) data set. The related primary and alternate key pairs can then be stored and processed as a second data set rather than as a sequential table that must be copied into memory before it can be processed. For a very large data set, a table in memory is often undesirable because of the storage requirements, increased processing time to copy into memory and then back to disk, and the difficulties caused by adding, deleting, and changing table entries.

```
Prior to the rewrite operation:   A0003005015030B0002010020C0001025

Following the rewrite operation:  A0004005015030020B0001010C0001025
```

Figure 8.1   The three records in the indexed alternate index.

There are six records with keys of 005, 010, 015, 020, 025, and 030 in the base indexed data set. There are three records in the second indexed data set with key fields of A, B, and C. The alternate key is the first field in each record. It is 1 byte in length.

The remaining portion of the three records contains the number of primary key values associated with the given alternate key and the actual primary key values. This alternate key indexed data set can contain either fixed or variable-length records. However, if an ISAM data set is to be processed in a COBOL program, variable length data will require that all records be padded to some maximum value.

Suppose the fourth record in the base data set is to be modified. During the update operation, the alternate key value is to be changed from B to A. The only physical record (block) in the second indexed data set is shown in Fig. 8.1, both before and after the rewrite operation. Each logical record consists of the alternate key, the number of associated primary keys (underlined), and the primary key values.

Example 3.   The six base records in Table 8.2 can also be processed using relative data sets for the base data set, the alternate index, or both. Because relative record numbers must be nonnegative integers, every alternate key is paired with an unsigned integer, A with 1, B with 2, C with 3, and Z with slot 26. The contents of slots 1, 2, and 3 in the alternate index are shown in Fig. 8.2, both before and after the same rewrite operation processed in Example 2.

Because relative data sets must contain fixed-length records, all slot locations following the final primary key are padded with zeroes. Notice that, following the rewrite operation, the primary key values associated with A have been kept in ascending order, unlike in the previous example where chronological order was used. The developer of the alternate index chooses either of the two approaches.

Primary and alternate key pairs can be stored in a wide variety of ways using various types of non-VSAM and VSAM data sets. This is further examined in Exercise 1. It is an excellent learning tool to write a comprehensive, dynamic

```
                    Prior to the                Following the
                 Rewrite Operation            Rewrite Operation

Slot 1: A0003005015030000.....000      A0004005015020030.....000
Slot 2: B0002010020000000.....000      B0001010000000000.....000
Slot 3: C0001025000000000.....000      C0001025000000000.....000
```

Figure 8.2   The three records in the relative alternate index.

master file update program using a second data set to support alternate key processing. This makes it both very easy to understand how comparable processing is implemented with VSAM, and to develop an appreciation for how little work is required when VSAM is used. Exercise 2 examines the common processing situations that must be performed with the alternate index data set used to support the secondary key.

Using Alternate Key Indexes with VSAM Data Sets

Most of the work with the alternate key approaches discussed with non-VSAM data sets is performed by an application programmer who must explicitly maintain two data sets. On the other hand, VSAM alternate key processing is usually much simpler, reducing alternate key processing to a very mechanical level.

Before a VSAM data set can be processed with an alternate key, three separate IDCAMS commands must be executed: DEFINE ALTERNATEINDEX, BLDINDEX, and DEFINE PATH. The DEFINE ALTERNATEINDEX command is used to create an Alternate Index (AIX) data set, which is then used to hold the alternate and primary key pair records. Each record in this alternate index consists of control information, the alternate key value, and all primary keys associated with it. Hence, the data component of an alternate index is structurally similar to the Variable Length Entries Table shown in Table 8.3.

An alternate index is stored as a KSDS, and its data component logical records hold the variable length key pair values. The alternate index has an index component with exactly the same format as other KSDSs. Rather than performing a binary search as discussed with the variable-length entries in Table 8.3, a standard KSDS index search is used to determine which control interval contains the logical record with the alternate key value.

Once the alternate index data component is sequentially searched, the corresponding primary values for the specified alternate key value are located. For the six records in Table 8.2, there are three logical records in the data component of the alternate index. The contents of the records are shown in hexadecimal on the left in Table 8.4. For clarity, the printable character values are also shown on the right, but generally, the first 5 bytes are not printable. Hence, a PRINT command with an alternate index often does not specify CHARACTER.

Carefully examine the Variable Length Entries Table in Table 8.3 and compare it with an actual VSAM alternate index. The only difference between the two is several additional overhead bytes in each record in the actual VSAM alternate index.

TABLE 8.4 Logical Records in a VSAM Alternate Index.

Record	Key	Hexadecimal Contents			Character Contents		
1	C1	01030003	01C1F0F0	F5F0F1F5 F0F3F0	.... .A00	5015	030
2	C2	01030002	01C2F0F1	F0F0F2F0	.... .B01	0020	
3	C3	01030001	01C3F0F2	F5	.... .C02	5	

The first 5 bytes in an alternate index record

Every alternate index record begins with 5 bytes of control information occupying four fields. The fields consist of 1, 1, 2, and 1 bytes respectively. Ordinarily, each field except the third one contains a value that remains constant for the life of the record. These three field values are also the same for every record in the data set. The value in the third field is a variable but it can always be determined from the RDF value.

Byte 1.   The first field specifies whether the alternate index is constructed over a KSDS or an ESDS and whether alternate key values must be unique or if base records can contain duplicates. The four possible values are identified in Table 8.5. Note that the records in Table 8.4 are part of an alternate index, which is constructed over a base KSDS (01) and that duplicate alternate key values are allowed (01). This chapter emphasizes alternate indexes over a KSDS. Alternate indexes over an ESDS are examined in detail in chapter 10.

Byte 2.   The second control field contains the length of the primary key field, which is 3 bytes in Table 8.4.

Bytes 3 and 4.   Two bytes are used to store the number of primary keys associated with the alternate key value. In Table 8.4, three records contain the first alternate key value (A); two contain the second value (B); and only one contains the third value (C). Theoretically, the maximum number of records in a KSDS or ESDS that can have the same alternate key value is 32,767. Consider the length of such a logical record in the alternate index data set. Questions related to the maximum and minimum size and structure of such records are examined in Exercise 5.

Byte 5.   The final control field byte contains the length of the alternate key field, which is 1 byte in Table 8.4.

When an alternate index is constructed over an ESDS, bytes 2, 3, and 4 have a slightly different meaning, which is described in chapter 10. In addition, byte 1 contains the value 80 or 81, depending on whether the alternate key values are unique.

Alternate index logical records

The remaining portion of each record consists of the alternate key value and the associated primary key values. Primary key values are not compressed in the

TABLE 8.5 Four VSAM Alternate Indexes.

Value	Type of Alternate Index
00	base KSDS and unique alternate key values
01	base KSDS and duplicate alternate key values allowed
80	base ESDS and unique alternate key values
81	base ESDS and duplicate alternate key values allowed

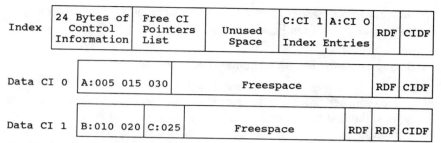

Index	24 Bytes of Control Information	Free CI Pointers List	Unused Space	C:CI 1 A:CI 0 Index Entries	RDF	CIDF

Data CI 0	A:005 015 030	Freespace	RDF	CIDF

Data CI 1	B:010 020 C:025	Freespace	RDF	RDF	CIDF

Figure 8.3 A complete VSAM alternate index structure.

data component of an alternate index. Otherwise, their identity would be ambiguous. Simple arithmetic with the values in the 5 bytes of control information can be used to determine the length of the logical record. In particular:

$$\text{Logical Record Length} = 5 +$$
$$\text{Value in byte } 5 +$$
$$\text{Value in byte } 2 * \text{value in bytes } 3 \text{ and } 4$$

Unless the record spans control intervals, the logical record length is also stored in the RDF. However, SPANNED cannot be specified when IDCAMS is used to create the alternate index. Furthermore, the records in an alternate index are stored as spanned blocked. A record in an alternate index must be contained within a single control area.

If a moderately large first subparameter value is specified with FREESPACE when the alternate index is built, very little data is written in control intervals during the load operation. In this case, a picture like that shown in Fig. 8.3 could accurately represent the data set. Note that the data component consists of three very small logical records—15, 12, and 9 bytes respectively. There is one RDF in CI0, and two RDFs in CI1. The RDFs contain the length values 15, 12, and 9 in their final 2 bytes. Obviously, the Freespace and Unused space are not drawn to scale.

Example 4.   The same processing in Examples 2 and 3 will be performed here. The logical record with a key of 015 is rewritten and, in the process, the alter-

Index	24 Bytes of Control Information	Free CI Pointers List	Unused Space	C:CI 1 A:CI 0 Index Entries	RDF	CIDF

Data CI 0	A:005 030	Freespace	RDF	CIDF

Data CI 1	B:010 020 015 C:025	Freespace	RDF	RDF	CIDF

Figure 8.4 The alternate index following the rewrite operation.

nate key value is changed from A to B. The status of the alternate index following the rewrite is shown in Fig. 8.4.

Detailed examination of VSAM alternate key processing

In this section, the specific steps required to perform VSAM alternate key processing are examined. For the base data set used to construct the alternate index in Fig. 8.3, the first record with an alternate key value of B is to be read. The application program specifies the value B and that the alternate key be used. VSAM employs seven major steps in locating the record. The steps are described and summarized in Table 8.6:

- In Step 1, the search key value is initially compared with A and then with C, which determines that, if the alternate key value is in the data set, it is in the second control interval. If there are multiple control areas in the alternate index, the search begins in the highest level index record.

- Steps 2 and 6 are performed in the same fashion because a KSDS is processed in both cases. Specific details are described in chapter 2.

- In Step 3, the RDF values are used to locate the individual logical records. Once the desired record is found, a record pointer is initialized to the next primary key paired with the alternate index value of B. Notice that this is superficially somewhat more complex than a base KSDS pointer (CRP) in that more information than just a record boundary must be saved.

- Steps 3 and 7 involve standard KSDS sequential searching using key values of B and 010 respectively. Once the record has been retrieved, VSAM returns a status code (02 in COBOL) specifying that there are additional records with an alternate key of B.

Suppose that the next command executed is a sequential read operation using the alternate key. The record pointer in the alternate index determines that the next primary key to process is 020. The associated record is retrieved from the

TABLE 8.6 Alternate Key Record Retrieval Steps.

Step	Processing Function
1	The alternate index sequence set record is read and searched.
2	The search moves from the index to data CI1, which contains the record with an (alternate) key value of B.
3	CI1 is searched, and the first logical record in the control interval contains the key value B. The record also contains the two associated primary key values of 010 and 020. The first value (010) is selected, and a pointer is set within the logical record identifying B:020 as the next key to be processed in ascending sequential order.
4	The search moves from the alternate index to the base cluster.
5	The index component in the base cluster is searched.
6	The search moves from the index component to the data control interval, which contains the record with primary key value 010.
7	The data control interval is sequentially searched, and the logical record with a key field value of 010 is located.

5 Bytes of Control Information	B	010	020	013

Figure 8.5   The alternate index record after it is rewritten.

base cluster using the same final four processing steps shown in Table 8.6. Although the records in the alternate index are sequentially processed in ascending key field order, a random retrieval is performed in the base cluster (Steps 5, 6, and 7). Following this, a status code (00 in COBOL) is returned identifying that this is the last record with an alternate key of B. Furthermore, because there are no more primary keys in the alternate index logical record, the next record pointer identifies the logical record with an alternate key value of C.

Suppose a random write operation is performed next. The record to be added contains a primary key of 013 and an alternate key of B. The record is added to the base cluster using standard VSAM processing. In addition, the B-010020 record in the alternate index must be rewritten. Figure 8.5 shows the logical record following the rewrite operation. Because the random add operation immediately followed the sequential processing, it is unclear what value should be placed in the alternate index's next record pointer following the add. Chapter 9 clarifies this point.

When the alternate index is initially loaded, the primary key values associated with a specific alternate key are stored in ascending order within the record. As the base data set grows, additional primary key values are added to the back of the record in chronological order.

A potential modification in future releases of VSAM would be to insert each additional primary key into its correct collating sequence location. What additional overheads would this create? Perhaps when adding records with duplicate key field values, the programmer could be given a choice between collating sequence or chronological order. This choice would be made when the alternate index is built and loaded, not with each subsequent add operation.

Constructing a VSAM Alternate Index

The three IDCAMS commands required to construct, load, and use an alternate index are now examined in detail in Table 8.7. Remember that an alternate index has the same structure as a KSDS. Hence, using DEFINE ALTERNATEINDEX to create an alternate index is almost identical to defining a KSDS. Loading records with BLDINDEX into an alternate index is very similar to using REPRO to load records into a KSDS. This analogy is summarized in Table 8.8. The PATH command supplies a logical interface to records in the base data set through the alternate index. Surprisingly, in addition to its major role with alternate indexes, the PATH command can also be used to create another name (an alias) for a VSAM data set. In this setting the Path name specifies a second name for the data set. However, it does not reorder the logical records.

TABLE 8.7   Functionally Comparable IDCAMS Commands.

Function	Creating, Loading, and Processing a KSDS	Creating, Loading, and Processing an Alternate Index
Create	DEFINE CLUSTER	DEFINE ALTERNATEINDEX
Load	REPRO	BLDINDEX
Process	DEFINE PATH (Optional)	DEFINE PATH

Processing alternate key indexes with IDCAMS commands

Because an alternate index is structurally and functionally identical to a KSDS, the DEFINE ALTERNATEINDEX command required to create an alternate index is very similar to the DEFINE CLUSTER command used to create a KSDS. Both commands use basically the same parameters. The few differences are noted in Table 8.9.

Once an alternate index is created, records are loaded into it with the BLDINDEX command, whose parameters are syntactically and functionally similar to the REPRO command. Thus, it should be carefully noted that Fig. 8.6 does not reflect the status of the alternate index following the DEFINE ALTERNATEINDEX command. Rather, the BLDINDEX command has been used to load the alternate index.

The BLDINDEX command causes all the records in the base cluster to be read. The primary and alternate keys in each record are paired and written into a table. The table is then sorted into ascending order using the alternate key value as the major sort key. Finally, all of the primary keys associated with a specific alternate key value are combined into a single record, and the sorted records are loaded into the alternate index data set—a KSDS structure. (See Fig. 8.7.)

TABLE 8.8   BLDINDEX Parameters.

Input Parameters	Required	REPRO Equivalent
INFILE(DDname) or INDATASET(data set name)		Identical with REPRO
Output Parameters	Yes	Identical with REPRO Except only 1 output data set
OUTFILE(DDname1 ... DDnameN) or OUTDATASET(data set name1 ... data set nameN)		
Sorting Parameters	All optional	No REPRO equivalent
EXTERNALSORT INTERNALSORT WORKFILES(DDname1 DDname2)	or	
Other Parameters	Optional	Identical with REPRO
CATALOG(Catalog Name)		

TABLE 8.9 DEFINE CLUSTER and DEFINE ALTERNATEINDEX Parameters.

Parameter	DEFINE CLUSTER Command			DEFINE ALTERNATEINDEX Command		
	Cluster	Data	Index	Cluster	Data	Index
NAME(entryname)	X*	X*	X*	X	X	X
SPACE ALLOCATION						
CYLINDERS(primary secondary)	X	X	X	X	X	X
TRACKS(primary secondary)	X	X	X	X	X	X
RECORDS(primary secondary)	X	X	X	X	X	X
VOLUMES(Volser1...VolserN)	X	X*	X*	X	X*	X*
RELATE(base cluster)				X		
UNIQUEKEY or NONUNIQUEKEY				X	X	
UPGRADE or NOUPGRADE				X		
ATTEMPTS(number or 2)	X*	X*	X*	X*	X*	X*
AUTHORIZATION(entrypoint string)	X*	X*	X*	X*	X*	X*
BUFFERSPACE(value in bytes)	X	X*		X	X*	
CODE(code)	X*	X*	X*	X*	X*	X*
CONTROLINTERVALSIZE(size)	X	X	X	X	X	X
CONTROLPW(password)	X*	X*	X*	X	X	X
DESTAGEWAIT or NODESTAGEWAIT	X	X*	X*	X	X	X
ERASE or NOERASE	X	X*		X	X	
EXCEPTIONEXIT(entrypoint)	X	X*	X*	X	X	X
FILE(DDname)	X*	X*	X*	X	X	X
FREESPACE(CI% CA%)	X	X*		X	X	
IMBED or NOIMBED	X		X	X		X
KEYRANGES(low1 hi1)...(lowN hiN)	X	X		X	X	
KEYS(length offset)	X*	X*		X	X	
MASTERPW(password)	X*	X*	X*	X	X	X
MODEL(entryname/password)	X	X	X	X	X	X
ORDERED or UNORDERED	X	X	X	X	X	X
OWNER(name)	X*	X*	X*	X	X	X
READPW(password)	X*	X*	X*	X	X	X
RECATALOG	X	X	X	X	X	X
RECORDSIZE(average maximum)	X*	X*		X	X	
REPLICATE or NOREPLICATE	X		X	X		X
REUSE or NOREUSE	X	X	X	X	X	X
SHAREOPTIONS(crossregion system)	X	X*	X*	X	X	X
SPEED or RECOVERY	X	X		X	X	
STAGE or BIND or CYLINDERFAULT	X	X*	X*	X	X	X
TO(yyddd) or FOR(days)	X*			X		
UNIQUE or SUBALLOCATION	X	X	X	X	X	X
UPDATEPW(password)	X*	X*	X*	X	X	X
WRITECHECK or NOWRITECHECK	X	X*	X*	X	X	X
INDEXED or NONINDEXED or NUMBERED or LINEAR	X					
SPANNED or NONSPANNED	X	X				
CATALOG(catalog name)	X	X	X	X	X	X

*Under "suitable conditions".

Even after the alternate index has been loaded, it cannot immediately be used by VSAM to process the records in the base VSAM data set. Rather, a logical interface called a path must be constructed. The DEFINE PATH command performs this function. When the records in the base cluster are to be processed using alternate key values, the path name is specified as the data set name, either in the accompanying JCL or IDCAMS commands. Thus, to support processing with a single alternate index, several additional catalog entries are required. The alternate index itself is a KSDS, or true VSAM data set. The

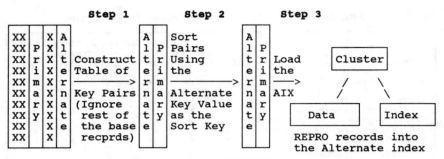

Figure 8.6 Three basic steps performed by the BLDINDEX command.

path is a logical connector to the base cluster by way of the alternate index. When the path data set is opened, the base cluster and alternate index are also opened.

IDCAMS can construct up to 255 alternate indexes over a base cluster. However, the overhead associated with alternate keys is both substantial and cumulative as the number of alternate keys increases. Hence, it is rare that more than several alternate indexes are built over one base cluster.

It is usually desirable to request that VSAM automatically maintain an alternate index and modify it to reflect all changes in the base cluster. This is done by making the alternate index a member of the "Upgrade Set" for the base cluster. When an alternate index is initially defined, it can be specified as belonging to the Upgrade Set. Set membership implies that when the base cluster is opened for "update" processing, every alternate index in the Upgrade Set will also be opened. Changes in the base data set are then reflected in the structure of each alternate index in the Upgrade Set.

An alternate index does not *have* to be made a member of the Upgrade Set, however. In fact, even an alternate index that belongs to this set can have its membership temporarily ignored. This is accomplished by the manner in which a path is defined over it. The ALTER command can be used to change membership status for an existing alternate index or path at any time.

```
//AIXBILD EXEC IDCAMS
//BASECLUS DD   DSN=MEDCAT.DOCTOR.CLINIC,DISP=SHR
//SDB      DD   VOL=SER=WORK06,UNIT=3390,DISP=OLD,AMP='AMORG'
//MDB      DD   VOL=SER=WORK03,UNIT=3390,DISP=OLD,AMP='AMORG'
//SYSIN    DD   *
  BLDINDEX INFILE(BASECLUS)                                    -
           ODS(MEDCAT.DOCTOR.CLINIC.AIX.CLUSTER                -
               MEDCAT.DOCTOR.CLINIC.AIX2.CLUSTER)             -
           WORKFILES(SDB MDB)                                 -
           EXTERNALSORT
/*
```

Figure 8.7 Loading records into alternate indexes.

Defining a VSAM Alternate Index Data Set

The DEFINE ALTERNATEINDEX (DEF AIX) command creates a VSAM alternate index over an existing, non-empty, base cluster. Recall the distinction between an empty and an unloaded VSAM data set. DEF AIX does not load records into the alternate index. The base cluster must be a KSDS or an ESDS. Currently, VSAM will not construct an alternate index over a RRDS or a non-VSAM data set. Future VSAM releases might permit an RRDS to be used as the base cluster. However, there would be an inherent contradiction in using an alternate index, which slows random response time appreciably over an RRDS, which is ordinarily used to provide rapid random processing.

An alternate index also cannot be defined over another alternate index. This restriction holds even though an alternate index itself is a KSDS. Also, if UNIQUE is specified with the DEFINE ALTERNATEINDEX command, the base cluster cannot be defined with the REUSE attribute.

Because an alternate index has the same structure as a VSAM KSDS, similar parameters are coded with both. The DEFINE CLUSTER command described in chapter 4 contains additional information on most of the parameters discussed in this section. The RELATE, UNIQUEKEY, and UPGRADE parameters are unique to the DEFINE ALTERNATEINDEX command and are discussed first. None of the three can be coded when creating a VSAM KSDS. RELATE and UPGRADE can only be coded with the cluster component of the alternate index. UNIQUEKEY may be coded with the data component or cluster component.

The RELATE(base cluster) (REL) (Cluster Only) parameter

The RELATE parameter identifies the alternate index's base cluster, which must be an existing nonempty KSDS or ESDS. If the base cluster is password-protected, the master password must be supplied with the RELATE parameter. RELATE is required. RELATE can also be used in another context, as discussed later in this chapter, to allow alias names to be created.

The UNIQUEKEY (UNQK) or
NONUNIQUEKEY (NUNQK) (Cluster or Data) parameters

The UNIQUEKEY parameter (Fig. 8.8) specifies that each record in the base cluster contain a unique alternate key value. UNIQUEKEY implies that the records in the alternate index are fixed-length. If UNIQUEKEY is specified and duplicate keys exist in the base cluster, the BLDINDEX command terminates during processing with an IDC sequence error message. If an attempt is made to add a duplicate alternate key value during an update of a base cluster, and UNIQUEKEY had been specified with the existing alternate index, a status code of 22 is returned to a COBOL application program. UNIQUEKEY and UNIQUE are unrelated parameters, and they perform totally diverse functions.

NONUNIQUEKEY means that records in the base cluster can have the same

```
DEFINE AIX(NAME(MEDCAT.DOCTOR.AIX2.CLUSTER)        —
            RELATE(MEDCAT.DOCTOR.CLINIC)           —
            MODEL(MEDCAT.DOCTOR.CLINIC.AIX.CLUSTER) —
            UNIQUEKEY                              —
            CYLINPER(1 1)                          —
            KEYS(5 99)                             —
            RECORDSIZE(37 37)                      —
            NOUPGRADE)                             —
        DATA(NAME(MEDCAT.DOCTOR.AIX2.DATA))        —
        INDEX(NAME(MEDCAT.DOCTOR.AIX2.INDEX))
```

Figure 8.8 Creating an alternate index with unique keys.

alternate key value. This implies that the alternate index contains variable-length records. NONUNIQUEKEY (Fig. 8.9) is the default value. With NON-UNIQUEKEY, it is important that the maximum RECORDSIZE value be large enough to contain the potential logical records keys that can be written in the alternate index. A maximum of 32,768 records can contain the same alternate key value. However, because RECORDSIZE also has a maximum value (default or user specified), under most circumstances, substantially fewer records can contain the same alternate key value.

The UPGRADE (UPG) or NOUPGRADE (NUPG) (Cluster Only) Parameters

The UPGRADE parameter makes the alternate index a member of the "Upgrade Set" for the base cluster named with the RELATE parameter. The Upgrade Set is defined as all alternate indexes that are opened whenever the base cluster is opened for a write, rewrite, or delete operation. The UPGRADE parameter does not take effect until after the alternate index is loaded. Following this, adds, deletes, and changes to the base cluster will cause the corresponding records in the alternate index to also be modified. If the

```
DEFINE AIX(NAME(MEDCAT.DOCTOR.CLINIC.AIX.CLUSTER)   —
            RELATE(MEDCAT.DOCTOR.CLINIC)            —
            NONUNIQUEKEY                            —
            UPGRADE                                 —
            VOLUMES(WORK02)                         —
            CYLINDER(4 1)                           —
            KEYS(2 3)                               —
            FREESPACE(20 20)                        —
            RECORDSIZE(1500 6000)                   —
            SHAREOPTIONS(2 3))                      —
        DATA(NAME(MEDCAT.DOCTOR.CLINIC.AIX.DATA)    —
            CONTROLINTERVALSIZE(4096))              —
        INDEX(NAME(MEDCAT.DOCTOR.CLINIC.AIX.INDEX)  —
            CONTROLINTERVALSIZE(1024))
```

Figure 8.9 Creating an alternate index with non-unique keys.

DEFINE ALTERNATEINDEX command is executed when the base cluster is already opened, the upgrading will begin the next time the base cluster is opened. This could lead to some initial data integrity problems.

Other DEFINE ALTERNATEINDEX Parameters

The remaining alternate index parameters are all also used with the DEFINE CLUSTER command. Chapter 4 contains the fundamental information for all of these parameters. Unless described otherwise, their basic role and their sub-parameter values are the same with both the DEFINE CLUSTER and DEFINE ALTERNATEINDEX commands. The NAME, VOLUMES, and space allocation parameters are required with both commands. These three parameters and RELATE are the only explicitly required parameters. Except for NAME, all of their values can be supplied with a MODEL parameter. The object being modeled must also be an alternate index.

The NAME(alternate index name) parameter

A data set name must be coded for the alternate index cluster component. The same syntax rules hold as when assigning a name to any VSAM cluster. The NAME parameter can be optionally coded with the data and index components. If values are not supplied, defaults will be generated for both. It is a good practice for all three names to be supplied by the programmer. Furthermore, the three names should show their own interrelationship and also an identification with the base cluster, as well as any future paths constructed over it.

The VOLUMES(volser1 volser2 ...) (VOL) parameter

Unless the MODEL parameter is coded, a specific volume(s) must be identified to hold the data and index components with the VOLUMES parameter. There is no default volume; either component can occupy multiple volumes. The data and index components can be placed on different volumes. Under some circumstances, access time is improved when this is done. Likewise, the base cluster and alternate index can be stored on the same or different volumes.

Space allocation parameters

Unless the MODEL parameter is used to provide the space allocation, one of these three parameters must be coded:

RECORDS (primary secondary) (REC) or
TRACKS (primary secondary) (TRK) or
CYLINDERS (primary secondary) (CYL)

There is no default value. Space can be requested via a parameter of the cluster, data, or index component and can be coded with multiple components. A value can be coded with the cluster component to determine space allocations for the data and index components. Recall that records in the data component of an alternate index consist of 5 bytes of control information, an alternate key, and one or more primary keys. Hence, large amounts of disk space are ordinarily not required. The index component of an alternate index clearly requires even less space than the data component. Exercise 10 examines extreme situations in the relationship between the size of an alternate index and the base cluster over which it is built.

The KEYS (length offset) parameter

The KEYS parameter, which can be coded with either the cluster or data component, identifies the length and location of the alternate key field within the records in the base cluster. When processing through the alternate index, the values specified with KEYS must match the values in an application program. If either value disagrees, the data set cannot be successfully opened.

An alternate index LISTCAT is examined. In addition to information concerning the alternate key field in the base cluster, which is provided by the KEY parameter, it specifies the KEYS information for the alternate index data set itself. This is a different value. In particular, the KEYS displacement value will always be 5, the initial field following the 5 bytes of overhead.

The FREESPACE (CI% CA%) (FSPC) parameter

The FREESPACE parameter specifies the amount of free space to be left in the control intervals and control areas when records are loaded into the data component. Both values are, in effect, with the primary and secondary allocations when the alternate index is loaded or extended, and optionally during any control interval and control area splits. FREESPACE can be coded with either the cluster or data component. A true extension of an alternate index would not commonly occur, but a load operation could be resumed.

The SHAREOPTIONS (Cross-Region Cross-System) (SHR) parameter

The same values are coded with the SHAREOPTIONS parameter as with a KSDS. The complete set of values and their meanings is given in chapter 4. It is important to realize that the most common type of alternate key processing consists of record retrieval only. Hence, some of the SHAREOPTIONS values might be inappropriate with an alternate index. Whether an alternate index is made a member of the Upgrade Set also effects the values coded here.

The SPANNED (cannot be coded) parameter

An alternate index data record can span control interval boundaries. Thus, the maximum RECORDSIZE value can be greater than the CISZ value. However, SPANNED cannot be coded in the DEFINE ALTERNATEINDEX command, although it is always in effect. In addition, two or more logical records or segments can be placed in the same control interval. Recall that specifying SPANNED with a KSDS or ESDS, results in unblocked spanned records. In non-VSAM terminology, an alternate index has a record format of VBS (variable blocked spanned), while a standard KSDS has a VS (variable spanned) record format.

The RECORDSIZE (average maximum) (RECSZ) parameter

The RECORDSIZE parameter can be coded with either the cluster or data component. The maximum RECORDSIZE value should be carefully selected when creating an alternate index that will allow duplicate key values. It is much more complicated than the DEFINE CLUSTER maximum RECORDSIZE value. The following formula is used to determine the maximum length of a logical record in an alternate index constructed over a KSDS. The comparable formula for an alternate index built over a base ESDS is examined in chapter 10.

MAX-RECSZ = 5 + alternate-key-length + (N*primary-key-length)

Here, MAX-RECSZ denotes the maximum logical record length, N is the maximum number of records in the base cluster containing the same alternate key value, and 5 denotes the number of bytes of control information that begin each alternate index data record. The average RECORDSIZE value is used only for documentation unless a space allocation for a specific number of logical records is requested with the RECORDS parameter in the DEFINE ALTERNATEINDEX command. If UNIQUEKEY is specified, N = 1 in the preceding formula, then value 5 + alternate-key-length + primary-key-length should be coded for both RECORDSIZE parameters.

Several numeric examples can be used to illustrate these formulas. Suppose a base KSDS has a 12-byte primary key and 5 and 30-byte alternate keys respectively. The 5-byte alternate key allows duplicate values. In particular, the same alternate key could occur up to 100 times within the base cluster records. The RECORDSIZE(maximum) value is 1,210 bytes for the nonunique alternate key and 47 bytes for the unique key. Note that the crucial value is the length of the primary keys, not the alternate key.

Comparing DEFINE CLUSTER and
DEFINE ALTERNATEINDEX

The syntax and function of the additional parameters that can be coded with DEFINE ALTERNATEINDEX is the same as the parameters used with DEFINE CLUSTER as described in chapter 4. This includes all of the parameters shown in Table 8.9, which are not discussed in the preceding section. The format in Table 8.9 illustrates those parameters that can be coded with one or more components. In addition, an asterisk after an X means, under "suitable conditions," the parameter value can be modified by the ALTER command. For more details on "suitable conditions" see the ALTER command section in chapter 6.

Note in Table 8.9 that the INDEXED and SPANNED parameters cannot be coded with a DEFINE ALTERNATEINDEX command, even though both are permitted with a DEFINE CLUSTER command. Conversely, there are three parameters that can only be coded with DEFINE ALTERNATEINDEX: RELATE, UNIQUEKEY, and UPGRADE. If UNIQUE is coded with the base cluster, REUSE is not allowed with the alternate index.

DEFINE ALTERNATEINDEX coding examples

Example 1. The DEFINE ALTERNATEINDEX command in Fig. 8.9 was used to create an alternate index over the base cluster created in Coding Example 1 in chapter 4 by the DEFINE CLUSTER command (the KSDS for the medical facility patient records). The alternate key is an insurance billing code in bytes 4 and 5. There are only 12 possible code values. Hence, many patient records contain the same code. For example, approximately one-third of the patients use Blue Cross/Blue Shield, which has a code of 01. Recall that the primary keys are 27 bytes in length, and there are approximately 5,000 records in the base cluster.

Because many of the records in the base cluster have the same billing code, the corresponding alternate index record is very large. For example, if 175 records have a billing code of 01, then a record of length $4732 = ((27 * 175) + 2 + 5)$ bytes is written in the data component of the alternate index. In this case, each of the logical record segments is placed in a different control interval. Because the maximum logical record size is 32K, there is an upper bound of approximately $32K/27 = 1200$ records with the same alternate key value.

Example 5. A second alternate index is to be built over the same base cluster. The DEFINE ALTERNATEINDEX command is shown in Fig. 8.8. Several significant modifications are to be included here. The alternate key is a 5-byte patient number containing unique values. NOUPGRADE is specified because the alternate index is to be resynchronized with the base cluster at a later time. This is sometimes done to improve response time when the base cluster is updated on-line. A batch program can then be run at a later time to update the alternate index when the on-line system is down. This is a somewhat questionable practice, which is further discussed later in this chapter and also in chapter 16 with CICS. Ordinarily, this is done with all the alternate indexes or none of them.

Notice that this alternate index can be modeled on the previously created structure of the same type. Because of the unique alternate key values, there is a dramatic change in the RECORDSIZE values. Here, the unique alternate key values minimize the effect of the very large primary keys. In the previous example, the average logical record in the alternate index was almost five times as large as an average logical record in the base cluster. Here, each alternate index record is 37 bytes in length, and there is the same number of records in the alternate index as in the base cluster. This alternate index is larger than the first one, both in terms of records and actual disk storage!

Loading an ALTERNATEINDEX – the BLDINDEX (BIX) command

The BLDINDEX command loads an empty alternate index with data taken from the records in the the base cluster. In particular, the base cluster records are read and just the primary and alternate key fields are copied from each record and written to a table. After all the base records are read, the key pairs in the table are sorted using the alternate key as the key field for the sort. Following this, pairs with the same alternate key value are combined or compressed into variable-length records, the sorted records are loaded (REPROed) into the empty alternate index data component, and the corresponding index entries are created.

The three basic steps in this process are depicted in Fig. 8.6. Notice that the alternate key is the first field in the key pair record built in Step 1. This makes the sort in Step 2 more efficient.

Unless the base data set is large, only two parameters must be coded with BLDINDEX—INFILE or INDATASET—to identify the input base cluster that BLDINDEX is to process. INFILE and INDATASET are described in detail with the REPRO command in chapter 5.

The output from the BLDINDEX command is loaded into an alternate index, which is identified with either an OUTFILE or OUTDATASET parameter. See the REPRO command section in chapter 5 for additional information. If the sort operation can be performed in memory, no other parameters need be coded. For a large base cluster, the sort might need to use work data sets. The complete list of parameters available with the BLDINDEX command is now described. Table 8.8 contains a summary of significant information associated with the parameters.

The INFILE (DDname for Base Cluster DD Statement) (IFILE)
or INDATASET (Base Cluster name) (IDS) parameters

INFILE identifies the DD statement that contains the name of the base cluster. Coding INDATASET causes the nonempty base cluster to be dynamically allocated. Either INFILE or INDATASET must be specified. The same advantages and disadvantages discussed previously regarding dynamic data set allocation apply here.

The OUTFILE (DDname1 for AIX DD Statement ... DDnameN) (OFILE)
or OUTDATASET (alternate index1 ... alternate indexN) (ODS) parameters

OUTFILE identifies the DD statement that contains the name of the alternate index. The alternate index must be related to the input base cluster with the

DEFINE ALTERNATEINDEX command.

Coding OUTDATASET dynamically allocates the alternate index, and either OUTFILE or OUTDATASET must be specified. No matter which parameter is coded, two or more alternate indexes can be loaded with one command by identifying multiple, alternate indexes with either parameter. For example, ODS(ALTNAME1 ALTNAME2) and OFILE(DDALT1 DDALT2) both load two alternate indexes. This results in a more complicated picture in Fig. 8.6. See Exercise 5. Each alternate index can have a different key field.

The EXTERNALSORT (ESORT) or INTERNALSORT (ISORT) parameter

The EXTERNALSORT or INTERNALSORT parameter determines whether, in the middle step in Fig. 8.6, the alternate key-primary key pairs are sorted internally or using external disk storage. INTERNALSORT is the default value. If insufficient storage is available for an internal sort, then an external sort can be performed. In this case, two work data sets are used for the sort operation. These are identified by DD statements with the default DDnames of IDCUT1 and IDCUT2. The IDCUTx data sets perform the same roles as the SORTWKxx data sets, which are used with the DFSORT/Sort-Merge (SYNCSORT) utility. *The VSAM Programmer's Guide* manual contains the details concerning the amount of storage required to perform the sort operation.

The WORKFILES (DDname1 DDname2) parameter

If the DDnames IDCUT1 and IDCUT2 are used to identify the two work data sets mentioned in the preceding section, the WORKFILES parameter is unnecessary. If other DDnames are selected, they must be specified with the

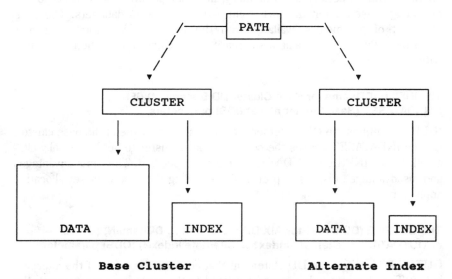

Figure 8.10   Relationship between base cluster, alternate index, path.

```
IDC0550I ENTRY(D)  MEDCAT.DOCTOR.CLINIC.AIX.DATA DELETED
IDC0550I ENTRY(I)  MEDCAT.DOCTOR.CLINIC.AIX.INDEX DELETED
IDC0550I ENTRY(G)  MEDCAT.DOCTOR.CLINIC.AIX DELETED
IDC0550I ENTRY(P)  MEDCAT.DOCTOR.PATH DELETED
IDC0050I ENTRY(D)  MEDCAT.DOCTOR.CLINIC.DATA DELETED
IDC0050I ENTRY(I)  MEDCAT.DOCTOR.CLINIC.INDEX DELETED
IDC0050I ENTRY(C)  MEDCAT.DOCTOR.CLINIC DELETED
```

Figure 8.11   IDCAMS messages following deletion of the base cluster.

WORKFILES parameters. This rarely needed occurance is included in Example 6.

Example 6.   The two alternate indexes using the code that was created in Examples 1 and 2 will now be loaded. With a relatively small base cluster such as this, an internal sort can usually be performed with the key pairs. However, to further illustrate the syntax and JCL available with the BLDINDEX command, an external sort is requested, and user DDnames are provided for the two work data sets. The four DD parameters coded with the work data sets are required.

Do not specify SYSDA as the UNIT value. Multiple volumes can be requested to guarantee sufficient storage. Because the DD statements for the work files identify VSAM data sets, the AMP parameter is coded. Note that both alternate indexes are loaded by the single BLDINDEX command. The complete codes are shown in Fig. 8.7.

The DEFINE PATH Command

The DEFINE PATH command creates a logical structure, called a path, which is an interface for processing base cluster records through a related alternate index. A path does not contain either a data or index component. When a program opens a path for processing, the associated alternate index and base cluster are also both opened.

When using an alternate index to either sequentially or randomly process records in the KSDS base cluster, all processing is performed using the primary key values. No RBA processing is permitted through the path.

Figure 8.10 illustrates the relationships among the seven cataloged entries required to process a VSAM KSDS through a single alternate index. Notice the relative sizes of the objects involved. In reality, the data component should be proportionally even bigger for a large base cluster than shown here, and the index component in the alternate index might be even smaller. Every additional alternate key adds four more entries to the structure in Fig. 8.10.

A LISTCAT or DELETE command that names the alternate index will cause all of the paths defined over it to also be processed. A single DELETE command with the name of the base cluster will delete all seven VSAM objects shown in Fig. 8.10. The resulting IDCAMS messages associated with deleting a structure like the one shown in Fig. 8.10 is given in Fig. 8.11.

The following sections describe the three parameters that can be coded with the PATH command—NAME, PATHENTRY, and UPDATE or NOUPDATE. Because a path is a control object rather than a true data set, a limited group of parameters are needed.

The NAME (path name) parameter

Unlike the DEFINE CLUSTER and DEFINE ALTERNATEINDEX commands, a path requires only one name because it has no data or index component. The DEFINE CLUSTER command in chapter 4 contains detailed information on coding data set names for any VSAM object. After the path is created, it can be referenced on a DD statement by coding DSN = pathname. When this is done, logical records will be retrieved from the base cluster using the key values in the alternate index. Likewise, several IDCAMS commands, including REPRO, PRINT, LISTCAT, ALTER, and DELETE, allow the path name to be specified explicitly.

EXPORT, IMPORT, and VERIFY commands are not used to process a path. On the other hand, all three commands can be used to process an alternate index. See chapter 6 for information on EXPORT/IMPORT with alternate indexes. Even the REPRO command can be used with an alternate index if needed.

The PATHENTRY (alternate index name)(PENT) parameter

The PATHENTRY parameter identifies the alternate index used to retrieve records from the base cluster. The name of the base cluster is not coded in the DEFINE PATH command. Recall that the RELATE parameter coded with DEFINE ALTERNATEINDEX identified it, and its name is stored in the cluster component of the alternate index.

The UPDATE (UPD) or NOUPDATE (NUPD) parameter

The UPDATE parameter, the default, determines whether the base cluster's Upgrade Set is to be allocated when the path is opened. UPDATE causes every alternate index in the Upgrade Set to be allocated and automatically updated to reflect changes in the base cluster.

NOUPDATE means that the path's base cluster will be allocated but not its Upgrade Set. NOUPDATE has precedence even if UPGRADE is coded for an alternate index over the base cluster.

It is possible to create two distinct paths over the same alternate index and specify UPDATE with one and NOUPDATE with the other. The ALTER command can be used to switch from UPDATE to NOUPDATE and vice-versa for a path. The relationship between UPGRADE and UPDATE is summarized in Table 8.10.

Even more complications are possible while trying to maintain synchronization among a base cluster and its alternate indexes. In particular, it is possible

TABLE 8.10 UPGRADE and UPDATE Parameters Relationship.

Path Parameter	Alternate Index Parameter	
	UPGRADE (Default)	NOUPGRADE
UPDATE (Default)	The associated alternate index is a member of the Upgrade Set and is allo- cated along with all the other Upgrade members.	The associated alternate index is not a member of the Upgrade Set. However, all members of the Upgrade Set are allocated.
NOUPDATE	Although the associated alternate index is a member of the Upgrade Set, changes in the base cluster will not be re- flected in the alternate index. Only record re- trieval is permitted through the path.	The associated alternate is not a member of the Upgrade Set. Further- more, none of the members of the Upgrade Set are allocated.

that changes can be made to the base cluster through an alternate index without initially allocating the base cluster. In this situation, the intent of UPGRADE and UPDATE are circumvented. Serious integrity problems can occur and go undetected. This is further discussed in chapter 17.

The non-IDCAMS alternatives to UPGRADE and UPDATE are nontrivial. If an application has to update an alternate index directly, it will have to be written in assembler. It will also require a strong knowledge of VSAM internal struc- tures. Many potential problems can occur in this environment.

The complete group of parameters available with the DEFINE PATH com-

Required Parameters

NAME(pathname)
PATHENTRY(alternate index name or cluster name)

Optional Parameters

UPDATE or NOUPDATE

Passwords—READPW, UPDATEPW, CONTROLPW, and MASTERPW
ATTEMPTS(number)
AUTHORIZATION(program string)
CODE(string)
FILE(DDname)
MODEL(existing Path Name)
OWNER(owner name)
RECATALOG or NORECATALOG
TO(date) or FOR(days)
CATALOG(catalog name)

Figure 8.12 DEFINE PATH parameters.

mand is shown in Fig. 8.12. Only PATHENRY and UPDATE are new commands that haven't already been thoroughly discussed in chapter 4 with DEFINE CLUSTER. Notice that, unlike other IDCAMS DEFINE commands, DEFINE PATH has no parameters for specifying data set properties or disk storage. Because there are no logical records to store, PATHENTRY can be loosely considered as an input parameter.

Five IDCAMS commands must be executed before the records in a KSDS or ESDS can be processed through an alternate key. DEFINE CLUSTER, REPRO, and DEFINE ALTERNATEINDEX must be performed in order. DEFINE PATH and BLDINDEX must then be executed. However, either can be done first. The base cluster must be a nonempty KSDS or ESDS. Because of this restriction, the following command order is invalid when trying to load an alternate index:

> DEFINE CLUSTER
> DEFINE ALTERNATEINDEX
> REPRO and then BLDINDEX or DEFINE PATH

Example 7. A path will be defined over the alternate index created in Example 4 that is password-protected. When the path is opened, every alternate index in the Upgrade Set of the base cluster will also be opened for processing.

Example 8. Four reports are to be printed. The records in the base cluster MEDCAT.DOCTOR.CLINIC.CLUSTER are to be printed in four different orders. First, they are to be listed in ascending order based on their alternate key value. This order results when the path name is coded on a PRINT statement. Next, the records in the base cluster are to be listed in ascending order on primary key value. Following this, the same logical records are to be printed in order by their RBA value in the base cluster. Finally, the records in the MEDCAT.DOCTOR.AIX.CLUSTER alternate index itself are printed.

Each of these records contains 5 bytes of overhead, an alternate key value, and all associated primary key values. Exercise 3 is an extension of this example, which requests a classification of all possible record orders generated by the base cluster, alternate index, and path.

Other uses of the DEFINE PATH command

Generally, a path can be constructed over a VSAM cluster of any type: KSDS (including alternate indexes), ESDS, and RRDS. If no alternate index is involved, the object identified on the PATHENTRY parameter is a "true" KSDS, ESDS, or RRDS. In this context, the DEFINE PATH command creates an alias for the "base" cluster. Although IDCAMS provides a DEFINE ALIAS command, the object receiving the alias name must be a non-VSAM data set or a user catalog. Thus, DEFINE PATH over a cluster, which is not an alternate index, is functionally similar to DEFINE ALIAS over a non-VSAM data set.

Example 9.   Several users of the MEDCAT.DOCTOR.CLUST KSDS have no legitimate processing to perform other than record retrieval with the primary key. In order to guarantee that no other types of processing will be performed, a PATH with a read only password is constructed directly over the KSDS. A master password is also coded to prohibit upward propagation of the read only password. Notice that it is meaningless to code UPDATE in this example. Both of the PRINT commands following the DEFINE PATH produce identical listings.

It is possible to create a KSDS to contain the same records as an existing KSDS except that, in the new KSDS, they are in order by alternate key value rather than by primary key value. Notice that this is not the same as processing the records in one data set in two different orders. Here, there are two distinct data sets, and each is ordered on its own primary key. The concept described here should be carefully thought through.

Example 10.   Use IDCAMS commands to create a KSDS to contain exactly the same records as the existing data set KSDS.PRIMARY.KEY.CLUSTER. The new data set should use the 10-byte field beginning at byte 25 as the primary key. This field is an existing alternate key with unique values. A path over the existing KSDS using the alternate key is used to simplify processing. Finally, the PRINT command is used to produce a list of the records in order by alternate key value in the old KSDS and by primary key value in the new KSDS.

Using Alternate Keys in Application Programs

One additional extremely important alternate index topic remains to be discussed. This is the use of alternate keys in an application program, most commonly COBOL. This topic is deferred to the chapters where application programming is discussed. Chapter 9 discusses alternate key processing with COBOL and numerous examples are used to clarify the discussion.

Example 11.   The LISTCAT command is used to print all the information contained in the cluster component of the alternate index constructed over the base cluster, which was examined in chapters 2 and 7. Most of the information is the same as that provided with a LISTCAT of a KSDS. See chapter 7 for more information on reading and understanding LISTCAT printouts. The actual IDCAMS command used was LISTCAT ENTRIES ( ) ALL.

Exercises

1. For each of the data set combinations listed in Table 8.11, describe the details of the alternate index structure and discuss the programming techniques required to process the records in the base data set through such an alternate index. The data set organizations for the base cluster and associated alternate index pairs are grouped into categories in the left-most

column in Table 8.11. For each row entry in the table, specifically describe how the alternate index is initially constructed and how it will be used to support the complete spectrum of processing performed during a standard, random master file update.

A more ambitious project would be to expand the scope to a dynamic update. For some of the entries, it is sufficient to note that most or all of the details of alternate index processing will be routinely performed by VSAM/IDCAMS. For other entries, an application program, utilities (IDCAMS, IEB/IEH, DFSORT), or both must be used to perform the equivalent of the DEFINE ALTERNATEINDEX, BLDINDEX, and DEFINE PATH commands.

For each table entry, identify and discuss potential problems caused by duplicate alternate key values. Discuss any additional problems that could occur if all application programming is done in COBOL. Some entries might be impossible to implement in COBOL; other entries are virtually impossible under almost all conditions.

2. The six records in the data set described in Table 8.2 are to be updated. The base cluster is a KSDS, and an alternate index and path over it have been constructed by IDCAMS using DEFINE AIX, BLDINDEX, and DEFINE PATH. Describe all of the basic details required to perform the processing functions listed in a. through j.

TABLE 8.11 Potential Base Data Sets and Alternate Index Structures.

General Processing Category	Base Cluster Data Set Organization	Alternate Index Data Set Organization	VSAM PATH Available
VSAM(Base) and VSAM(AIX)	KSDS	VSAM Alternate Index	Yes
	ESDS	VSAM Alternate Index	Yes
	KSDS	VSAM Alternate Index	No
	RRDS	VSAM Alternate Index	Yes
	RRDS	KSDS	No
	Alternate Index	VSAM Alternate Index	No
	KSDS	RRDS	No
VSAM(Base) and Non—VSAM (AIX)	ESDS	ISAM	
	KSDS	ISAM	
	KSDS	QSAM	
	KSDS	Relative	
Non—VSAM (Base) and Non—VSAM (AIX)	ISAM	ISAM	
	ISAM	ISAM Alternate Index	
	ISAM	Relative	
	ISAM	Direct	
	Relative	ISAM	
	Relative	Relative	
*VSAM(AIX)	ISAM	KSDS	No

Assume UPGRADE and UPDATE have been coded. All operations using DEFINE AIX, BLDINDEX, and DEFINE PATH are performed successfully on the base cluster:

 a. Add a record. No existing records have the same alternate key value as the new record.
 b. Add a record. One or more existing records have the same alternate key value as the new record.
 c. Delete a record. No other existing records have the same alternate key value as the record to be deleted.
 d. Delete a record. One or more existing records have the same alternate key value as the record to be deleted.
 e. Rewrite a record. No key field values are to be changed. No other existing records have the same alternate key value as the record to be modified.
 f. Rewrite a record. No key field values are to be changed. One or more existing records have the same alternate key value as the record to be modified.
 g. Rewrite a record. In the process, change the alternate key value. Discuss the required processing in four situations depending on whether the initial alternate key value is unique, and whether the value it is to be changed to already occurs in the alternate index. If multiple operations (Add, Delete, and Change) are required, specify the order in which they should be performed. For example, a modification is to be implemented as an add and a delete operation. Suppose that neither NOUPGRADE or NOUPDATE is in effect when each of the preceding operations is performed. What occurs in each situation?
 h. Retrieve the records in the base data set in ascending order based on alternate key value.
 i. Retrieve the records in the base data set in descending order based on alternate key value.
 j. For each of the nine processing situations described here, what change will occur if the base KSDS is replaced by an ESDS?

3. Suppose an alternate index and a path have been created over a KSDS base cluster. Describe the output produced by each of the PRINT statements listed in Fig. 8.13. Identify the records printed and the format of the output. Five distinct groups of records are printed. Within a group, the individual records can be printed in a different order or be prefaced with a different type of identifier (RBA, prime key, alternate key, etc.).

 After discussing alternate indexes over an ESDS in chapter 10, reclassify the output produced by the nine PRINT commands, assuming the base cluster is an ESDS.

4. What are the probable reasons why VSAM uses a variable-spanned blocked record format with the logical records in an alternate index data compo-

```
PRINT INDATASET(base cluster KSDS)
PRINT INDATASET(data component of the base cluster)
PRINT INDATASET(index component of the base cluster)
PRINT INDATASET(alternate index cluster)
PRINT INDATASET(data component of the alternate index)
PRINT INDATASET(index component of the alternate index)
PRINT INDATASET(path)
PRINT INDATASET(data component of the path)
PRINT INDATASET(index component of the path)
```

Figure 8.13 All possible printed reports for a KSDS and AIX.

nent? Recall that, if SPANNED is coded in the DEFINE CLUSTER command, a variable spanned unblocked record format is used with a KSDS and an ESDS. Why is SPANNED not an optional parameter with the DEFINE ALTERNATEINDEX command?

5. For a VSAM KSDS with an alternate index constructed over it, what is the maximum number of logical records, which can contain the same alternate key value? Why is this particular value used as the upper limit? Does the answer change if the base cluster is an ESDS? Describe a situation where VSAM will permit less than 500 base records to contain the same alternate key value. Hint: Control area size and key length are important factors. What is the minimal number of records that can contain the same alternate key value where one more will cause an error?

6. Is it possible that the same load module code is used by VSAM with both the REPRO command and the BLDINDEX command to load the sorted key pairs into the alternate index? Present a justification for your answer.

7. Examples 1 and 2 describe using two indexed and two relative data sets respectively as the base and alternate index data sets. What structural changes will occur if the data sets are replaced by their VSAM equivalent. For example, two KSDSs (neither a true alternate index) in Example 1 and two RRDSs in Example 2.

8. Each record in an alternate index begins with 5 bytes of control information. Classify each of these bytes as containing data that is either constant or variable for the life of the alternate index. For those bytes whose contents can be changed, describe the manner in which the value can be changed. Can ALTER be used to effect any of the changes?

9. Construct an experiment to determine if the order of the primary key values in an alternate index data record are reordered during a control interval or control area split. For a control interval split, this will involve three basic steps:

    1. Building a record in the alternate index where the primary key values do not occur in ascending logical order.
    2. Causing a control interval split to occur in the alternate index.
    3. Examining the same logical record before and after the split.

10. Describe a base data set and its corresponding alternate index where the data component of the alternate index is larger than the data component of the base cluster. How much bigger can the alternate index data component ever be? What is the relationship in the sizes of the index components for the two data sets? How much bigger can the alternate index component ever be than its corresponding index component in the base cluster? Can the same data set satisfy both criteria, i.e., the alternate index data and index components are both larger than their corresponding components in the base cluster.

11. Use BLDINDEX to perform an external sort while loading an alternate index. Examine the two work files following the completion of the BLDINDEX command.

12. A university administrator wants to create a "database" where student records can be retrieved using almost any field within the records as a key, including name, address, city, state, zip, age, classification, major, courses taken, and grades. You have been asked to implement this system. Identify significant limitations that must be considered. There are 25,000 student records.

13. Export an alternate index to tape. Identify any structural distinctions between an exported KSDS and an exported alternate index.

14. Identify all structural differences between an alternate index and a true KSDS.

9

Processing VSAM Data Sets in a COBOL Application Program

Chapters 3 through 7 in Part 2 and chapter 8 in Part 3 describe how the IDCAMS utility can be used to perform a wide range of processing with a VSAM data set. However, most IDCAMS commands affect the status of the entire data set. Only a few IDCAMS commands allow just some of the individual logical records to be processed. Even these commands, such as REPRO and PRINT, have very limited capabilities for identifying specific records.

In order to process individual records within a VSAM data set and perform the complete range of available I/O operations, an application program must be used. The three major languages—COBOL, PL/I, and assembler—can all perform a wide range of VSAM I/O operations, but because COBOL is the most heavily used language, processing a VSAM data set in a COBOL program is emphasized throughout Part 3. Only a very small percentage of VSAM data set processing is performed in PL/I or assembler programs.

Unfortunately, COBOL also has the most limited processing capabilities of the three languages. Hence, numerous important VSAM features that are available in PL/I and assembler have still not been implemented in COBOL. More than likely, most of the missing features will eventually become available with COBOL. Even COBOL II does not support many of these features. These missing features are listed and described in a later section in this chapter. Most of them are available with a COBOL program that uses Command Level CICS, which is discussed in chapter 16.

Until 1985, there was but one COBOL available on large IBM computer systems. In 1985, a dramatically revised COBOL was released. It is called COBOL II or NEW COBOL. Hence, the existing COBOL became "OLD" COBOL. A later section in this chapter identifies the distinctions between the two

COBOLs with regards to processing VSAM data sets. Unless specifically qualified, all material in this chapter applies to OLD and NEW COBOL.

This chapter is divided into seven major topics. The first four topics examine those portions of a COBOL program that relate to processing VSAM data sets: the SELECT statement, the FD statement, exceptional conditions and error processing, and the actual I/O operations that can be performed. Next standard KSDS processing situations are described. Following this, significant VSAM features not available with COBOL are discussed. Finally, several very lengthy and comprehensive examples are given.

COBOL VSAM Processing

There are four major parts of a COBOL program that affect the processing of a VSAM data set. A general overview of the role of each of these four parts is given in Table 9.1. The remaining portions of a COBOL program are the same whether processing a VSAM or a non-VSAM data set.

There is a fundamental distinction between processing VSAM and non-VSAM data sets. It is extremely rare that a VSAM-related problem will cause a COBOL program to abend, even though a comparable situation with a non-VSAM data set will result in an abend. Throughout this chapter, the major emphasis is on using a COBOL application program to process a KSDS. Although an ESDS and RRDS are briefly discussed in several places in this chapter and the detailed syntax of their I/O statements is included here, these two types of data sets are examined in complete detail in chapters 10 and 11 respectively. Various coding examples illustrating fundamental processing in COBOL programs are given in both chapters. Finally, additional information on the material discussed in this chapter can be found in IBM manuals (4), (5), and (6).

The SELECT Statement

The SELECT statement for a VSAM data set usually contains a large number of clauses, some of which cannot be coded with a non-VSAM data set. All of the allowable SELECT statement clauses are shown in Fig. 9.1. Other than the SELECT clause itself, the clauses can be coded in any order. The RECORD KEY and ALTERNATE KEY clauses can have subordinate clauses associated with them. These are the PASSWORD clause with both RECORD KEY and ALTERNATE KEY and WITH DUPLICATES with the ALTERNATE KEY only. PASSWORD and WITH DUPLICATES can be coded in any order. The ALTERNATE KEY clause cannot be coded with an ESDS or RRDS.

The basic functions of the SELECT statement are the same with both VSAM and non-VSAM data sets. SELECT identifies the connection between the COBOL file description (FD) coded with file-name and the DD statement coded with DDname, which identifies the actual name of the data set. The SELECT

TABLE 9.1   COBOL Program Portions Involving VSAM Processing.

Part of Program	General Description of VSAM Related Processing
SELECT Statement	This statement specifies the most important properties of the data set. It also identifies various related fields in the WORKING-STORAGE and/or LINKAGE SECTIONs and one or more DD statements in the accompanying JCL for the job step. Two additional VSAM data set entries can be coded in the I-O-CONTROL SECTION and are described in a separate topic in this chapter following the SELECT statement.
FD and 01 Statements	The FD provides the VSAM equivalent of some of the DCB values specified with a non-VSAM data set. The 01 level information describes the fields in the logical records in the VSAM data set.
Exception Processing and Error Detection	Detecting and handling errors and exceptional conditions, along with program debugging techniques are exceedingly important notions when processing VSAM data sets. The major topics in this category are VSAM status codes, the role of the DECLARATIVES SECTION with VSAM I/O operations, the AT END clause, the INVALID KEY clause, and a transaction log of every I/O operation involving a VSAM data set. The available information is substantially increased with COBOL II.
I/O Verbs	Eight statements are available to perform I/O operations with a VSAM KSDS and RRDS: OPEN, CLOSE, READ(random), READ NEXT(sequential), WRITE(random or sequential), REWRITE(random or sequential), DELETE(random or sequential), and START (random). READ(random), WRITE(random), REWRITE(random), DELETE, and START cannot be used with an ESDS. The Conceptual Record Pointer (CRP) is available with a KSDS and RRDS when sequential and random processing are mixed together. Identifying the key of reference is an essential notion with a KSDS which allows processing through an alternate index. Generic processing can be performed using the START statement with a KSDS or RRDS. Here, generic means that only part of a key field value or relative record number is specified.

statement classifies the data set as either non-VSAM or VSAM, and also identifies the specific data set organization within each class. It also identifies:

- The key field(s).
- Passwords.
- The type of processing to be performed.
- Buffer information.
- The name of the field that will contain the status codes.

The file-name is the COBOL FD structure used to process the records in the VSAM data set. There is nothing coded within the FD itself that explicitly (or implicitly) duplicates the information provided by the SELECT statement.

```
            SELECT Statement Syntax for KSDS and RRDS

SELECT file-name
      ASSIGN TO DDname              (//DDname DD DSN=Cluster Name)
      ORGANIZATION IS data-set-organization
      ACCESS IS type-of-access
      RECORD KEY IS record-key-field (KSDS only)
           PASSWORD IS password1-field
  or RELATIVE KEY IS relative-key-field (RRDS only)
           PASSWORD IS password1-field
      FILE STATUS IS status-code-field
      RESERVE integer AREAS
      ALTERNATE KEY IS alternate-key-field (KSDS only)
           WITH DUPLICATES
           PASSWORD IS password2-field
      . . .
      (Multiple ALTERNATE KEY clauses are allowed with a KSDS.
      Each may contain WITH DUPLICATES, PASSWORD, or both.)

I-O-CONTROL.
      RERUN ON DDname EVERY n RECORDS OF file-name
      SAME (RECORD) AREA FOR file-name, file-name2, ...

            SELECT Statement Syntax for ESDS

SELECT file-name
      ASSIGN TO AS-DDname           (//DDname DD DSN=Cluster Name)
      The default data-set-organization is SEQUENTIAL
      The default type-of-access is SEQUENTIAL
      RECORD KEY is not coded with an ESDS
      RELATIVE KEY is not coded with an ESDS
      However, PASSWORD is the same as with a KSDS and RRDS
      FILE STATUS is the same as with a KSDS and RRDS
      RESERVE is syntactically the same as with a KSDS and RRDS
      ALTERNATE KEY is not coded with an ESDS

I-O-CONTROL clauses are the same as with a KSDS and RRDS
```

Figure 9.1 The SELECT statement for a VSAM data set.

SELECT Statement Clauses

The ASSIGN clause

The syntax of the ASSIGN clause is much simpler than when coded with a non-VSAM data set. With a KSDS or RRDS, only the DDname should be coded. Recall that ASSIGN TO DA-I-DDname is coded with an ISAM data set, and with a sequential data set, ASSIGN TO UT-S-DDname is coded. Device type (DA, UT, UR, etc.) and data set organization (I, S, etc.) are not identified with the ASSIGN clause. A VSAM data set organization is specified in the ORGANIZATION IS clause. The device type is always direct access. Note that the SELECT statement for an ESDS specifies ASSIGN TO AS-DDname. If the AS- is not included (a very common occurrence), an S213 abend might occur when attempting to open the data set.

There must be an accompanying DD statement with the DDname value coded in the JCL with the step in which the program is executed. It must contain, at a minimum, the DSN and DISP parameters:

//DDname DD DSN = cluster-name,DISP = SHR or DISP = OLD

Because the VSAM data set already exists and is cataloged, a bare minimum of JCL is needed. Most frequently, when processing a VSAM data set, only DSN and DISP parameters are necessary on the DD statement. Occasionally, the AMP parameter must also be coded. This is discussed in chapter 13, along with additional information concerning the DD parameters that can be coded with a VSAM data set.

The ORGANIZATION clause

The ORGANIZATION clause identifies the type of VSAM data set. INDEXED, RELATIVE, and SEQUENTIAL are coded to identify a KSDS, RRDS, and ESDS respectively. The default is SEQUENTIAL. When the ORGANIZATION clause is coded for a file, the COBOL compiler interprets it as a VSAM data set. Hence, the ORGANIZATION clause should not be coded with a non-VSAM data set.

The ACCESS clause

The ACCESS clause specifies one of three methods, SEQUENTIAL, RANDOM, or DYNAMIC. COBOL permits only SEQUENTIAL access with an ESDS. Both a KSDS and an RRDS permit all three types of access. SEQUENTIAL and RANDOM access have the same basic meaning whether processing VSAM or non-VSAM data sets.

With SEQUENTIAL access, the records in the data set are processed in order beginning with the first record in the data set or the last record when extending the data set or reading backwards. Within the SELECT statement, SEQUENTIAL is used in two different contexts. The word SEQUENTIAL identifies the method of processing with the ACCESS clause and the data set organization with the ORGANIZATION clause.

RANDOM access allows any individual record in the data set to be processed without processing the records that precede it. DYNAMIC access permits a COBOL program to process a VSAM data set both sequentially and randomly using just one SELECT and one FD statement. The application program can switch back and forth between the two methods of access.

In order to process a non-VSAM data set both sequentially and randomly in the same program, it is necessary to code two SELECT and two FD statements Furthermore, with a non-VSAM data set, the processing of the two separate files must be carefully coordinated. Example 1 describes the basic manner in which dynamic processing is performed.

Example 1.   As shown in Fig. 9.2, two control intervals contain 5 and 3 logical records respectively. The numeric value within each rectangle is the record key. When DYNAMIC access is used, a wide range of operations can be performed with a single file (FD).

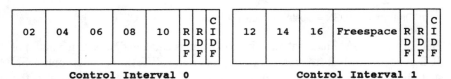

Figure 9.2   Eight logical records in two control intervals.

The record with a key value of 14 is to be randomly retrieved. The second control interval is copied into one of the application program's buffers. Following this, the fields in the 01-level contain the data in the seventh logical record. The next I/O operation is to randomly retrieve the record with a key value of 04. After the first control interval is read into a buffer, the second logical record can then be processed in the 01-level.

Following this, sequential processing is performed. A READ NEXT operation retrieves the record with a key value of 06 which is the next record in logical order. A second sequential READ NEXT operation retrieves the record with a key value of 08. Following this, random processing can be immediately resumed, and a record with a key value of 15 is added to the data set as the third record in the second control interval. A subsequent READ NEXT operation then retrieves the record with a key value of 10—the next record following the last one read sequentially. In other words, sequential processing is resumed at the point where it was last performed.

One required overhead because of the flexibility of a VSAM data set is the requirement that a READ statement specify whether an operation is sequential or random. With DYNAMIC access, the WRITE statement always specifies a random operation. There are, however, additional system overheads associated with dynamic processing. Hence, if the I/O operations in a program for a data set will be either all sequential or all random, there is no reason to request dynamic processing. In this case, either sequential or random access should be specified. This reduces the use of system resources and simplifies programming logic.

The RECORD KEY and RELATIVE KEY clauses

With a KSDS, the RECORD KEY clause identifies the field in the logical record that is used as the primary key. RECORD KEY is replaced by a RELATIVE KEY clause with an RRDS, and no KEY clause is coded with an ESDS. In a batch COBOL program, the RECORD KEY field must be contained within the first (or only) 01 structure under the associated FD and must be either a group or an elementary item. Unlike processing an ISAM data set, there is no NOMINAL KEY field used with a KSDS.

The RECORD KEY field can be any COBOL data type(s) and can be as large as 256 bytes. VSAM treats the key value as a pure hexadecimal number. A RELATIVE KEY clause must identify a PIC S9(8) COMP field not contained in any 01 structure coded with the FD.

When the program opens a KSDS, the length and the offset of the RECORD KEY field in the 01 structure are compared with the two KEYS subparameter values that are stored in the cluster component. If either cluster subparameter contains a different value than the comparable value in the COBOL program, the KSDS cannot be processed. In this case, a status code of 95 is returned following the open, and no further processing is performed.

Any COBOL data type is considered valid by IDCAMS. Although an incorrect data type will allow the KSDS to be opened successfully, most I/O operations will produce incorrect results. The information supplied from a COBOL program (SELECT and FD) must be consistent with the corresponding values stored in the data set's cluster component. Just as with ISAM, the values placed in the record's key field must be unique. Otherwise, VSAM detects an exceptional condition. Likewise, when sequentially writing records to a KSDS or RRDS, the records must be added in ascending order based on key values or relative record numbers.

The PASSWORD clause

The PASSWORD clause provides a low level of protection for a VSAM data set. The PASSWORD clause applies to all processing that uses the primary key with a KSDS or the relative key with an RRDS. An application program processing a VSAM data set must supply an appropriate password value that matches a value stored in the data set's cluster component.

DEFINE CLUSTER and/or ALTER can be used to assign passwords to a VSAM data set. When the data set is opened, the COBOL data name coded with the PASSWORD clause must contain one of the four actual password values. Only one of the four password levels can be specified in a COBOL program with the primary key, and it determines the type of file processing permitted.

Recall that each level of password protection allows different types of operations to be performed with the records in a data set. The CONTROLPW value is not supported with a COBOL program, and the full power of the MASTERPW value is not accessible. Each alternate key allows one additional password to be specified. Currently, a literal cannot be coded with the PASSWORD clause. If the system is protected by RACF or a comparable security package, the password value might be ignored.

The FILE STATUS clause

The FILE STATUS clause identifies a 2-byte field in the program, where VSAM places a status code following every I/O operation involving the data set. This field is usually coded in the WORKING-STORAGE SECTION. However, it can also be coded in the LINKAGE or FILE-CONTROL SECTION. It is defined as PIC 99 or PIC XX. After every I/O operation, the value in the status code field should be checked.

An unsuccessful VSAM I/O operation almost never causes a program to abend. Rather, VSAM places a nonzero numeric character value in the status code field that identifies why the operation could not be successfully performed. It is then the responsibility of the application programmer to examine the status code values. If this is not done, major problems might go undetected. A COBOL program can execute and return a condition code of zero for the job step even though none of the requested VSAM I/O operations were successfully performed.

Suppose some of the information in a COBOL program that describes a VSAM data set disagrees with one or more values coded in the DEFINE CLUSTER command when the cluster was created. This could be a result of several causes:

- A key is specified in a different record location in each place
- The key lengths are different in each place.
- Alternate keys are identified as unique in one of the two places and nonunique in the other.
- The maximum logical record sizes disagree.
- The data set organizations are different.

In these situations, a status code of 92 or 95 results when the data set is opened or an attempt is made to process a record. After either of these status code values appear, VSAM appears to execute every requested I/O operation. In reality, however, most or all of the I/O operations are not performed. In fact, a program detects that when an open operation produced a status code of 92 or 95, it is usually best to skip all additional processing with the data set.

The RESERVE clause

The RESERVE clause specifies that "integer" additional buffers are to be allocated for processing the records in a data set. With VSAM, the RESERVE clause is meaningful only with an ESDS and a KSDS that is to be processed sequentially. In addition to the two default buffers that are provided, 1 to 254 additional buffers can be specified. The RESERVE clause is ignored with an RRDS, where only 1 buffer is provided. Other methods for requesting buffer space are discussed in chapter 13, as well as the importance of sufficient buffers in chapter 17.

SELECT statement clauses for KSDS
alternate key processing

Alternate indexes and secondary keys tremendously expand the number of ways in which records can be easily retrieved from a VSAM data set. This is one of the most significant differences between VSAM and non-VSAM data set

```
        SELECT STUDENT-RECORD-FILE
            ...
            RECORD KEY IS SS-NUM
            ALTERNATE KEY IS LAST-NAME
                PASSWORD IS SECRET
                WITH DUPLICATES
            ALTERNATE KEY IS EMPLOYEE-NUM
            ALTERNATE KEY IS SEX-CODE
                WITH DUPLICATES
            ...

01  STUDENT-RECORD-FILE.
    05  LAST-NAME              PIC 9(9).   First Alternate Key
    05  SS-NUM                 PIC X(14).  Primary Key
    05  non-key fields         PIC ...
    05  SEX-CODE               PIC X.      Second Alternate Key
    05  more non-key fields    PIC ...
    05  EMPLOYEE-NUM           PIC 9(6).   Third Alternate Key
```

Figure 9.3 SELECT statement and 01 structure used to process a KSDS.

organizations. VSAM supports simplified data base processing from within a COBOL application program. The same end results can usually be achieved in a non-VSAM environment as well. However, with VSAM, it is considerably simpler. Chapter 8 is devoted entirely to alternate indexes and related processing exclusive of the coding details within a COBOL application program.

Example 2 shows the relationship among the fields in a logical record and the primary and alternate keys identified in the SELECT statement. The WITH DUPLICATES and PASSWORD clauses can be used to qualify the ALTERNATE KEY clause.

Example 2.   A COBOL program is processing logical records that contain the fields identified in the next paragraph. The records are contained in a KSDS, over which three alternate indexes have been constructed. The RECORD KEY and ALTERNATE KEY clauses in the SELECT statement in Fig. 9.3 identify the four key fields contained in the 01 level. The four key fields can be located in any order within the 01-structure and the results will remain the same.

Because of the SELECT statement and underlying alternate index structures, a record in the KSDS can be retrieved using either the SS-NUM, LAST-NAME, EMPLOYEE-NUM, or SEX-CODE field as the key. Records can be retrieved either sequentially or randomly with any of the four keys. There can be only one RECORD KEY clause and its key values must be unique. However, up to 255 additional alternate keys can be specified. The KEY clauses can be coded in any order.

WITH DUPLICATES clause.   A particular alternate key field within the data set might permit the same value to occur in two or more records. If an alternate key allows duplicate values, the clause WITH DUPLICATES should be coded in the SELECT statement. The equivalent information should also be stored in the cluster component of the alternate index. This requires coding NONUNIQUEKEY with the DEFINE ALTERNATEINDEX and/or ALTER command.

To illustrate, suppose the SEX-CODE field contains only two valid values: M and F. If an I/O command is executed to randomly retrieve a record with SEX-CODE = 'F', the first female record in the data set is read. A following sequential READ NEXT operation will retrieve the second record with 'F' in the SEX-CODE field. As each record is read, a status code value is returned specifying whether there are additional records with the same alternate key value. When the final record with a key of 'F' is read, the returned status code identifies it as the last record with that particular alternate key value.

In some processing situations, complications can occur when duplicates exist on two or more alternate keys at the same time. The single status code field identifies the existence of duplicates for all of the alternate keys listed in the SELECT statement. The specific alternate key cannot be determined, and the status code by itself is not enough to drive the program logic. There is no relationship between the order in which the ALTERNATE KEY clauses in the SELECT statement are coded and the fields they reference in the 01 record description in the FD.

Each ALTERNATE KEY clause requires one additional DD statement, and the order in which the ALTERNATE KEY clauses are coded determines the DDname on their accompanying DD statements. DD statements can be coded in any order. The relationship between DDnames and alternate index processing in a COBOL program is further discussed in the next section.

Passwords can be used specifically for alternate key access. Access through an alternate key is permitted only if the password associated with the particular key is coded. This is a password value associated with the path, not an alternate index password. Hence, some users might not be permitted all of the possible accesses to the records in a KSDS. In many situations, only record retrieval is permitted using an alternate key. In fact, it is quite common to permit only record retrieval through an alternate key.

Example 3.   The SELECT statement and its referenced WORKING-STORAGE values used to process a KSDS are shown in Fig. 9.4. The same four key fields are used as in the previous example. The accompanying FD entry is shown in Example 4. The value in ALPHA contains the update password, and the SECRET value allows read only processing.

DD statements for alternate key processing with COBOL

In a COBOL application program, each alternate key used to process a KSDS requires one additional DD statement, which identifies the name of the path. The DDname coded for the path must be a concatenation of (1) the value coded on the ASSIGN clause for the FD associated with the base cluster and (2) an

```
       SELECT STUDENT-RECORD-FILE
           ASSIGN TO MASTER
           ORGANIZATION IS INDEXED
           ACCESS IS DYNAMIC
           RECORD KEY IS SS-NUM
               PASSWORD IS ALPHA
           FILE STATUS IS STATUS-CODE
           ALTERNATE KEY IS LAST-NAME
               PASSWORD IS SECRET
               WITH DUPLICATES
           ALTERNATE KEY IS EMPLOYEE-NUM
           ALTERNATE KEY IS SEX-CODE
               WITH DUPLICATES.

WORKING-STORAGE SECTION.

01  ALPHA                        PIC X(7) VALUE 'BIZARRE'.
01  SECRET                       PIC X(8) VALUE 'AARDVARK'.
01  STATUS-CODE.
    05  GENERAL-CLASS            PIC 9.
    05  SPECIFIC-STATUS-VALUE    PIC 9.
```

Figure 9.4   SELECT statement and related WORKING-STORAGE fields.

unsigned integer. The integer must identify the relative position of the associated ALTERNATE KEY clause in the SELECT statement among the (possible) other ALTERNATE KEY clauses.

Example 4.   A VSAM KSDS has been created and loaded, and three alternate indexes and paths have been constructed over it. The paths allow processing on last name, sex code, and employee number, respectively. The relevant clauses in the COBOL SELECT statement are shown in Fig. 9.5 along with the four required DD statements referenced in the SELECT statement.

The JCL required with the base KSDS and three alternate indexes consists of four DD statements with DDnames of ABC, ABC1, ABC2, and ABC3. The four DD statements can be coded in any order within the job step and need not be adjacent. The DDname coded in the ASSIGN clause must identify the KSDS base cluster. The same DDname with the integer 1 concatenated to it must identify the path associated with the first ALTERNATE KEY clause coded in the SELECT statement. Likewise, the same DDname concatenated with the unsigned integer N must identify the path associated with the N-th ALTERNATE KEY clause coded in the SELECT statement. Up to 255 ALTERNATE KEY clauses can be coded in the SELECT statement.

JCL syntax does not permit a DDname to exceed eight characters. If the base cluster DDname is too long to allow the concatenation of additional integers, the right-most characters in the DDname should be truncated, and the concatenation then performed, yielding a name of exactly eight characters. For example, suppose the SELECT statement shown in Fig. 9.5 had contained the clause ASSIGN TO ABCDEFGH. The four DDnames in the JCL would then become ABCDEFGH, ABCDEFG1, ABCDEFG2, and ABCDEFG3. If a tenth or hundredth alter-

```
      SELECT STUDENT-RECORD-FILE
          ASSIGN TO ABC
          ORGANIZATION IS INDEXED
          ACCESS IS DYNAMIC
          FILE STATUS IS STATUS-CODE
          RECORD KEY IS SS-NUM (PRIMARY KEY)
          ALTERNATE KEY IS LAST-NAME (First Alternate Key)
              WITH DUPLICATES
              . . .
          ALTERNATE KEY IS SEX-CODE (Second Alternate Key)
              WITH DUPLICATES
              . . .
          ALTERNATE KEY IS EMPLOYEE-NUM (Third Alternate Key)

//ABC       DD   DSN=KSDS-Cluster-Name,DISP=OLD or SHR
//ABC1      DD   DSN=PATH-For-Last-Name,DISP=SHR
//ABC2      DD   DSN=PATH-For-Sex-Code,DISP=SHR
//ABC3      DD   DSN=PATH-For-Employee-Num,DISP=SHR
```

Figure 9.5 SELECT statement and associated DD statements required to process on a primary key and three alternate keys.

nate key was identified in the SELECT statement for processing over the base KSDS, their paths would be identified by DDnames of ABCDEF10 and ABCDE100 respectively. It is remotely possible that 10 or more alternate indexes might exist over the same base KSDS, although 100 or more will probably never occur.

Why are these rather strange and special rules necessary? The answer is primarily historic. The COBOL language is more than 10 years older than VSAM. The developers of COBOL did not allow provisions for the type of multiple key processing provided by VSAM. Hence, DDname and integer concatenation probably appeared to be an easy way to support the processing.

Another potential approach would be to code a separate SELECT for each alternate index even though each SELECT could identify the same FD. Although such an approach would involve some extra coding, any arbitrary values could be used as DDnames. PL/I and Assembler allow this method. Hence, to process the KSDS defined in the last example, four DECLARE DDname FILE statements would be needed with PL/I. Likewise, a Command Level CICS program written in any language allows an arbitrary DDname to identify the path over a KSDS. See chapter 16 for more details.

If the DDname identifying the path is not coded in the JCL for each alternate key specified in an application program, the following IEF message is printed in the JES log when the FD for the data set is opened: MISSING DDNAME ABC2. VSAM returns a status code of 96, and subsequent processing of the data set cannot occur.

Because COBOL does not presently allow an ESDS to be processed through an alternate index, special DDname conventions are not necessary with an ESDS. It will be interesting to see if a different set of rules are selected when alternate key processing for an ESDS is eventually supported in COBOL or, for that matter, for a KSDS.

The AIXBLD COBOL PARM option

It is possible to build an alternate index within an executing COBOL program. This is requested by specifying PARM = (AIXBLD,other PARM options) on the EXEC statement for the compile step. This causes the IDCAMS program to be dynamically invoked during the execution of the application program. Because the IDCAMS message data set must be opened, it is necessary to include a DD statement with a DDname of SYSPRINT during execution. The SYSPRINT DDname should not be used for any other purpose. Likewise, if an external sort must be performed while loading the alternate index, the work data sets IDCUT1 and IDCUT2 are needed.

Because of the size of the IDCAMS program, a much larger region is required to build the alternate index. Therefore, it is usually preferable to complete the IDCAMS processing before running the COBOL program that performs processing using the alternate index. However, there are some rare situations where AIXBLD can significantly improve processing efficiency.

I-O-CONTROL SECTION Parameters

The I-O-CONTROL SECTION parameters contain two clauses that can be coded with any type of VSAM data set. See Fig. 9.1. If checkpoints are to be written during processing, the RERUN clause is used. After n records in the VSAM data set have been processed, a checkpoint record is written to the data set named on the DD statement identified by DDname in the RERUN clause, not the VSAM data set itself, which is identified by file-name in the SELECT clause. In theory, a program that terminates prematurely can be restarted from a checkpoint at a later time.

The SAME AREA clause allows two files to share the same buffers. Like checkpoints, SAME AREA is a rarely used feature. It reduces the amount of storage required for buffers during program execution. It may also be coded as SAME RECORD AREA, and all files coded with the statement can be opened at the same time.

The FD statement and associated 01 level structure

Unlike the SELECT statement, which is substantially more complicated for a VSAM data set, the FD for a VSAM data set is simpler than the FD for a comparable non-VSAM data set. The only FD clauses that are commonly coded with a VSAM data set are LABEL RECORDS, RECORD CONTAINS, and DATA RECORD. There is no coding order among the FD clauses. Figure 9.6 illustrates a typical FD.

The logical record description is the same with both VSAM and non-VSAM data sets. Likewise, the LABEL RECORDS, RECORD CONTAINS, and DATA RECORDS clauses do not distinguish between VSAM and non-VSAM

```
FD   File-name-for-VSAM-data-set   (Matches SELECT name)
     LABEL RECORDS ARE STANDARD or OMITTED
     RECORD CONTAINS clause
     DATA RECORD clause.
01   Logical Record Description.
     05  ...
```

Figure 9.6 FD statement for VSAM processing.

data sets. The LABEL RECORDS clause is required, but it is treated as documentation. However, STANDARD is usually coded with a VSAM data set. The DATA RECORDS clause is optional and identifies the OI record descriptions associated with the FD. Both LABEL RECORDS and DATA RECORDS are rumored to be dropped in the next release of COBOL.

The RECORD CONTAINS clause is optional and is coded for two reasons: documentation and programmer confirmation of logical record size. With any type of variable-length records, the overhead bytes are not included with the values in the RECORD CONTAINS clause. Hence, RECORD CONTAINS x to y CHARACTERS identifies the range of actual data bytes.

Neither a BLOCK CONTAINS nor a RECORDING MODE clause is ordinarily coded with a VSAM data set. The BLOCK CONTAINS clause is meaningless with VSAM because control intervals are used rather than blocks. In addition, the data set always exists before processing begins, and the control interval size is stored in the cluster component. For non-VSAM data sets, BLOCK CONTAINS 0 RECORDS is coded to retrieve the BLKSIZE value from the data set labels or JCL. It's treated as documentation with a VSAM data set.

The RECORDING MODE clause is unnecessary because every KSDS and ESDS has a variable-length record format. The spanned/non-spanned indicator is stored in the cluster component. All records in an RRDS are fixed length. If FD values conflict with cluster component information, the data set cannot be opened successfully.

```
FD   STUDENT-RECORD-FILE
     RECORD CONTAINS 32 TO 87 CHARACTERS
     LABEL RECORDS ARE STANDARD
     DATA RECORDS ARE STUDENT-RECORD, FIXED-PART-OF-RECORD.
01   STUDENT-RECORD.
     05   LAST-NAME            PIC 9(9).
     05   SS-NUM               PIC X(14).
     05   SEX-CODE             PIC X.
     05   EMPLOYEE-NUM         PIC X(6).
     05   NO-OF-BILLS          PIC S9(2) COMP-3.
     05   BILLS                OCCURS 0 TO 11 TIMES
                               DEPENDING ON NO-OF-BILLS
                               PIC 9(3)V99.
01   FIXED-PART-OF-RECORD     PIC X(32).
```

Figure 9.7 FD and 01 statements for VSAM processing.

TABLE 9.2   Significant Error and Exception-Handling Techniques.

Error or Exceptional Related Topic	Role with VSAM Data Sets	Role with Non-VSAM Data Sets
VSAM File Status Codes	A wide range of values deal with the standard processing situations.	A limited group of values are used with QSAM data sets only.
AT END and INVALID KEY	Can be used in addition to the file status codes.	Heavily used for basic processing situations.
DECLARATIVES SECTION Processing	Available with all types of VSAM data sets and all types of processing.	A somewhat more limited processing range is supported.
Printed Exception Report	Status code values of 21, 22, and 23 generate exception report entries.	Same basic report as with VSAM; but generated by INVALID KEY entries.
Log of I/O Operations	Monitor I/O operations and their outcome.	Infrequently used because abends occur during comparable processing.

Example 5. The complete FD and 01 level referenced in the previous examples is shown in Fig. 9.7.

Error Detection and Error Handling in a COBOL Program

It might seem surprising that error detection and error handling are one of the four major components of a COBOL program related to VSAM processing. With non-VSAM data sets, not nearly as much importance is attached to this topic. Five significant subtopics are examined here. The role of each topic with VSAM and non-VSAM data sets is summarized in Table 9.2. Extended 6-byte file status codes are now available with COBOL II.

VSAM file status codes

The most important aspects of error handling with a VSAM data set involve the status codes returned after every I/O operation. As mentioned previously, these codes should be examined following every I/O operation. It is absolutely essential to realize that a nonzero status code for an I/O operation specifies an error or exception condition.

If status codes are not examined, the programmer might assume that the program worked perfectly when, in actuality, no VSAM I/O was performed. The *COBOL Programmer's Guide* summarized it this way:

> If status codes are not examined after every I/O operation and the program itself does not abend, the programmer may be unaware of serious problems which occur while processing the VSAM data set. An abend always warns the programmer of major problems.

Almost every production program that uses VSAM data sets maintains a log of the (nonzero) status codes associated with every I/O operation. It is a matter of personal preference as to whether each file has its own individual status code field or whether several files share the same field. The single threaded nature of batch COBOL guarantees that only one I/O operation is outstanding at any time.

The complete list of possible status codes produced by an executing COBOL program, along with the most common reasons why they are generated, is given in Table 9.3. Some status codes will cause an accompanying IDC or IEC message to print in the JES log or with the allocation messages. Note that the status code values decompose into two, single-digit numbers. The left-most digit denotes the general "category" to which the value belongs.

For example, a status code beginning with a 2 corresponds to an INVALID KEY condition with non-VSAM data sets (ISAM, Relative, and Direct), and a status code beginning with a 9 denotes a serious error. The right-most digit gives the specific meaning within the "category." Therefore, the status code field is occasionally represented as a group item as illustrated in Fig. 9.4 in Example 3.

Note in Table 9.3 that, in several cases, the second digit also identifies a specific condition. Status codes of 24 and 34 denote an out-of-space condition during an output operation. If the logical end of the data set is exceeded during a sequential input operation (read past end of file), a status code of 94 results.

The 02 and 22 status codes identify records that contain duplicate keys. A status code of 22 specifies a duplicate primary key or relative record number. A status code of 02 following a READ operation means there are additional records with the same alternate key value. A value of 02 is provided until the final record with the alternate key value is processed.

When the last record is read, a status code of 00 might be generated. A status code of 02 following a WRITE operation means the record was successfully added to the data set and had an alternate key that matched the key of an existing data set record. All status codes whose second digit is a 0 identify a "catch-all" entry for the general category identified by the first digit.

Program logic can be written to utilize the values returned in the status code field in a variety of ways. For example, when sequentially processing a data set, a status code of 10 results when the end of the data set has been detected on a READ operation. An IF statement or a PERFORM statement can be written to use the status code value to terminate processing input records in several ways, two of which are shown here:

```
PERFORM TRANSACTION-LOOP UNTIL TRANS-STATUS-CODE = 10 or
IF TRANS-STATUS-CODE = 10 THEN ...
```

When randomly adding, deleting, and updating records in a KSDS or RRDS, status codes of 22 and 23 denote a duplicate master record and a missing master record respectively. Often, the associated transaction records are to be written

TABLE 9.3   VSAM Status Codes Returned by COBOL Program.

Status Code- First Digit	General Classification	Status Code- Second Digit	Specific Meaning within the General Classification
0	Successful completion of the I/O operation	0 2	No further information. A duplicate key is found, and the alternate key in the application program contains the WITH DUPLICATES clause.
1	AT END (no more logical records) or an OPTIONAL file not available at OPEN time.	0	No further information.
2	Invalid key conditions. These (*) are similar to INVALID KEY conditions with an ISAM file. Several other errors fall into this category. 24 means out of space.	0 1* 2* 3* 4*	No further information. Sequence error. A duplicate key is found but duplicate keys are not allowed on either the primary or an alternate key. (Duplicate master condition.) No record found with this key. (Missing master condition.) Boundary violation on a WRITE to a KSDS or RRDS. No space is available to add the requested record. (With some effort, this can be overcome). A REWRITE with a KSDS can also cause this code.
3	Permanent error (data check, parity check, transmission error). Such errors rarely occur.	0 4	No further information. Boundary violation on a WRITE to an ESDS. This is similar to 24 above. There is no space to add the record.
9	Other errors. Most 9x errors are very serious and identify major problems with the applica- tion program. The 90 is an exception to this statement.	0 1 2 3 4 5 6 7	No further information. Some relatively 'obscure' errors fall into this category. Password failure. Logic error. Resource not available. No CRP for a sequential request. Invalid or incomplete file. No DD statement for the file. The data set was not properly closed; an implicit verify has therefore been issued, and the file then successfully opened.

to an exception report. Program logic can use the status code values to accomplish this:

```
IF MASTER-STATUS-CODE = 22 OR MASTER-STATUS-CODE = 23
   PERFORM EXCEPTION-ROUTINE-PROCESSING.
```

When loading records into a KSDS or RRDS, a status code of 21 identifies a record whose key or slot number respectively is out of order or duplicates a previously loaded value. Program logic can be used to generate a report of all such records:

```
WRITE NEW-MASTER-RECORD FROM WORKAREA-RECORD
IF MASTER-STATUS-CODE = 21 PERFORM BAD-INPUT-PROCESSING
```

AT END and INVALID KEY clauses

If the status code values are used in the manner illustrated in the previous section, it is not necessary to code AT END and INVALID KEY clauses when processing a VSAM data set. However, both clauses can still be coded as a supplement or an alternative to status codes. One reason for doing this is to display additional information whenever any of the relevant conditions occur. As mentioned before, the AT END condition is equivalent to a status code of 10. An INVALID KEY condition is equivalent to a status code of 21, 22, 23 or 24.

Using the DECLARATIVES SECTION

A DECLARATIVES SECTION can be coded in a COBOL program to handle errors and exceptional conditions that occur when processing VSAM data sets. This is done in much the same manner as when processing some types of non-VSAM data sets. Although the DECLARATIVES SECTION can be coded with non-VSAM and VSAM data sets alike, a wide range of status codes can be used only with VSAM data sets and a somewhat more limited range with sequential non-VSAM data sets.

Other types of processing can also be performed in the DECLARATIVES SECTION. The DECLARATIVES SECTION of the PROCEDURE DIVISION can be used when exceptional situations occur during I/O processing. If an error or exceptional condition occurs, control is transferred to the appropriate SECTION in the DECLARATIVES part of the PROCEDURE DIVISION. Figure 9.8 illustrates the overall format used to do this.

EXCEPTION and ERROR are equivalent and can be used interchangeably. Exactly one of INPUT, OUTPUT, I-O, or EXTEND can be coded for a file. However, any number of file (FD) names can be specified with USE AFTER.

VSAM I/O logs and exception reports

Exercise 11 at the end of this chapter describes a subroutine that can be used to produce a log containing all relevant information for VSAM I/O operations. A simpler log is used in most data processing environments. The importance of monitoring the outcome of VSAM I/O operations cannot be overstated. Likewise, exception reports are routinely generated with all types of processing.

```
PROCEDURE DIVISION.
DECLARATIVES.
Section-name1 SECTION.
      USE AFTER STANDARD ERROR or PROCEDURE ON INPUT      or
                         EXCEPTION              OUTPUT     or
                                                I-O        or
                                                EXTEND     or
                                                fd-name1,
                                                fd-name2...

      MOVE KSDS-REC TO EXCEPTION-REPORT.
      DISPLAY EXCEPTION-REPORT.
Section-name2 SECTION.
      . . .
      PERFORM UPDATE-EXCEPTION-STATISTICS
      . . .
END DECLARATIVES.
```

Figure 9.8 DECLARATIVES SECTION for VSAM I/O processing.

COBOL I/O Statements Available with VSAM Data Sets

Eight statements are available in a COBOL program to perform I/O operations with a VSAM data set. These eight statements are identified and their functions briefly described in Table 9.4. READ KEY is a special form of the READ statement, which is meaningful only when alternate key processing is to be performed. It is not a 9th statement type.

An Access Control Block (ACB) is constructed and used for processing a VSAM data set in somewhat the same manner that a data control block (DCB) is used with a non-VSAM data set. An overview of the contents of an ACB and other important VSAM control blocks, along with the details of processing, can be found in the IBM manual[2].

For each of the three VSAM data set organizations a detailed syntax analysis is presented that illustrates how the statements are coded. The final example in this chapter illustrates the range of I/O operations allowed with a KSDS. Chapter 10 and chapter 11 illustrate the comparable I/O operations available with an ESDS and RRDS respectively. Basically, the I/O statements can be categorized as associated with one or more of the three data set organizations and the type of accesses allowed with the data set organization, as illustrated in Table 9.5.

With both a KSDS and an RRDS, access can be sequential, random, or dynamic. Table 9.5 shows that, for both the KSDS and RRDS, dynamic access provides a combination of all statements available with either sequential or random access. Only sequential processing is permitted with an ESDS. Sequentially adding records to an ESDS and a KSDS requires either OUTPUT or EXTEND to be coded on the OPEN statement, depending on whether records are added at the front or back of the data set. EXTEND cannot be coded with an RRDS. When a KSDS or an RRDS is opened for I-O processing with ACCESS IS DYNAMIC, all six possible I/O operations are available.

TABLE 9.4 COBOL Statements Used to Process VSAM Data Sets.

I/O Verb	Basic Syntax Details	General Description
OPEN	OPEN INPUT file-name or OUTPUT file-name or I-O file-name Or EXTEND file-name	Prepare the data set for processing. When the data set is opened, all relevant information is combined.
CLOSE	CLOSE file-name	Finish processing. At this point, cluster control information is updated.
READ NEXT	READ NEXT file-name	A sequential read operation with a KSDS and an RRDS. NEXT is needed with dynamic access.
READ	READ file-name	A random read using the current key of reference with a KSDS and slot number with an RRDS. A sequential read operation with an ESDS.
READ KEY	READ file-name (KEY IS key-field)	A random KSDS read operation using either the primary key or an alternate key.
WRITE	WRITE record-name	Add a record to the data set. Random or sequential operation.
REWRITE	REWRITE record-name	Modify a record in a data set. Random or sequential operation.
DELETE	DELETE file-name	Physically delete one logical record from a KSDS or RRDS. Random or sequential operation.
START	START file-name (KEY IS key-field)	Establish position in data set. No record is read or written.

Notice in Table 9.5 that some variety is possible depending on the mode of access. With dynamic access, sequential processing requires that NEXT be coded with READ. With sequential access, NEXT is optional, but NEXT is explicitly prohibited with random access.

Detailed VSAM Statement Syntax

Table 9.6 contains the complete exact syntax of VSAM I/O statements. Capitalized words are COBOL-reserved words, and underlined words are required. Clauses within brackets are optional.

For each of these statements, COBOL II permits an end of scope delimiter clause to be coded. These are of the form END-READ, END-WRITE, END-DELETE, etc. No delimiters are shown in the examples here.

The conceptual record pointer (CRP)

The current (or conceptual) record pointer (CRP) is a major concept that must first be understood before examining the way in which the I/O statements are used to process the records in a VSAM data set. The CRP is used with all three types of VSAM data sets. It is most important with a KSDS accessed dynamically and least important with an ESDS. The CRP identifies the next record to be processed sequentially. Hence, the CRP is meaningless if ACCESS IS RAN-

TABLE 9.5 COBOL I/O Operations with the Three VSAM Data Sets.

	ESDS I/O Operations	KSDS I/O Operations	RRDS I/O Operations	Data Set Opened
Sequential Input Operations	READ	READ START	READ START	INPUT
Sequential Output Operations	WRITE	WRITE	WRITE (OUTPUT only)	OUTPUT or EXTEND
Sequential I-O Operations	READ REWRITE	READ [NEXT] START REWRITE DELETE	READ [NEXT] START REWRITE DELETE	I-O
Random Input Operations		READ	READ	INPUT
Random Output Operations		WRITE	WRITE	OUTPUT
Random I-O Operations		READ WRITE REWRITE DELETE	READ WRITE REWRITE DELETE	I-O
Dynamic Input Operations		READ READ NEXT START	READ READ NEXT START	INPUT
Dynamic Output Operations		WRITE	WRITE (OUTPUT only)	OUTPUT or EXTEND
Dynamic I-O Operations		READ READ NEXT START WRITE REWRITE DELETE	READ READ NEXT START WRITE REWRITE DELETE	I-O

TABLE 9.6   Syntax for VSAM Processing Statements.

```
                    Statement                          Data Set

              Sequential READ Statement

READ file-name {NEXT} RECORD {INTO identifier}
     {AT END imperative statement}
     For dynamic access with a KSDS and RRDS,
        NEXT is required.

Random READ Statement

READ file-name RECORD {INTO identifier}
     {KEY IS data-name}                        <—KSDS only
     {INVALID KEY imperative-statement}         <—KSDS and RRDS only

START Statement:

START file-name                                <—KSDS and RRDS only
     {KEY IS EQUAL TO {    }      data-name}         or
     {KEY IS GREATER THAN         data-name}         or
     {KEY IS NOT LESS THAN        data-name}         or
     {INVALID KEY imperative-statement}

WRITE Statement:

WRITE record-name {FROM identifier}
     {INVALID KEY imperative-statement}         <—KSDS and RRDS only

REWRITE Statement:

REWRITE record-name {FROM identifier}
     {INVALID KEY imperative-statement}         <—KSDS and RRDS only

DELETE Statement:

DELETE file-name RECORD                         <—KSDS and RRDS only
     {INVALID KEY imperative-statement}
```

DOM is coded because no sequential processing is performed. Likewise, with ACCESS IS SEQUENTIAL, records are always processed in order by key field, relative record number, or RBA value depending on the type of data set. The value of the CRP can be changed by any of five COBOL I/O statements: OPEN, CLOSE, READ, READ NEXT, and START. The manner in which a value is assigned to the CRP by each type of I/O operation is identified in Table 9.7. The

TABLE 9.7   I/O Operations Affecting the CRP Value.

I/O Statement	Record the CRP Identifies for Processing Next
OPEN	The initial record in the data set.
CLOSE	The CRP for the data set is no longer defined.
READ	The logical record following the one retrieved during the present random READ operation.
READ NEXT	The logical record following the one retrieved. during the present sequential READ NEXT operation.
START	The logical record identified by the partial or complete key value in the START operation.

basic function of the START statement is to assign a value to the CRP. It does not cause a record to be read.

With COBOL II, the term *Conceptual Record Pointer* has been replaced with *File Positioning Indicator (FPI)*. Although not yet widely used, this term is expected to become more common. Therefore, both CRP and FPI are used throughout this book. IBM has documented an SAA version of COBOL for all hardware platforms. It also uses FPI. Unfortunately, it is not yet available.

Note that the three random output operations—WRITE, REWRITE, and DELETE—never change the value of the CRP. With sequential processing, the WRITE operation adds records to the end of the data set. Only one CRP is maintained for a KSDS, even if alternate keys are used. However, a separate CRP is provided with each alternate index. This additional CRP is essential in automatically and logically reordering the records in the base KSDS and processing them in their alternate key value order.

Random writing, rewriting, and deleting

As discussed in chapter 2, writing, rewriting, and deleting all cause the effected control interval to be rewritten. Likewise, control interval and control area splits can occur during a write operation and are even possible during a rewrite. With a KSDS, all three of these random output operations must be performed using the primary key. With both random and dynamic access, it is unnecessary to read a record before rewriting it or deleting it. There are numerous situations where a record should be read prior to deleting it, and it is almost always necessary to read a record prior to changing it.

For the next several examples, assume that two control intervals in a VSAM KSDS contain eight logical records. The key values for each logical record are shown in Fig. 9.9.

Example 6. Various valid and invalid random I/O operations are attempted using the records in the KSDS in Fig. 9.9. Notice that the contents of the 01 level is undefined after most of the I/O operations. Table 9.8 traces the processing performed. Examine it carefully, as the same format is used throughout this chapter.

Example 7. Dynamic access is to be used to process the records shown in Fig. 9.9. The results are summarized in Table 9.9. If a random read operation (READ) is executed with the key field set to 06, Control Interval 0 is copied into

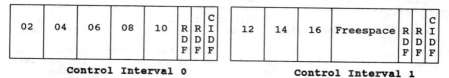

Figure 9.9 Logical records used in examples 6, 7, 8, and 9.

TABLE 9.8   Tracing VSAM Processing Operations in a COBOL Program.

Random Operation	CRP Points To Record	Status Code	Contents of 01 Level	Actual I/O Performed
OPEN for I-O	Key=2	00	Undefined	File Opened
WRITE KEY=6	Key=2	22	Undefined	Duplicate Record
WRITE KEY=7	Key=2	00	Undefined	Valid Add
READ KEY=12	Key=14	00	Key=12Record	Record Read
REWRITE	Key=14	00	Undefined	Record Rewritten
READ KEY=9	Key=14	23	Undefined	Record Not Found
REWRITE	Key=14	92	Undefined	Logic Error
DELETE KEY=6	Key=14	00	Undefined	Record Deleted
DELETE KEY=3	Key=14	23	Undefined	Record not Found

one of the data control interval buffers, and the third record in the data set can be processed in the 01-level. The CRP points to the fourth record (key field 08). If a sequential read (READ NEXT) is then executed, the fourth record is read, and following this, the CRP points to the fifth record, with a key field of 10. If an additional READ NEXT is performed, the last record in Control Interval 0 is retrieved, and the CRP points to the first record in Control Interval 1. One more READ NEXT causes Control Interval 1 to be copied into memory.

Example 8.   Table 9.10 summarizes the results of several consecutive I/O operations beginning with a random read operation and continuing with sequential processing using the records shown in Fig. 9.9.

After the third READ NEXT operation is executed, there is no change in any of the table entries until a different record is referenced. Recall that attempting a sequential read operation with non-VSAM data sets after end of file is detected usually causes an abend. In a COBOL program, the abend is classified as a QSAM, QISAM, or BSAM error depending on the data set organization.

Example 9.   The KSDS shown in Fig. 9.9 is to be extended by sequentially adding records to the end of the data set. The results are summarized in Table 9.11. Notice that the first and last WRITE operations both fail because each record's key value causes a sequencing error to occur. For these two situations, the status codes could be switched and the results would still seem meaningful! Comparable sequencing problems occur with ISAM data sets.

TABLE 9.9   Processing a KSDS Sequentially.

Operation	CRP Value	Status Code	Contents of 01 Level	Actual Processing
READ KEY=06	Key=08 record	00	Third record key=06	CIO read
READ NEXT	Key=10 record	00	Fourth record	Logical read
READ NEXT	Key=12 record	00	Fifth record	Logical read
READ NEXT	Key=14 record	00	Sixth record	CI1 read

TABLE 9.10   Sequential Processing and Detecting End of File.

Operation	CRP Value	Status Code	Contents of 01 Level	Actual I/O Performed
READ Key=14	Key=16 record	00	Seventh record key=14	Disk read
READ NEXT	End-of-file	00	Eighth record key=16	Logical read
READ NEXT	Undefined	10	End of file detected (same value or garbage)	None
READ NEXT	No change	94	No change	None
READ NEXT	No change	94	No change	None

The START statement

The primary function of the START statement is to assign a specific value to the conceptual record pointer. Hence, after opening a KSDS or RRDS for INPUT or I-O processing, START is executed preliminary to beginning sequential processing. A random READ can also assign a value to the CRP prior to sequential processing. START cannot be coded with an ESDS or when randomly processing a KSDS or RRDS.

Example 10.   The results of performing a START followed by a READ NEXT can often be duplicated by coding a single, random READ operation. This can only occur with dynamic access. Note that performing either of the sections of code shown in Table 9.12 gives the same results. Hence, the random READ operation is equivalent to the START and READ NEXT operations.

In Example 10, there is no advantage to coding a START followed by a READ NEXT. Because this is the case, when should START be used? The START statement has two processing options not available with a random READ statement. First, START allows generic key values to be specified. In this context, generic means that only part of the key value must match a record key in the KSDS or slot number in an RRDS. Generic keys are illustrated in Example 11. Second, the START statement allows conditions other than just equality to be specified with the key value coded to identify a record in a KSDS or RRDS. Greater than ($>$) or not less than ($> =$) can be specified.

Generic key fields and non-equal key value comparisons can be used together or separately. Various possible combinations are illustrated in Example 12. Although generic keys and non-equal comparisons are available with the START statement but not the READ statement in batch COBOL, both are supported

TABLE 9.11   Extending a KSDS.

Operation	CRP Value	Status Code	Results
OPEN EXTEND	Undefined	00	Successful open of file.
WRITE Key=13	Unchanged	92	Logic error, key value < 16.
WRITE Key=18	Unchanged	00	Record added successfully.
WRITE Key=17	Unchanged	21	New record key out of sequence.

TABLE 9.12 Comparing READ and START Operations.

Operation	CRP Value	Status Code	Contents of 01 Level
READ Key=12	Key=14	00	Eighth record Key=12 <─┐
or			
START Key=12	Key=12	00	Undefined
READ NEXT	Key=14	00	Eighth record Key=12 <─┘

with the CICS READ command. With CICS, however, several additional features are available with the START(BR) command, which READ does not support. Hence, even with CICS, the START(BR) is still important and distinctive from a random READ.

Example 11. Suppose the RECORD KEY clause specifies the group item FULL-NAME in the 01 level associated with the FD for a KSDS. Several potential generic key fields are identified in Table 9.13. Depending on the generic key or full key named with the START statement, different records can be identified in the data set even though FULL-NAME contains the same value.

Note that four data names can be used with the START statement. FULL-NAME identifies the complete key. The READ statement must use the value in FULL-NAME. LAST-NAME-AND-INIT, LAST-NAME-ONLY, and LINIT all supply partial key values for generic processing. Every generic key must contain values beginning on the left-most boundary of the full key. These are the so-called high-order bytes.

For example, LAST-NAME-AND-INIT occupies the first 17 bytes; LAST-NAME-ONLY occupies the first 15 bytes; and LINIT the first byte. Fields like REST-OF-FIRST and FIRST-LETTER cannot be used as generic keys. Up to 26 distinct

TABLE 9.13 Possible Key Fields Available with the START Verb.

COBOL Name for the Key Field	Key Type	Length in Bytes	Length of Other 10 Levels	Length of Other 15 Levels	Length of Other 20 Levels
FULL-NAME	Full	27	--	--	--
LAST-NAME-AND-INIT	Partial	17	10	--	--
LAST-NAME-ONLY	Partial	15	--	2	--
LINIT	Partial	1	--	--	14

```
      05  FULL-NAME.                          <────────-FULL-NAME────────->
          10  LAST-NAME-AND-INIT.             <LAST..INIT><REST><MID>
              15  LAST-NAME-ONLY.             <LAST><  ><  >
                  20  LINIT          PIC X.
                  20  FILLER         PIC X(14).
              15  FILLER             PIC X.
              15  FIRST-LETTER       PIC X.
          10  REST-OF-FIRST          PIC X(9).
          10  MIDDLE-INIT            PIC X.
      05  ALPHA    REDEFINES FULL-NAME.
          10  NAME                   PIC X OCCURS 27 TIMES.
```

```
The Complete 27-Byte Key Field Value

   Record    Last      First
   Number    Name      Name        MI

      N       SMITH     JOHN        Q
     N+1      SMITH     ROBERT      A
     N+2      SMITHE    SUSAN       D
     N+3      SMYITHE   MARIE       D
     N+4      SMYTHE    DONNA       M

      Although the same 17 leading bytes are used, each of
the START verbs coded below positions the CRP to a different
record.

MOVE 'SMITH            R' TO LAST-NAME-AND-INIT.
START KEY IS EQUAL TO LAST-NAME-ONLY.
The CRP points to record N.

MOVE 'SMITH            R' TO LAST-NAME-AND-INIT.
START KEY IS NOT LESS THAN LAST-NAME-AND-INIT.
The CRP points to record N+1.

MOVE 'SMITH            R' TO LAST-NAME-AND-INIT.
START KEY IS GREATER THAN LAST-NAME-ONLY.
The CRP points to record N+2.

MOVE 'SMITH            R' TO LAST-NAME-AND-INIT.
START KEY IS GREATER THAN LAST-NAME-AND-INIT.
The CRP points to record N+2.
```

Figure 9.10 Generic keys and non-equal key field values.

generic key field values are possible in this example. The REDEFINES clause illustrates how additional generic keys can be created. The REDEFINES clause cannot, however, be used within the RECORD KEY to create generic keys.

Regardless of whether the full key or a generic key is used with the START statement, the key in the retrieved record can exactly match the value in the search key. It can be the first value greater than or the first value greater than or equal to the search key value. Hence, in Example 8, to find the first record in the data set whose key starts with a letter in the second half of the alphabet, specify 'N' as a 1-byte partial key, (LINIT = 'N'), and perform a START with the NOT LESS THAN option.

Example 12.   Six consecutive records in a KSDS contain the primary key values listed in Fig. 9.10. The key field is the 27-byte FULL-NAME field used in the previous example. The record number is used only to simplify identification. Although the same 17 leading bytes are used, each of the START statements coded in Fig. 9.10 positions the CRP to a different record.

Determining the key of reference with a KSDS

In addition to generic keys and non-equal key field comparisons, the START statement can be used to change the key of reference. Both the START statement and the random READ statement allow a key of reference to be selected with the KEY IS clause. Key identification can be coded in the three ways—primary, alternate, and generic:

READ file-name KEY IS primary-key, alternate-key or a generic-key
START file-name KEY IS primary-key, alternate-key or a generic-key

Hence, either START or READ file-name KEY IS alternate-key switches processing to the specified alternate key. The alternate key field must have been named in the SELECT statement with an ALTERNATE KEY clause.

Exactly three statements can be used to select the key of reference, START, READ, and OPEN. The OPEN statement always selects the primary key. The key of reference effects only sequential processing, random reads, and starts. Writing, rewriting, and deleting is always performed using the primary key, regardless of which key is currently the key of reference.

If sequential processing is resumed following any of these random operations, the key of reference retains its value prior to the operation. Hence, it is often said that the key of reference is ambiguous or undefined during a random operation.

VSAM Processing Options Not Available with COBOL

There are several significant processing features supported in CICS, PL/I, and Assembler that cannot be used in a COBOL program:

- Sequentially reading backwards.
- Mass record insertion.
- Accessing a record via its relative byte address.
- Processing an ESDS through an alternate key.
- Using FREESPACE values after the initial load is completed.
- Control interval processing.

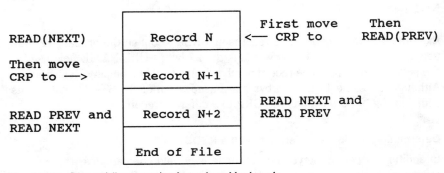

Figure 9.11 Sequentially processing forwards and backwards.

- Skip sequential processing
- Assigning multiple strings to a single file (data set).
- Asynchronous processing.

Each of these unsupported features is briefly discussed in the following sections. There are two reasons for doing this. First, it is worthwhile to know that all these features exist. Second, if one or more of these features are essential to an application, an alternative to COBOL should be used for programming.

Sequentially reading backwards

VSAM allows sequential processing both in a forward (READ NEXT) and a backward (READ PREV) direction. This processing is possible with all types of VSAM data sets.

Example 13. Suppose that the CRP correctly points to record N. At present, READ PREV is not supported in batch COBOL programs. PL/I, assembler, and CICS allow backward sequential processing. The pair of statements in Fig. 9.11 reads the same record twice.

In this case, the READ PREV operation sets the CRP to its last previous value before the READ NEXT, and then performs the READ operation. Following the READ PREV operation, the CRP remains pointing at the record that was just read. The CRP does not advance after the operation is completed. Hence, performing READ PREV and READ NEXT in order also reads the same record twice.

To begin sequential processing with the first record in the data set, the data set need merely be opened. If LOW-VALUES is specified as the key field value with a START NOT LESS THAN statement, the first record is also identified. In order to read the entire data set in reverse order, it is necessary to first establish positioning beyond the last record in the data set, but not abend in the process. More details of reverse sequential processing are given in chapter 16.

When dynamic access is specified, sequential processing is preceded by an OPEN, (random) READ, or START operation. Each of these operations assigns a CRP value, which is used during subsequent processing.

Mass record insertion

VSAM can use a mass insertion technique to add two or more records to a KSDS when all of the records are to be placed in the same general location, and the records are in ascending order based on their primary key value. When these two conditions are met, mass insertion is much more efficient than performing a true random write operation with each record to be added.

In particular, the involved control intervals in the data and index components are held by the application program until processing is completed. After the first record is written, it is unnecessary for VSAM to search the index component during subsequent write operations. Likewise, control interval buffers need not be repeatedly copied to disk following each write operation. Mass insertion is discussed in more detail in chapter 16.

Accessing a record via its relative byte address

Both Assembler and PL/I allow an application program to retrieve the relative byte address (RBA) value where a logical record is written. This value can be saved and used in subsequent processing. RBA processing is currently not permitted with batch COBOL but is supported with CICS. RBA processing is discussed in detail in chapter 10. It is widely used with several major system software packages.

Processing an ESDS through an alternate key

Both Assembler and PL/I allow an ESDS to be processed both randomly and sequentially through an alternate index. This is not currently permitted with batch COBOL but is supported with CICS. Using alternate keys with an ESDS is discussed in detail in chapter 10. Alternate key ESDS processing is widely used with several major system software packages. In fact, it is often also more efficient than alternate key processing over a KSDS.

Using FREESPACE values after the initial load is completed

The two FREESPACE values associated with a KSDS are always in effect during the initial load. With a COBOL application program, the FREESPACE values are not used during subsequent processing. With Assembler and PL/I, both values can be used when control interval and control area splits occur. For example, if FREESPACE(66 60) is in effect and a control interval split occurs, each control interval involved in the split should contain approximately two-thirds freespace following the split. Hence, multiple free control intervals are required to perform the split operation.

This same logic is in effect for the number of free control intervals in a control area following a control area split. Here, 60 percent of the control intervals in a control area must be free after the split is completed. The application program specifies whether the FREESPACE values should be used following the load operation. The default with COBOL is not to use the FREESPACE values during subsequent splits. The default with IDCAMS is to use the values.

Example 14. Suppose FREESPACE(75 80) is in effect with a KSDS. Two possibilities exist: either the values are used only during the initial loading of the data set or they remain in effect whenever a control interval and control area split occurs. Suppose FREESPACE remains in effect after the initial REPRO completes. The KSDS consists of 2,048-byte control intervals, 250-byte logical records, and a control area composed of 200 control intervals. Following a control interval split, 75 percent of the data control interval's data area (1,500 bytes) should be free space. This will require at least three, free control intervals for each split. Following a control area split, 80 to 90 percent of the control intervals (160) must be free. This will require five new control areas to be allocated during the split.

Control interval processing

Control interval processing allows the entire control interval, including the CIDF and RDF fields, to be accessed in an application program. During this mode of processing, it is the responsibility of the application to update these fields to reflect any record changes in the control interval. Although control interval processing is not directly supported in COBOL, a technique to implement it can be used. It consists of accessing individual components of the data set as if they are non-VSAM sequential data sets. These values override the values stored in the data set labels for the duration of the job step.

Skip sequential processing

Skip sequential processing is an alternative to standard random and sequential processing, although it has functional similarities of both. Skip sequential processing is used only with "randomlike" input operations. Furthermore, the records to be retrieved must be requested in ascending key field order. The first record to be retrieved is located using all the levels in the index component as described in chapter 2. All subsequent retrievals are accomplished using the sequence set records only. Skip sequential processing is permitted with PL/I, Assembler, and CICS, and is discussed in greater detail in chapters 16 and 17.

Assigning multiple strings to a single file

VSAM allows a single program to record concurrently at two or more locations within the same data set. Each location is identified by a VSAM string. Whenever a program begins execution, a maximum number of strings is assigned to each VSAM data set. Each string identifies one processing location in the data set and one set of control blocks. The string number can be modified each time the program is executed. String numbers are usually insignificant with batch programs. In fact, such processing would require multiple SELECT and FD statements for the same VSAM data set.

Asynchronous processing

VSAM I/O operations can be performed either synchronously or asynchronously. The distinctions between the two are discussed with Assembler language programming. Synchronous implies coordinated training between operations while asynchronous identifies operations performed on an ad hoc basis. There is nothing really comparable to either with a COBOL program.

```
SELECT KSDS-MASTER
    ASSIGN TO KSDSDD
    ORGANIZATION IS INDEXED
    ACCESS IS DYNAMIC
    RECORD KEY IS PRI
        PASSWORD IS ...
    ALTERNATE KEY IS ALT
        WITH DUPLICATES
    FILE-STATUS IS STATUS-CODE
    ...

FD  KSDS-MASTER
    LABEL RECORDS ARE STANDARD.
01  KSDS-RECORD.
    ...
    05  ALT             PIC 999.
    ...
    05  PRI             PIC 99.
    ...
```

Figure 9.12   SELECT and FD statements for example 15.

Tracing Execution in a COBOL Program

Example 15. A KSDS has been created and loaded with 5 records. IDCAMS has also been used to build (and load) an alternate index and path over the base cluster and load the alternate index. The relevant clauses coded in the SELECT and FD statements used to process the records in the data set are shown in Fig. 9.12.

The 5 records loaded into the KSDS have the primary and alternate key values shown in Table 9.14. In the processing that follows, a record can be identified by its record number, primary key value, and alternate key value, provided it is a unique value.

A very wide range of I/O operations are to be performed with the KSDS. The operations are performed as part of a COBOL dynamic master file update application program, and they build upon one another.

At this point, the I/O operations and their effect on the data set are described. For every I/O operation listed in Table 9.15, five values are specified.

1. Key of Reference (either PRI or ALT).

2. Logical record in the 01 level (part of the data component buffer) identified by its record number.

3. CRP value (identified by record number).

TABLE 9.14   Primary and Alternate Keys for Tracing Example.

Record Number	Primary Key Value (PRI Field)	Alternate Key Value (ALT Field)
1	15	110
2	25	070
3	35	030
4	45	070
5	55	050

TABLE 9.15   Analyzing I/O Operations on a KSDS.

Type of I/O Operation and Key Field Values	Key of Ref	01 Level Buffer	CRP Value	Status Code	Results of Operation	Further Remarks
1 OPEN I-O	PRI	none	1	00	Successful	(a)
2 READ NEXT	PRI	1	2	00	Read record 1	
3 READ NEXT	PRI	2	3	00	Read record 2	
4 MOVE 45 TO PRI READ	PRI	4	5	00	Read record 4	(b)
5 MOVE 15 TO PRI REWRITE	PRI	1	5	00	Rewrite rec 1	(c)
6 MOVE 030 TO ALT READ KEY IS ALT	ALT	3	5	00	Read record 3	(d)
7 READ NEXT	ALT	5	2	00	Read record 5	(e)
8 READ NEXT	ALT	2	4	02	Read record 2	
9 MOVE 65 TO PRI MOVE 130 TO ALT WRITE	ALT/ PRI	6	4	00	Add record 6	(f)
10 READ NEXT	ALT	4	1	00	Read record 4	
11 MOVE 75 TO PRI MOVE 130 TO ALT WRITE	ALT/ PRI	7	1	00	Add record 7	
12 MOVE 65 TO PRI START KEY IS PR	PRI	-	6	00	Point to rec 6	
13 MOVE 45 TO PRI DELETE	PRI	-	6	00	Delete rec 3	
14 MOVE 25 TO PRI MOVE 130 TO ALT REWRITE	PRI	2	6	00	Rewrite	(g)
15 MOVE 85 TO PRI REWRITE	PRI	-	6	23	Not found	
16 WRITE KEY IS ALT	This statement will cause a syntax error during compilation					
17 MOVE 130 TO ALT READ KEY IS ALT	ALT	6	7	02	Read record 6	
18 READ NEXT	ALT	7	2	02	Read record 7	
19 READ NEXT	ALT	2	EOF	00	Read record 2	
20 READ NEXT	ALT	EOF	none	10	EOF detected	
21 READ NEXT	ALT	none	none	94	CRP undefined	
22 MOVE 90 TO PRI START KEY IS PRI	PRI	none	EOF or none	92	Key too big	(h)
23 READ NEXT	PRI					
24 MOVE 130 TO ALT MOVE 37 TO PRI WRITE	PRI	8		00	Add record 8	x

4. Status code produced by the operation.

5. Result of the I/O operation.

Some additional explanatory comments to clarify some aspects of a specific operation are identified by footnotes. Some of the most interesting statements are identified by the numbers on the left-hand side and described in more detail following Table 9.15:

(a) An OPEN statement always establishes the primary key as the key of reference and initializes the CRP to the RBA of the first record in the data set. When a data set is initially opened, the contents of the 01 level (buffer) is undefined.

(b) Following the two previous sequential read operations, the CRP is assigned a new value as a consequence of the random read.

(c) Following the rewrite operation, the CRP retains the same value that it had prior to the operation.

(d) Because the CRP value is always reset by a random read operation, it is coincidental that the CRP contains the same value before and after the operation. The key of reference for subsequent sequential operations remains the alternate key until changed by a random READ or START statement with a KEY IS clause.

(e) In the alternate index, the record following the one with a key of 30 has a key of 50, and the next one has a key of 70. The alternate key value of 70 is associated with the two records with primary keys of 25 and 45.

(f) In this situation, the key of reference remains the alternate key following the operation, even though the operation is performed using the value in the primary key. The same statement applies to I/O operation 11.

(g) After record 2 is rewritten, there are three logical records with an alternate key value of 130. Because the entry for record number 2 was created last, it follows the entries for records 6 and 7. This ordering accounts for the results shown in I/O operations 17, 18, and 19.(h) Because the START operation is unsuccessful, the following operation also fails.

If all the logical records in the KSDS are contained in two control intervals and all the records in the data component of the alternate index are in the same control interval, then actual disk I/O operations are only performed with several of the preceding operations. Try to determine which ones?

Exercises

1. For each clause that can be coded with an FD statement, identify the DEFINE CLUSTER command parameter(s) that specify the comparable information. Explain the manner in which comparable information is pro-

vided by the clauses in the SELECT statement and their DEFINE CLUS-
TER equivalent? In conjunction with this, determine which FD and
SELECT clauses do not have an equivalent DEFINE CLUSTER parame-
ter.

2. Identify five properties associated with a KSDS or the records it contains.
The property can be assigned different values in the DEFINE CLUSTER
(DEFINE ALTERNATEINDEX and ALTER) command and a COBOL
application program that will result in a status code of 92 or 95 when the
data set is opened for processing.

3. Recall that for a non-VSAM data set, the value in the application program
has precedence, and the value in the data set labels is ignored. Why would
the same technique not also be used with VSAM data sets?

4. Among the values that can be coded to describe a VSAM data set with
either the DEFINE CLUSTER command or in a COBOL application program, identify those that can also be specified on an associated DD statement? See also chapters 4 and 13.

5. Determine the process used by VSAM to construct the control block
(ACB) to associate with a data set that is comparable to the data control
block (dcb) constructed for processing a non-VSAM data set. Note that,
with both VSAM and non-VSAM data sets, values are provided from three
sources: the (application) program itself, the associated DD statement, and
the data set labels. The cluster component contains "Label" information
for a VSAM data set. When a VSAM data set is modified, discuss the
details of modifying control blocks and rewriting 'Label' information in the
cluster component. (Note: Some of the material will be expanded upon in
chapter 13.)

6. Discuss the specific role of the relative byte address (RBA) with each of the
I/O statements available in a COBOL program. In particular, discuss the
use, assignment, and modification of RBA values during a successful execution of an I/O operation.

7. Can a COBOL application program retrieve the value in the FPI or assign a
value to it without performing an I/O operation of any type? What is the
maximum number of FPI assigned to a single FD?

8. A KSDS contains five records with keys of 02, 04, 06, 08, and 10. For each
segment of code in Fig. 9.13, determine the nonzero status code(s) that
results when processing is attempted and give the reason for the code(s).
Assume that ACCESS IS DYNAMIC is coded in the SELECT statement
unless stated otherwise.

9. Write a COBOL program to read the records in the data component of a
KSDS. Rather than the cluster component, the data component itself
should be identified on the accompanying DD statement. Consequently, it
is essential to inform the COBOL program that the records are not part of a

```
a.   OPEN EXTEND

b.   OPEN I-O
     MOVE 7 TO PRI-KEY
     READ NEXT
     MOVE 6 TO PRI-KEY
     READ random

c.   OPEN EXTEND
     READ NEXT
     REWRITE

d.   OPEN OUTPUT
     MOVE 12 TO PRI-KEY and values to other 01-fields
     WRITE
     MOVE 12 TO PRI-KEY and values to other 01-fields
     REWRITE
     MOVE 10 TO PRI-KEY and values to other 01-fields
     WRITE

e.   START PRI-KEY = 11
     READ NEXT

f.   DELETE KEY = 1x (Generic Key)

g.   OPEN I-O
     MOVE 12 TO PRI-KEY
     READ
     MOVE 15 TO PRI-KEY
     REWRITE

h.   MOVE 6 TO PRI-KEY
     READ random
     DELETE
     WRITE
```

Figure 9.13 Determining the results of VSAM operations.

KSDS but rather a single data set of some type. Likewise, the dcb values should not necessarily reflect those associated with the logical records in the data component. Perform the same type of processing with the index component also.

Furthermore, after reading an index record, modify information in the CIDF and RDFs so that it no longer reflects the actual contents of the control interval, and rewrite the control fields. Now, attempt to process the records in the data control interval. Use the same general technique to change the update number associated with one segment of a spanned record.

10. Alternate indexes verses linked lists as an alternative to standard VSAM alternate key processing. Linked lists are frequently useful in some applications. Suppose every record in a KSDS contains a 2-byte field containing a

special code that can contain one of ten distinct values. A second field contains the key of the next record in the group with the same special code value. Hence, if a record with a special code of X is read, it contains a value that can be moved to the RECORD KEY field to retrieve the next record. Write the code to create and implement such a structure. Perform a master file type update with the records in the KSDS.

11. Develop an external subroutine to produce a report (log) tracing all the processing performed with a VSAM data set. In particular, the subroutine should be called after every I/O operation and a variety of values passed to it. These should include the transaction identifier, type of operation, key of reference, status code value, description of the processing results, etc.

12. Suppose an alternate index has gotten out of synchronization with its base cluster because NOUPGRADE or NOUPDATE was coded. Discuss the IDCAMS commands and COBOL application code that could resynchronize the alternate index. How can it be resynchronized? Is it necessary to completely rebuild the entire alternate index?

13. Why are the master password and control password rarely, if ever, needed when processing a VSAM data set within a COBOL application program?

14. Perform a standard sequential master file update where the base data set is actually processed in ascending, alternate key order because the transactions have been sorted into that order. The update program should contain a combination of valid and invalid retrieval, addition, rewrite, and delete operations. As with any sequential update of this type, a new master file must be created.

15. Can the rules used by the COBOL compiler to construct a DDname for a path over a base cluster lead to any problems with the other DDnames that are coded in the same job step?

16. Write the complete group of DD statements required during execution of a COBOL program where a KSDS is to be updated and an alternate key is to be used, check points taken, and the alternate index built and loaded within the COBOL program. While building the alternate index, an external sort must be performed. One exception occurs whenever the records being used to build the alternate index are to be edited. For a discussion of this situation, see the COBOL progammers guide.

10

Entry Sequenced Data Sets

Both this chapter and chapter 11 are organized so that they both provide a detailed study of one specific type of VSAM data set organization. The topics in chapters 4, 5, 6, 7, 8, and 9 are restricted to just an ESDS in this chapter and to only an RRDS in chapter 11. Material in both chapters is grouped into four general categories. First, an overview of the data set organization is given. In this chapter, an ESDS; in the next, an RRDS. This includes a physical description, processing capabilities, advantages and disadvantages, and structural/syntax limitations. This is followed by a discussion of how IDCAMS commands are used to create and process an ESDS or RRDS. Third, batch COBOL processing is discussed in detail, including a thorough evaluation of all possible I/O operations and programming concepts. Finally, several actual implementation situations are analyzed for each data set organization and various random ESDS processing techniques are examined.

Some of the material in chapters 10 and 11 overlap material in other chapters of the book. However, the intent is to try and gather the significant information about ESDSs and RRDSs together in one place, even if some duplication with earlier material results.

Processing Non-Indexed Data Sets

There are probably still a few programmers left in the world who still think of VSAM as "V-ISAM," a new and improved version of ISAM. Such a viewpoint classifies VSAM and KSDS as more-or-less equivalent. Although the KSDS is the most important of the four, two other VSAM data set organizations, the Entry Sequenced Data Set (ESDS) and the Relative Record Data Set (RRDS), are also powerful and flexible. The ESDS is examined in detail in this chapter, and the RRDS in chapter 11. Linear Data Sets (LDS), which are structurally similar to an ESDS, are discussed in chapter 15.

Unlike a KSDS, both the ESDS and RRDS consist only of the cluster and data components. Because there is no index, neither data set organization can be processed using a primary key field, as can a KSDS. This feature is both the major advantage and disadvantage of both the ESDS and RRDS. Without an index, the types of processing that can be performed become somewhat limited unless substantially more work is done by the programmer. This is partially balanced by the fact that the processing time and disk storage overheads required with an index are not present.

Random record processing is possible with both an ESDS and an RRDS. In fact, random processing is the rule with an RRDS, and it is the exception with an ESDS. Because no index is available, the records are accessed differently than with a KSDS. Random processing is also much faster with an RRDS and only somewhat slower with an ESDS than with a KSDS.

Because the records in an ESDS and RRDS can be processed randomly at speeds comparable to, or faster than, a KSDS, and because neither contains an index, why are the ESDS and RRDS used less frequently than a KSDS? Primarily because most collections of records cannot readily be stored as an ESDS or an RRDS in a convenient format for random processing. There is no field in the records whose values can easily be used for random processing. Often, a hashing algorithm must be used to determine the specific disk location to associate with a record. Considerably more program design is usually required with an RRDS or when doing random processing with an ESDS.

Overview of ESDS Processing

An ESDS is the appropriate VSAM data set organization to use when all, or almost all, subsequent processing will be sequential. When sequentially processing logical records in an application program, there are very few differences between an ESDS and a QSAM data set. For example, in a COBOL program, the identical I/O statements are used with both types of data sets.

The ESDS generally does not provide many significant advantages over non-VSAM sequential data set organizations. This is especially true when almost all programming is done in COBOL. Consequently, programmers in many COBOL shops see little reason to convert their QSAM data sets to ESDSs. In fact, QSAM data sets have the advantage of being stored in PDS libraries and entire groups of PDS members can be processed together.

Even when COBOL is used, an ESDS has several advantages over a QSAM data set. A very limited group of status codes (00, 10, 92) are available with non-VSAM data sets. Abends occur while processing QSAM data sets partly because of this. In a comparable situation, this does not occur with a VSAM data set and it occurs less frequently with COBOL II because a much wider range of status codes is available. See Table 9.3. Non-VSAM sequential data sets can only be processed sequentially. However, RBA values are accessible with VSAM data sets, and several important non-sequential processing techniques are possible with an ESDS.

ESDS Processing Limitations

Records in an ESDS cannot be accessed with a primary key or a relative record number. In fact, no type of true, straightforward random access is possible. Once an ESDS is created, it is a very inflexible structure. When compared with an RRDS, a totally different category of limitations hold with an ESDS. See chapter 11.

Internal Structure of an ESDS

There are numerous similarities in the internal structure of the data components of an ESDS and a KSDS. Both variable and spanned record formats are available with each, and variable length is the default. A record cannot be split across control interval boundaries unless SPANNED is coded. The RDF and CIDF control fields contain exactly the same types of information. Two initial tracks in an ESDS are shown in Fig. 10.1.

It is impossible to determine if a data set is a KSDS or ESDS merely from examining the control intervals in Fig. 10.1. However, it clearly cannot be an RRDS or LDS. There are some very significant differences between a KSDS and an ESDS data component. A control interval split can never occur in an ESDS. Once an ESDS control interval is filled, any unused space remains unused, and a "true" control area split cannot occur. However, secondary extentions can be allocated both when creating and later extending a data set.

When writing records to an ESDS, as much of every control interval is filled as possible. An ESDS does not contain true free space, but a control interval can contain permanently unused space. The area with Xs in Fig. 10.1 represents unused space. The unused space is followed by the RDFs and CIDF. For example, if 200-byte records are written to an ESDS where the control intervals are 512 bytes, there will be 102 unused bytes in each control interval containing the records, except for possibly the last one. Without free space, records cannot be inserted, deleted, or have their length changed during a rewrite operation.

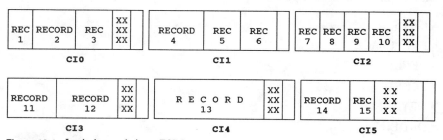

Figure 10.1 Logical records in an ESDS.

Once a control interval is initially filled, the two CIDF values do not change. A record can be replaced but only by another record of exactly the same length. The existing record must first be read sequentially and then rewritten. A record can be logically deleted, but it is entirely the responsibility of the application to create and detect deleted records. Because of these processing restrictions, the RBA value associated with a record never changes. This is not the case for a record in a KSDS. Furthermore, the RDF values describing an ESDS record cannot be changed except possibly in two cases: for records in the final control interval when a data set is extended and incrementing update numbers for spanned records. As described later in this chapter, an ESDS record can also be randomly accessed in various ways using its RBA value.

The same programming considerations used with non-VSAM sequential data sets apply when sequentially processing an ESDS. In particular, additional buffer space might be requested to hold a designated number of data control intervals rather than the default value of 2. VSAM can do the same automatic multiple level buffering that QSAM employs with non-VSAM data sets. Finally, the AMP DD parameter can be used to request additional buffers before program execution.

Using IDCAMS Commands with an ESDS

The material in chapters 4, 5, 6, and 7 is reexamined in this section from the viewpoint of processing an ESDS. All of the Big Eight IDCAMS commands allow a more limited range of processing (parameters) with an ESDS than with a KSDS.

Creating an ESDS with DEFINE CLUSTER

An ESDS can be created with the DEFINE CLUSTER command. Most parameters can be coded with either the CLUSTER or the DATA component; they have the same effect in both places. The NONINDEXED parameter is required to create an ESDS. The only other required parameters are cluster NAME, VOLUME, and Space Allocation. RECORDSIZE can specify variable or fixed records, and SPANNED can be coded. A DEFINE CLUSTER command to create an ESDS is illustrated in Example 1. The following parameters can be coded with a KSDS but are not permitted with an ESDS:

- KEYS
- FREESPACE
- REPLICATE
- IMBED
- KEYRANGE
- ORDER
- INDEX

```
DEFINE  CLUSTER(NAME(ESDS.MASTER)        -
                NONINDEXED               -
                SHAREOPTIONS(2 3)        -
                FOR(365)                 -
                RECORDSIZE(100 100)      -
                CISZ(8192)               -
                BUFFERSPACE(81920)       -
                VOLUME(DISK27)           -
                CYLINDER(1 1)            -
                SPEED)                   -
           DATA(NAME(ESDS.MASTER.DATA))
```

Figure 10.2 DEFINE CLUSTER code to create an ESDS.

Example 1. A data set is to be created that will hold approximately 50,000 fixed-length, 100-byte records. Some additional records might be added to the data set at later times. Although most subsequent processing will be sequential, an alternate key will be used for random retrieval. The alternate key field allows duplicate values, and therefore, is not a potential candidate for a primary key. Field concatenation, or something comparable, would be required to construct a primary key. Based on the preceding criteria, the ESDS is selected as the appropriate data set organization to store the records. The code in Fig. 10.2 is used to create the ESDS.

In Fig. 10.2, all the parameters coded with the CLUSTER component, except NONINDEXED, could alternatively be coded with the DATA component and the results would be the same. If all subsequent processing will be sequential, an even larger CISZ value might be appropriate. Likewise, if most processing will be random, smaller CISZ and BUFFERSPACE values should be coded. If most processing will be random, however, an ESDS becomes a questionable choice for holding the records. A control area occupies 1 cylinder, which, on a 3380 disk, consists of 75 control intervals and 6,075 records. Notice that, because there is no freespace to consider and the records are fixed length, it is easy to determine the exact number of records loaded into a control area. Hence, the data set occupies 8 control areas (cylinders) following the REPRO operation. This occurs because 50,000 divided by 6,075 gives a quotient greater than 7 but less than 8.

ESDS Processing with the IDCAMS Commands

The role of each of the major (The Big Eight) IDCAMS data set and system commands, specifically restricted to an ESDS, are examined in this section. This information should be considered a supplementary subset of the detailed explanation of the eight commands presented in chapters 5 and 6.

With the REPRO command, the valid parameters for identifying the initial record to process are FROMADDRESS, SKIP, and FROMKEY. FROMKEY is used only when processing the ESDS through a path over an alternate index. The valid parameters for identifying the final record to process are TOAD-DRESS, COUNT, and TOKEY. TOKEY can only be used through a path. REPLACE involves random inserts and changes and is meaningless with an ESDS. REUSE can be coded to set the HI-USED-RBA to zero and subsequently load a new group of records into the data set. If OUTFILE is used, REUSE overrides coding DISP = MOD on the DD statement for the ESDS.

All of the relevant capabilities and restrictions in the previous paragraph concerning the REPRO command parameters also hold with the PRINT command. When FROMADDRESS and COUNT are coded, each record is printed preceded by its RBA value. When FROMKEY is coded, each record is preceded by its alternate key value. As always, the values coded with FROMADDRESS and TOADDRESS must identify the initial byte in a record.

ALTER performs the same role with an ESDS as with a KSDS. DELETE is also identical to its use with a KSDS except there are only two components to delete, and two messages are printed. Likewise, EXPORT and IMPORT perform the same functions with every type of VSAM data set. However, REPRO is a somewhat more viable alternative for exporting and importing an ESDS than it is with a KSDS. VERIFY is syntactically the same as with a KSDS. However, with an ESDS, only the HI-USED-RBA value can be incorrect. Subsequent recovery is much easier because of the processing limitation associated with an ESDS. Example 2 illustrates using most of the major IDCAMS commands to process an ESDS.

Example 2. The records contained in the catalogued data set ALPHA.BETA are to be loaded into the ESDS created in the previous example. The initial record in ALPHA.BETA is not to be copied because it is a control record that is not used with the ESDS. The IDCAMS code in Examples 1 and 2 is valid no matter which data set organization ALPHA.BETA has.

Once the data set is loaded, the first 50 records and the final 50 records should be printed. Likewise, all of the cluster information for the data set is to be printed. If all the previous commands executed successfully, the name of the ESDS is to be changed to ESDS.ALPHA.BETA. A backup copy of the data set should be created on tape. If the backup is successful, the original data set is deleted and its space overwritten with binary zeroes. Notice that dynamic allocation is used throughout Fig. 10.3 except for the EXPORT command.

The types of printed listings of ESDS records and a LISTCAT for an ESDS, such as in Example 1, should be carefully examined and the following points noted. Although the cluster name is specified with the first PRINT command, each record is prefaced by its RBA value exactly as if the data component had been coded. Also, the LISTCAT contains various data values and parameters, which are completely meaningless with an ESDS but appear anyway. For example, there is no sense in mentioning NOREPLICATE, NOIMBED, and zero-percent freespace.

```
      REPRO IDS(ALPHA.BETA)                              -
            ODS(ESDS.MASTER)                             -
            SKIP(1)
      PRINT IDS(ESDS.MASTER)                             -
            COUNT(50)
      PRINT IDS(ESDS.MASTER.DATA)                        -
            SKIP(49950)
      LISTCAT ENT(ESDS.MASTER) ALL
      IF MAXCC = 0 THEN                                  -
            DO
            ALTER  ESDS.MASTER                           -
                   NEWNAME(ESDS.ALPHA.BETA)
            EXPORT ESDS.ALPHA.BETA                       -
                   OFILE(DDTAPE)
         END
         IF LASTCC <= 4 THEN                             -
               DELETE ESDS.MASTER PURGE ERASE
      ELSE

      //DDTAPE   DD   DSN=TAPE.BACUP,DISP=(NEW,KEEP),UNIT=CART,
      //              VOL=SER=100170
```

Figure 10.3   Basic IDCAMS processing with an ESDS.

COBOL Syntax for ESDS Processing

Tables 9.4 and 9.5 summarize all permissible I/O operations for processing an ESDS in a COBOL program. Like a KSDS, an ESDS can be opened for INPUT, OUTPUT, I/O, or EXTEND processing. Certain restrictions hold with each of the four. In particular, I/O processing allows a very limited range of operations when compared to a KSDS or an RRDS. ACCESS IS SEQUENTIAL must be implied or explicitly coded in the SELECT statement, no matter how the data set is opened. COBOL does not permit random and dynamic access with an ESDS.

Because the range of COBOL processing with an ESDS is so limited, it is possible to illustrate every type of processing situation with very few lines of COBOL code. Initially, an ESDS is created (OPEN OUTPUT); closed; opened for additional output records (OPEN EXTEND); closed; opened for update processing (OPEN I/O); closed; and finally, opened to retrieve and print all the records (OPEN INPUT).

Sequential record retrieval can take place in either direction in both PL/I and assembler using READ NEXT and READ PREV commands. COBOL allows only a standard forward READ operation. Hence, READ implies a forward sequential read operation. Generic processing is not permitted with an ESDS. The START statement cannot be used. Because dynamic access is not allowed, the CRP is not a significant concept for programmer interaction. The WRITE operation with an ESDS is sequential, and records can only be added to the end of an existing data set (OPEN EXTEND) or overwrite records at the beginning of the data set (OPEN OUTPUT).

TABLE 10.1   Random Processing Methods Used with an ESDS.

Processing Technique	Implementation of the Random Processing Technique
VSAM Alternate Index	A VSAM alternate index and path can be constructed by IDCAMS with an ESDS as the base cluster. DEFINE AIX, BLDINDEX, and DEFINE PATH are used.
User-Built Alternate Index	The RBA of a record can be used to identify the record during reading, writing, and rewriting operations. This approach is not limited to an ESDS; it can also be used with a KSDS.
Pseudo-Relative Record Data Set	A relativelike data set organization can be superimposed on an ESDS. This approach illustrates several different file processing techniques that can be performed with an ESDS.
Linked List	Standard linked-list processing techniques are easy to implement with an ESDS. In this context, (logical) record insertions and deletions are permitted with an ESDS. Every record length can be changed.

Random Processing with an ESDS

Several methods for randomly processing an ESDS are examined in this section. Random ESDS processing is the exception in batch application programs, where the great majority of processing is sequential. However, major IBM program products, including IMS and CICS, use ESDSs for random processing.

Various techniques are available to support random processing with an ESDS. Four significant approaches are described in Table 10.1. Each of these four techniques is discussed and illustrated with examples in the next four sections. References are also made to all four techniques with an RRDS in the next chapter. The first two approaches are much more difficult to implement with an RRDS. The third approach is irrelevant with an RRDS, which, by definition, uses relative numbering. The fourth approach is of equal difficulty with both and implemented differently with both.

A VSAM/IDCAMS alternate index over an ESDS

An alternate index structure built and maintained by VSAM is usually associated with secondary key processing over a KSDS. However, IDCAMS can also construct a VSAM alternate index over a base ESDS. With this approach, any field within an ESDS record can be used for sequential processing in alternate key order and random record retrieval. There is very little structural difference between an alternate index built over an ESDS or one built over a KSDS. In both cases, the alternate index itself is a KSDS. This is the most important fact to keep in mind when trying to determine how an alternate index functions. Every VSAM alternate index is built and loaded with the DEFINE AIX and BLDINDEX commands. Processing takes place through a path constructed with the DEFINE PATH command.

The logical records in an alternate index over a KSDS contain a secondary key value and all the primary keys associated with it. When an ESDS is used as the base cluster, the alternate key value is paired with the RBA values of the ESDS records, which contain the alternate key. Hence, a data record in the alternate index has 5 bytes of overhead, the alternate key value, and the associated RBA values, each of which is 4 bytes in length. (See Table 8.4 in chapter 8 on constructing an alternate index over a KSDS.) The records in a data control interval in the alternate index contain comparable values to those shown in Fig. 10.4. RBA values are in decimal for readability.

Chapter 8 contains a thorough discussion of the 5 bytes of overhead that begin each logical record in an alternate index. In Fig. 10.4, the first byte in each record contains 81, which identifies the alternate index as (8) having been constructed over an ESDS, and (1) that duplicate alternate key values are allowed. The length of the RBA field is 4 bytes, which is the second value (byte 2) in each record. Three logical records are associated with the alternate key value A (C1). The corresponding base records have RBA values of 00000000, 00000300, and 00000675. The base record at RBA 1,024 has an alternate key value of C2 (B). The value in the last of the five overhead bytes is the length of the alternate key, here 1 byte.

The rules for choosing an alternate key field are the same as with a KSDS except there is no primary key overlap to consider, and the same key field limitations apply. (See chapter 8.) Not all I/O operations are permitted with an alternate index over an ESDS. Clearly, deletions and insertions cannot be performed. As a general rule, if an I/O operation can be performed directly with the base ESDS, then it is also possible through the alternate index. This is substantially different than with a KSDS, where a record can be retrieved through its alternate key value and then, by using the associated primary key, delete or rewrite the record.

Example 3. An alternate index is to be constructed over the ESDS created in Example 1. A 9-byte Social Security number beginning in byte 6 is to be the unique alternate key field. Each record in the alternate index is 18 bytes in length: 5 bytes overhead, a 9-byte key, and a 4-byte RBA field. Any alternate key related changes made to the base cluster should be immediately reflected in the alternate index. Such changes might occur when existing ESDS records are rewritten and when additional records are added to the end of the data set. The

5 Bytes of Overhead	AIX Key	Associated RBA Values (8 Hexadecimal Digits)	Character Equivalents For Entire Record
8104000301	C1	00000000 00000300 00000675	.... .A.. ....
8104000201	C2	00001024 00002048	.... .B.. .... ..
8104000301	C3	00000000 00000392 00009876	.... .C.. ....

Figure 10.4 An alternate index record associated with a base ESDS.

```
DEFINE AIX(NAME(ESDS.MASTER.AIX)            -
           RELATE(ESDS.MASTER)              -
           UNIQUEKEY                        -
           UPGRADE                          -
           KEYS(9 5)                        -
           FREESPACE(10 20)                 -
           CYLINDER(1 1)                    -
           VOLUME(DISK28)                   -
           SHAREOPTIONS(2 3)                -
           RECORDSIZE(18 18)                -
           CISZ(4096))                      -
        DATA(NAME(ESDS.MASTER.AIX.DATA))    -
        INDEX(NAME(ESDS.MASTER.AIX.INDEX))

BLDINDEX IDS(ESDS.MASTER)                   -
         ODS(ESDS.MASTER.AIX)

DEFINE PATH(NAME(ESDS.MASTER.PATH)          -
            PATHENTRY(ESDS.MASTER.AIX)      -
            UPDATE)
```

Figure 10.5 Building an alternate index and path over an ESDS.

IDCAMS code to create and load the alternate index and path is shown in Fig. 10.5.

An ESDS with an alternate index over it is an excellent data set organization choice when most processing is sequential but some random processing is required. Choosing an ESDS rather than a KSDS as the base cluster optimizes the sequential processing because the index records required with a KSDS are not present.

An alternate index is constructed by IDCAMS and is language-independent. ESDS batch processing through an alternate index, however, must be done in PL/I or assembler. COBOL does not presently support it. Alternate key ESDS processing can also be performed with CICS.

An ESDS can be created to store a collection of records that do not contain any field with unique values and, hence, cannot readily be stored as a KSDS. One or more of the fields with duplicate values could be defined as alternate keys and used for random processing. This is a possible alternative to concatenating a counter field to a potential primary key field that contains duplicates in order to create a KSDS.

Using RBA values for random record retrieval

When a record is written to an ESDS or KSDS, the application program can retrieve the RBA value where the (beginning of the) record is placed from VSAM. A specific, 4-byte field is used for this purpose. The program can then save this RBA value for future processing, in which case, usually the RBA and one field value from the record are written as a logical record in a second data set. The selected field can then be used as the "key" field during subsequent random processing.

VSAM provides the RBA value when the record is first added to the data set. It is entirely the programmer's responsibility to construct and maintain the data set of RBA value key field pairs. When random record retrieval is required, the second data set is searched for the particular key value. The corresponding RBA value is then used for the actual random retrieval. Random retrieval and subsequent access using RBA values are not supported with COBOL, but are permitted with PL/I, assembler, and CICS.

When RBA values are used in this way, the ESDS is processed through an alternate index built and maintained by the programmer rather than using IDCAMS to build and maintain one. Clearly it requires less work to allow VSAM to construct and maintain the alternate index. However, a programmer-constructed alternate index can be customized to take advantage of any special characteristics of the data set in order to optimize processing.

In particular, suppose that some records are accessed an inordinately large percentage of the time. Then such an approach could be very efficient. A second approach would be to maintain two alternate indexes, one programmer-created for high-priority records and a standard IDCAMS for all others. If the data set containing the RBA and user key pairs can be kept in memory during processing, only one I/O operation is necessary to retrieve an ESDS record. This contrasts with searching the index first and then reading the desired data component record when a VSAM alternate index is used before accessing the ESDS.

The data set containing the RBA and user key pairs should be maintained so that it optimizes locating a particular key value. If it is ordered on the key values using the EBCDIC collating sequence, then a binary search might be possible. If update operations are performed, the data set itself will have to be periodically reorganized. Clearly, updating is a limited process with the base ESDS.

Complications can result if there are multiple records with the same key value. The records in the index data set can be stored as variable-length records. This is how VSAM maintains alternate index records. However, VSAM does not use a binary search to locate a specific alternate key value. The particular type of application and the records themselves determine the best approach. Whatever is decided upon, it should be determined if it is actually an improvement over a standard VSAM alternate index.

Although RBA processing is discussed here with Entry Sequenced Data Sets, it can be used in the same way with a KSDS, but results in considerable complications with an RRDS. However, because a KSDS and an RRDS contain a primary key and relative record number respectively, there are fewer situations where it is necessary to retrieve records based on RBA values. This is especially true for an RRDS where RBA values cannot be explicitly specified.

Using an ESDS to simulate an RRDS structure

Unlike the previous two techniques, using an ESDS to simulate an RRDS structure is rarely used in an actual programming situation. It does, however, illustrate several interesting processing techniques available with VSAM data sets.

When all logical records have the same length, an ESDS can be created in a format that allows RRDS types of I/O operations with a sequential data set. Records in a relative data set must have the same length. The technique employed to locate a record will consist of using its displacement from two (previous) positions in the data set. This is the same approach used by VSAM with an RRDS.

To illustrate, suppose all logical records are 100 bytes in length and the CISZ is 2,048. Furthermore, the DEFINE CLUSTER command specified a fixed-length record size of 2,000. Hence, VSAM determines that each control interval contains one record. The one VSAM record actually contains 20 of the 100-byte logical records known to the application program. See Fig. 10.6. The data set, which is initially preformatted with dummy records, can be loaded sequentially by building and writing the 2,000-byte records in an application program. A true individual logical record can then be read or written randomly.

Suppose the record with a "relative key" of 36 is to be written or rewritten. Dividing 36 by 20, the number of records in a control interval, results in a quotient of 1 and a remainder of 16. The two values are interpreted as a request to read the second control interval (the quotient is a displacement to skip over one control interval) and then move the fields for the record with key 36 to bytes 3,548 (2,048+1,500) through 3,647 (2,048+1,599).

In Fig. 10.6, (16-1)*100 results in the displacement within the 2,000-byte record. The 2,000-byte record would then be rewritten by VSAM. Retrieval would work the same way as insertion. Efficiency is similar to actual VSAM processing, where the entire control interval is rewritten following an update to a single logical record.

It is certainly unreasonable to use this approach if most of the data set processing was not sequential. VSAM can create an actual RRDS and do the preceding easier and more efficiently than the average programmer could do it. Before the RRDS was fully supported on MVS systems (sometime in late seventies), this type of approach could be used with COBOL and PL/I to simulate relative record processing.

CIO – First Record							CI1 – Second Record							
REC01	REC02	REC03		REC19	REC20	RDFs	CIDF	REC21	REC22	REC23		REC36	REC39	REC40	RDFs	CIDF

0000   2048   3548

Figure 10.6   Using an ESDS as a simulated RRDS.

Three Initial Records in Order by "Key Field" Value

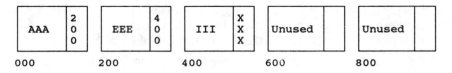

Same Data Set Following Record Insertions and Deletions

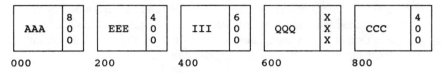

Figure 10.7 Linked list processing with an ESDS.

Linked list processing with an ESDS

Linked lists are a data structure that allows records stored in an arbitrary physical order to be processed in a sequential order. Record insertions and deletions can be made without creating a new master data set. Linked lists allow ESDS records to be retrieved in a sequential order, which is different than the actual physical order. Each record must contain one additional field to hold a 4-byte RBA value identifying the next record to be processed. This is illustrated in Fig. 10.7. The field used as a record key is shown in the left rectangle. The right rectangle contains the RBA of the next record. Notice that the second record (key = EEE) is deleted and the two new records become the second (key = ccc) and last (key = QQQ) in the data set.

If speed is an important processing criteria, linked list processing might not be a good idea. Linked list processing incurs two noticeable overheads. The first overhead is the 4 additional bytes in each record, which are an acceptable cost for the flexibility. The second overhead is the slow processing time associated with traversing a linked list, where each record must be randomly accessed. Using RBA values does not allow logical records to be blocked together in the order in which they are to be processed.

Future ESDS Developments

It is reasonable to expect that most of the ESDS processing features not presently supported in COBOL will eventually be added to the language. Likewise, a wider range of IDCAMS processing will also be most likely to be added. Restrictions on FROMADDRESS and TOADDRESS could be weakened to allow any byte rather than the first byte to specify the initial and final records to copy.

Exercises

1. Identify five significant structural or functional similarities between an ESDS and the data component of a KSDS. Identify five significant structural differences between an ESDS and the data component of a KSDS.

2. Construct a programmer-built alternate index over an ESDS using any command but the IDCAMS DEFINE AIX command. Use the alternate index to perform a limited dynamic master file update. Records can be modified, (logically) deleted, and added (to the end of the data set). Furthermore, the records can be retrieved in ascending key order and the alternate key values can be modified. Discuss any complications that might occur because of nonunique alternate key values. Identify the data set organization and logical record format associated with the alternate index.

3. The processing requirements identified in the previous exercise are to be implemented using an alternate index and path built and maintained by IDCAMS. Does the IDCAMS one or the "homegrown" approach allow the widest range of I/O operations? Which approach allows the I/O operations with the alternate keys to be performed most efficiently?

4. Implement the RRDS structure as an ESDS, which is described in Fig. 10.6. Perform whatever standard I/O operations are possible.

5. Use the EXPORT command to unload an ESDS to tape or disk. Dump the records in the exported data set, and examine their contents. In particular, identify any differences between the logical records in the ESDS and in the exported data set.

6. A linked list structure is to be used to store records. Could the linked list be implemented as a KSDS? What are the significant advantages of using an ESDS versus a KSDS for linked list processing?

7. Suppose RBA processing is supported in a programming language but not alternate key processing over any ESDS. Try to determine the most efficient/easiest way to implement record retrieval and modification using an alternate key value.

Comprehensive IDCAMS exercises for an ESDS

Create an ESDS to store card image (80-byte) records. Use a control area size of 2 tracks. Specify an update password, owner identification, expiration date, and allow only one user to process the data set at one time.

Load a sufficient number of records into the data set to place some records on each track in the minimal primary allocation. Use PRINT and LISTCAT (independently!) to confirm that the data set has been created according to these specifications.

Change the name of just the data component, and nullify both the password and retention period. Furthermore, any number of concurrent users should now be allowed to access the data set for any type of processing permitted.

Load a second group of exactly 10 records into the data set, in the process causing the contents of all the records presently in the data set to be lost. Print out the 10 new records in the ESDS. Try to print out some of the other records that were formerly contained in the data set prior to the second REPRO operation. Assume that not all of the initial records were overwritten by the second REPRO operation.

EXPORT the ESDS to tape. Delete the original copy of the ESDS and allow any subsequent modifications to be made to the records in the exported copy. Use the PRINT command to display the complete exported copy of the data set and analyze the information it contains.

IMPORT the exported data set back to the original system and have it replace the initial ESDS. Following this, delete the data set.

11

Relative Record
Data Sets (RRDS)

The last of the three original VSAM data set organizations is thoroughly examined in this chapter. The material is grouped into four general areas. First, an overview of the RRDS is given. This includes a physical description, processing capabilities, advantages and disadvantages, and structural/syntax limitations. Next, IDCAMS commands are used to create and process an RRDS. Third, batch COBOL programming with an RRDS is described. This includes a detailed evaluation of most relevant processing features used to load and dynamically update an RRDS. Finally, various applications using an RRDS are evaluated and constructed.

Overview of RRDS Processing

An RRDS is the disk data set counterpart to an array or table in memory. Each RRDS record has an integer associated with it called its relative record number. The relative record number identifies a disk location called a slot, which is equivalent to one table entry. A slot is either empty or contains exactly one logical record. The relative record number is processed as a 4-byte binary value, i.e., an S9(8) COMP field in COBOL. The initial location in the data set is slot number 1, and successive slot numbers are each one greater than their predecessor. See Fig. 11.1, where each track contains three control intervals and each control interval holds four slots.

To randomly access a slot in an RRDS, its relative record number must be identified or specified. In COBOL, the value should be moved to a designated 4-byte key field in WORKING-STORAGE before an I/O operation is attempted.

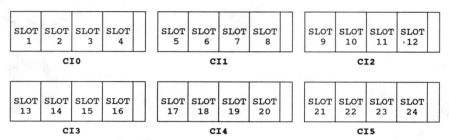

Figure 11.1   Initial tracks and slots in an RRDS.

VSAM calculates the location of the slot in the data set, and retrieves or supplies the contents of the slot in exactly one I/O operation.

The basic reason for using an RRDS is that any individual record can be randomly read or written in exactly one I/O operation. This should be contrasted with a minimum of two I/O operations to random process a record in a KSDS (three is more common).

Whenever rapid random access time is the most important processing criteria for a group of records, a relative data set organization should always be considered. If a collection of records can be readily stored in a relative format, it is usually possible to perform random I/O operations much faster than if the same group of records is stored as a KSDS or an ESDS. This occurs because an RRDS does not contain an index component, which, in turn, provides two advantages over a KSDS. No index structure needs to be searched, and no separate disk storage is required to hold the index.

RRDS Processing Limitations

When compared with a KSDS or even an ESDS, it initially appears that an RRDS suffers from several significant processing limitations prohibiting its use with many collections of records. All records in an RRDS must be the same fixed length. Relative byte address (RBA) processing is not allowed with an RRDS. Once an RRDS is initially created and loaded, its size cannot be increased. IDCAMS will not construct an alternate index over an RRDS. Most important, very few collections of records are "appropriate" candidates for storage as an RRDS without a substantial amount of planning and work on the programmer's part.

Many of these disadvantages can be overcome with careful programming, a great deal of system resources (hardware, money, etc.), or both. The major RRDS processing limitations are discussed in the following six sections in approximate increasing order of importance. They are:

1. Only fixed-length records are allowed.

2. RBA processing is not supported.

3. The size of an RRDS is fixed once it is loaded.

4. Much storage allocated to an RRDS can never be used.

5. Standard IDCAMS alternate key processing (DEFINE AIX, BLDINDEX, DEFINE PATH) is not supported.

6. The slot number to associate with a record is often difficult or nearly impossible to determine.

Several additional minor disadvantages associated with RRDS processing include: generic processing is inconsequential, a COBOL program cannot open an RRDS for EXTEND processing, and contents of deleted records are difficult to recover.

Variable-length records

Because of the technique VSAM uses to locate a specific slot, it is an essential requirement that relative records must be fixed length. However, it is possible to pad variable-length records with a fill character. Whenever all the records are approximately the same size, or it is absolutely essential that a relative data set organization be used, padding is a reasonable cost to pay. The RRDS simulation discussion in chapter 10 illustrates that, for a single collection of records, logical record length can have different meanings with different applications.

It is also important to remember that with an RRDS a complete control interval must be read (and perhaps rewritten) to randomly process a single logical record. Non-VSAM relative data sets require fixed-length, unblocked records. Hence, to mimic the non-VSAM relative data set organization, each individual record could be padded to fill the smallest control interval large enough to hold it. With COBOL II, a feature has been added to allow a simulated variable length RRDS. The padding is performed automatically.

Relative byte address processing

Relative byte addresses are used with each component for all three types of VSAM data sets. The RBA values for an RRDS cannot be explicitly processed by an application program or even IDCAMS commands. However, there are several straightforward relationships between RBA values and relative record numbers. An important formula value is SLOTS-PER-CI, which is a constant obtained by dividing the control interval size by the record size and discarding the remainder. The formulas are shown in Fig. 11.2.

```
            SLOTS-PER-CI = INTEGER {CISZ/RECORDSIZE}
             SLOT-NUMBER = (Q * SLOTS-PER-CI)+ R + 1
     RELATIVE-BYTE-ADDRESS = (Q * CISZ)          +(R * RECORDSIZE)

where RBA/CISZ = Q + R/CISZ Q is the Relative Control Interval
```

Figure 11.2 Conversion formulae between RBA and slot number.

```
SLOTS-PER-CI = INTEGER {2048/500} = 4
RBA/CISZ     = 5596/2048 = 2 + 1500/2048 and Remainder/500 = 3
   Thus    Q = 2 and R   = 3
SLOT-NUMBER  = (2 * 4) + 3 + 1 = 12 (the fourth slot in the third CI)
```

Figure 11.3 Illustrating the formulae in Fig. 11.2.

These formulas can be illustrated using an RRDS, where the logical records are 500 bytes in length and the control interval size is 2,048. One specific record is stored at RBA value 5,596. As shown in Fig. 11.3, the record is stored in slot 12. Conversely, suppose that a record is stored in slot 12. Then:

RELATIVE-BYTE-ADDRESS = 2 * 2048 + 3 * 500 = 5596

Notice that any unusuable bytes in the CI following the records along with CIDF and RDF space is transparent in the calculations. In addition to showing the arithmetic involved in RBA processing, these formulas illustrate how VSAM actually locates records in an RRDS. The basic issue is which of the two is more user friendly and easy to work with: the RBA value or the relative record number. Most people would overwhelmingly pick the relative record number. Hence, the inability to perform RBA processing is of almost no consequence.

Extending an RRDS

There are two distinct issues to extending an RRDS: sequentially extending an RRDS and randomly updating when most slots are filled. If an RRDS becomes "filled," it is difficult to add additional records. COBOL does not permit an RRDS to be opened for EXTEND processing. Typically, when a KSDS runs out of space, a DEFINE CLUSTER command is used to create a second KSDS larger than the existing one. The records in the old KSDS are then copied to the new one, and the old cluster is deleted. Finally, the new cluster is renamed to the old cluster name.

With an RRDS, it is very likely that the slot where a record is currently stored will have to be changed when a new, larger RRDS is loaded. A simple REPRO command probably cannot be used. Hence, a new technique must often be developed to determine the slot in which to place a record. Some common hashing algorithms are discussed in the examples and exercises later in the chapter.

Storage space in an RRDS

An extremely large RRDS can initially be created to guarantee that there will always be sufficient storage for the data set and no extends will be necessary. However, this strategy often results in a large amount of wasted disk storage. Various "experts" propose a percentage of allowable wasted storage which they feel is a reasonable overhead to pay for using an RRDS.

Alternate key processing

Although IDCAMS will not explicitly construct an alternate index over an RRDS, secondary key processing can be performed in a straightforward manner. The same basic approach of using the RBA to identify an ESDS record described in chapter 10 can be used by an application program to build and maintain a user-customized alternate index structure. In this case, each logical record in the alternate index contains an alternate key value and the relative record number(s) of those records that contain the alternate key value.

Unlike an ESDS, it is difficult to use the RBA value rather than the relative record number. However, as discussed in a preceding section, there is no real advantage to processing records in an RRDS with their RBA values. The slot number/key pairs can be stored in a data set in a programmer-selected ordering on the alternate key, such as ascending key order, chronological, most frequently referenced, etc.

Multiple (relative) records can contain the same alternate key value. One straightforward approach is to create a KSDS and use it as the alternate index for the RRDS. The KSDS can be relatively easily maintained in an application program. This comes extremely close to how VSAM actually builds and maintains an alternate index. A KSDS simplifies the existence of duplicate keys and modifications to the alternate index. Realistically, some synchronization problems are more likely to occur when error and exceptional situations arise than if a true VSAM alternate index was available for use. Furthermore, the entire notion of multiple alternate indexes and an upgrade set increase complications substantially.

A programmer-maintained alternate index can also be used with a base ESDS or KSDS. For some rare applications, it might be possible to do this more efficiently than the generalized machinery of VSAM can do it. Several examples in chapter 10 illustrate this with an ESDS. User-created alternate indexes with a KSDS and ESDS are quite rare.

Example 1. Last Name is to be used as an alternate key for processing the records in an RRDS. The same Last Name value can occur up to 10 times in the data set. The Last Name field is 20 bytes in length. The alternate index is stored as a KSDS, and the maximum RECORDSIZE value is specified as 62 ($= 2 + 20 + (10 * 4)$), where the initial 2 bytes identify the number of records that contain the Last Name Value. See Exercise 4.

In order to load the alternate index, each record in the base RRDS is read and the Last Name and Slot Number are combined and written as a two-field record in a temporary disk data set. The temporary data set is sorted using Last Name as the key.

These functions can be easily performed using a combination of utility programs such as IEBGENER, DFSORT, and, of course, IDCAMS itself. An application program is then required to combine the duplicate alternate keys into a single record and calculate the value placed in the two overhead bytes. No standard utility program performs this function. After this, the alternate index records are immediately loaded into the KSDS by the application program or with REPRO in a later step.

Determining the slot number for a record

The previous five sections have discussed how some of the apparent substantial limitations associated with an RRDS can be minimized or overcome in one way or another. However, the single major obstacle remains to be considered. Is a particular collection of records a viable candidate to be stored as an RRDS? In order for this to be the case, there must be a field within the records whose value can be used to determine the slot number where a record will be stored. Ideally, the field value must directly or indirectly identify a unique positive integer, which should be neither too small nor too large. If it is possible for two distinct records to be assigned to the same slot, substantial programming complications might occur. Another significant but somewhat less serious problem occurs if the slot numbers are lightly distributed over a very wide range. In this case, the data set might be unnecessarily large and a substantial percentage of the disk storage allocated for the data set never used. In addition, this leads to somewhat slower sequential processing.

Example 2.   It is extremely unusual to find a data set with a field that directly determines the slot number with no duplications, or almost none, and at the same time is "semi-dense," meaning a moderate percentage of slots will contain records. Suppose Social Security number is used to directly identify the slot number. Clearly, each record will be stored in a unique slot. However, the data set will require space for 1 billion (1,000,000,000) slots. Perhaps the main Internal Revenue Service data center would be able to fill several hundred million of these slots with the records of all current and deceased taxpayers. With most groups of records, far more than 90 percent of this disk storage would never be used.

When the decision is made to create an RRDS, care should be given to selecting the algorithm that will assign a record to a slot. The same algorithm is then used to subsequently retrieve the record. A vast theory of techniques for associating a record with a slot have been developed. Such algorithms are often referred to as "hashing" algorithms. There is no universally best hashing algorithm. Each collection of records must be considered on an individual basis. Hashing algorithms are discussed in more detail in data structures and file design textbooks.

Using IDCAMS to Process an RRDS

The material in chapters 4, 5, 6, and 7 is now reexamined in the following section. Here, all IDCAMS commands are used with an RRDS, paralleling the comparable section in chapter 10 with an ESDS.

DEFINE CLUSTER with an RRDS

As with every VSAM data set, an RRDS can be created with the DEFINE CLUSTER command. The NUMBERED parameter must be coded. RECORDSIZE should specify fixed-length records, and SPANNED should not be coded. Once an RRDS is created, it cannot be extended. However, secondary allocations can be coded and used during the initial load. If almost all processing will be random, a smaller control interval size might be appropriate than would be used with the same records stored as a KSDS. Likewise, a buffer space value for exactly one buffer is specified and is sufficient only for random processing. No CI splits can occur.

When the data set is first opened, the primary disk storage allocation is preformatted, and each record slot is described by its own RDF. The first byte of the RDF consists of control information and the record length is in the last two bytes. One control information bit is comparable to the delete byte in an ISAM, relative or direct access data set, specifying whether the slot is empty or contains a record. With an RRDS, the program does not need to explicitly test for an active record.

Example 3.   The DEFINE CLUSTER code to create an RRDS is shown in Fig. 11.4. The Cluster NAME, NUMBERED, VOLUME, and Space Allocation parameters are required. Approximately 5,000 logical records, each 50 bytes in length, will be stored in the data set. The hashing algorithm used to process the RRDS results in approximately 80 percent of the slots remaining empty. Hence, a total of slightly more than 25,000 slots will be allocated. This excess results because the track containing slot 25,000 will be completely formatted.

Major IDCAMS commands

The role of the remaining major IDCAMS commands is now discussed specifically with regard to RRDS processing. All of this information should be considered as supplementary to the discussion of the Big Eight commands in chapters 5 and 6.

```
DEFINE  CLUSTER(NAME(NEW.RRDS.MASTER)       -
                NUMBERED                     -
                SHAREOPTIONS(2 3)            -
                RECORDSIZE(50 50)            -
                RECORDS(25000)               -
                CISZ(1024)                   -
                TO(94365)                    -
                VOLUME(DISK23))              -
           DATA(NAME(NEW.RRDS.MASTER.DATA)))
```

Figure 11.4   DEFINE CLUSTER code to create an RRDS.

The valid REPRO command parameters for identifying the first record to process are FROMNUMBER and SKIP, while the valid parameters for identifying the final record are TONUMBER and COUNT. In particular, FROMKEY, TOKEY, FROMADDRESS, and TOADDRESS are not valid. REPLACE performs the same basic functions as with a KSDS except that input records will replace existing records with the same relative record/slot number in their designated slots. REUSE will set the HI-USED-RBA to zero. Data encryption is the same as with a KSDS and ESDS.

The preceding comments concerning the initial and final REPRO parameters supported with an RRDS are exactly the same with the PRINT command. PRINT precedes each record by its slot number. Likewise, a LISTCAT ALL for an RRDS includes several fields that do not make sense with a KSDS LISTCAT. These include NOREPLICATE, NOIMBED, FREESPACE, and KEYS.

The ALTER, DELETE, EXPORT, and IMPORT commands with an RRDS function in the same way as with a KSDS and ESDS. These commands also adhere to the basic information provided in chapters 5 and 6. VERIFY syntax is identical for a KSDS and an RRDS. However, a VERIFY is a far less dramatic situation with an RRDS than with a KSDS, or even an ESDS because the HI-USED-RBA rarely changes during standard RRDS random processing.

Example 4. A variety of IDCAMS commands are used in Fig. 11.5 to process the RRDS created in Example 3. It is to be loaded with the records stored in the data set OLD.RRDS.MASTER. Because the input data set is also an RRDS, the active records are copied to the corresponding slots in the new data set. Because the output data set is empty, it is meaningless to code REPLACE and REUSE.

Following the REPRO operation, the first five records are printed, along with a complete LISTCAT for the data set. Both PRINT commands list the records in the same order with the same format.

```
REPRO    IDS(OLD.RRDS.MASTER)                      -
         ODS(NEW.RRDS.MASTER)
PRINT    IDS(NEW.RRDS.MASTER)          COUNT(05)
PRINT    IDS(NEW.RRDS.MASTER.DATA)  COUNT(05)
LISTCAT  ENT(NEW.RRDS.MASTER)  ALL
IF MAXCC = 0 THEN                                  -
    DO
         DELETE    OLD.RRDS.MASTER
         ALTER     NEW.RRDS.MASTER                 -
                   NEWNAME(OLD.RRDS.MASTER)
         ALTER     NEW.RRDS.MASTER.DATA            -
                   NEWNAME(OLD.RRDS.MASTER.DATA)
    END
```

Figure 11.5 Basic IDCAMS command processing with an RRDS.

Finally, if all of the prior commands were successful, the old RRDS is deleted, and the new RRDS has its name changed to that of the deleted data set. Note that two ALTER commands are required but only one DELETE command is needed.

COBOL Programming Considerations with an RRDS

In this section, the COBOL programming material in chapter 9 is reexamined as it relates to an RRDS. When an RRDS is initially created, all the slots are marked as empty. When a record is written to a slot, the control bit in the RDF is changed to identify an active record in the slot.

A COBOL program can load records into an RRDS either sequentially or in a pseudo-random manner that shares some similarities with skip sequential processing during an input operation. Both sequential and pseudo-random require that ACCESS IS SEQUENTIAL be coded in the SELECT statement. During a true sequential data set creation, the first record is written in slot number 1, the second record in slot number 2, etc.

A RELATIVE KEY clause can optionally be coded with the SELECT statement. After a record is written, the number of the slot where it was stored is placed in the RELATIVE KEY field if it is coded. Otherwise, this information will be lost unless the program has some other way to determine it.

A pseudo-random creation requires that records be loaded in ascending slot number order. Otherwise, VSAM returns a status code of 21. Before a record is written, the designated slot number is moved to the RELATIVE KEY field. After the fields in the 01 level are assigned values, the record is written. A random load operation works the same way except the input records need not be in order by slot number. When non-VSAM relative data sets are pseudo-randomly created, dummy records are written with the same data placed in the next slot with an active record.

With subsequent random and dynamic processing, the slot number where a record is to be stored must also be moved to the RELATIVE KEY before the WRITE and REWRITE statement is executed. In all cases, the field identified with RELATIVE KEY does not need to be contained within the logical record. If the slot is empty, a WRITE operation adds the record to the data set. If the slot contains a record, VSAM returns a status code of 22.

An application program must be used to randomly or pseudo-randomly sequentially load records into an RRDS from sequential input. IDCAMS cannot perform this function because there is no way to identify the slot in which to store the record. See Exercise 9. Likewise, the complete range of random processing must be performed in an application program. REPRO can randomly copy records from one RRDS to a second RRDS. Either REPLACE or NOREPLACE can be specified to determine whether strictly record additions are performed (NOREPLACE) or if changes are also possible (REPLACE).

TABLE 11.1 Using COBOL to Process Records in an RRDS.

VSAM I/O Operation	Contents of Relative Key	CRP	Status Code	Explanation of the Processing Results
READ	50	–	23	Missing master record
WRITE	50	–	00	Record added
REWRITE	50	–	00	Record changed
WRITE	50	–	22	Duplicate master record
READ	50	55	00	Valid random read
DELETE	50	55	00	Record deleted
DELETE	50	55	23	Missing master record
READ	50	55	23	Missing master record
START >= 50	50	55	00	CRP Points to slot 55
READ NEXT	55	60	00	Valid sequential read

Example 5.   Table 11.1 shows the results of performing I/O operations with an RRDS. Assume that, prior to the first operation, slot 50 is empty. ACCESS IS DYNAMIC has been specified and the data set opened successfully. The first two active records following slot 50 have relative numbers of 55 and 60 respectively.

After an RRDS is loaded, it can be processed in much the same manner as a KSDS. In a COBOL program, an RRDS can be accessed sequentially, randomly, or dynamically. A variant of skip sequential access is also possible with PL/I and assembler. The syntax of the COBOL statements used to process a KSDS and an RRDS are almost identical. The slot number is identified by the RELATIVE KEY field in the same way that the KSDS logical record is identified by the RECORD KEY field.

Records can be added, deleted, and rewritten both sequentially and randomly. A record can only be added to an empty slot. Because an RRDS cannot be extended after it is initially created, OPEN EXTEND cannot be coded. Every deletion is physical in the sense that, after a record is deleted, VSAM will not subsequently retrieve it. A rewritten record cannot have its length changed. For sequential processing, the READ...NEXT format must be specified with dynamic access, and NEXT is optional with sequential access. The syntax of the START statement is similar to that used for processing a KSDS. Generic keys and non-equal key value comparisons can be used.

When sequentially processing the records in an RRDS, it is unnecessary to read every slot and determine whether a given slot contains a record. Rather, during sequential processing, VSAM supplies only active records. To retrieve the contents of every slot regardless of its active/deleted status, the technique of processing just the data component as a non-VSAM data set with an undefined record format can be used.

Dynamic COBOL Update Program

Several detailed COBOL coding situations are examined in this section. An RRDS usually is loaded using pseudo-sequential processing (OPEN I/O). The

RRDS can then be dynamically updated. (If variable length records are used as input, padding would be required.) Likewise, programming parallels the comparable programming with a KSDS in chapter 9. Here, the application itself loads the RRDS, rather than the REPRO command. Every VSAM command available with a KSDS can be used with an RRDS.

Standard RRDS applications

When should an RRDS be used? Several applications are presented to illustrate when using an RRDS might be appropriate. In the first application, the data set consists of records that are "ideal" candidates for storage as an RRDS. In the second application, hashing is used out of necessity to build an RRDS. The third application, which requires the most sophisticated programming techniques of the three, uses a separate overflow area to resolve collisions. Finally, linked list RRDS processing is mentioned. The format throughout these sections is to identify a processing situation and then show an example where an RRDS is used to address the problems.

An "Ideal" RRDS

There are 10,000 fixed-length records. Each record contains a 5-byte field, whose values are unique positive integers ranging from 1 to 20,000. These records are to be randomly processed almost exclusively, and no future additions to the data set will result in duplicate values in the 5-byte field. These records are an "ideal" candidate for being stored as an RRDS. They are almost too good to be true. If these records are to be processed only sequentially, then there is no reason to store them as an RRDS no matter how ideal they are. If subsequent additions will result in duplicates assigned to the same slot, an RRDS might still be a good choice, but it is no longer ideal.

Example 6.   An RRDS is created with 20,000 slots. After the records are loaded, half of the slots will be empty. This is considered a very acceptable overhead for the speed and ease of random access the RRDS provides. The record with the number N in the 5-byte field will be written in the Nth slot. To retrieve the record, N is moved to the RELATIVE KEY and a random READ is executed. No collisions should ever occur and an acceptable percentage (50 percent) of the RRDS contains active records.

Hashing and duplicate keys (collisions)

An existing data set contains 10,000 records. The size of the data set is expected to increase at a rate of 50 percent per year. There is only one field in the records that contains unique values—a 9-digit Social Security number. It is decided to store the records in an RRDS and to use the Social Security number to determine the records' slot. It is reasonable to expect that the data set will be reorganized on a periodic basis because of growth. This application illustrates some of the significant problems that can arise with RRDS processing involving a group of records that are not "ideal" but are also not worst-case scenario.

Example 7. Because there are 1 billion distinct, 9-digit numbers, a direct relationship between Social Security number and slot number is impractical. Instead, the Division/Remainder algorithm should be used to transform a Social Security number to a slot value between 1 and 20,000. For a given record with Social Security number N, N is divided by 19,999. The quotient is discarded, but the remainder, R, is kept.

The record will be associated with slot number $R + 1$. This gives a range of 1 to 19,999 for the slot number. The same algorithm is also used to retrieve an existing record. The value 20,000 is selected because of projected data set growth and to reduce the chances that two records will be sent to the same slot. An even larger value might be appropriate, although this will produce more empty slots.

This approach functions very smoothly unless two or more records end up being associated with the same slot. When such a "collision" occurs, programming becomes more complicated. The second record cannot be stored in its designated slot. Where should it be placed?

One common approach is to write it in the next available empty slot in ascending sequence in the data set. Hopefully, if the record cannot be placed in its designate slot X, then slot $X + 1$ is empty. This is sometimes called the *worst neighbor policy*. This is because, if a record associated with slot $X + 1$ is to be added later, it cannot be placed in its assigned slot because it is occupied by a record that does not belong in the slot.

A designated number of slots can be examined to determine if there is a free slot near the calculated hashing value. In fact, there are several approaches for finding the next available slot. Successive random READ operations can be done until a status code of 23 occurs. Alternatively, the first slot located with a READ NEXT can be evaluated. If an empty slot "relatively" close to the calculated value cannot be found, the data set might require reorganization and a new hashing routine.

It is possible that a collision record will be written in a slot and a later record to be added actually hashes to the slot. This forces the new record to another slot. An alternative approach is to restrict adds during the initial load to only those records that go to their designated slots. The records involved in collisions can be temporarily stored and then later randomly written to the data set, attempting first to add to slot $X + 1$, if it is assigned to slot X.

The approach used to write a record must be repeated when retrieving a record. Dynamic processing is very convenient for doing this (START followed by a READ NEXT loop). The record key, along with the slot number, is used to place and then locate a given record. Because of all the complications generated by the collisions, it is questionable as to whether a relative data set of the selected size is appropriate for this group of records.

Separate overflow areas for record collisions

Other approaches than the ones listed in the preceding section exist to deal with collisions. Suppose the same group of records considered in the last example is used but, as an alternative to the worst neighbor policy, a general overflow area can be built to handle collision records.

If a record is hashed to a slot containing a record, the new record is placed in the general overflow area. A pointer can be attached to the base record to show where a collision record is stored in the overflow area. Thus, there is no significance as to which slot in the overflow area a record is placed in.

This method is similar to the overflow areas used with ISAM. In fact, most overflow processing techniques mimic the way ISAM maintains its cylinder and independent overflow areas. The overflow area used might be a portion of the RRDS, or it could be a second independent RRDS. In either case, the overflow area could be the same size as the base data set or smaller.

There is no limit to how elaborate or complicated an overflow area can be. In theory, it could be the same size as the base RRDS. In particular, each slot in the overflow area would be initially associated with exactly one slot (the same location) in the base RRDS.

Example 8.   The same group of records considered in the previous example is to be stored as an RRDS. It has been determined that about 60 percent of the records hash to a unique value; about 35 percent are resulting in a collision with 1 other record; 4 percent are involved in collisions involving two other records; and the remaining 1 percent are involved in collisions with three or more records.

It is decided to store the records in two separate data sets, where the 60 percent of the records not involved in collisions will be stored in RRDS1, along with a flag specifying whether other records were hashed to the same slot. The first record later hashed to the slot resulting in a collision will go in the same slot number in RRDS2. Hence, RRDS2 is an overflow data set. Furthermore, RRDS2 is bigger than RRDS1 and will contain a general overflow area for those 5 percent of the records not placed in RRDS1 or in a primary slot (the actual hashed value) in RRDS2.

Linked list processing

Linked lists are easy to build and process using the records in an RRDS. One additional 4-byte field is added to each record. It contains the slot number of the next record in the linked list. Because slot numbers are easier to work with than RBA values, a linked list is simpler with an RRDS than with an ESDS.

Example 9.   The records in Example 8 are to be linked together so that they can be processed in ascending order by Social Security number. In this case, each active record contains two pointer fields, one for the next record with ascending key value in the linked list and one for the overflow record assigned to a slot. These data sets can be processed in COBOL but this is not possible with ESDS linked lists because RBA processing is not supported.

Future RRDS Developments

Several major improvements could be made to RRDS processing. IDCAMS should be available to build and manage an alternate index over an RRDS. A programmer could then make the decision as to whether this "contradictory" structure is appropriate for a specific application. When copying records from a non-relative data set into an RRDS with REPRO, a parameter could be optionally coded to identify the slot where the record is to be written. As KEYS with a KSDS, it could contain two parameters—length and location. Specifying KEYS(4 0) or SLOT(4 0) and NUMBERED would imply that the first 4 bytes in each record identify the slot in which to write the record. The four bytes themselves could optionally be written within the new record.

Exercises

1. Identify five significant similarities between an RRDS and a KSDS. Identify five significant differences between an RRDS and a KSDS. Determine five significant similarities and differences between an RRDS and an ESDS. Categories to consider include disk representation, permissible I/O operations, processing overheads, access speeds, etc.

2. A specific field in an RRDS contains unique values. It is to be used as a secondary key field. Construct an alternate index over an RRDS and perform a dynamic master file update. It should be possible to add, delete, and change records based on either their relative record number or alternate key value.

3. One significant change is made to the hypotheses in the previous exercise. Duplicate alternate key values are allowed. Identify all additional complications that can occur because of nonunique alternate keys.

4. The alternate index described in Example 1 did not include the 5 bytes of overhead for each logical record that an IDCAMS alternate index record would contain. Which of the five bytes are unnecessary in this case? Which of these four fields are unnecessary in general? Discuss the processing that occurs in the alternate index as records in the base RRDS are added, deleted, and changed.

5. Three common hashing algorithms are quotient—remainder, folding, and double hashing. Evaluate the appropriateness of all three algorithms using first a worst neighbor policy and then an independent overflow area for processing an RRDS where Social Security number is to be used to determine the slot number. There are 1 million records. Are any modifications necessary if almost every Social Security number begins with a 3?

6. Implement Example 6 using a worst neighbor approach to reduce collisions.

Use the quotient-remainder hashing algorithm. How can careful preprocessing before loading the data set result in a larger percentage of records being placed in the slot to which they are initially hashed? Determine the number of records involved in collisions. How many slots are involved in 3, 4, or more records hashing to them?

7. How can IDCAMS be used to print the deleted records in an RRDS? How can this be done in an application program? Can COBOL be used or is it necessary to use PL/I or assembler?

8. Export an RRDS to tape or disk. Dump the records in the exported data set, and examine their contents. In particular, which records were exported and how are slots identified? Identify any differences between the logical records in the RRDS and in the exported data set.

9. Develop a utility program to load (REPRO) records into an RRDS, either pseudo-sequentially or randomly from a sequential data set. Note that IDCAMS REPRO cannot do this. Note that this is more complicated than the final comments in the last section in the chapter.

Comprehensive exercises for an RRDS

1. Use IDCAMS to create an RRDS that contains sufficient slots for storing up to 5,000 logical records, each 100 bytes in length. Actual storage will depend on the type of disk. Assume that approximately half of the slots in the data set will always be empty. Specify a minimum number of slots in each control interval. Try to create the entire data set with just the primary allocation, but do not overallocate. Otherwise, the storage will be wasted. Hint: There are two approaches, use numeric calculations or overallocate and then determine how much storage was actually required. This information can be found in a LISTCAT report.

2. Write a short application program in COBOL (or PL/I or assembler) to load the RRDS. To simplify logic, write an active record in each odd-numbered slot. Each record should begin with four bytes containing the slot number and 96 bytes of filler, such as an asterisk. Use LISTCAT to confirm that the 5,000 records have been loaded correctly. Print out the first 10 and the final ten active records in the RRDS.

3. Create a second data set identical to the first one in every way except for the cluster and data component names. Modify the application program to write 2,500 records into the new RRDS, placing them in the 1st, 5th, 9th, etc., slots. Each record should begin with four bytes containing the slot number and 96 bytes of filler, such as a dollar sign. Now, copy from the first RRDS to the second, replacing records or adding records depending on whether there is an active record in the target slot. Confirm that the processing was successful by examining a LISTCAT and printing out the records in a typical cross section of the second RRDS, such as all slots from 1500 to 2500.

4. Export the second RRDS to cartridge. Retain the original (pre-exported) copy and allow any type of processing to be made to it. Import the exported data set back to the original system. Verify the original data set and delete all objects involved in this exercise.

Part

4

12

VSAM
Catalog Structure

No matter how you might work with VSAM, some knowledge of VSAM catalogs is helpful. This chapter covers the overall system catalog structure and the interrelations among catalogs and volumes on the system, as well as a general description of the internal structure of an individual catalog. Evolving catalog structures used with VSAM are strongly related to the actual release of VSAM concurrently available with a given catalog structure. This evolving history of VSAM and the various catalog structures, as well as the volume data set, are discussed. Throughout the chapter, various comparisons between the two primary types of catalog structures are made.

Early VSAM Eras

As with other major software products and data set organizations, VSAM has undergone significant structural changes throughout the more than two decades of its lifetime. Knowing how VSAM has changed results in a better understanding of present-day VSAM. This history is strongly related to various VSAM catalog structures.

There have been several fundamental eras in the history of VSAM, beginning with the announcement and introduction of VSAM in 1973. Originally, VSAM consisted of the KSDS and ESDS structures, a collection of IDCAMS commands for processing them, and the original VSAM catalog structure to manage them. Several years later, a new release called *Enhanced VSAM* was developed. Enhanced VSAM added many of the basic features associated with VSAM today. In particular:

- The RRDS.
- Alternate indexes.
- A new catalog structure.
- Index component processing.
- Catalog recovery commands.
- Reusable data sets.
- Spanned records.
- A much wider range of IDCAMS commands.

Clearly, the Enhanced VSAM features continue to form the crucial nucleus for much of today's VSAM processing. These major features have been discussed in detail in earlier chapters, and much of the material in chapters 1 through 11 has remained virtually the same with Enhanced VSAM and its successors.

The third significant era in VSAM processing consisted not so much of additions, but modifications to the existing features. In conjunction with this, the third truly significant VSAM release was meant to correct some of the most glaring deficiencies found in Enhanced VSAM. Most problem areas centered around the VSAM catalog structure and the methods used by VSAM to allocate and manage disk storage. In particular, a new catalog structure was introduced called the *Integrated Catalog Facility (ICF)* that gave users a variety of catalog choices: (Enhanced) VSAM Catalogs, ICF Catalogs, and even CVOLs. All of these catalog types can be used together in the same system.

CVOLs are non-VSAM objects themselves, and VSAM objects cannot be cataloged in them. The CVOL is in the endangered catalog structure category and is rarely encountered today. Enhanced VSAM catalogs are also finding themselves on the same endangered list. The distinction between UNIQUE and SUBALLOCATION was described earlier in chapter 4. This is intimately related to catalog concepts. A catalog recovery area that approximately doubled the efforts of catalog management was also discarded and was altered substantially in newer releases.

(Enhanced) VSAM catalog problems

Catalogs are one of a handful of absolutely fundamental components on which VSAM is built. The basic role of catalogs has already been discussed at various locations throughout the book. The catalog structure provided with Enhanced VSAM centered around the notion of "volume ownership." Every disk volume that stored VSAM data sets was assigned or paired with one specific VSAM catalog, almost always a user catalog, but possibly the master catalog. The selected catalog was then said to "own" the DASD volume. Any VSAM data set placed on a disk volume must then be cataloged in the specific catalog that owned it. Furthermore, the catalog that owned the volume did not need to reside on the volume.

Volume ownership probably seemed like a good idea in the mid to late 1970s when the IBM 3330 was the state-of-the-art and most widely used disk volume in the world. It was envisioned (and routinely implemented) that an entire 3330 volume would be dedicated to a specific application system, or group of programmers. All catalog/data set management associated with this volume could then be consolidated into a single user catalog.

The 3330 had considerably smaller data capacity than its successor the 3350. (The 3330 was also removable and, hence, truly portable.) Fewer applications and groups of programmers had cause to routinely use the capacity of an entire 3350 volume. However, any unused space could not be managed by a second catalog and remained unused and wasted. Hence, in the post-3330 disk world, it seems unreasonable to force every data set placed on a disk volume to be cataloged in the same catalog.

Volume ownership became an even more convoluted notion when the 3380 and 3390 disks were developed. Why not allow a somewhat arbitrary pairing between a catalog and disk volumes? This is but one illustration of how technology caused a significant VSAM feature in the 1970s to become outdated and wasteful today. The obvious solution to this problem was to greatly modify the volume ownership requirement. ICF catalogs use volume management rather than volume ownership.

A second problem with the standard VSAM catalog structure was that all catalog information for an object was placed in the same level of importance. In retrospect, it seems reasonable to divide such information into several distinct classifications. One high-level grouping consists of more-or-less permanent information (it almost never changes) and temporary information (it changes on a frequent basis). Permanent information includes associated objects, security information, identification, disk volumes, etc. Temporary information includes volatile values such as processing statistics, allocation information, CI and CA split statistics, and various RBA values, such as HURBA.

It seems reasonable to store (temporary) information in a location where it can be readily modified whenever the underlying data set is changed. One possible location would be on the volume where the data set itself is stored. With Enhanced VSAM, such information is stored in a catalog that is frequently located on a different volume than the data set. On the other hand, permanent information could be maintained in a location far removed from the data set itself. One obvious potential solution to this problem is to have a catalog structure with at least two disjoint component parts.

A third significant problem concerned the inflexibility of the Enhanced VSAM catalog structure itself. A programmer could specify very few parameters when a catalog was created. Parameters such as CISZ, BUFFERSPACE, and INDEX allowed almost no flexibility in their possible values. RECORDSIZE and KEYS values were fixed. Parameters such as REPLICATE and IMBED could not be coded, even though the catalog was a KSDS. Amazingly, even the INDEX parameter could not be coded. The name coded with DEFINE CLUSTER became the Data Component name while a fixed name was generated for the index component. Very little additional information could be specified when processing the catalog, and it seemed reasonable to allow programmers to have more of a role in creating and processing a catalog. As a consequence, a much wider range of programmer processing options (parameters) became available for ICF catalogs using the DEFINE USERCATALOG command. The cluster name was called *Binary Zeroes* in order to be the first entry in the catalog.

There were a number of additional problems with the catalog structure and disk storage management, but these were certainly among the major ones. Consequently, ICF solutions were dramatic and effective, and the notion of volume ownership by a single catalog was discarded.

Although one enhanced VSAM catalog could still "own" the volume, with an ICF structure, up to 36 catalogs could share the ownership of a single disk volume. If both Enhanced VSAM catalogs and ICF catalogs were used, up to 37 catalogs could have entries for objects on the volume. Enhanced VSAM and ICF catalogs entries could not be mixed, and all related objects were cataloged in one type or the other.

The integrated catalog facility is unintegrated in that one part of it was stored as a true cataloglike structure while the rest of the catalog information was moved to the volumes where the data sets with entries in the catalog were stored. The portion of the catalog that contains the stable information (unlikely to change) is called the *Basic Catalog Structure (BCS)*, where every cataloged data set has information stored in the BCS. The more volatile catalog information was stored on the disk volume in the VSAM *Volume Data Set (VVDS)*, a special type of data set required with ICF catalogs. Each volume that contained one or more VSAM objects under ICF had a VVDS on it. The name of this data set was standardized; it was always SYS1.VVDS.Vvolser. Its role with VSAM data sets, which are cataloged in an ICF catalog, is analogous to the Volume TABLE of Contents (VTOC) with non-VSAM data sets.

The next section describes how pseudo-unique eliminated the SUBALLOCATION and UNIQUE VSAM data sets and the concept of shared disk storage management that existed with Enhanced VSAM. Several other major changes occurred in the transition from Enhanced VSAM to ICF catalogs. Related objects had their information stored together rather than separately. In addition, several catalog and data set diagnostic tools were introduced with the ICF catalog structure, including DIAGNOSE. The notion of reclaiming a control interval that had all of its records deleted was introduced.

UNIQUE and SUBALLOCATION revisions

Classifying clusters as unique and suballocated, one of the fuzzier Enhanced VSAM notions, was reevaluated and a much needed revision done. The revision consisted of discarding both of these classifications and replacing them with a new, storage allocation category called *pseudo-unique*.

Pseudo-unique is an appropriate name because the ICF approach is closer to unique than suballocation. Because suballocation ceased to exist, there was no reason to provide a DEFINE SPACE command to reserve storage areas on disk volumes, and it was removed from IDCAMS. In fact, it is not possible to specify UNIQUE, SUBALLOCATION, or pseudo-unique with DEFINE commands used with ICF catalogs. However, a DEFINE PAGESPACE command remains, and each VSAM object that contained records is an object in its own right, the same as any non-VSAM disk data set. However, the resulting pseudo-unique object differs from an Enhanced VSAM unique object in several significant ways.

First, pseudo-unique allows up to 122 secondary allocations—the same as suballocation—rather than the 15 secondary allocations available with unique. In addition, each requested control area, which is less than 1 cylinder, is actually created with its specified size rather than rounded up to 1 cylinder, as is the case with unique. Hence, pseudo-unique shares many properties with non-VSAM data sets. With pseudo-unique, the Data (and Index for a KSDS) components have an entry in the VTOC on the volume on which they are stored. This is not the case for suballocation. Finally, with the ICF structure, the DEFINE USERCATALOG command supplies a wider range of processing options, providing the programmer with some additional flexibility.

The Most Recent Major VSAM Era

The fourth major date in VSAM history occurred in late 1988 with the announcement of the Storage Management System (SMS) and a variety of related features. The Storage Management System was an attempt to update VSAM and its disk processing management in the 1980s. Note, not the 1990s. This will probably not occur for at least another 10 to 12 years. The changes introduced with era four are as dramatic as those in each of the three eras that preceeded it.

The SMS era includes several truly profound changes in VSAM structure and processing. A fourth VSAM data set was introduced, the *Linear Data Set (LDS)*, sometimes called the *Linear Sequenced Data Set (LSDS)*. This is imprecisely described as an "ESDS-like" data set meant to be used in a variety of completely new processing situations, including DB2. In addition, it became possible to create and delete VSAM data sets via the JCL DD statement.

As an alternative to DEFINE CLUSTER, it is now possible to code DISP = (NEW,CATLG) for a newly created VSAM data set. As an alternative to the IDCAMS DELETE command, code DISP = (OLD,DELETE) can be used to scratch and uncatalog a VSAM data set. It is also now possible to make some general performance and management-related specifications when creating a data set without having to worry about an overwhelming amount of technical details.

In conjunction with these last two points, the notion of data set models was greatly expanded upon. An installation could create a group of models that could then be referenced through various DD statement parameters. In addition to these three major innovations, various other important changes were made.

As noted in chapter 1, a major advantage of VSAM data sets and the IDCAMS utility is that very little JCL is required. Still, if the past 15 to 20 years is any indication, either some people prefer using JCL to coding IDCAMS or, at the least, would like a choice between the two methods. This choice is now available. Although JCL has become substantially more user friendly since VSAM was first introduced, it is still not in a class with IDCAMS. But, for a variety of reasons, IDCAMS features are now being moved into JCL rather than vice versa. The major movement concerns the DEFINE CLUSTER and DELETE command features.

To accommodate the additional JCL support for VSAM data sets, a number of additional DD parameters have been created. The major points that must be addressed when using JCL to process VSAM data sets are very similar to those with non-VSAM data sets. In addition, the IDCAMS MODEL parameter has been mimicked in JCL to allow a substantial amount of information to be supplied from a minimum of JCL coding. The following DD parameters are available when creating a VSAM data set with JCL:

- DSN = Cluster
- DISP = (NEW,CATLG)
- SPACE =
- UNIT and VOL
- AMP

The Name (DSN = Cluster) Default names are generated for components only. The DISP = (NEW,CATLG) parameter is inflexible, and with SMS, CATLG = KEEP. The SPACE = (amount,(primary,secondary)) can have CYL, TRK, blocksize, or recordsize coded. Recordsize is new with SMS. The UNIT and VOL parameters should be identified together. DCB is not permitted with a VSAM data set, but AMP is comparable. Other parameters with no Non-VSAM equivalents include:

- STORCLAS
- DATACLAS
- MGMTCLAS

Today, it is uncertain what potential changes will be associated with the next (fifth) VSAM era.

Catalogs—Their Purpose, Creation, and Management

There are three several good reasons for catalogs. They:

- Are convenient.
- Require less work from a programmer.
- Supply relevant information about data sets.

As a general rule, permanent data sets should always be cataloged (if possible). There are several exceptions to this rule. If two data sets contain the same name, only one of them can be cataloged in a single, specific user catalog. Some processing situations might require that a data set not be cataloged.

The DEFINE USERCATALOG command

A VSAM user catalog is created much like a standard VSAM KSDS. The IDCAMS DEFINE USERCATALOG (DEF UCAT) command is used, and the same three parameters required when creating any VSAM data set must be provided: cluster name, volume, and space allocation. MODEL can be used to supply the later two values. Because both Enhanced VSAM catalogs and ICF catalogs can be created with the DEFINE UCAT command, the VSAMCATA-LOG (Enhanced) and ICFCATALOG (ICF) parameters are provided to identify the type of catalog. VSAMCATALOG is the default.

The NAME parameter has a different role with the DEFINE UCAT command than with any other DEFINE command. The value specified for the cluster name actually becomes the name of the data component of the catalog. The index component name should not be coded, and it is always generated as CATINDEX.Tbbbbbbb.VIDyyddd.Taaaaaaa.

A cluster name of 44 bytes of binary zeroes is generated. This convention guarantees that the cluster name is the first catalog entry in the EBCDIC collating sequence. The cluster entry will always appear first in a LISTCAT for the entire catalog. Recall that the complete catalog structure consists of one BCS and one or more VVDS entries. Hence, the value specified with NAME identifies, in a sense, all of the objects grouped together. A separate DEFINE (CLUSTER) command is required for each VVDS that must be created. An overview of the relationship among the BCS and VVDSs is shown in Table 12.1.

Although a user catalog is a KSDS, the role of some DEFINE parameters are either prohibited or more restrictive than with a standard KSDS. INDEXED, KEYS, SPEED, NOREUSE, and RECOVERABLE cannot be coded. The structure of the index is completely determined by virtue of being a user catalog. The keys are always the first 45 bytes in each record—44 bytes for the name of the data set and 1 byte to identify record extensions. A catalog is always preformatted for a load operation. Hence, RECOVERY is used rather than SPEED. An ICF catalog is reusable and can be reloaded at any time. It

TABLE 12.1   Comparing the BCS and a VVDS.

Catalog Property	BCS	VVDS
Data Set Type	KSDS	ESDS
How Created	DEFINE USERCATALOG	DEFINE CLUSTER
Number of Objects	One per catalog	One or more per catalog
VOLUME Location	With DEFINE UCAT	With DEFINE CLUSTER

cannot, however, be specified as recoverable because basic recoverable structures ended with Enhanced VSAM.

Unlike with Enhanced VSAM catalogs, which have a very inflexible structure and cannot be tuned, most remaining KSDS parameters can be specified when creating an ICF catalog:

- REPLICATE and IMBED can be coded.
- RECORDSIZE, CISZ, and BUFFERSPACE allocations can be coded.
- FREESPACE can be selected.

The following final four parameter values can have a significant effect on processing efficiencies with a catalog, but none of them can be coded with an ICF catalog.

Example 1.   An ICF user catalog is to be created on volume MAST23. It is expected to contain only a small number of objects. However, a substantial amount of creations and deletions will take place. The IDCAMS code is shown in Fig. 12.1.

The VVDS

With an ICF catalog structure, each volume contains a VSAM Volume Data Set (VVDS). This is a required data set that must be on the volume before any additional VSAM data sets can be stored on the volume. The VVDS can be explicitly created before placing any VSAM data sets on the volume that are cataloged in an ICF catalog. It can also be implicitly created in conjunction with placing the very first such data set on the volume.

The VVDS itself is an ESDS and must have the required name of SYS1. VVDS.Vvolser. The VVDS can be pictured as shown in Fig. 12.2. Note that a VVDS is meaningful only with an ICF catalog structure.

The first field in the VVDS is the VSAM Volume Control Record (VVCR), which identifies all the basic catalog structures that share in managing the VVDS. For one VVDS, there can be up to 36 such ICF catalogs. The VVCR consists of two components, each 2,048 (2K) bytes in length. The first ICF catalog to assume management of an object on the volume creates the VVDS, and with it, the VVCR. As other catalogs assume management of a data set on the

```
DEFINE  USERCATALOG(NAME(APPL2.CTLGTAXS)  -
        ICFCATALOG                         -
        VOLUME(MAST23)                     -
        CYLINDER(1 1)                      -
        FREESPACE(25 33)                   -
        CISZ(2048))
```

Figure 12.1 Creating an ICF catalog.

VSAM Volume Control Record	Self Describing VSAM Volume Record (VVR)	VVR1	VVR2	VVR3	. . .	VVRN

Figure 12.2   The VSAM volume data set (VVDS).

volume, the first field in the VVCR is updated. The second field in the VVCR is a bit map, which is used to manage storage throughout the rest of the VVDS. The 16K available bits can then manage a huge number of control intervals.

The VVCR is followed by the self-describing VVR, which contains the information that describes the VVDS. The VVR is a VSAM data set and, hence, must have a VVR entry. The VVDR and SD-VVR is structurally the same as the other VVRs and describes other objects such as:

- Clusters
- Non-VSAM data sets
- Alternate indexes
- Generation data groups
- Paths
- Aliases

A VVR is associated with each object cataloged in an ICF catalog-managed data set on the volume. This includes the data and index components for VSAM data sets. Hence, the KSDS will have multiple VVRs associated with it. The VVR holds the information associated with the object that is most likely to be modified. The less volatile information is stored in the BCS.

The only objects with entries in the VVDS are those VSAM objects cataloged in one of the managing ICF catalogs. In particular, a non-VSAM data set will not have a VVR entry describing it. For a non-VSAM data set cataloged in an ICF catalog, all catalog information is stored in the BCS. Additional information is stored in a standard format-1 DSCB in the VTOC. Likewise, a VSAM data set cataloged in an Enhanced VSAM catalog will not have a VVR entry. A VVR entry for a data set further decomposes into entries called sphere records.

Example 2.   A VSAM volume data set is to be created on volume DISK24. Space should be allocated 1 cylinder at a time, resulting in a control area size of 1 cylinder. Notice in Fig. 12.3 that the name coded with DEFINE CLUSTER

```
DEFINE  CLUSTER(NAME(SYS1.VVDS.VDISK24)    -
                NONINDEXED                  -
                VOLUME(DISK24)              -
                CYLINDER(1 1))
```

Figure 12.3   Creating a VSAM VOLUME DATA SET (VVDS).

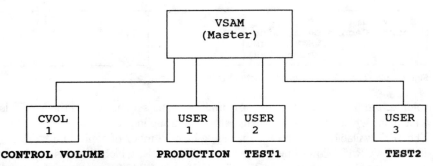

Figure 12.4 Typical system catalog structure.

identifies the data set as the VVDS for the volume. NONINDEXED, a space allocation, and specifying the volume as DISK24 are all required.

System catalog structure

A somewhat "typical" modern VSAM catalog structure is pictured in Fig. 12.4. It consists of a master catalog and several user catalogs—either ICF catalogs or Enhanced VSAM catalogs. The entries in a master catalog can be any of the following types of objects:

- User catalogs of any type (found only in the master catalog).
- Alias names for VSAM and ICF user catalogs.
- CVOL catalogs.
- VSAM data sets of all four types.
- Components of VSAM data sets.
- Alternate indexes and paths.
- Non-VSAM data sets of any type.
- Generation data group base table and generation data sets.
- Assorted other exotic objects.

A user catalog can contain every type of entry except for the first one. For most operations, be they defining, deleting, or retrieving a data set, the hierarchy of catalog search is the following:

1. IDCAMS CATALOG parameter explicitly coded
2. STEPCAT/JOBCAT (concatenation is allowed with both)
3. First qualifier of data set name:
   – is it the name of a user catalog?
   – is it an alias of a user catalog?
4. The master catalog (always a VSAM catalog)

When generic catalog operations are performed, this hierarchy becomes more involved. Table 12.2 is a list of the types of cataloged objects.

GDG processing can also be considered a special case. The existing VSAM catalog structure is being replaced by the ICF catalog structure on most large MVS systems. ICF stands for Integrated Catalog Facility. Some fundamental distinctions between these two structures are identified below Table 12.3 on the next page. The types of information stored in catalogs for a non-VSAM data set include:

- DSNAME
- UNIT
- VOLUME
- File Sequence Number

All other information describing an existing non-VSAM data set is found in its format-1 DSCB. The following types of information for a VSAM data set can be found in a VSAM catalog:

- Ownership
- Security
- Volume information
- Space allocation
- DCB-like characteristics
- Processing statistics

Why have multiple user catalogs instead of only the master catalog?

- Smaller sized catalogs results in better efficiency.
- Less damage to system if only one catalog becomes damaged or destroyed.
- Master catalog less susceptible to problems.

A summary of the most significant properties in an ICF catalog is as follows:

TABLE 12.2   Types of Cataloged Objects.

```
User Catalogs of Any Type (found only in Master catalog)
Alias Names for VSAM and ICF User Catalogs
CVOL Catalogs
VSAM Data Sets of all Four Types
Components of VSAM Data Sets
Alternate Indexes and Paths
Non-VSAM Data Sets of Any Type
Generation Data Group Base Table and Generation Data Sets
Assorted Other Exotic Objects
```

- Standard KSDS with spanned records.
- Use the DIAGNOSE command to determine catalog errors.
- Sphere Records CLUSTER + AIX grouped together—CDG likewise.
- Fewer I/O operations are needed for catalog request.
- No concept of volume ownership.
- Multiple ICF catalogs can have entries on the same volume.
- Multiple ICF catalogs can reside on the same volume.
- DEFINE command has a RECATALOG parameter.
- Can be combined with VSAM and CVOL catalogs.
- One ICF catalog can be shared by loosely coupled CPUs.
- Provides improved performance with tuning parameters.

Table 12.3 contains a listing of the standard abbreviations and terms used when describing an ICF catalog structure.

Exercises

1. Identify the four basic eras that VSAM processing can be divided into. Identify the approximate dates of each era and the significant changes from the previous era. Conjecture what changes could be associated with a fifth VSAM era.

2. Use IDCAMS to create a User Catalog and two VSAM Volume Data Sets. Use LISTCAT ALL to examine the information stored in the user catalog. Create several VSAM and non-VSAM data sets on each of the two volumes where the VVDS were created. At this point, use a second LISTCAT ALL to reexamine the catalog information.

3. What "crucial" parameters must be coded with a DEFINE USERCATALOG command to optimize subsequent processing. Classify standard KSDS parameters in three categories; those that can be coded with:

TABLE 12.3   Terms and Abbreviations Used with ICF Catalogs.

BCS	– Basic Catalog Structure, a standard KSDS. Each catalog contains one BCS. The BCS contains information of a static nature.
VVDS	– VSAM Volume Data Set, a standard ESDS. Each disk volume contains one VVDS. The VVDS contains information of a volatile nature. It consists of two types of records: a VVCR and VVRs
VVCR	– A VSAM volume control record. It is the first record in the VVDS.
VVR	– VSAM volume record, like a format-1 DSCB in the VTOC.
Cell	– A VVR is composed of cells.
Sphere	– Related catalog entries.

- An ICF and an Enhanced VSAM catalog.
- An ICF but not an Enhanced VSAM catalog
- Cannot be coded with an ICF catalog.

4. Identify the role of the "Big Eight" IDCAMS commands with an ICF user catalog. In particular, use REPRO, PRINT, LISTCAT, ALTER, DELETE, EXPORT, IMPORT, and VERIFY to process a user catalog. Try to identify the differences between user catalog processing and comparable processing with standard VSAM data sets.

13

The Relationship
between VSAM Data Sets
and MVS JCL

This chapter discusses a variety of topics related to processing both VSAM and non-VSAM data sets within the larger MVS environment. The topics examined in the first half of the chapter are somewhat traditional. They include the historic role of JCL with VSAM data sets, necessary DD parameters, sorting VSAM data sets, using non-IDCAMS utilities to process VSAM data sets, the DEFINE NONVSAM and DEFINE ALIAS IDCAMS commands, and VSAM work data sets. The first half of the chapter describes the non-SMS, pre-1990 environment. The second half of the chapter focuses on the SMS environment that will eventually become prevalent.

DD Statements for VSAM Data Sets

A limited number of DD parameters can be meaningfully coded with VSAM data sets. The role of each of the major DD parameters is discussed. Note that, for a dynamically allocated data set, no DD statement is coded. Most of the remaining parameters not discussed here are either invalid or ignored when coded with a VSAM data set.

DSNAME = data set name parameter
DSN = 1st-Level-qualifier.2nd-Level-qualifier.3rd-Level-qualifier.---

DSN must be coded for each VSAM data set not dynamically allocated. Temporary data set names (&&name or &name) are not permitted, because every

VSAM data set must be cataloged. Support for generic names on DD statements are not yet permitted in most JCL situations, although eventually it probably will be. A present exception is GDGs, where with some applications the base GDG name identifies all the data sets in the group. This is discussed in the next chapter. The role of the individual data set name qualifiers is now examined.

First level qualifier
(DSN = XXXXXXXX.yyyyyyyy.zzzzzzzz.---)

The initial qualifier can identify a VSAM user catalog through either its true name or alias. It is also used in conjunction with security packages, such as RACF, to control the types of access to a data set. MASTER, ALTER, UPDATE, and READ are the four basic levels of access to select from. Programs like RACF provide an alternative to password protection. With TSO users, the first level qualifier identifies the TSO user-ID.

Second level qualifier
(DSN = xxxxxxxx.YYYYYYYY.zzzzzzzz.---)

The second qualifier identifies all of the data sets in an entire project group in an environment where multiple groups share the same user catalog. This results in a global subgrouping.

Third, or lower level qualifiers
(DSN = xxxxxxxx.yyyyyyyy.ZZZZZZZZ.---)

Lower-level qualifiers can specifically identify an individual user or project. Local identification is provided by these qualifiers:

DISP Parameter DISP = (before step,after step,after step abends)

The possible subparameter values that can be used are limited by three factors:

1. A VSAM data set ordinarily exists before the job step begins.

2. It must be cataloged.

3. It cannot be deleted through JCL.

Hence, the permissible first subparameter values are OLD, SHR, and MOD. Because the default for the first DISP subparameter value is NEW, one of these three must be coded. The only relevant second and third subparameter values are KEEP and PASS, which are discussed as follows. Note that NEW, CATLG, UNCATLG, and DELETE should not be coded with VSAM data sets.

OLD—The job has exclusive control of the data set until the step ends or the program releases the data set. The SHAREOPTIONS parameter values are ignored when DISP = OLD is coded.

SHR—The data set can be shared. When DISP = SHR is coded, the actual status is determined by the SHAREOPTIONS values stored in the catalog entry. Hence, SHR does not necessarily imply a shared data set. Default values are used if none are coded.

MOD—With a VSAM data set, MOD has the same basic meaning as OLD, except the data set can be extended by adding records after the last one in the data set. MOD can be used with a KSDS and an ESDS only.

KEEP—The status of the data set remains unchanged. KEEP is the default value for the second DISP subparameter with a VSAM data set.

PASS—A VSAM data set cannot be passed, and PASS is interpreted as KEEP.

Hence, the pass mechanism (formerly called the pass table) is probably an endangered species on future MVS systems. This will actually make for a more efficient search technique for data sets on future MVS systems. As it is now, whenever a DD statement contains just a DSN parameter and DISP = OLD or DISP = SHR, the pass table is initially examined. Whenever a pass entry is not located, catalogs are then searched. This is always the case with VSAM data sets.

UNIT parameter

The UNIT parameter is coded to help locate the I/O device associated with the data set. UNIT is not required on a DD statement for a VSAM data set. Furthermore, the comparable information (the FILE parameter) need not be coded with the DEFINE CLUSTER command. MVS provides the UNIT information dynamically in all cases.

VOLUME parameter

The VOLUME parameter is not required on a DD statement for an existing VSAM data set. The VOLUME parameter is always required with the DEFINE CLUSTER parameter. This is the trade-off from not having to code a UNIT value. It would seem to be a viable alternative in the future to offer VSAM users the option of coding a UNIT(device) class parameter rather than a specific volume, VOLUME(volser) within the DEFINE CLUSTER.

SPACE parameter

The SPACE parameter is never required on a DD statement for an existing VSAM data set. A space allocation is always required with the DEFINE CLUSTER command (CYL, TRK, or RECORD). None of the SPACE sub-parameters options other than unit and primary and secondary allocations are used with VSAM data sets. VSE systems provide an allocation in terms of blocks. It is unlikely that a block size allocation will ever be added to the DEFINE CLUSTER parameter with MVS.

DCB parameter

The DCB parameter is specifically prohibited with VSAM data sets. Default values are available for most "DCB-type" subparameter values (LRECL, BLKSIZE, RECFM, DSORG) if they are not explicitly coded with the DEFINE CLUSTER or ALTER commands.

LABEL parameter

There is no reason to code the LABEL parameter with a VSAM data set. Only the fifth subparameter values are meaningful, and retention period and expiration date can be specified with the DEFINE CLUSTER and ALTER commands.

VSAM and the SORT/MERGE (SYNCSORT and DFSORT) Programs

Records in an ESDS or KSDS can be sorted using standard sort/merge utility programs. Two points should be noted. First, any VSAM data set to be sorted is assumed to contain variable-length records. Second, 4 bytes must be added to the starting location of each field, just as with non-VSAM variable-length records. The sort/merge program uses the RDF values to create a standard, 4-byte, non-VSAM Record Description Field that precedes each record.

Example 1.   Figure 13.1 shows the code to sort the records in an ESDS into ascending order based on the value in bytes 10 to 25 and load the sorted records into a KSDS. The sorted records are initially loaded into a second ESDS.

Notice that the first FIELDS value is 14, which is four greater than the actual beginning location of the key field in the records. This results from the sort program turning the VSAM records into the equivalent of non-VSAM, variable-length records preceded by a 4-byte RDW (record descriptor word). The 16 bytes of character (CH) data are used to sort the records into ascending (A) order.

```
//A          EXEC   SORTD
//SORTIN     DD     DSN=INPUT.UNSORTED.ESDS,DISP=SHR
//SORTOUT    DD     DSN=OUTPUT.SORTED.ESDS,DISP=SHR
//SYSIN      DD     *
    SORT FIELDS=(14,16,CH,A)
/*
//B          EXEC   IDCAMS
//SYSPRINT   DD     SYSOUT=A
//DD1        DD     DSN=OUTPUT.SORTED.ESDS,DISP=SHR
//SYSIN      DD     *
    REPRO   INFILE(DD1)   OUTDATASET(NEW.KSDS)
/*
```

Figure 13.1 Sorting ESDS records and loading a KSDS.

```
//A           EXEC  PGM=ADRDSSU
//SYSPRINT DD     SYSOUT=A
//SYSIN      DD    *
   DUMP                          -
   DATASET(ALPHA.BETA)           -
   DEVTYPE(3390)
/*
```

Figure 13.2   Analyzing the disk structure of a KSDS.

VSAM Work Data Sets

VSAM work data sets are frequently required with the BLDINDEX command. Work data sets are also used in many other contexts. Currently, VSAM data sets are not the default in most of the other contexts, but it is reasonable to assume that they eventually will be. For the present, a VSAM work data set should be identified by a DD statement coded as:

```
//WORKDATA DD UNIT = unit-value,VOL = SER = volser,
//    AMP = 'AMORG',SPACE = (actual amount requested)
```

The AMP parameter contains the AMORG value to identify the VSAM data set. The remaining parameters are similar to those used with a non-VSAM work data set.

The ADRDSSU Utility Program

The ADRDSSU utility program is an excellent tool for studying data sets in general and VSAM data sets in particular on MVS systems. In particular, this program can be used to print out the total disk structure of any data set, VSAM or non-VSAM. This includes the disk COUNT fields and the VSAM CIDFs and RDFs. These items are not displayed by IDCAMS commands.

Example 2.   Figure 13.2 shows the code to dump out all the control intervals in the KSDS ALPHA.BETA. The KSDS is stored on the 3390 disk volume DISK23.

Describing VSAM Data Sets with the AMP DD Parameter

The AMP parameter is used to identify a variety of processing options for a VSAM data set. The comparable non-VSAM equivalent is the DCB parameter. Several of the AMP subparameters are used almost exclusively with ISAM data sets, which are to be converted to VSAM via the interface program. These subparameters are not discussed here.

The AMP parameter is meant to be used exclusively with VSAM data sets. The five most important AMP subparameters are AMORG, BUFSP, BUFND,

BUFNI, and STRNO. AMORG is used when one of several exceptional processing situations with a VSAM data set is to be performed. BUFSP, BUFND, and BUFNI are used to specify the amount of buffer space to allocate to the data set during the job step. STRNO determines the amount of concurrent processing the application can perform on the data set during the job step. Each AMP subparameter is further described and illustrated in one or more examples in the following sections.

AMORG subparameter

The AMORG subparameter is used to specify three basic functions:

1. Either an ISAM data set is to be processed through the VSAM interface, a historic artifact no longer in wide usage.

2. A VSAM work data set is to be used. This is discussed in a separate section in this chapter.

3. DUMMY is specified on the DD statement. DUMMY has the same meaning with both VSAM and non-VSAM data sets. In particular, during input processing, DUMMY means an end of file is detected on the initial read operation. No records are read. During an output operation, using DUMMY with the data set means no record is ever actually written.

Example 3:.   A DUMMY data set, a work data set, and an ISAM data set are to be processed as VSAM data sets. The three DD statements are:

```
//NOVSAMIO DD DUMMY,AMP = 'AMORG'
//WORKVSAM DD UNIT = SYSDA,VOL = SER = WORK01,AMP = 'AMORG'
//ISAMVSAM DD DSN = ISAM.DATA.SET,DISP = OLD,AMP = 'AMORG'
```

Buffer requirements

BUFND = D, indicates the number of buffers allocated to the data component. BUFSP, BUFND, BUFNI are subparameters. BUFNI = I, the number of buffers allocated to the index component. BUFSP = N, the number of bytes allocated for the data sets buffers.

BUFNI should be coded only with a KSDS. Either BUFND or BUFSP can be coded but not both. If both are coded, a variety of tests are made to determine which has precedence. If BUFSP is coded with a KSDS, the value specified is divided among the data and index components.

Example 4.   Two buffers are to be allocated to the data component and four buffers to the index component of a KSDS.

```
//KSDSBUFR DD DSN = KSDS,DISP = SHR,AMP = (BUFND = 2,BUFNI = 4)
```

Hierarchy of specifying buffer values

The number of buffers allocated for processing a VSAM data set can be specified in a number of ways. They are identified in order from lowest to highest priority:

- *VSAM (System) defaults*. Two data buffers and one index buffer (KSDS only) are allocated.

- *IDCAMS commands*. The BUFFERSPACE parameter with DEFINE CLUSTER or ALTER can specify the total number of bytes to reserve for buffers. Although a LISTCAT report shows that all buffers are allocated to the data component, this value applies to both components for a KSDS. ALTER also supports coding BUFND and BUFNI to specify the number of buffers for each component. IDCAMS values override the system defaults.

- *AMP parameter*. This is coded on the DD statement for the data set and is in effect for the job step only.

- *Application program*. This can be done in Assembler (ACB = ...) and COBOL (RESERVE n AREAS) with the SELECT statement.

When the AMP parameter is coded, it overrides the default and/or the value stored in the catalog entry for the single job step only. The system default is only in effect if nothing else is specified. Note the analogy with constructing the data control block with non-VSAM data sets as regards to the priority of the information provided. Sources for the BUFFERSPACE subparameter values are defaults, data set labels, DD statement, and application program.

String number subparameter

The string number subparameter, STRNO, identifies the maximum number of strings assigned to the data set for the duration of the job step. With most batch programs, a default value of 1 will suffice. STRNO cannot be assigned a value with an IDCAMS command. The reason for this is that STRNO is in the same category as specifying type of access or how the data set is to be opened. This type of information is only meaningful in the context of a specific application.

Example 5. A single KSDS is to be concurrently processed sequentially from two different points in the data set. In a COBOL program, two distinct START(BR) statements are used to establish positioning. Because sequential processing is to be performed, five buffers are associated with each string.

```
//KSDSTOPT DD DSN = KSDS.DATASET,DISP = SHR
//     AMP = (STRNO = 2,BUFND = 10)
```

TABLE 13.1   DD Parameters Vs. DEFINE NONVSAM Parameters.

DD Statement *Parameters and Values*	DEFINE NONVSAM Command *Parameters and Values*
DSN=data set name	NAME(data set name)
DISP=(NEW,CATLG)	NEW and CATLG are the defaults
UNIT=device type	DEVICETYPE(device type)
VOL=SER=volser	VOLUME(volser)
SPACE=(amount,(pri,sec))	No DEFINE NONVSAM Equivalent
LABEL=(n,SL)	FILESEQUENCENUMBER(n)
LABEL=RETPD=nnnn or	TO(days) or
=EXPDT=yyddd	FOR(date)
No JCL Equivalent	OWNER(name)

IDCAMS Commands For Processing Non-VSAM Data Sets

The two commands discussed in the next section are used with Non-VSAM data sets. The DEFINE NONVSAM command is used to create a cataloged, non-VSAM, sequential data set. The DEFINE ALIAS command is used in exactly two settings: with non-VSAM data sets and VSAM user catalogs. Only the first use is discussed here. Catalog aliases are discussed in chapter 12.

The DEFINE NONVSAM command

IDCAMS provides a command to create a catalog entry for a non-VSAM data set. This function is typically performed by a DD statement with a DISP parameter value of CATLG, specified or implied. The DEFINE NONVSAM command is comparable in that it catalogs the data set but does not write any records in it. The IDCAMS equivalents of DSN, UNIT, and VOL must be provided with the command.

A comparison between DEFINE NONVSAM parameters and DD statement parameters is illustrated in Table 13.1. Multiple volumes and units can be coded with both the IDCAMS command and the DD statement. Most of the DEFINE NONVSAM parameters have exactly the same meaning as when coded with the DEFINE commands discussed previously, such as DEFINE CLUSTER and DEFINE AIX. One new parameter is DEVICETYPE, which is coded to identify the general category of I/O device.

```
DEFINE NONVSAM          -     //DISK  DD DISP=(NEW,CATLG),
    NAME(ALPHA)         -     //         DSN=ALPHA,
    VOLUME(WORK01)      -     //         VOL=SER=WORK01,
    DEVICETYPE(3390)    -     //         UNIT=3390,SPACE=(TRK,1)
DEFINE NONVSAM          -     //TAPE  DD DISP=(NEW,CATLG),
    NAME(BETA)          -     //         DSN=BETA,
    VOLUME(123321)      -     //         VOL=SER=123321,
    DEVICETYPE(CART)    -     //         UNIT=CART,
    FILESEQUENCENUMBER(1)     //         LABEL=(1,SL)
```

Figure 13.3 Comparing DEFINE NONVSAM commands with DD statements.

TABLE 13.2   Objects that Permit Alias Names.

Object	Method of Creating Alias
VSAM user-catalog	DEFINE ALIAS command
VSAM data set	DEFINE PATH command
non-VSAM data set	DEFINE ALIAS command
PDS library member	(1) Linkage editor; or (2) an IEB/IEH utility; or (3) DEFINE ALIAS command

FILESEQUENCENUMBER is used only with tape data sets, which must be IBM standard label. Thus, coding FILESEQUENCENUMBER(2) is equivalent to LABEL = (2,SL) on a DD statement.

Unlike with JCL, an initial space allocation cannot be made at the same time IDCAMS catalogs the data set. This is because DEFINE NONVSAM creates a catalog entry, not a format-1 DSCB entry on a disk volume. A space allocation is necessary to create a format-1 DSCB. Even coding SPACE = (TRK,0) or (CYL,0) is sufficient.

Example 6.   Create two cataloged data sets called ALPHA and BETA on disk and tape respectively. Two approaches are used to do this. The DEFINE NON-VSAM commands are coded on the left and the DD statements are used on the right in Fig. 13. 3.

The DEFINE ALIAS command

What is an alias? An alias is an alternate name for a data set of some type. The original object over which the alias is defined is often referred to as the "true name" object. On MVS systems, there are numerous places where an alias can be used. Four important locations where aliases are employed along with the IDCAMS command that can be used to create the alias are shown in Table 13.2.

Creating an alias name for a VSAM data set is discussed in chapter 8 along with secondary keys and alternate indexes, although it probably seemed out of place there. Likewise, placing an alias on a PDS member cannot be done with the DEFINE ALIAS command. Hence, DEFINE ALIAS is used with two entries from Table 13.2: user-catalogs and non-VSAM data sets. In both cases, the name of the alias and the name of the existing object must be specified. A second set of security attributes can be specified for the alias rather than those associated with the original object.

```
DEFINE  ALIAS NAME(READONLY.NONVSAM.DATASET)   -
           READPW(LOWLEVEL)                     -
           UPDATEPW(HILEVEL)                     -
           RELATE(NONVSAM.MASTER)
```

Figure 13.4   Creating various access levels for a non-VSAM data set.

```
DEFINE ALIAS NAME(ACSSTU) RELATE(SYS1.ACSCTLG1) -
             CATALOG(SYS1.ACSCTLG1/TOPSECRT)
DEFINE ALIAS NAME(ACSFAC) RELATE(SYS1.ACSCTLG1) -
             CATALOG(SYS1.ACSCTLG1/TOPSECRT)
DEFINE ALIAS NAME(LJB)    RELATE(SYS1.ACSCTLG1) -
             CATALOG(SYS1.ACSCTLG1/TOPSECRT)
```

Figure 13.5   Generating alias names for a user catalog.

Example 7.   The code in Fig. 13.4 creates an alias over the sequential data set NONVSAM.MASTER. When the alias is specified, read only processing is permitted. Hence, an update password is coded that will not be provided to people supplied with only the alias name. The RELATE parameter identifies the underlying base object.

Example 8.   Several aliases are to be created for an existing user catalog. The actual name of the catalog is SYS1.ACSCTLG1. The aliases ACSSTU, ACSFAC, and LJB are created in Fig. 13-5. Notice that common parameter information cannot be factored onto a single command.

Performing Data Management Functions with IDCAMS and JCL

Many important data management functions that must be performed on an MVS system with non-VSAM data sets can be done with either IDCAMS or through JCL with the DD statement. Twelve of the most important functions are summarized in Table 13.3. For each function, it is shown how it is performed with IDCAMS and with JCL whenever each or both is possible. All of the table entries apply only to non-VSAM data sets. In particular, functions 1, 8, 9, 11, and 12 do not apply to VSAM data sets. Furthermore, 2 is automatic with VSAM data sets.

The Storage Management System (SMS)

The announcement of the Storage Management System in the late 1980s marked the beginning of a new era in VSAM processing. The complete name of this complex product is DFSMS, however, it is almost always called SMS. Even if not explicitly stated, SMS is required for all of the features discussed throughout the remainder of this chapter.

The basic intent of SMS is to allow users to create and manage VSAM data sets much more effectively than was previously possible and with a lot less effort. Many functions that required considerable programmer expertise or effort, pre-SMS, can now be completely automated. In this chapter, the role of SMS with the DD statement to process VSAM data sets is described. This in itself is an extremely significant notion. Except for perhaps those rare individuals who just recently began working with VSAM, creating and deleting VSAM data sets has always been completely separate from JCL processing.

TABLE 13.3 Basic Non-VSAM Data Set Processing Functions.

Specific Function to Perform	IDCAMS	JCL
Create Only (not cataloged)	-	DISP=(NEW,KEEP)
Create and Catalog	DEF NONVSAM	DISP=(NEW,CATLG)
Catalog an Existing data set	DEF NONVSAM	DISP=(OLD,CATLG)
Uncatalog	DELETE	DISP=(OLD,UNCATLG)
Delete or Scratch only	DELETE	DELETE+UNIT and VOL
Uncatalog and Delete	DELETE	DISP=(OLD,DELETE)
Rename a Data Set	ALTER	Impossible
Delete a PDS Member	DELETE	Impossible
Rename a PDS Member	ALTER	Impossible
Generic Processing	ALTER	
	LISTCAT	Only with GDGs
	DELETE	Only with GDGs
Add a Member to a PDS	REPRO	DISP=OLD
Replace a Member in a PDS	REPRO	DISP=MOD

This chapter does not discuss the total SMS picture, but deals with the parts most relevant to VSAM and the typical application programmer instead. Along with the linear data set (chapter 15), this material is the leading edge of VSAM technology; a cornerstone of future VSAM development. Incidentally, much of this material is also applicable to non-VSAM data sets, provided they meet the qualifications of being an SMS-managed data set, as outlined in the next section.

The following discussion requires two significant prerequisites. First, SMS must be installed on a computer system. Second, SMS must be active. If these conditions are not met, the power and sophistication described in the remainder of this chapter are not available. However, if both conditions in the ESA environment are not in effect and any of the SMS parameters are coded, they are syntax-checked and then ignored. Obviously, this can lead to subsequent processing problems with the data sets.

Managing data sets with SMS

Not all types of data sets qualify for management under SMS. Basically, only those disk data sets for which IBM has projected a long-term future are qualified. This includes ICF VSAM data sets of every type, partitioned and sequential data sets, and generation data groups. Even long-term, non-disk are omitted. Non-SMS data set types include ISAM, tape, print, and Enhanced

TABLE 13.4 SMS vs. Non-SMS-Managed Data Sets.

SMS Managed Data Sets	Non-SMS-Managed Data Sets
DFP VSAM data sets	Enhanced VSAM data sets
(KSDS, ESDS, RRDS, LDS, AIX, etc.)	Enhanced VSAM catalogs
ICF catalogs (master and user)	Tape data sets
PDS libraries	Print data sets (SYSOUT)
Sequential data sets	In-stream data sets (*)
Generation data sets	Non-cataloged data sets
VIO data sets	ISAM data sets

VSAM. The remainder of this chapter applies only to SMS-managed data sets. SMS data set management classification is categorized in Table 13.4, which is not an all-inclusive list.

All SMS data sets must be cataloged. For this reason, coding DISP = (NEW,KEEP) creates a cataloged data set, non-VSAM or VSAM. Coding DISP = (OLD,DELETE) both uncatalogs and deletes a data set before converting to SMS, a disposition of DELETE was ignored with VSAM data sets. This can lead to problems with the JCL in existing production jobs. Some jobs contained DELETE as a disposition because it functioned the same as KEEP. This will no longer be the case.

At a computer center of any size, SMS requires one additional job function. This is a storage administrator whose job is to implement and manage SMS-related concepts.

New JCL Parameters

There are several new parameters that have been added to MVS JCL to specifically support the creation of VSAM data sets. These include RECORG, AVGREC, KEYLEN, and KEYOFF. Each of these four new parameters supplies one specific property. The LIKE parameter is also new and is a functional combination of the DEFINE CLUSTER MODEL parameter and the JCL refer-back.

Even more important, three very powerful parameters have been created to provide most of the significant information that must be specified for VSAM data set creation: the DATACLAS, STORCLAS, and MGMTCLAS parameters. Each of these parameters supplies a large group of properties. With SMS, the specified properties for a VSAM data set are classified into four categories:

1. Actual data set structure (DATACLAS).

2. Location (STORCLAS).

3. Automated management (MGMTCLAS).

4. STORGRP, which cannot be accessed by an application programmer and does not have a DD statement equivalent. The STORGRP is used to place groups of disk volumes into various classes for comparable processing, including allocation and backup.

RECORG parameter

Whenever a VSAM data set is created with JCL, the RECORG parameter can be used to identify the data set organization. The four RECORG values that can be coded are shown in Table 13.5. If RECORG is not coded, its value can be provided from either the DATACLAS or LIKE parameter. If RECORG, DATACLAS, and LIKE are not coded, a default data set organization is selected based on the values coded with the SPACE parameter. There are two possible

TABLE 13.5   Identifying VSAM Data Sets.

Value	Type of Data Set	DEFINE CLUSTER Parameter
KS	Key Sequenced Data Set (KSDS)	INDEXED
ES	Entry Sequenced Data Set (ESDS)	NONINDEXED
RR	Relative Record Data Set (RRDS)	NUMBERED
LL	Linear Data Set (LDS)	LINEAR

non-VSAM default values: partitioned and non-VSAM sequential. Hence, there are several ways to specify a VSAM data set type:

- Code RECORG explicitly.
- Reference a value with LIKE.
- Use a DATACLAS parameter.
- Receive a default ACS value.

Notice that, if none of these methods are used, a VSAM data set will not be created by default. There is no reason to code RECORG with an existing data set. Data set organization type can always be determined from the catalog and it cannot be altered.

Example 9.   Create a KSDS called ALPHA.BETA.GAMMA. Many of its properties will be copied from a data class and a storage class model. However, the data set type in the model will be overridden by explicitly coding RECORG.

```
//DDA DD DSN = ALPHA.BETA.GAMMA,DISP = (NEW,KEEP),
//    DATACLAS = TOPSECRET,RECORG = KS,STORCLAS = TOPSECRET,
      AVGREC = ...
```

AVGREC parameter

The AVGREC parameter for storage allocation is used in conjunction with the SPACE parameter. It specifies how the primary and secondary values coded with SPACE are to be interpreted. AVGREC is used to request storage based on the size of the average, logical record length. Coding AVGREC causes the SPACE storage allocation values to be interpreted as a specific number of logical records. There are three values that can be specified with AVGREC: U, K, or M. These values identify the multiplying factor to be associated with both the primary and secondary allocations.

AVGREC = U The values coded are the actual amounts.
AVGREC = K The values coded are to be multiplied by 1,024 (1K).
AVGREC = M The values coded are to be multiplied by 1,048,576 (1M).

Example 10.   Storage is to be allocated for approximately 5,000 records averaging 150 bytes in length. The largest records are 200 bytes. Because the number of records is a very rough approximation, a secondary allocation of 1,000 records will also be requested. This can be accomplished by coding either set of parameters:

```
//DDB1 DD AVGREC = U,SPACE = (150,(5000,1000)),...
//DDB2 DD AVGREC = K,SPACE = (150,(5,1)),...
```

Control interval or block size information is supplied from some other source. The comparable DEFINE CLUSTER parameters are RECSZ(150 150) and RECORDS(5000 1000). Note that coding SPACE = (150,(5000,1000)) without specifying AVGREC will generate a different storage allocation. In this case, the 150 is interpreted as the BLKSIZE value rather than the LRECL value.

Example 11. An RRDS is to be created and slots should be reserved for approximately 2 million, 90-byte records with a record density of approximately 50 percent of the total storage. This means half of the slots will be empty.

```
//DDC DD DSN = RRDS.SMSDS,DISP = (NEW,KEEP),
//     RECORG = RR,AVGREC = M,SPACE = (90,(4)),DATACLAS = MOD3
```

KEYLEN and KEYOFF parameters

The KEYLEN and KEYOFF parameters can be used to specify the key length and key location respectively when creating a KSDS. Neither parameter should be coded with the other three types of VSAM data sets. As with any KSDS, a key length value from 1 to 255 can be specified. The offset is a value relative to 0 that identifies the initial byte in the key. The offset value can range from 0 to 32,760.

KEYLEN and KEYOFF can be specified in two contexts. When a KSDS is initially created, they can be used to provide key field information. For an existing KSDS, they can be used to override the values specified with the cluster component or the key length and offset provided by the DATACLAS parameter. When a KSDS is initially created by means of a DD statement, the key length and offset can be supplied in a number of ways. By:

- Coding them explicitly on the DD statement.

- Providing them with a DATACLAS parameter.

- Using the LIKE parameter.

- Specifying an ACS default.

Although ordinarily coded together, KEYLEN or KEYOFF can be coded by itself. Unlike the DEFINE CLUSTER KEYS parameter, KEYLEN and KEYOFF do not have default values.

Example 12. Create a KSDS called ALPHA.BETA.GAMMA most of whose properties will be copied from the DATACLAS model BIGKSDS. However, key field information, space allocation, and record size are to be explicitly coded and will override the corresponding values in the model. The first 5 bytes in each record contain the key. The KEYLEN and KEYOFF values in a data class model are routine candidates to be overridden. Note that KEEP with an SMS-managed data set implies cataloged.

```
//DDD DD DSN = ALPHA.BETA.GAMMA,DISP = (NEW,KEEP),
//    DATACLAS = BIGKSDS,KEYLEN = 5,KEYOFF = 0,
//    AVGREC = K,SPACE = (300,(125,10))
```

LIKE parameter

The LIKE parameter can be used to assign values to a data set similar to DATA-CLAS. When a data set is created, properties can be copied from the existing data set, identified as the model with LIKE. With DATACLAS, a true model is used rather than an actual data set. Only a cataloged data set can be coded with LIKE. Because the system requires unit and volume information to locate a data set, and neither parameters can be coded as part of LIKE, a catalog must be used to provide their values. Notice that the programmer can use LIKE without obtaining information from the storage administrator concerning the permittable values to code.

LIKE is similar to the MODEL parameter used with various IDCAMS DEFINE commands. LIKE also shares similarities with older DD statement parameters that allow the name of a cataloged data set to be specified as an alternative to actual properties. Both DCB = (dsname) and VOL = REF = dsname allow this approach. Just as with the DEFINE commands, MODEL parameter, and the DD statement DCB parameter, LIKE allows actual properties to be specified in addition to the data set name. These properties override the comparable values provided by the model. They can be coded in any order on the DD statement.

The following seven properties can be copied from the cataloged data set model identified with LIKE:

1. RECORG—To identify one of the four types of VSAM data sets.

2. RECFM—The record format.

3. LRECL—The (maximum) size of logical records.

4. AVGREC—Used with primary and secondary storage allocations.

5. SPACE—The amount of disk storage requested.

6. KEYLEN—The length of a KSDS key.

7. KEYOFF—The offset of the key in a KSDS record.

Notice that every one of these values is also provided with DATACLAS. DATACLAS, however, also provides the expiration date or retention period, volume-count, SHAREOPTIONS, FREESPACE, CISZ, IMBED, and REPLICATE.

The final five parameters are meaningful only with VSAM data sets. Hence, LIKE is meant to serve a broader spectrum of data set types than DATACLAS.

Example 13.   Create a KSDS and use LIKE to supply values for all seven properties listed previously except for AVGREC and SPACE, which are to be explicitly coded.

```
//DDE DD DSN = NEW.KSDS,DISP = (NEW,KEEP),STORCLAS = LONGTERM,
//    LIKE = EXISTING.KSDS,AVGREC = K,SPACE = (200,(10,1))
```

DATACLAS parameter

The DATACLAS parameter is one of the three major SMS parameters for creating VSAM data sets with JCL for specifying cluster properties. The DATACLAS parameter can be used to specify a wide group of values for a new data set being created—both VSAM and non-VSAM. VSAM's only properties include REPLICATE, IMBED, CISZ, FREESPACE, and SHAREOPTIONS. This is the only way these five parameters can be assigned values through JCL. Additional property values that, under some conditions, are also meaningful with various types of non-VSAM data sets include:

- Expiration date (EXPDT) or retention period (RETPD), but not both.
- Disk storage allocation (SPACE and AVGREC).
- Key length and key offset (KEYLEN and KEYOFF).
- VSAM data set organization (RECORG).
- Logical record length (LRECL).
- Record format (RECFM).
- Volume-count (number of volumes).

If any of these parameters are specified on the same statement with DATACLAS, they override the values contained in the DATACLAS value. Note that seven of the values can also be provided by the LIKE parameter.

Those values coded with DATACLAS are generated by naming a value provided by the storage administrator. If an automatic class selection (ACS) is available and a DATACLAS parameter is not coded, then ACS can select a data class for the data set.

```
//DDF1   DD   DSN=NEW.KSDS,DISP=(NEW,KEEP),DATACLAS=KSDSTYPX,
//            STORCLAS=WORKDATA,MGMTCLAS=M123
//DDF2   DD   DSN=NEW.ESDS,DISP=(NEW,KEEP),DATACLAS=ESDSTYPY,
//            AVGREC=M,SPACE=(80,(2))
//DDF3   DD   DSN=NEW.RRDS,DISP=(NEW,KEEP),DATACLAS=RRDSTYPZ,
//            MGMTCLAS=RRDSSTUF
```

Figure 13.6   Creating VSAM data sets with JCL.

Example 14. A KSDS, an ESDS, and an RRDS are to be created in Fig. 13.6. All three are to have a variety of their properties specified through various DATACLAS models. With ESDS, the SPACE allocation information is overridden, and with both the ESDS and RRDS, a default storage class is provided by ACS.

STORCLAS parameter

The STORCLAS parameter is one of the three major SMS parameters for processing VSAM data sets with JCL to specify unit and volume-type information. The STORCLAS parameter can be used to specify information about where to store a data set. In particular, it is similar to the UNIT and VOL DD statement parameters. It serves as an alternative to coding UNIT and VOL parameters on the DD statement or VOLUME and FILE with DEFINE CLUSTER.

The storage administrator is responsible for creating a group of storage class values from which a programmer can select the appropriate value. None of the information provided by the STORCLAS values can be overridden. As with DATACLAS and MGMTCLAS, STORCLAS's syntax is checked and ignored if SMS is not installed and active and is used to create a new data set. The information supplied by STORCLAS can be provided for non-VSAM data sets by the UNIT and VOL parameters.

If all the criteria for using STORCLAS are met but no value is coded, then it is still possible that a default value will be assigned when a new data set is created. An automatic storage class (ACS) routine can be used to select appropriate values.

Example 15. A KSDS is to be created and placed on a 3390 disk volume identified as part of the MAJOR storage class:

```
//DDG DD DSN = ALPHA.BETA.GAMMA,DISP = (NEW,KEEP),
//    STORCLAS = MAJOR,DATACLAS = KSDSTYPX MGMTCLAS
```

Managing VSAM Data Set Parameters

MGMTCLAS is one of the three major SMS parameters for processing VSAM data sets through JCL. The other two are DATACLAS and STORCLAS. These three parameters identify a powerful new collection of processing options to associate with a new data set.

MGMTCLAS parameter

The storage administrator is responsible for creating the values specified with the MGMTCLAS parameter. MGMTCLAS can only be used with SMS and SMS-managed data sets. If these conditions are not met, or MGMTCLAS is coded with an existing data set, its syntax is checked and then ignored. Furthermore, the information provided by MGMTCLAS cannot be specified with any

TABLE 13.6 Important DD Parameters with VSAM Data Sets.

```
RECORG  - To identify one of the four types of VSAM data sets.
RECFM   - The record format.
LRECL   - The (maximum) size of logical records.
AVGREC  - Used with primary and secondary storage allocations.
SPACE   - The amount of disk storage requested.
KEYLEN  - The length of a KSDS key.
KEYOFF  - The offset of the key in a KSDS record.
```

other DD statement parameter. Quite simply, existing JCL is not designed to provide the type of information associated with MGMTCLAS.

After a data set is created, the values in a management class determine subsequent action, including data set migration and data set backup. Data sets can be migrated from primary disk storage to DFHSM-owned storage (secondary storage), as well as archived storage. Management information related to backup includes the time intervals for performing backup, the number of backup copies to retain, and the length of time a back-up copy is to be kept. Notice that none of this information overlaps anything available with DATACLAS and STORCLAS.

If all the criteria for using MGMTCLAS are met but no value is coded, it is possible that a default value will be assigned when a new data set is created. This can occur if the storage administrator has defined an automatic storage class routine (ACS). The ACS routine can assign a management class to the data set.

Example 16.   A KSDS is to be created that is to be migrated from primary to secondary storage after 30 days if it is not accessed. Backups are to be made every week, and three backups are to be kept. Notice that none of this information is apparent from reading the DD statement.

```
//DDH DD DSN = IMPT.DATASET,DISP = (NEW,KEEP),STORCLAS = XYZ,
//    MGMTCLAS = PQR,DATACLAS = KSDSTYPX
```

Exercises

1. Use JCL to create the equivalent of the VSAM data set constructed in each of the four coding examples at the end of chapter 4.

2. Classify each of the major DD statement parameters into one of three categories: used exclusively with VSAM data sets, used exclusively with non-VSAM data sets, and used with both VSAM and non-VSAM data sets. Refer to Table 13.6.

14

Generation Data Groups

A generation data group (GDG) is frequently used for processing data sets that are created on a regular basis at specific time intervals. They are often created by a program that is run every week, month, quarter, etc. Many transaction-driven master file update programs fall into this category. When a GDG is used, it is unnecessary to assign and keep track of unique names for the data sets in the GDG. Rather, all data sets in a GDG have exactly the same name, and the same DD statement can be used to create each of them. This means that an identical job step can be run every time the program must be executed, with no JCL changes whatsoever regarding data set creation. The same is true for data set retrieval.

Because every data set in a GDG has the same name, they can be uniquely identified if their name is qualified by a relative generation number. The generation number is functionally similar to a subscript or superscript. The current generation is identified as DSN = GDGname(0). The next oldest generation can be referenced as DSN = GDGname(−1), and the second oldest as DSN = GDGname(−2), etc.

Basically, a GDG provides a way of grouping together related data sets that share similar functional or physical properties. Currently, all the data sets in a GDG must be cataloged, non-VSAM data sets. It is reasonable to guess that VSAM data sets will be eventually permitted. It is also a certainty that GDGs will continue to indefinitely coexist with VSAM data sets. The same statement can be made regarding PDS libraries and VSAM data sets.

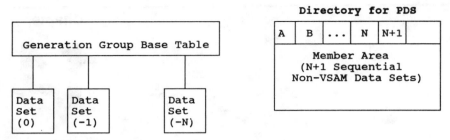

Figure 14.1 A GDG and a PDS each containing N + 1 data sets.

Grouping Multiple Data Sets

There are many similarities between a GDG and a partitioned data set (PDS). Both structures contain a table of contents or directory that identifies a number of data sets that each manages. A graphic comparison between the two structures is shown in Fig. 14.1, and a detailed comparison of their respective properties is given in Table 14.1. Additional information concerning partitioned data sets can be found in chapter 12 in MVS JCL and utilities.

Note that in Fig. 14.1, the GDG consists of a base table or data set index and N + 1 data sets, with relative numbers ranging from 0 to −N. The PDS also consists of N + 1 data sets, which are all sequential and contained in the member area. Member names are unrelated to one another. The members are managed by the BPAM access method (see chapter 1) using the information in the directory. The data sets in the GDG are managed by IDCAMS. Table 14.1 compares and contrasts GDGs and PDSs.

Using IDCAMS to Create a GDG

There are two possible ways to create a generation data group. Either by using the IDCAMS DEFINE GENERATIONDATAGROUP (DEF GDG) command or the IEHPROGM utility. Almost every installation now uses IDCAMS for this function. The complete set of parameters available with the DEFINE GDG command are listed in Fig. 14.2. Those parameters not described or that have a different role or meaning with DEFINE GDG are then described. In actuality, the only data set created with the DEFINE GENERATIONDATAGROUP command is the base table, and this must be done before the first GDS can be created.

The rules for coding a name for a GDG have one significant difference from those permitted with standard data set names. A GDGname can contain a maximum of 35 characters. This allows room for an additional nine characters to be concatenated to it when forming the absolute name of a GDS. Hence, the ''absolute'' name, which is discussed later, will contain less than, or equal to, 44 characters—the limit with MVS JCL.

The LIMIT value, which specifies the maximum number of generation data sets permitted in the GDG, can range from 1 to 255. Once the limit is reached,

TABLE 14.1   Comparison of Properties between a GDG and a PDS.

Generation Data Group	Partitioned Data Set
A GDG consists of a base table, which is a separate data set, and from 0 to 255 Generation Data Sets, each of which has its own VTOC entry on the volume where it resides. Each generation data set has a catalog entry, all of which are contained in the same user or master catalog.	A PDS consists of a directory and an essentially unlimited number of sequential data set members. The entire PDS, directory and members, has just one VTOC entry and one catalog entry, if cataloged. The directory occupies the beginning of the PDS is fixed in size following its creation.
The base table is a separate data set, and it must be cataloged.	The directory is a part of the PDS. Under some circumstances it can be processed independently of the member area.
Each GDS must be cataloged.	A PDS may be temporary, cataloged kept, or passed, or a combination. Most DISP values do not apply to individual members.
Each individual GDS can be referenced by a combination of name and relative number; for example DSN=GDGname(+N).	Each individual member can be referenced by dsname qualified by member name; for example DSN=PDSname(member name).
Coding DSN=GDGname results in every GDS in the GDG being concatenated and process together.	Coding DSN=PDSname references the entire PDS, both the members and the directory.
The IDCAMS DEFINE GDG command or IEHPROGM utility is used to create a GDG base table.	Coding SPACE=(x,(y,z,w)) on a DD statement specifies creation of a PDS.
A GDS in a GDG can be sequential, ISAM, BDAM, or partitioned.	Each PDS member must be a sequential data set.
Each GDS can have different DCB values. The model DSCB described in a later section can be used to simplify coding DCB values on the DD statement.	All PDS members should have the same DCB values. However they can have totally different values if only one member is processed at a time and correct values are specified.
A GDS can reside on disk or tape.	A PDS must reside on disk.

```
DEFINE   GDG(NAME(GDGdsname)          -
         LIMIT(limit-value)           -
         SCRATCH or NOSCRATCH         -
         EMPTY or NOEMPTY             -
         TO(value) or FOR(value)      -
         OWNER(owner-name)            -
         CATALOG(catalog name))
```

Figure 14.2   The DEFINE GENERATIONDATAGROUP(GDG) command parameters.

the status of the oldest existing data sets in the GDG is determined by the SCRATCH or NOSCRATCH parameters.

When SCRATCH is specified, a data set bumped from the GDG because the LIMIT value is exceeded is also scratched from the VTOC of the volume on which it resides. When NOSCRATCH is specified, the oldest data set is still bumped from the GDG when the LIMIT value is exceeded. However, the data set is not deleted from the volume, and it can still be referenced if UNIT and VOLUME values are coded on its accompanying DD statement along with its complete (absolute) name.

Like SCRATCH and NOSCRATCH, the EMPTY and NOEMPTY parameters are effective only when the number of data sets in the GDG exceeds the LIMIT value. When this occurs, EMPTY causes the entry for every GDS to be removed from the GDG. The base table then contains no entries. The SCRATCH parameter controls whether the generation data sets whose entries are removed from the base table are themselves also deleted from the VTOC (volumes) that contain them. If NOEMPTY is coded, only the oldest data set entries are removed from the GDG. This is further explained in examples that follow.

TO, FOR, OWNER, and CATALOG have the same functions as when using IDCAMS to create other objects. Their values apply to the GDG base table, not to a GDS. Once the DEFINE GDG is executed, the base table becomes a cataloged entry in the specified VSAM catalog. Ordinarily, this is a user catalog, although it can be the system master catalog.

In order to successfully perform GDG processing, it is necessary to know the volume on which the base table resides. Note that the identity of the volume cannot be specified with the DEFINE GDG command. However, a LISTCAT command can be used to identify the actual volume where the catalog resides.

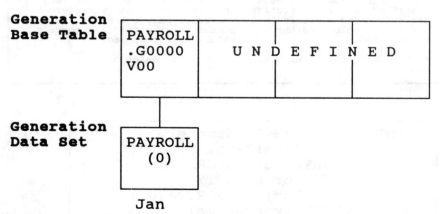

Figure 14.3   GDG base table and one generation data set.

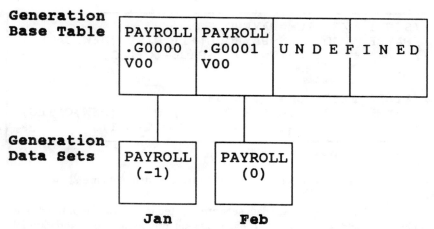

Figure 14.4   GDG base table and two generation data sets.

Creating Generation Data Sets

As mentioned previously, GDGs are usually associated with data sets that are chronologically related. This is not, however, an absolute requirement. To illustrate the standard environment in which a GDG is used, a common programming situation is considered. Suppose a company pays their employees on a monthly basis. Hence, at the end of each month, a payroll program is run. The program is always the same, and the output consists of the payroll information associated with each employee. The use of a GDG with the payroll system is implemented for the first time during January. The data set holding the payroll information is identified by a DD statement containing:

```
//PAYREC DD DSN = PAYROLL(+1),DISP = (NEW,CATLG),
//    UNIT = 3390,SPACE = (CYL,1)
```

For purposes of illustration, suppose that a GDG is created with a LIMIT value of 4. Hence, at most, four GDSs can be contained in the GDG. In addition, NOSCRATCH and NOEMPTY are also specified. The GDG is used to hold a copy of the payroll data set that is generated every month. The DD statement to create the GDS contains DSN = PAYROLL(+1),DISP = (NEW,CATLG),... After the January payroll job completes, the GDG appears as shown in Fig. 14.3.

In February, the identical job is run, and the DD statement for the payroll data set is the same as for January. After the job ends, the GDG is updated as shown in Fig. 14.4.

In March, the payroll program is run twice in the same job. The first run produces the standard monthly payroll, and the second run to pay a quarterly bonus. The two runs are performed in separate steps in the same job. In this

```
//STEP1 EXEC PGM=PAYPROGM
//PAYREC   DD   DSN=PAYROLL(+1),DISP=(NEW,CATLG),
//               UNIT=3390,SPACE=(CYL,1)
  . . .

//STEP2 EXEC PGM=PAYPROGM
//PAYREC   DD   DSN=PAYROLL(+2),DISP=(NEW,CATLG),
//               UNIT=3390,SPACE=(CYL,1)
```

Figure 14.5 Creating two generation data sets.

case, the relevant DD statements to create the two data sets are shown in Fig. 14.5.

Notice that because the two data sets are created in the same job, the relative numbers +1 and +2 are used. If each data set was created in a separate job, both would have used +1. After the job finishes, the GDG base table is updated. The final (bonus) data set created is identified by the relative number 0 in the base table and the slightly older data set by the relative number −1. At this point, each of the table entries as shown in Fig. 14.6 references a data set.

In April, another payroll data set is created as PAYROLL(+1). Once the job ends, it is stored as PAYROLL(0). Because the base table is filled, the oldest data set entry is bumped from the table. The January payroll data set is uncataloged, but it is not deleted because NOSCRATCH is in effect. It can still be processed if its absolute name is coded on a DD statement along with UNIT and VOLUME values. If SCRATCH had been coded,the data set would have been uncataloged and deleted. If EMPTY had been specified, every existing data set in the GDG would have been uncataloged and its entry bumped from the base table. In this case, every GDS would also be deleted.

Subscript Conventions

All new generation data sets created using relative number notation must be coded with positive subscripts. There are no exceptions. Duplicate, positive relative numbers should not be used in the same job unless the COND or RESTART parameters, or something comparable, are used to determine the flow of execution.

As a general rule of thumb, relative numbers should not be skipped when creating multiple data sets in a job. Although this is syntactically permissible, it can lead to processing problems in subsequent jobs. Thus, if a job creates N generation data sets, they should be named X(+1), X(+2), ..., X(+N), where X is the name of the generation base table. If any of the new data sets are referenced later in the same job stream in which they were created, they are identified by the positive relative number even though the DISP parameter value specifies an existing data set.

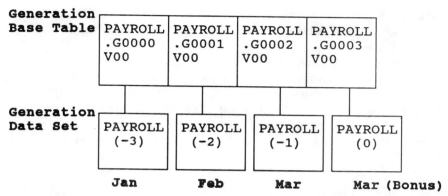

Figure 14.6 GDG base table and maximum number of data sets.

With the exception of creating a generation data set and processing it in a later step in the same job, existing GDSs are referenced using relative numbers $0, -1, -2, ..., -(n-1)$, etc. Here, n is the value coded with LIMIT with the DEFINE GDG command, which created the GDG:

X(0) is the newest data set in the GDG, which was created in an earlier job.
X(−1) is the next newest data set.
X(−n) is the oldest in the GDG.
X(−(n+1)) has been bumped from the base table or never existed.

Defining a Model Data Set Control Block (DSCB)

Before a generation data set can be created or processed, a model data set control block (DSCB) must first be defined. A model DSCB is a standard format-1 DSCB located in the Volume Table of Contents (VTOC) of a disk volume. A format-1 DSCB is often referred to as the data set label for a disk data set. In particular, it contains the DCB values associated with the data set. The model DSCB can be used to assign values to a new generation data set or an existing generation data set.

The model DSCB must be created before the first generation data set. It can be created before or after the GDG base table. The model DSCB must be defined on the same volume that contains the catalog with the entry for the base table. The model DSCB can be defined in the same IDCAMS job step in

```
//PAYREC  DD  DSN=PAYROLL,DISP=(NEW,KEEP),
//              UNIT=3390,VOL=SER=volser,
//              SPACE=(TRK,0),
//              DCB=(LRECL=xxxx,BLKSIZE=yyyy,RECFM=zz,...)
```

Figure 14.7 Creating a GDG model data set control block.

which the DEFINE GDG command is coded or in a separate IEFBR14 job step. No matter where it is placed, the DD statement to create a model DSCB is coded as shown in Fig. 14.7.

Several important points should be noted. The DSN value for the model DSCB must be the same as the name of the base table. The second DISP subparameter value cannot be CATLG because a catalog entry for the GDG base table with the same name already exists. The disk volume must be the same volume where the user catalog is stored. No disk space is required for logical records. Hence, the primary space allocation is zero. Any collection of DCB parameters can be coded.

Absolute GDG Names

The GDG base table uses relative subscripts to identify generation data sets. The base table also contains the corresponding absolute names discussed in this section. However, the catalog and VTOC entries do not contain the subscript entries. Rather, they contain the name of the data set in a format much like the standard DSN value used with MVS JCL.

The first several data sets in the PAYROLL GDG will have the absolute names shown in Table 14.2. A maximum of 44 total characters, separated by periods into qualifiers of 1 to 8 alphanumeric characters, are available. Specifically, the absolute generation data set name has a final level of qualification of the form GnnnnVmm. Here, nnnn is the absolute generation number and can be any value from 0000 to 9999. The absolute version number, mm, can be any value from 00 to 99.

If relative numbers are coded when a data set is created, the absolute generation number becomes one larger that the last previous absolute generation number created (provided it does not create a duplicate data set name). The absolute version number is set to 00. A version number other than 00 can only be specified when creating a data set and coding an absolute generation name or by renaming an existing data set. Renaming is discussed in the last section in this chapter. Creating absolute data names can be done as follows:

```
DSN = PAYROLL.G0001V00,DISP = (NEW,CATLG),... or
DSN = PAYROLL.G0123V75,DISP = (NEW,CATLG),...
```

TABLE 14.2   Absolute Names for the First N PAYROLL Data Sets.

Data Set Created	Absolute Name
First	PAYROLL.G0001V00
Second	PAYROLL.G0002V00
Third	PAYROLL.G0003V00
Nth	PAYROLL.G000nV00

```
First Job Executed

//DD1    DD    DSN=PAYROLL.G0007V23,DISP=(NEW,CATLG),...
//DD2    DD    DSN=PAYROLL(+2),DISP=(NEW,CATLG),...

Second Job Executed

//DD1    DD    DSN=PAYROLL(0),DISP=SHR
//DD2    DD    DSN=PAYROLL(-1),DISP=SHR
```

Figure 14.8 Mixing absolute and relative generation names.

When an absolute name is used to create a generation data set, the same name can also be coded to subsequently reference the data set. In addition, a relative number is also associated with the data set. Using absolute names complicates GDG processing and is infrequently used. There are, however, some situations where absolute names are convenient.

When absolute names are coded during data set creation, generation and version numbers might be skipped and coded out of sequence. This is not good programming practice. Likewise, it is permissible to skip relative numbers during data set creation, but this is also not recommended.

The interaction between relative and absolute is illustrated in Fig. 14.8, where DD1 and DD2 reference the same data sets in both jobs. Here, both relative and absolute notation is used to create and retrieve generation data sets in two separate jobs.

Using IEHPROGM to Create Generation Data Groups

Prior to the development of IDCAMS, the IEHPROGM utility was used to create a GDG base table. IEHPROGM is still supported and, at some installations, it is used for GDG base table creation. Most installations, however, now require that IDCAMS be used to create a GDG base table. In fact, IEHPROGM is on the endangered utilities list because all of its functions can now be performed by IDCAMS.

Concatenating Generation Data Sets

A GDG name can be coded without specifying either a relative number or an absolute name. If this is done where the GDG name is associated with a DD statement used for an input operation, all the generation data sets in the GDG are concatenated. For example, if the GDG name is coded on the SYSUT1 DD statement with IEBGENER and IEBPTPCH or the DDname DD statement identified with INFILE with the IDCAMS utility, the generation data sets are concatenated. Reading a data set in an application program also permits the same type of concatenation. The data sets in the GDG are then processed in reverse chronological order from the most recently created first and oldest last.

```
DELETE     (GDGname.*)
DELETE     (GDGname)        GDG
```

Figure 14.9 Delete all GDG data sets and the base table.

An analogy can be made to specify the name of a PDS with a DD statement that is processed as an input data set. For example, with IEBPTPCH, the SYSUT1 DD statement would contain DSN = PDSname, and the PRINT control statement would specify TYPORG = PO. Most operations with IEBCOPY process every member in an input PDS. More than likely, some of the functions that process every member in a PDS with an IEB utility will eventually become available with IDCAMS.

A second important point should be made concerning concatenation of (generation) data sets. All of the data sets in the concatenation should, essentially, have the same DCB values (LRECL, BLKSIZE, RECFM). If the model DSCB is used to provide these values when each data set is created, the DCB properties will be the same. If different block size values are used, the largest block size must be used with the newest data set, which is the first data set processed in the concatenation.

Manually Deleting Generation Data Sets

An individual data set can be deleted from a GDG the same as any cataloged disk or tape data set can be deleted (Fig. 14.9). Either IEFBR14, IEHPROGM, or IDCAMS (the DELETE command) can be used. To delete every data set in a GDG, the generic properties of the IDCAMS DELETE command can be used. The code in Fig. 14.9 can be used to delete every member in the GDG.

The order of these two control statements cannot be reversed. If the GDG base table is deleted first, each data set must be individually deleted because they are no longer cataloged data sets.

Renaming Generation Data Sets

Both IDCAMS and IEHPROGM can be used to rename the data sets in a GDG. With IDCAMS, generic processing using the ALTER command can cause every data set in the GDG to be renamed (Fig. 14.10). The GDG base table can also be renamed. Generic renaming is similar to generic deletion with IDCAMS. The code in Fig. 14.10 can be used to rename all of the PAYROLL data sets and also the base table.

```
ALTER GDGname.*    NEWNAME(newGDGname.*)
ALTER GDGname      NEWNAME(newGDGname)
```

Figure 14.10 Renaming all of the data sets in a GDG.

Exercises

1. Create a generation data group that can hold a maximum of three data sets. During the same job, add two data sets to the GDG. Reference both of the members in a subsequent job. Now, add two additional data sets to the GDG in another single job. Reference both of these data sets during subsequent steps during the same job. Hence, they are created in an early step(s), and they exist in a later step(s).

2. Print out the records in the single data set that was bumped from the GDG base table during the processing in the previous exercise. How and why are these records still accessible? What are the relevant GDG parameters that permit the processing?

15

Linear Data Sets

The overall organizational structure of this chapter is somewhat similar to chapters 10 (ESDS) and 11 (RRDS), although on a simpler scale. It contains a general description of the Linear Data Set (LDS). Various IDCAMS commands are used to process an LDS, and unlike chapters 10 and 11, there is no discussion of the use of "standard" COBOL application programs to process an LDS. This is because, for the most part, an LDS is not directly processed but rather indirectly processed through DB2 or some other comparable approach. Here, High-Level Callable Services are used and COBOL programming with an LDS is deferred until near the end of the chapter. The two terms *DIV object* and *Data-in-Virtual* are used to identify an LDS. Finally, a more general framework for using the LDS is described.

Unlike the other three VSAM data set organizations, the LDS has not yet achieved widespread popularity. This chapter and earlier references in the book imply a crucial connection between DB2 and the LDS. Although this is true, the LDS has usage in many other contexts. Individuals and installations are just now beginning to utilize the various LDS facilities. For more information on LDS programming, consult the *MVS/ESA Callable Services for High Level Languages*.

General Description of the LDS

The fourth type of VSAM data set was introduced in 1988—the Linear Data Set (LDS), or LSDS. It is sometimes imprecisely categorized as a special type of ESDS. This is misleading. The LDS has a structure and a set of processing rules completely different from the three older VSAM data set organizations. Although Linear Data Sets can, in theory, be used in a wide variety of processing situations, they are most commonly associated with IBM's relational database management system product DB2.

The LDS contains the data tables for DB2, which are processed by the various SQL commands. Generally, the LDS is an example of a new type of disk processing that is supported by an MVS/XA product called Data-In-Virtual (DIV). The term *DIV Object* is sometimes used to identify an LDS. LDS programming uses a DIV assembler macro to provide a wide variety of processing options.

Internal structure of the LDS

Like the ESDS and RRDS, the LDS consists of a cluster and data component. The data component consists of control intervals that must be 4,096 bytes in length. The entire control interval is available to hold data. There is never any unused VSAM space or control fields, no CIDF and no RDFs. The concept of logical records is not relevant, which precludes the need for RDFs. Figure 15.1 contrasts the structure of an ESDS and an LDS. A comparable KSDS contains freespace rather than unused space. Clearly, the extremely simple physical structure of an LDS is not appropriate for many standard programming applications.

The LDS is created by IDCAMS, but IDCAMS is not commonly used for any subsequent processing. With the other VSAM data set organizations and non-VSAM data sets, an access method is used to perform functions such as blocking, deblocking, buffer management, and read ahead/processing. By not using the traditional approach of an access method to process a disk data set, more efficient processing is possible.

LDS processing is implemented using system paging routines. Hence, LDS processing is related to ESDS processing in the same way that UNIT = VIO is related to UNIT = SYSDA with disk data sets in general. Any LDS discussion should also mention two other major related MVS/ESA processing concepts, data spaces and hiperspaces. Because an LDS is accessed using control interval processing, READPW and UPDATEPW are not appropriate with an LDS. Genuine control interval processing in assembler language is possible, but rarely performed. See Table 15.1.

Standard ESDS (or KSDS) Control Interval

Record 1	Record 2	Record 3	Unused Space (Freespace)	RDF3	RDF2	RDF1	CIDF

LDS Control Interval

Data Stream Without Record Boundaries or Control Information

Figure 15.1 Comparing ESDS and LDS control interval structures.

TABLE 15.1   Methods of Processing an LDS.

```
Standard IDCAMS Commands
Control Interval Processing in Assembler Language
Using the DIV Macro in Assembler
Callable Services for High Level Languages
Using a DBMS or TP Monitor as an Interface to Callable
  Services
```

Using IDCAMS with an LDS

Most IDCAMS commands have been modified in order to process an LDS. Some IDCAMS commands have a very limited role with an LDS, including EXPORT, IMPORT, and VERIFY. No new commands were created for use strictly with an LDS. A patchwork approach seems to have been used for command modification. In the *Access Method Services* manual, several additional lines have been added to the end of the descriptions of the relevant commands and parameters qualifying and describing their use with Linear Data Sets. The appearance is that of a hastily thrown together add-on. Therefore, this book is at the opposite extreme of the manual, where the ESDS and RRDS are organized into separate chapters.

DEFINE CLUSTER with an LDS

Among the four VSAM data set types, the most limited set of parameters are available with an LDS. In particular, every parameter that can be coded with an LDS can also be used with an ESDS, except for LINEAR, which replaces NONINDEXED. With an LDS, the CISZ must always be 4,096 bytes and need not be coded. RECORDSIZE is meaningless, and SPANNED should not be coded. As with any DEFINE CLUSTER command, the NAME, VOLUME, and Space Allocation values are required. MODEL can be used to provide the volume and space allocation values. Initially, only SHR(1 3) was permitted with an LDS, but this restriction has been lifted and any permissible cross-region value can be specified. However, 3 is the only value that can be specified for the cross-system subparameter value. Hence, there is no cross-system read or write integrity. Furthermore, cross-region values other than 1 place additional processing complications on the applications using the LDS.

Example 1.   A Linear Data Set is to be created on volume PERM23. It is estimated to require 15 cylinders. To allow for possible future expansion, a secondary allocation of 3 cylinders is requested. The control area size is 1 cylinder. Any number of users should be able to concurrently process the data set for input along with one job processing for output. The data set should be reusable. The DEFINE CLUSTER command is shown in Fig. 15.2.

The Big Eight IDCAMS commands

The REPRO command allows very few parameters with an LDS. The input and output parameters use the same syntax as other types of VSAM data set. The

```
DEFINE  CLUSTER(NAME(EMPLOYEE.MASTER.LINEAR)    -
               LINEAR                           -
               VOLUME(PERM23)                   -
               CYL(15 3)                        -
               MASTERPW(DB3)                    -
               SHR(2 3)                         -
               REUSE)                           -
          DATA(NAME(EMPLOYEE.MASTER.LINEAR.DATA))
```

Figure 15.2 Creating a linear data set.

only parameters available to identify the beginning and the end of the input to be
copied are FROMADDRESS and TOADDRESS. Even SKIP and COUNT can-
not be used because they apply to logical records. The RBA values specified
with FROMADDRESS and TOADDRESS should only be multiples of 4,096.
REUSE can be coded, but REPLACE cannot be used. Encryption is also supported. Exactly the same parameters as with REPRO are available for identifying the initial and final data processed with the PRINT command.

There are no data set organization-specific comments concerning LDS processing with the LISTCAT, ALTER, and DELETE commands. A LISTCAT of an
LDS is smaller than other VSAM data set types. EXPORT and IMPORT are
available to unload and reload LDSs. However, the extremely simple structure
of the LDS and the small amount of DEFINE CLUSTER code makes REPRO a
very viable alternative to both EXPORT and IMPORT. Finally, VERIFY has an
extremely limited role with an LDS.

Example 2.   In Fig. 15.3, various IDCAMS commands are used to process an
LDS. Records are copied from an existing LDS to the LDS created in Example
1. After the copy is completed, the third through fifty-first control intervals in
the newly created copy are to be printed in character format. The name of the

```
REPRO  IDS(EXISTING.LDS)                     -
       ODS(EMPLOYEE.MASTER.LINEAR)
PRINT  IDS(EMPLOYEE.MASTER.LINEAR)           -
       FROMADDRESS(8192)                     -
       TOADDRESS(204800)                     -
       CHARACTER
ALTER  EMPLOYEE.MASTER.LINEAR                -
       NEWNAME(NEW.EMPLOYEE.LDS)
ALTER  EMPLOYEE.MASTER.LINEAR.DATA           -
       NEWNAME(NEW.EMPLOYEE.LDS.DATA)        -
       BUFFERSPACE(20480)
LISTCAT ENT(NEW.EMPLOYEE.LDS)  ALL
```

Figure 15.3 Processing a linear data set.

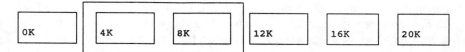

Figure 15.4 8K window (offset 1 and span 2) into an LDS.

data component is changed, and five buffers are to be provided for subsequent processing. Finally, all information in the cluster component is to be displayed.

The General LDS Picture

The previous sections do not identify the complete scope of linear data sets. Basically, it is possible for applications to view selected portions of an LDS through a "window" into virtual storage. The window provides a temporary access within the users address space to a portion of the LDS disk data. It allows a group of contiguous 4K blocks within the LDS to be processed. The processing can be read only or update. There are actually three possible locations associated with processing an LDS:

1. True disk storage.
2. A scroll area.
3. The program area.

The application must provide two values, the location and the size of the window area within the LDS. These must be identified as (1) an offset from the beginning of the LDS, and (2) a span that specifies the amount the window is open. Both values are specified as integers to identify the number of 4,096-byte blocks.

For example, an offset of 6 and a span of 3 identifies 12K bytes beginning at relative byte address 24K. An application can move the window to other locations within the LDS and can change the window span. Intuitive window concepts are illustrated in Figs. 15.4 and 15.5. In Fig. 15.4, the values 1 and 2 are

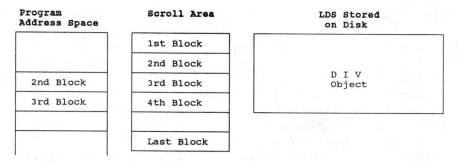

Figure 15.5 Mapping a DIV object which has a scroll area.

parameters identifying the location and size respectively of the window. In Fig. 15.5, a more general situation is identified. In addition to the window in the program area, there is also a scroll area in which the data can be processed.

Utilizing the window

The DIV macro can be used to perform a wide range of processing with the data contained in the window. However, the use of the DIV macro is restricted to assembler language. DIV processing capabilities include initial access to the data set, viewing and modifying data, refreshing data, and eventually freeing the data set.

In order to perform comparable processing in high-level languages such as COBOL and PL/I, the data window services (DWS) facility can be used. DWS provides two basic features. First is the type of processing provided by the DIV macro through a facility known as *Callable Services*. The *MVS/ESA Callable Services for High Level Languages (HLL)* manual describes the facilities. The manual contains numerous coding examples written in COBOL, PL/I, FORTRAN, Pascal, and C/370. Second, DWS allows objects other than just LDSs to be processed in comparable fashion. The significant additional objects are called data spaces and hiperspaces.

Data Spaces and Hiperspaces

Data spaces and hiperspaces are available with MVS/ESA. Both structures allow I/O to be performed faster and more efficiently on an MVS system. On large MVS systems, a tremendous amount of disk and terminal I/O is constantly being performed. All such processing occurs at considerably slower speeds than central memory processing. Data spaces and hiperspaces are part of the solution to the I/O processing bottleneck and both can be used by application programs and system software. Many of the HLL Callable Services commands do not distinguish among an LDS, data space, or hiperspace.

Data spaces

Data spaces are objects in virtual storage that can be used to hold data. Address spaces in virtual storage are usually associated with programs. Data spaces can contain only data, not an executing program. Consequently, they have very little overhead compared to the address space for a program. They can, however, be used for any programmer-selected functions. Locations in data spaces are byte addressable, and the maximum size of a data space is 2 gigabytes. One executing program can process multiple data spaces. Data spaces can be created before usage by a program or dynamically. Data spaces can be stored in any of three locations: central memory, extended storage, or true auxillary storage. Central memory is the new ESA name for what used to be called main memory. Extended storage is a type of memory that could be categorized as second class memory. Access times are slower than central memory. Ordinarily, there is much more extended storage than central storage.

Hiperspaces

Hiperspaces are also new with ESA. A hiperspace provides more potential storage than a data space. Hiperspaces can only be referenced in increments of 4,096 (4K) bytes, unlike a data space reference where individual bytes can be accessed. Unlike a data space, a hiperspace can only be found in extended memory or disk storage.

There are two basic types of hiperspaces: standard and expanded storage only. A standard hiperspace can reside in either expanded storage or disk. An ESO (expanded storage only) can only reside in expanded storage. A standard hiperspace is associated with scroll-type operations with the HLL statements.

Callable Services Call Functions

There are five types of HLL CALL statements, each beginning with CSR followed by 3 or 4 additional letters:

- CSRIDAC
- CSRVIEW
- CSRREFR
- CSRSAVE
- CSRSCOT

Each statement has a parameter list that must be specified. CSRIDAC is usually initially employed. CSRIDAC is used to request access to a data object when processing begins and also to terminate access to a data object when processing is completed. A data object can be an LDS, data space, or hiperspace.

CSRVIEW is used to view an object. CSRVIEW maps a window to one or more blocks within a data object. CSRREFR is used to refresh the data contained in a window, a scroll area, or a temporary object. Basically, it allows processing to continue without any explicit reinitialization.

CSRSAVE and CSRSCOT are used to make changes to an object. CSRSAVE is used with permanent objects, and CSRSCOT is used with objects in a scroll area. If scrolling is being used, the window is mapped to the scroll area and the scroll area is mapped to the object. Without scrolling, the window is mapped directly to the object.

HLL call statements with COBOL

Example 3. The HLL CALL statements can be embedded in a COBOL application program. In order to actually execute this code, the load modules used to implement the HLL statements must be link edited to the compiled COBOL code. These modules would be ordinarily stored in the system load module library, SYS1.LINKLIB or the COBOL automatic call library, SYS1.VSCLLIB (SYS1.COB2LIB). Processing can include a data object is accessed, several blocks in the object are viewed, and some are eventually modified. Finally, the changes are saved and the object is released. The various methods available for processing an LDS include:

- Standard IDCAMS commands.
- Control interval processing in Assembler language.
- Using the DIV macro in Assembler.
- Callable services for high-level languages.
- Using a DBMS or TP monitor as an interface to callable services.

Notice that the use of IDCAMS commands is one of the least flexible.

Exercises

1. Why are SKIP and COUNT not allowed with the REPRO and PRINT commands when processing an LDS?

2. In Example 1, why is a secondary allocation of 3 cylinders used when the control area size is always, at most, 1 cylinder? For example, allocating 3 cylinders will create 3 separate control areas.

3. Use IDCAMS to create an LDS. Load data in the LDS and print out the resulting contents of the LDS. Finally, modify several cluster component properties and print out all the information in the cluster component.

4. Write a complete COBOL application program to build and load an LDS using HLL commands. In a second COBOL application, update the information in the LDS.

16

VSAM Processing with CICS

There are few, if any, software products that are as crucially involved with VSAM as is Customer Information Control System (CICS). The CICS processing environment is totally different from the batch COBOL environment. CICS allows a wide range of processing options of which many are not permitted in a batch COBOL program. This chapter covers the 11 CICS commands for VSAM processing in detail. Each command is illustrated with numerous coding examples. The final two topics of the chapter cover alternate key processing in a CICS application and handling exceptional conditions.

File Processing Operations with a TP Monitorlike CICS

CICS is one of the most widely used program products in the world. It is often categorized as either a mini-operating system or a teleprocessing (TP) monitor. CICS allows terminal users to process records in a VSAM data set. This processing is almost always randomly performed, one record at a time. Except for the beginning paragraphs, only the VSAM processing component of CICS is discussed. CICS is an even more complex product than VSAM, and there are numerous excellent books on the subject.

Several important features are typical of most CICS application programs. These characteristics are ''almost'' as important as it is for the program to produce correct results! First, response time, the elapsed time from when a person strikes a key to transmit data from a terminal until the response is visible on the screen, is an extremely important factor in determining the quality of an on-line program. Generally, whenever a person enters data on a terminal screen and strikes a key to transmit, they expect something close to an instantaneous response time. In some situations, response time is considered as important as accurate results! This point is further discussed with alternate key processing.

Second, preserving data integrity is a very significant and complicated issue with CICS. Several people at different terminals might want to concurrently access the same logical record or modify two different records in the same control interval. A very large number of terminal users might want to process a VSAM data set at the same time. Two distinct CICS users should not be permitted to modify the same logical record concurrently. However, the operating system considers every terminal user processing with CICS as being part of the same job. CICS uses various types of "locks" to provide some data integrity.

Third, an additional complicating factor is that records in a VSAM KSDS are more commonly processed using their alternate key values with on-line CICS processing than with batch processing. Alternate key processing has various hidden costs.

Some methods must be provided to allow multiple users a variety of concurrent accesses and yet still protect the integrity of the data and guarantee a reasonable response time. The techniques used by CICS and VSAM to accomplish these goals are necessarily more complex than those used with VSAM data sets in a strictly batch processing environment. Hence, CICS provides an additional layer of data management software. This software is called the *File Control Program (FCP)* and is a major CICS subroutine. The relative location of various types of software used in processing a VSAM data set in both a batch program and with CICS is shown in Table 16.1.

In a batch processing environment, coding DISP = OLD on a DD statement gives exclusive control of an entire VSAM data set to one job. Coding DISP = SHR permits any number of jobs to access a data set simultaneously. Minimally, access control defaults to the SHAREOPTIONS values stored in the catalog. The DISP parameter and the SHAREOPTIONS values stored in the

TABLE 16.1 Comparing Batch and CICS VSAM Processing.

Application Programs to Process VSAM Data Sets	
Batch Program (single user)	**CICS Application (multiple users; considered one job)**
VSAM Routines Access Method	CICS Routines (File Control Program)
	VSAM Routines Access Method
Disk Data Set Control Intervals	Disk Data Set Control Intervals

cluster component completely determine how a VSAM data set can be shared by batch programs. Obviously, a more extensive set of rules are necessary to control the access of a VSAM data set processed by CICS.

The complicating factor is that the operating system considers all terminal users (tasks) signed onto CICS a group tied together into a single batch job, which, at any given time, could include several hundred people. Hence, both VSAM and CICS must monitor the I/O operations performed. It is no wonder then that, with its various management functions with terminals, VSAM data sets, and other system entities, CICS is frequently called a mini operating system. In this role, there are many similarities between CICS, MVS, and other operating systems.

All the information concerning individual VSAM I/O operations performed with CICS applies to every language that can be used with CICS. Because the I/O operations are language-independent, several important VSAM features that are not available with a batch COBOL program can be used with a Command Level CICS COBOL program.

VSAM I/O Operations with CICS

The CICS program itself is a very large and sophisticated batch program. Assume, for simplicity, that the CICS program itself is written in a high-level language like COBOL or PL/I. For every VSAM data set that a CICS user might want the CICS program to process on their behalf, a SELECT...ASSIGN statement in COBOL or a DECLARE...FILE statement in PL/I is required within CICS itself (not the user's program). This statement associates the file in the program with a DD statement in the JCL. The same basic idea holds in the assembler language in which the CICS program is actually written. VSAM data sets processed by CICS applications are allocated when the batch CICS start-up program executes. Consequently, because they are defined to CICS, a person at a terminal in a session with CICS can process records in the data sets. Individual users cannot, however, define or allocate VSAM data sets to CICS. Defining and maintaining data sets is done by the system support staff.

A CICS user does not ordinarily open or close any data sets in their program. All existing data sets are opened automatically when CICS is started up. Actually, beginning with Release 1.7, the data set is opened when the first I/O operation is executed. New data sets can be allocated while CICS is running, although this is usually not done by an application programmer. Conversely, if a data set allocated to CICS must be reorganized, it must first be deallocated, because reorganization requires DISP = OLD processing. An IDCAMS batch job can then be run and the data set reallocated to CICS and opened.

Example 1.   Suppose that four VSAM data sets have been defined to CICS. In a simplified manner, their accompanying JCL can be thought of as shown in Fig. 16.1. DD statements are used on an MVS system, and DLBL statements are used on a VSE system. One or more of these data sets are used in almost all of

```
//A          EXEC PGM=DFHCICS
     . . .
//DD1KSDS    DD   DSN=CICS5.DD1KSDS,DISP=SHR   with MVS JCL
//DD2ESDS    DD   DSN=CICS5.DD2ESDS,DISP=SHR
//DD3RRDS    DD   DSN=CICS5.DD3RRDS,DISP=SHR
//DD4PATH    DD   DSN=CICS5.DD4PATH,DISP=SHR

//   DLBL    DD1KSDS,'CICS5.DD1KSDS',,VSAM       with VSE JCL
//   DLBL    DD2ESDS,'CICS5.DD2ESDS',,VSAM
//   DLBL    DD3RRDS,'CICS5.DD3RRDS',,VSAM
//   DLBL    DD4PATH,'CICS5.DD4PATH',,VSAM
```

Figure 16.1 JCL for VSAM data sets defined to CICS.

the processing examples of VSAM data sets with CICS. Assume that the name of the batch program that is CICS is DFHCICS.

As always, the first three VSAM data sets are created with the DEFINE CLUSTER command and initialized with the REPRO command. They are then allocated to CICS. Unlike batch VSAM processing, at least one record should be loaded into a VSAM data set before actual processing by CICS. The record can then be subsequently deleted. The CICS5.DD4PATH data set is a path over the base cluster CICS5.DD1KSDS.

Because all of the VSAM data sets allocated to CICS are allocated before user processing begins, an application can, at any time, perform any of the standard I/O requests including (random or sequential) read, write, rewrite, and delete operations.

For an input or output operation, the verb syntax identifies whether the processing is sequential or random. Unlike a batch program, this choice is made with each individual I/O operation rather than a SELECT...ASSIGN statement. Application programs that use CICS do not contain their own SELECT or DECLARE...FILE file name statements. Hence, CICS uses dynamic access with every VSAM data set allocated to it. Recall that, with a batch program, the actual name of the data set being processed does not occur anywhere within the application code. The same is true with a CICS application program. With each I/O operation, the data set is identified by its DDname in the accompanying JCL. Hence, to add a record to the KSDS CICS5.DD1KSDS, the CICS command would contain the following code:

```
EXEC CICS WRITE
    DATASET('DD1KSDS')
    other parameters
    END-EXEC
```

EXEC CICS is required to identify the beginning of a CICS command in every programming language, and the END-EXEC is required with COBOL. PL/I and assembler use different CICS command delimiters. The DATASET parameter contains the DDname value that identifies the data set, and it should be enclosed in quotes if it is a literal. A rare application where quotes should not be used is to develop system software to retrieve records from any arbitrary data set or to scroll the records in an arbitrary data set. There is an analogy between the DATASET parameter with a VSAM operation and MAPSET when transmitting data to or from a terminal.

Suppose it is necessary to delete a data set allocated to CICS and then redefine and load it. In order to do this, the data set must first be deallocated from CICS. Following this, a batch IDCAMS job can be run to delete and recreate the data set. Finally, IDCAMS or another program can be used to load the new data set. Furthermore, while it is deallocated, the name of the data set can be changed or moved to a different volume. When this processing is done, the necessary information describing the data set must be updated in one of the major control tables used by CICS, the *File Control Table (FCT)*.

Ordinarily, DISP = SHR is specified with data sets processed by CICS. Every terminal user communicating with CICS is grouped together and considered a single batch job by the operating system. When SHR is coded and appropriate SHAREOPTIONS values are supplied, other batch jobs or on-line systems can also use the data set concurrently as long as they do not specify DISP = OLD— either explicitly or implicitly. If a second job specifies DISP = OLD with a data set allocated to CICS, the second job will wait for the data set or eventually be cancelled.

There are two common programming situations where OLD is implicitly specified. When using the IDCAMS PRINT and REPRO commands, an attempt can be made to dynamically allocate a data set. With these commands, dynamic allocation occurs when either INDATASET or OUTDATASET is coded. For a data set defined to CICS, the system returns the message that the data set is not available to the new job. VSE/IDCAMS does not allow dynamic allocation. A second on-line system (TP monitor) might want to process the data set exclusively. In this case, DISP = OLD is coded when the job that defines the on-line system is started. This can be done with some on-line systems but it is not common with CICS.

CICS Data Set Organizations

Five types of data set organizations were formerly allowed with CICS. ISAM cannot be used with the last several releases of CICS, beginning with release 1.6 in 1985 and BDAM is on the endangered data set organization list. This is one of several strategies used by IBM to strongly "encourage" users to convert from non-VSAM to VSAM data sets.

It is expected that the use of non-VSAM data sets with CICS will soon become virtually nonexistent. All types of VSAM data sets except linear are available with CICS. Because most on-line processing involves random record retrieval, the KSDS is the most popular, while ESDS is the least-frequently used with CICS. Few CICS applications require only standard sequential processing. Paths and alternate indexes can also be used for processing the records

TABLE 16.2   CICS Methods to Process VSAM Data Sets.

	KSDS	RRDS	ESDS
Random	Primary key Alternate key RBA	Relative record number	Alternate key RBA
Sequential	Primary key Alternate key	Relative record number	RBA Alternate key
Skip Sequential	Primary key Alternate key		

in a KSDS or ESDS. Recall that a path is a logical entity located in a VSAM catalog that processes records in the base cluster using the alternate key values.

CICS allows records in a VSAM data set to be processed in almost every permissible manner. There are three basic access techniques for processing records in a VSAM data set: random, sequential, and skip sequential. Records in a KSDS can be randomly accessed in three ways:

1. Using the primary key

2. Using the relative byte address (RBA).

3. Through a path and alternate index (AIX) constructed over the base KSDS.

Records in an ESDS can be randomly accessed using their RBA and through a path and alternate index constructed over the base ESDS. Records in an RRDS can be randomly accessed only by their relative record number (RRN). Recall that an alternate index cannot be constructed over an RRDS. All three VSAM data set organizations can also be processed sequentially. Both forward and backward processing are possible with all three types. Skip sequential processing is possible with a KSDS. Table 16.2 summarizes the methods available with CICS to process records in a VSAM data set.

Most installations have an on-line transaction that allows specific individual records to be displayed from any data set defined to CICS. Depending on the data set organization, a record can be identified by primary key, alternate key, RBA, RRN, or sequential processing. Some transactions of this type also support random additions, changes, and deletions. The CECI system transaction supplied with CICS performs all of these functions. Several third-party software vendors provide transactions that allows almost every conceivable I/O operation to be easily performed without using an application program.

CICS Syntax for Processing VSAM Data Sets

Although a CICS application program written in COBOL does not contain a SELECT...ASSIGN statement for a VSAM data set, a 01-level structure describing the logical records in the data set is coded in either the WORKING-STORAGE or LINKAGE SECTION. With most operations, it is the combination of the logical record area, the DDname coded with the DATASET parameter of the CICS command, the type of I/O operation, and a key field area that determines the type of processing that takes place. In several instances, the key field area might not be needed for a command. With an RRDS, the key field is replaced by a field that holds the relative record number.

Example 2.   To read a record from the VSAM KSDS identified in Example 1 into an area in WORKING-STORAGE called MASTER-REC, the code shown on the left-hand side in Fig. 16.2 can be used. The code on the right-hand side can be used to read the same record into a structure in the LINKAGE SECTION.

The COBOL data area coded with RIDFLD must identify a field in either the WORKING-STORAGE SECTION or the LINKAGE SECTION. The RIDFLD data area need not be contained within the structure coded with the INTO clause and it must not be within the area pointed to by the address specified with SET. Recall that most batch processing requires that the primary key be contained within the 01-level record structure used to process the KSDS.

The size of the KSDS-KEY field must be the same as the length value stored in the KEYS parameter in the data set's cluster component. In addition, the 01-level structure coded with INTO and identified by the SET address should contain a field with the same length and at the same offset as the two KEYS parameter values stored in the cluster component. It deserves some thought as to why this approach (similar to the NOMINAL KEY with an ISAM data set) is used rather than the batch KSDS approach, where the only key field is the RECORD KEY in the 01 structure.

After the READ command is executed, the control interval containing the requested logical record is read into one of the CICS buffers. If INTO is coded,

```
Move Mode Processing              Locate Mode Processing
WORKING-STORAGE SECTION.
                                  01   POINTER1   PTR.
                                  01   REC-LEN S9(4) COMP.
                                  01   KSDS-KEY        PIC 9(9).
                                  LINKAGE SECTION.
01  MASTER-REC.                   01   MASTER-REC BASED(POINTER1).
    ...                                ...
    02  REC-KEY PIC 9(9).              02  REC-KEY CHAR(9).
    ....                               ...

    ....                          01  ...

01  KSDS-KEY    PIC 9(9).
    EXEC CICS READ                    EXEC CICS READ
        DATASET('DD1KSDS')                DATASET('DD1KSDS')
        INTO(MASTER-REC)                  SET(POINTER1)
        RIDFLD(KSDS-KEY)                  RIDFLD(KSDS-KEY)
        ...                               LENGTH(REC-LEN)
```

Figure 16.2   Random record retrieval with a KSDS.

the record is then moved to MASTER-REC in WORKING-STORAGE. The fields the record contains can then be processed within the CICS program.

The SET parameter can be coded as an alternative to INTO. INTO specifies MOVE mode processing, and SET identifies LOCATE mode processing. With SET, the 01-level used to identify the fields in the record following the READ command must be in the LINKAGE SECTION. Because it is outside the bounds of the application program, a pointer identifies it instead of the area specified by a variable name. In this case, the record is processed in a CICS buffer.

With both MOVE and LOCATE mode processing, the basic steps identified in Fig. 16.3 are performed. With both types of processing, the area acquired with the Getmain is used as a buffer. With MOVE mode, the record is copied from the buffer into WORKING-STORAGE prior to the processing in B). With LOCATE mode, the address of the Getmain area is passed to the program prior to B) and the record is processed in the buffer itself.

The File Control Table (FCT)

CICS attempts to perform processing operations as quickly as possible to reduce response time. Hence, accessing system catalogs and VVDS entries (data set labels) should be minimized, if not completely avoided. Unnecessary I/O operations are time-consuming. To help reduce processing time, much of the essential information contained in data set labels and catalogs is maintained in memory in the File Control Table (FCT). For each specific data set, the FCT also identifies the types of I/O operations permitted with it. For example, all possible I/O operations might be allowed with a KSDS, but only establishing position and sequential record retrieval are permitted with the path and alternate index constructed over it. A second KSDS might permit Add and Change operations but not record deletion. Likewise, an RRDS might be defined to permit only record retrieval and rewriting of existing records.

Although each data set defined to CICS contains a large number of entries in the FCT, only the most important fields are described in Table 16.3. Generally,

CICS Application Program	CICS File Control Program (FCP)	VSAM Access Method
A) READ Record for UPDATE	(1) Getmain for Storage (2) Enque on the Logical Record (3) Issue VSAM GET	(4) Control Interval Lock
B) Modify Fields		
C) REWRITE the Record	(5) Issue VSAM PUT	(6) Update the Control Interval (7) Release the Lock

Figure 16.3 Details of VSAM processing with CICS.

TABLE 16.3   Important File Control Table (FCT) Entries.

FCT Field	Description
DDname*	Used to locate and identify other table entries The FCT is organized on the DDname values. DDname must be coded with every VSAM command.
Data Set Organization	Type of data set—KSDS, RRDS, ESDS, or PATH. A PATH must be built over a base KSDS or ESDS. Alternate index entries are not placed in the FCT.
Data Set* Name	The cluster name of the VSAM data set.
Allowable$ Operations	Only those operations listed can be performed. Invalid operations raise an INVREQ condition.
String Numbers	String number information. There are two values, the total and the number currently in use.
Status$	Opened, Closed, Allocated, Deallocated, Undefined.
"DCB-Like" Values	Processing characteristics of the data set. This includes the key length and offset, maximum logical record size, and record format.
Buffer Information	Data component value and index component value for a KSDS.
Location	UNIT and VOLUME information, but not the actual location on volume.
Processing Statistics	Number of add, delete, change, and read operations performed on the data set.
Journaling Permitted	JFILEID=number, where number is an integer value between 2 and 99. Used with automatic journaling.
Journaling Operations	Types of operations that will cause a journal entry to be written, e.g., RU, WN, WU, D, etc.
Dynamic Transaction Backout	LOG=YES identifies a recoverable file.

much of the information contained in the FCT is also found in either the cluster component—BCS and VVDS—or VSAM control blocks.

FCT field entries identified with a dollar sign in Table 16.3 can be displayed and modified using CEMT, a system transaction provided with CICS. An asterisk denotes an entry that can be displayed but not modified using CEMT. Table 16.3 is not an all-inclusive listing.

CICS Commands for Processing VSAM Data Sets

CICS provides 11 commands for processing the records in a VSAM data set. The *CICS Application Programmers Reference* manual lists 10, considering

READ UPDATE a special case of READ. OPEN and CLOSE cannot be coded in a command level CICS application program. Rather, a system utility transaction such as CEMT is used to open and close data sets. Furthermore, these utilities can allocate and deallocate data sets. With CICS, a data set is closed before it is deallocated and allocated before it is opened.

The reason so many commands are available with CICS (versus batch) is because of multiple terminal users wanting to access records in the same data set simultaneously. Furthermore, terminal users expect a very rapid response time. Therefore, additional commands are needed to process VSAM data sets and to implement these two somewhat conflicting goals.

The 11 I/O commands and, in some cases, their equivalent batch verbs, are listed in Table 16.4. Commands fall into two categories. Those that:

1. Perform random or sequential processing of logical records, including the READNEXT command, which allows skip sequential processing.

2. Allocate or deallocate resources, with READ UPDATE, STARTBR, REWRITE, and RESETBR falling into both categories. In one situation, DELETE can also deallocate resources. The same holds for WRITE in an allocation situation. The + identifies skip sequential processing.

TABLE 16.4   VSAM I/O Commands Available with CICS.

CICS Command	Batch Equivalent	Process Type or Function	General Description
READ	READ	Random	Read only operation
READ UPDATE	READ	Random and Allocate	Read and later rewrite; Also allocates resources
STARTBR	START	Random and Allocate	Positioning operation; Also allocates resources
RESETBR	START	Random and Allocate	Repositioning operation; Transfers resources
READNEXT	READ NEXT	Sequential+	Logical record pointer used
READPREV	READ PREV	Sequential	Logical record pointer used
WRITE	WRITE	Random and Allocate	Random only; Use a batch program or MASSINSERT for sequential processing.
REWRITE	REWRITE	Random and Deallocate	Follows READ UPDATE only; Releases string and CI lock
DELETE	DELETE	Random and Deallocate	No READ need be executed; Rather, READ is optional.
ENDBR	none	Deallocate	Releases control of a VSAM string
UNLOCK	none	Deallocate	Releases exclusive lock on a control interval

+ Skip Sequential Processing Also Permitted

TABLE 16.5   Keyword Parameters Used with VSAM Commands.

Group 1 Input Commands
The Read and Browse Commands

Parameters	READ READ UPDATE	STARTBR RESETBR	READNEXT READPREV
DATASET(data-value)	R	R	R
RIDFLD(data-area)	R	R	R
SET(pointer)｜INTO(data-area)	R	X	R
LENGTH(data-value)	O	X	O
KEYLENGTH(data-value)	O	O	O
GENERIC	O	O	X
RBA｜RRN	O	O	O
GTEQ｜EQUAL	O	O	X
REQID(data-value)	X	O	O
UPDATE	R or X	X	X

Group 2 Output Commands
The WRITE, REWRITE, and DELETE Command

Parameters	WRITE	REWRITE	DELETE
DATASET(data-value)	R	R	R
FROM(data-area)	R	R	X
RIDFLD(data-area)	R	X	O
LENGTH(data-value)	O	O	X
KEYLENGTH(data-value)	O	X	O
RBA｜RRN	O	X	O
MASSINSERT	O	X	X
GENERIC(NUMREC(data-area))	X	X	O

Group 3 Deallocation Commands
The UNLOCK and ENDBR Commands

Parameters	UNLOCK	ENDBR
DATASET(data-value)	R	R
REQID(data-value)	X	O

R - a required parameter
O - an optional parameter
X - the parameter should not be coded with the command

Detailed Command Parameters Syntax

Based on either syntax or functionality, the 11 commands can be grouped into one of three general categories—input, output, and deallocation commands:

1. Input commands. READ, READ UPDATE, STARTBR, RESETBR, READ-NEXT, and READPREV share many of the same keyword parameters.

2. WRITE, REWRITE, and DELETE are output commands and share several syntactical similarities, with all three commands resulting in a control interval being rewritten.

3. Deallocation commands. UNLOCK and ENDBR can be grouped together as deallocation commands because they are the only two commands that do not perform an I/O operation.

The three command groups are shown in Table 16.5. For each of the three groups of commands, the possible parameters that can be coded with all of the commands in the group are listed on the left-hand side. Underneath each command, an R, O, or X is used to identify whether the parameter must be coded with the command (Required), coded with the command (Optional), or is prohibited with the command (X). (The same type of chart is used to categorize the parameters of other related groups of commands throughout the text.)

An OR bar (|) means exactly one of the two values can be coded. With each of the three groups, required parameters are listed first and not indented. A data-area must be a field in the WORKING-STORAGE SECTION or LINKAGE SECTION. A data-value can be a data-area or a literal that has the correct size and attributes.

The GENERIC parameter means that generic processing is possible with the command. Four of the read and browse commands permit generic processing: READ, READ UPDATE, STARTBR, and RESETBR. The DELETE command also permits generic processing.

Neither of the commands in the Deallocation group perform any I/O operations with logical records. An argument can be made that STARTBR and RESETBR also do not "process" logical records.

VSAM Input Operations with CICS

Random record retrieval—READ and READ UPDATE commands

The two CICS random READ commands have exactly the same syntax except for the UPDATE parameter. It is convenient to consider them as two distinct commands because their functions are quite different. The READ command retrieves a record. Once the record is read, no related resources remain tied up by the program that read the record. Hence, READ implies a read only operation. READ UPDATE also retrieves a record. However, it is assumed that the record is to be further processed.

Obtaining and releasing READ UPDATE resources

Following a READ UPDATE, other CICS users might try processing that could modify records in the control interval of a record read for updating. It is permissible for another program to read a record in the control interval. A second copy of the control interval is supplied by VSAM to any program performing read operations. However, any operation that can change the contents of the control interval is suspended, including READ UPDATE, WRITE, and DELETE commands. It is impossible for another program to try to rewrite a second record in the control interval because a REWRITE must follow a READ UPDATE.

A string is assigned to a program (task), which executes a READ UPDATE. The string is held until processing is completed by the execution of a second command or the program ends. Each string identifies a data set user. A predefined maximum number of strings are assigned to a data set, often quite small. Whenever possible, an application should try to restrict itself to holding only one string for each VSAM data set it is processing. However, a single program may hold two or more strings for the same VSAM data set.

In summary, the READ UPDATE command can clearly have a significant effect on other CICS users who wish to process the data set for two reasons, one local and one global. Locally, they are locked out of a specific control interval, and globally there is one less string available for the entire data set. These two reasons make the READ UPDATE command extremely important to system contention.

After the READ UPDATE command is executed, one of three additional commands must be issued to complete processing the record—REWRITE, DELETE, or UNLOCK. Until this occurs, no additional modification processing can be done to the other control interval records.

Usually, the REWRITE command is used to modify the record. The RIDFLD parameter should not be coded with the REWRITE command because its function is to modify the 1 outstanding record in the data set previously read for update. A record read for update can also be deleted. This is discussed with the DELETE command later. Finally, the control interval containing the record can be released without executing a REWRITE or DELETE command. The UNLOCK command is used for this purpose.

All three commands free the control interval holding the record and release the string. Even if none of these three commands is executed, when a program ends, either normally or abnormally, the control interval and the string are also released. A program cannot execute two consecutive READ UPDATE commands on the same data set. Rather, the first record retrieved must be rewritten, deleted, or unlocked before issuing the second READ UPDATE command. However, two records, each in different data sets, can be read for update without rewriting the first one.

Both READ and READ UPDATE place the retrieved record into the WORKING-STORAGE or the LINKAGE SECTION, depending on whether INTO or SET is coded respectively. If an RRDS is being processed, the RRN parameter must be coded. If a record in a KSDS or ESDS is to be retrieved using its relative byte address, then RBA must be coded. RRN and RBA are mutually exclusive, and RBA cannot be used with an RRDS.

LENGTH need not be coded with fixed-length records, which are read into a data area of the correct size. Otherwise, LENGTH should be specified with the READ commands. With the INTO parameter, the largest possible record size should be coded for variable-length records. With the SET parameter, the data area coded with LENGTH contains the size of the record retrieved by the

READ operation. In this situation, LENGTH can be coded even though it is not required.

When retrieving a record from a KSDS using a complete key value, the RIDFLD parameter should identify a field in the WORKING-STORAGE or LINKAGE SECTION that is the same length as the KEYS(length) value that is stored in the data set's cluster component. The key field can be part of the 01-level structure identified with INTO (but not SET) that holds the retrieved logical record. With an RRDS, the RIDFLD keyword should identify a 4-byte binary field that is not part of the 01-level structure identified with INTO or SET. Unlike the key field in a KSDS, there does not have to be a field in the RRDS record that contains the slot number of the records. When retrieving a record from a KSDS or ESDS using the RBA value, RIDFLD should also identify a data-area field defined as 4-byte binary. This is because the RBA is processed as a 4-byte number.

KEYLENGTH and GENERIC are used for retrieving a record when a complete key is not specified with RIDFLD. When GENERIC is coded, KEYLENGTH must also be coded. However, the converse is not true. KEYLENGTH is not needed when a full key value is used on a local system, but KEYLENGTH is required to retrieve a record on a remote CICS system. Local and remote are discussed later in this section.

With CICS, the term *generic processing* is used to describe retrieval using less than a full key value. When less than the full number of characters in the key are specified, the characters must be the most significant, or left-most, in the key field. The value supplied with KEYLENGTH determines the number of characters in the RIDFLD data area to use as generic key. These characters are compared with the left-most bytes of the record keys. When specifying a generic key, RIDFLD must still identify a data area large enough to hold the full key of the record retrieved. With many commands, the full key value will be placed in the RIDFLD data-area after command execution is complete.

GTEQ and EQUAL are used to determine whether the partial or complete value coded with RIDFLD must exactly match the comparable portion of the key field of an existing record. EQUAL is the default value. When EQUAL is specified, an exact match must be found for the complete or generic key coded in RIDFLD. GTEQ will retrieve the first record with a key greater than, or equal to, the value coded in RIDFLD. This holds whether it is a complete key or a partial key.

For example, if READ...KEYLENGTH(1) GENERIC GTEQ RIDFLD(LAST-NAME) is coded and a partial key of 'N' is specified, the first last name record in the second half of the alphabet will be retrieved. If there is any record in the data set with a last name that starts with 'N', it will begin with an N. Otherwise, it will begin with a letter that follows N.

The local CICS system is the one on which the transaction was invoked. When there are multiple CICS systems, the others are categorized as remote, even though a remote system can be physically contained in the same computer as a local system. Specifically, each CICS has its own FCT. Files defined on a

```
Version 1               Version 2               Version 3

EXEC CICS READ          EXEC CICS READ          EXEC CICS READ
DATASET('DD1KSDS')      DATASET('DD1KSDS')      DATASET('DD1KSDS')
RIDFLD(KSDS-KEY)        RIDFLD(KSDS-KEY)        RIDFLD(KSDS-KEY)
INTO(MASTER-REC)        INTO(MASTER-REC)        SET(LS-POINTER)
LENGTH(REC-LEN)         LENGTH(REC-LEN)         KEYLENGTH(TWO-CHAR)
END-EXEC                UPDATE                  GENERIC
                        END-EXEC                EQUAL
                                                END-EXEC
```

Figure 16.4   Three methods for reading a KSDS record.

remote CICS system must have an entry in the local FCT identifying where they are located. Most other FCT information is not present for such a file.

Example 3.   Three variations of random record retrieval are shown in Fig. 16.4. A record in a KSDS is to be read with all three. Because the UPDATE parameter is not coded with the first and third versions, a read only operation is performed. In the first and second versions, the record is read into WORKING-STORAGE. In the third, it is identified in the LINKAGE SECTION, where it is processed in a buffer pointed to by the address in LS-POINTER. In the third version, generic processing is used. The first 2 bytes of the record key must exactly match the first 2 bytes in KSDS-KEY. In the first and second versions, variable-length records are read, and REC-LEN should contain the maximum record size. In Version 3, the LENGTH parameter could be coded to obtain the length of the record retrieved by the read operation.

To modify the commands in Fig. 16.4 to retrieve records from an RRDS, several changes are necessary. The LENGTH parameter should be omitted, and the DATASET and RIDFLD values changed. These modifications are shown in Fig. 16.5.

Full and Partial Keys and Generic Processing

The Random Read (READ and READ UPDATE) and Browse (STARTBR and RESETBR) commands contain two fundamental options for identifying the initial record to be retrieved.

```
EXEC CICS READ
DATASET('DD2RRDS')
RIDFLD(REL-SLOT-NO)
INTO(FIXED-LENGTH-FIELD) or SET(POINTER)  ..
RRN
END-EXEC
```

Figure 16.5   Reading a record in an RRDS.

TABLE 16.6 Full, Partial, and Generic Keys.

	Full Key Specified	Partial Key Specified
	The Default	*KEYLENGTH and GENERIC*
The Default *Complete* *Match (EQUAL)*	All N bytes must match or the NOTFND condition is raised.	From 1 to N-1 of the most significant (left-most) bytes must match.
Need not *Match (GTEQ)*	Any complete key equal to or greater than the search key value.	Any partial key (1 to N-1 bytes) equal to or greater than the value.

1. A complete or partial key can be coded with RIDFLD. KEYLENGTH should be coded with a partial key value to identify the length of the search key.

2. A match on the key field value or the first record with a greater than or equal to value can be specified with GTEQ. These concepts apply to both a KSDS and an RRDS. With a KSDS, they hold whether the primary key or an alternate key is coded with the RIDFLD parameter. These concepts also apply to an ESDS processed through an alternate key.

The four basic categories for identifying a record are categorized in Table 16.6. Assume an N byte key field. N must be less than 9 with an RRDS:

1. KEYLENGTH can be coded with DELETE to identify a generic delete operation. GENERIC must also be coded along with KEYLENGTH.

2. KEYLENGTH can be coded with READ NEXT. However, GENERIC should not be coded. Only complete keys are used with sequential and skip sequential processing.

Deadly embrace situations

A situation called a deadly embrace can occur when two distinct CICS tasks each want to read the same two records for update before continuing with processing. Clearly, each of the records must be in a distinct data set. Suppose the data sets have DDnames of ALPHA and BETA and the two records have key fields of 'X' and 'Y' respectively. In Fig. 16.6, the READ UPDATE commands in the two programs are identical but are executed in the reverse order within the program.

The first READ UPDATE command in each program completed before the second READ UPDATE command in the other program executed. Once the second commands are executed, each program is suspended while waiting for a record in a control interval held exclusively by the other program. Both programs will wait indefinitely until one of them is cancelled.

The two logical records that are to be processed by one of the programs need not be the same records processed by the other program. Rather, for each data set, the two records must be in the same control interval. Furthermore, the second READ UPDATE command in each program could be replaced by a WRITE or DELETE command involving a record in the control interval held by the other program.

Installation standards to prevent a deadly embrace

It is important for a CICS system to have some method of prohibiting deadly embrace situations or resolving them if they do occur. Unfortunately, CICS cannot do the job entirely by itself. One widely implemented technique is to assign a specific order in which to read from the two data sets. For example, they should be read in collating sequence order of their DDname values. Exercise 2 at the end of the chapter continues the discussion of deadly embraces.

Browse Operations—The STARTBR and RESETBR Commands

With CICS, the word *browse* is used to identify sequential processing. Before records in a data set can be browsed, the starting location for record retrieval must be identified. Either the STARTBR or RESETBR command can be used for this purpose. Both commands use exactly the same group of parameters, all of which are available with the random READ commands, except for REQID.

The STARTBR or RESETBR commands

Identifying the location at which to begin a browse is a random operation. Once a browse begins, all subsequent processing is sequential or skip sequential. With all three types of processing, records can be retrieved either in logical order or reverse logical order. Hence, the browse can be ordered on an ascending or descending key value, relative record number, or relative byte address.

```
                    Program 1                      Program 2

First        EXEC CICS READ              EXEC CICS READ
Command           UPDATE                      UPDATE
Executed          DATASET('ALPHA')            DATASET('BETA')
                  RIDFLD('X') ...             RIDFLD('Y') ...
                  END-EXEC                    END-EXEC

Second       EXEC CICS READ              EXEC CICS READ
Command           UPDATE                      UPDATE
Executed          DATASET('BETA' )            DATASET('ALPHA')
                  RIDFLD('Y') ...             RIDFLD('X') ...
                  END-EXEC                    END-EXEC
```

Figure 16.6 Two tasks locked in a "deadly embrace."

Version 1	Version 2	Version 3
EXEC CICS STARTBR DATASET('DD1KSDS') RIDFLD(KSDS-KEY) REQID(+0) END-EXEC	EXEC CICS STARTBR DATASET('DD1KSDS') RIDFLD(END-KEY) REQID(+1) END-EXEC	EXEC CICS RESETBR DATASET('DD1KSDS') RIDFLD(END-KEY) REQID(+1) KEYLENGTH(TWO-CHAR) GENERIC END-EXEC

Figure 16.7   Commands used to begin or reposition a browse.

The REQID parameter can be coded with STARTBR and RESETBR (Fig. 16.7), but it is not needed with the random READ commands. REQID is necessary only when a program is performing multiple concurrent browse operations with the same data set. REQID assigns a numeric value to identify each of the browses. If REQID is not coded, a default value of 0 is assigned. For example, a program might begin a forward browse from the beginning of a data set and a concurrent browse backwards from the end of the data set looking for some correlation between records at the extreme ends of the data set. These are some programming applications where multiple concurrent browse operations on the same data set are either necessary or convenient.

Each browse operation requires a separate string. The program holds the string until the browse is ended. Installation standards can prohibit multiple concurrent browses to avoid the possibility of no available strings.

The ENDBR and RESETBR commands

As with a READ UPDATE, there are several ways to end a browse. These include executing the ENDBR or RESETBR commands, normally or abnormally ending the program, and processing the last (or first) record in the data set. ENDBR ends an existing browse. The RESETBR command ends an existing browse and starts a new browse at another location in the data set. Whenever possible, coding RESETBR is preferable to maintaining two concurrent browses.

As mentioned previously, all the parameters except REQID have the same basic role as both the READ commands when beginning a browse operation. Because records are not actually read when beginning a browse, LENGTH, INTO, and SET parameters are not needed. It is the subsequent READNEXT or READPREV command that causes a record to be retrieved. The same type of generic processing is possible when starting a browse as when reading a record. Likewise, GTEQ can be specified with either STARTBR or RESETBR. Browsing can be done with any of the three VSAM data set organizations or through an alternate index over a KSDS or ESDS.

To begin a browse with the first record in a data set, STARTBR can contain an RIDFLD value of binary zeroes or KEYLENGTH(0) can be coded. Likewise, to begin a backward browse at the end of a data set, binary ones can be specified.

In this case, the Conceptual or Current Record Pointer (CRP) identifies End of File.

Example 4. The three READ commands illustrated in the last example are now replaced in Fig. 16.8 by the comparable code required to begin a browse operation. Assume that Version 1 and Version 2 identify concurrent browses on the same data set. This is to illustrate the REQID parameter, not a recommendation that this practice be routinely done. Version 3 ends the browse in Version 2 and starts a new browse using a generic key value.

Sequential processing—the READNEXT and READPREV commands

Sequential processing involves the READNEXT and READPREV commands, which browse the logical records in a data set. Both commands have exactly the same set of parameters, all of which, except for REQID, are also parameters with the random read commands. REQID is used to identify a specific browse when multiple concurrent browses are in progress. When an application has only one active browse in a given data set, REQID has a default value of 0 and need not be coded. SET, INTO, and LENGTH have the same meaning as when coded with a random read command. EQUAL, GTEQ, and GENERIC cannot be coded, but KEYLENGTH can. However, if KEYLENGTH is not coded, the browse retrieves each successive record in order. If KEYLENGTH is coded with either command, the next record retrieved by the browse has a key field value that matches the RIDFLD value. Further details are described in the next section. The RIDFLD should contain the same data name as that coded when the browse began. If a READNEXT and READPREV are executed in order, the same record is read twice.

Example 5. Two browses are to be performed concurrently. The STARTBR commands that identified the beginning records were coded in the last example as Version 1 and Version 2. The first browse will use ascending key values and the second descending key values. The Version 3 browse operation uses locate mode processing to read a variable-length record. It is not performed concur-

Version 1	Version 2	Version 3
EXEC CICS READNEXT DATASET('DD1KSDS') RIDFLD(KSDS-KEY) REQID(+0) INTO(MASTER-REC) LENGTH(REC-LEN) END-EXEC	EXEC CICS READPREV DATASET('DD1KSDS') RIDFLD(END-KEY) REQID(+1) INTO(MASTER-REC) LENGTH(REC-LEN) END-EXEC	EXEC CICS READNEXT DATASET('DD1KSDS') RIDFLD(KSDS-KEY) SET(LS-POINTER) LENGTH(REC-LEN) END-EXEC

Figure 16.8 Syntax used to browse records in a VSAM data set.

rently with the other two browses. The code for all three browse operations is shown in Fig. 16.8.

Skip sequential processing

CICS browse operations can specifically request that skip sequential processing be performed rather than true sequential processing. Skip sequential processing is an intermediate between random and true sequential processing in how it works. To request skip sequential processing during a browse operation, a value can be moved to the RIDFLD prior to a READNEXT command, and KEY-LENGTH coded with the command. (If this is not done, READNEXT processing is always sequential.)

The value placed in RIDFLD must be at least as large as the value placed in the field by the previous READNEXT command. Hence, to use skip sequential processing to read a group of records, the record keys must be specified in ascending, collating sequence order. Otherwise, another STARTBR or a RESETBR must be executed to move the browse operation to another location in the data set. The overhead of these two alternatives should be carefully compared.

Skip sequential processing can only be performed in a forward direction with a KSDS or RRDS. It is not permitted with the READPREV command. With a KSDS, this is because the pointers in the sequence set records that skip sequential processing uses are all forward pointers. In addition, generic processing cannot currently be performed with skip sequential processing.

Example 6. In Fig. 16.9, a group of logically adjacent records are retrieved using sequential processing. Following this, program logic specifies that skip sequential processing be performed. Note that browse operations are one CICS processing situation where standard structured programming is often emPployed. CICS has a reputation for unstructured coding practices.

Random VSAM Operations with CICS

Rewriting records

The REWRITE command is used to modify logical records. The REWRITE command has a simple syntax. Very few parameters can be coded. Usually, only the DDname and the area in WORKING-STORAGE or the LINKAGE SECTION that holds the record to be rewritten are used. The LENGTH parameter must also be coded when changing the length of a variable-length record. Some batch processing allows a rewrite operation to be performed without first reading the logical record. With CICS, a READ UPDATE command must be executed prior to a REWRITE command.

Unless the file has been designated as recoverable, the REWRITE command unlocks the control interval and releases the string. Recoverable files maintain the control interval look until the program itself explicitly releases it.

```
    PERFORM BROWSE-LOOP UNTIL (no more records to process)
    . . .
BROWSE-LOOP.
    process the previously read record
    EXEC CICS READNEXT
        DATASET('DD1KSDS')
        RIDFLD(KSDS-KEY)
        INTO(MASTER-REC)
        END-EXEC

Program logic causes a switch to skip sequential processing

    MOVE KSDS-KEY TO CHANGE-KEY-VALUE.
    MOVE KEY-VALUE TO SKIP-SEQ-FLAG.

    EXEC CICS READNEXT
        DATASET('DD1KSDS')
        RIDFLD(KSDS-KEY)
        KEYLENGTH(KEY-VALUE)
        INTO(MASTER-REC)
        END-EXEC
```

Figure 16.9 Switch from sequential to skip sequential.

Example 7. In Fig. 16.10, the record read in Example 3 is to be rewritten. The code shown here can be used only in conjunction with Version 2 in that example. This is because the other versions do not contain the UPDATE parameter. If the length of the record is to be changed, the code in Version 2 in Fig. 16.10 is used.

Deleting records

The DELETE command physically deletes records from a KSDS or RRDS. DELETE cannot be coded with an ESDS. There are three distinct ways in which a record can be deleted. The DELETE command can be executed with RIDFLD containing a complete key value. If the data set contains a record with a matching key value, the record is deleted. If the DELETE command is executed with RIDFLD containing a partial key value, a generic delete is performed. All records whose leading key characters match the value in RIDFLD are deleted. Finally, if a READ UPDATE is executed, the record read can be deleted by issuing a DELETE command where the RIDFLD parameter is not

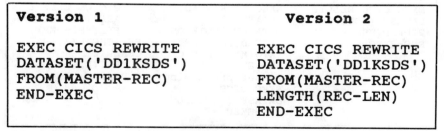

```
Version 1                    Version 2

EXEC CICS REWRITE            EXEC CICS REWRITE
DATASET('DD1KSDS')           DATASET('DD1KSDS')
FROM(MASTER-REC)             FROM(MASTER-REC)
END-EXEC                     LENGTH(REC-LEN)
                             END-EXEC
```

Figure 16.10 Syntax used for rewriting records.

coded. Records in a KSDS are physically deleted. Record slots in an RRDS are marked as empty. Their contents cannot be accessed by an application program.

Following a generic delete, the data-area coded with NUMREC contains the number of records deleted. Generic deletion should be done with the greatest of care. The number in the KEYLENGTH parameter determines the number of bytes in the RIDFLD value to use as the partial key. A mistake of one digit in the KEYLENGTH value could produce disasterous results. It is a simple exercise to write the necessary code to perform a generic delete in a batch application program.

Example 8. Three versions of the DELETE command are coded in Fig. 16.11. Version 1 deletes a single logical record, whose complete key matches the value coded with RIDFLD. Version 2 deletes the same record after it had been previously read for update. In this case, RIDFLD should not be coded with DELETE. Version 3 deletes every record whose three, left-most key field bytes match the value in the first three bytes in KSDS-KEY. Unlike previous examples, a literal is coded with KEYLENGTH in Version 3.

The records in an RRDS can also be deleted. With some minor changes, the three examples shown in Fig. 16.11 are also valid with an RRDS. The KSDS-KEY field must be replaced by a field with S9(8) COMP attributes. The KEYLENGTH value cannot be greater than 8, and the RRN parameter must be included with all three versions of the command. The following summarizes the three basic versions of the DELETE command:

1. Delete a KSDS record that has not been read for update:

    EXEC CICS DELETE DATASET('DD1KSDS') RIDFLD(PRI-KEY) END-EXEC

2. Delete a KSDS record that has been read for update. Note: RIDFLD should not be coded, or an INVREQ condition will be raised:

    EXEC CICS DELETE DATASET('DD1KSDS') END-EXEC

```
Version 1            Version 2              Version 3

EXEC CICS DELETE     EXEC CICS READ         EXEC CICS DELETE
DATASET('DD1KSDS')   UPDATE                 DATASET('DD1KSDS')
RIDFLD(KSDS-KEY)     DATASET('DD1KSDS')     RIDFLD(KSDS-KEY)
END-EXEC             RIDFLD(KSDS-KEY)       KEYLENGTH(3)
                     INTO(MASTER-REC)       GENERIC
                     END-EXEC               NUMREC(DEL-COUNT)
                     (other processing)     END-EXEC
                     EXEC CICS DELETE
                     DATASET('DD1KSDS')
                     END-EXEC
```

Figure 16.11 Syntax used to delete records from a KSDS.

```
EXEC CICS DELETE DATASET('DD1KSDS')
                 RIDFLD(KSDS-KEY)
                 KEYLENGTH(NUMBER-OF-BYTES) GENERIC
                 NUMREC(NUMBER-DELETED)
                 END-EXEC
```

Figure 16.12 A complete generic delete command.

3. Generically delete a group of logical records from a KSDS. Reading for update is not relevant in this context. After command execution is completed, NUMBER-DELETED will contain the number of records deleted. Both the KEYLENGTH and NUMREC fields should be half-word binary values. A generic delete is coded in Fig. 16.12.

All three versions of the DELETE command are also valid with an RRDS. The RRN parameter must be coded, the RIDFLD data-value must identify a full-word binary integer, and the KEYLENGTH value must be less than 8 for a generic delete.

Records can be deleted during a browse operation. Either DELETE or DELETE...RIDFLD can be used. In either case, the browse should be terminated prior to the delete.

Writing records

The WRITE command is used to randomly add records to a KSDS or RRDS data set. The name of the data set, the RIDFLD value, and the area in the application program containing the contents of the record to be written must always be coded. The rules for coding LENGTH are the same as performing a READ operation. With a KSDS or RRDS, the record is added to the data set in the location determined by the key value or relative record number. With an ESDS, the record is always added at the end of the data set. Following the WRITE operation with an ESDS, the RIDFLD contains the RBA of the record just written. This value can then be used in subsequent random read operations.

Example 9. Records are to be added to a KSDS, ESDS, and RRDS respectively. The code for all three is very similar and is shown in Fig. 16.13.

```
Version 1-KSDS         Version 2-ESDS         Version 3-RRDS

EXEC CICS WRITE        EXEC CICS WRITE        EXEC CICS WRITE
DATASET('DD1KSDS')     DATASET('DD2ESDS')     DATASET('DD3RRDS')
RIDFLD(KSDS-KEY)       RIDFLD(ESDS-RBA)       RIDFLD(RRN-VALUE)
FROM(MASTER-REC)       FROM(MASTER-REC)       FROM(MASTER-REC)
LENGTH(REC-LEN)        RBA                    RRN
END-EXEC               LENGTH(REC-LEN)        END-EXEC
                       END-EXEC
```

Figure 16.13 Syntax to add a record to a KSDS, ESDS, and RRDS.

Using the RIDFLD parameter value with a WRITE command. With a KSDS, the application supplies the key field value prior to the WRITE. With an RRDS, the application provides the slot number value prior to the WRITE. With an ESDS, CICS returns the RBA where the record was written after the WRITE is completed.

Using the MASSINSERT parameter with the WRITE command. The The MASSINSERT parameter can be coded when several records are to be added in succession. Furthermore, if keys are used, the records should be written in ascending key order. MASSINSERT retains in memory the buffer that contains the control interval until it is completely filled or the last record in the group is written. The buffer is then copied to disk. MASSINSERT is functionally similar to performing sequential processing in the middle of a data set. MASSINSERT can be used only with a KSDS. Mass insertion operations can also be performed during batch processing.

Example 10. In Fig. 16.14, a group of three or more records are to be inserted into a KSDS. All of the records have consecutive key field values. The input records are being provided from a CICS temporary storage queue. After all the records are added, the UNLOCK command terminates the MASSINSERT processing mode.

Deallocating resources

The UNLOCK and ENDBR commands do not perform I/O operations. Rather, they release resources that were allocated by previous commands. In the prevalent programming style used with CICS, called *non-conversational*, these two commands are infrequently used.

The UNLOCK command is used in two situations. First, it is coded following a READ UPDATE command, when it is decided not to perform the update (or delete) operation. Program logic determines when an UNLOCK command should be executed. After the UNLOCK is executed, the control interval that

```
        PERFORM ADD-LOOP UNTIL (no more records to process)
        . . .
        EXEC CICS UNLOCK
            DATASET('DD1KSDS')
            END-EXEC
ADD-LOOP.
        Read a Record from a Temporary Storage Queue.
        Move Temporary Storage Queue Record Fields to MASTER-REC.
        EXEC CICS WRITE
            DATASET('DD1KSDS')
            RIDFLD(KSDS-KEY)
            FROM(MASTER-REC)
            MASSINSERT
            END-EXEC
```

Figure 16.14 Inserting multiple records into a KSDS.

Version 1	Version 2	Version 3
EXEC CICS UNLOCK DATASET('DD1KSDS') END-EXEC	EXEC CICS ENDBR DATASET('DD1KSDS') REQID(+1) END-EXEC	EXEC CICS UNLOCK DATASET('DD1KSDS') END-EXEC

Figure 16.15 Deallocating control intervals and strings.

holds the record and the associated VSAM string are both released and available for other applications. Second, UNLOCK is also coded to end a MASSINSERT operation. Hence, any following WRITE commands will be processed randomly. Only the name of the data set needs to be specified with the UNLOCK command.

The ENDBR command is used to end a browse operation. The string associated with the browse, which is held by the task, is released. Two parameters can be coded with ENDBR. The name of the data set is required. If multiple browses are in progress with the same data set, then REQID must be coded to identify a specific browse.

Example 11.   A record has been read for update in a KSDS and it is decided not to perform the update. Hence, an UNLOCK is issued. Later, in the same data set, two browses are taking place. One of them is ended by the ENDBR command shown in Version 2 in Fig. 16.15. Still later a MASSINSERT operation is to be terminated. This is shown in Version 3.

Alternate Key Processing with CICS

Alternate indexes are extremely important in an on-line programming environment. Several specific comments relevant to alternate key processing with CICS are made here. This section primarily discusses syntax; program logic is examined in the next section.

The FCT contains an entry for each path defined over a base cluster. This is in addition to the base cluster FCT entry. The alternate index itself is not defined in the FCT.

It is unnecessary to create a separate 01-level structure to hold the records retrieved via an alternate index. Rather, a single, 01-level structure should be included in your program. No matter whether a logical record is retrieved directly from a base cluster or through an alternate index, the record structure remains the same. Thus, the only differences in the READ command occurs in the DATASET parameter where the base cluster and path are specified respectively and in the RIDFLD parameter. The RIDFLD value coded with a path should reflect the length of the associated alternate key. With both the locate and move mode, it is the DATASET value that determines how the base record is actually accessed. On the average, accessing a record through an alternate index will take approximately twice as long as accessing it directly through the

Version 1	Version 2	Version 3
EXEC CICS READ	EXEC CICS READ	EXEC CICS READ
DATASET('DD1KSDS')	DATASET('DD4PATH')	DATASET('DD4PATH')
RIDFLD(KSDS-KEY)	RIDFLD(AIX-KEY)	RIDFLD(AIX-KEY)
INTO(MASTER-REC)	INTO(MASTER-REC)	SET(POINTER1)
LENGTH(REC-LEN)	LENGTH(REC-LEN)	LENGTH(REC-LEN)
END-EXEC	END-EXEC	END-EXEC

Figure 16.16 Commands for processing through an alternate index.

base cluster. If UPGRADE is specified and there are multiple alternate indexes, it could take even longer.

Example 12. Fig. 16.16 shows the code to read records from a base KSDS using the primary key in Version 1 and through an alternate index in Version 2 (move mode) and Version 3 (locate mode). Note that there are exactly two differences between Version 1 and Version 2.

Program design

Often, a CICS program is sequentially processing records that have the same alternate key value and the program ends before the complete group of records is processed. This routinely occurs with non-conversational programs. When the program resumes execution, it is difficult to commence reading at the exact location where processing previously terminated. This results because a read operation specifying the alternate key value used during the previous execution now retrieves the first record with this as the alternate key value. A unique value (primary key or RBA) should be used to locate the last record processed by the previous task. With a KSDS, this is not exceptionally difficult. It is somewhat more complicated with an ESDS.

Alternate key processing with CICS is conducive to data integrity problems. Unlike batch processing, an alternate index or path is often created with NOUPGRADE or NOUPDATE specified. It is common to process a base cluster and its alternate indexes with NOUPGRADE specified because response time is superior. However, users often become suspicious of a CICS system that retrieves a record using the primary key but cannot find the record when the alternate key is used. Remember, response time can be more important than correctness.

Adding a single alternate index approximately doubles the processing time for an operation through the alternate index and its associated path. Adding N alternate indexes increases the processing time by a factor of approximately $N+1$ for add, delete, and change operations if UPGRADE is specified. Processing time is still only doubled for record retrieval.

A group of records with the same alternate key value is processed in exactly the same order, regardless of whether READNEXT or READPREV is used. In other words, alternate key processing reflects the record order produced by the BLDINDEX command and the chronological additions and deletions that followed, no matter which direction processing occured. Results such as this occur because of the way an alternate index record is built and managed by VSAM.

Browsing through an alternate index is not nearly as fast as using a primary key or RBA value. Although browsing is a sequential operation, every record must be randomly retrieved when an alternate index is used. This should be considered when response time is crucial.

Exceptional CICS Conditions

In a batch processing environment, an exceptional condition results in a non-zero status code, even though the program continues to execute. With CICS, the standard default option for almost every exceptional condition is to abend the program. However, the default value can be overridden if the application program specifies a routine to be performed whenever a specific condition occurs. RESP codes and HANDLE CONDITIONS can occur when processing a VSAM data set with CICS. An RESP code is more-or-less equivalent to a batch VSAM status code. A HANDLE CONDITION is an earlier technique that eventually accomplishes the same results.

Table 16.7 shows the VSAM related exceptional conditions that can be raised (occur) with CICS and the commands with which the exceptional condition might occur. CICS conditions are even more important than batch status codes because the results are more dramatic if they are not effectively dealt with. There are two layers in Table 16.7. The first group of conditions are the most significant; the second group is included for completeness.

TABLE 16.7   VSAM Exceptional (HANDLE) Conditions with CICS.

VSAM/CICS Exceptional Condition	READ or READ UPDATE	STARTBR or RESETBR	READ NEXT or PREV	WRITE	REWRITE	DELETE	UNLOCK	ENDBR
DUPKEY	X		X					
DUPREC					X			
ENDFILE			X					
ILLOGIC	X	X	X	X	X	X	X	X
INVREQ	X	X	X	X	X	X		X
IOERR	X	X	X	X	X	X	X	
LENGERR	X		X	X	X			
NOSPACE				X	X			
NOTFND	X	X	X		X	X		
DSIDERR	X	X	X	X	X	X	X	X
NOTOPEN	X	X	X	X	X	X	X	X
SYSIDERR	X	X	X	X	X	X	X	X

VSAM exceptional conditions

The most common reasons for each of the exceptional conditions occurring in Table 16.7 are described in this section. This is not an all-inclusive list, however. Consult the *CICS Application Programmer's Reference Manual (Command Level)* for more details.

DSIDERR   The data set is not defined to CICS. The value coded with DATA-SET must be an entry in the FCT. A comparable situation in a batch environment, will result in a JCL error. Every VSAM-related command can cause this condition.

DUPKEY   DUPKEY can only occur when reading records through an alternate index. It means that there are additional records that contain the same alternate key value as the record just read. However, DUPKEY will not occur when reading the last record in the group with the same value. This indicates that another sequential operation will retrieve a record that contains a different alternate key value. Unless dealt with by an RESP field or HANDLE CONDITION by the programmer, a DUPKEY condition will cause a program to abend. Note that this is a much more severe response than that which results in a batch program when records with duplicate alternate key values are read.

DUPREC   With a KSDS, DUPREC means that an existing record contains the same key as the RIDFLD parameter identified on a WRITE statement. With an RRDS, the record slot identified by RIDFLD contains an active record. DUPREC can also occur when processing a KSDS with an alternate index over it if a duplicate alternate key is contained in a record about to be written, and UNIQEKEY is specified in the cluster component for the alternate index.

ENDFILE   ENDFILE can only occur during a browse operation. With READ-NEXT, it means that end of file has been reached. With READ-PREV processing it means that the front of the data set has been reached. In either case, the browse should then terminate. A sequential input operation (READNEXT or READPREV) can cause an ENDFILE condition to occur with any type of VSAM data set.

ILLOGIC   ILLOGIC can occur with every VSAM command. It is a catch-all condition that is raised when a VSAM error occurs that is not covered by any of the other exceptional conditions. Often, additional CICS control fields must be examined to determine the specific cause of the condition.

INVREQ A VSAM command cannot be performed for one of any number of reasons. Several common situations would include A READ UPDATE command that was not issued but a REWRITE or a DELETE without an RIDFLD is attempted. A READNEXT, READPREV, ENDBR, or RESETBR is issued but no browse operation is in progress. An operation is requested for a data set, but the operation is not listed as valid in the FCT. Two READ UPDATE commands are executed successively on the same data set without an intervening command to end the first one. REWRITE, DELETE, or UNLOCK must be used for this purpose. An attempt is made to begin a browse with a REQID value that already exists.

IOERR   Like ILLOGIC, IOERR is a catch-all condition for VSAM I/O errors that are not covered by other exceptional conditions. In fact, IOERR is assigned to those situations that get by ILLOGIC.

LENGERR LENGERR results from a number of common processing situations. LENGTH is not coded with a MOVE mode input or output operation with variable-length records. An attempt is made to write a record bigger than the maximum logical record value stored in the FCT. An incorrect length is specified when processing fixed-length records. A record is read using MOVE mode, which is bigger than the maximum logical record value stored in the FCT.

NOSPACE No storage is available in which to write a record. This can occur with any of the three types of VSAM data sets. A rewrite of a variable-length record in a KSDS can also cause this to occur.

NOTFND NOTFND usually occurs when trying to perform a READ or STARTBR command. The data set does not contain a record that matches the RIDFLD value coded. NOTFND can also occur when specifying a key value with a DELETE command and no matching record can be found. If a record is read for update and its RIDFLD is changed, NOTFND could occur on a REWRITE operation.

NOTOPEN The data set named in the command is not open. Often, external help is required to correct the problem. NOTOPEN will result when a data set is temporarily deallocated in order to perform batch processing such as reorganization.

Exercises

1. Describe the results that occur when each of the group of CICS VSAM commands in Fig. 16.17 are attempted. Each set of commands is independent of

```
a) EXEC CICS READ UPDATE DATASET('X') RIDFLD(KEY1-FIELD) END-EXEC
   EXEC CICS READ UPDATE DATASET('Y') RIDFLD(KEY2-FIELD) END-EXEC
   EXEC CICS REWRITE DATASET('Y') END-EXEC
   EXEC CICS REWRITE DATASET('X') END-EXEC

b) EXEC CICS READ UPDATE DATASET('X') RIDFLD(KEY1-FIELD) END-EXEC
   EXEC CICS DELETE DATASET('X')        RIDFLD(KEY2-FIELD) END-EXEC
   EXEC CICS REWRITE DATASET('X') END-EXEC

c) EXEC CICS READ UPDATE DATASET('X') RIDFLD(KEY1-FIELD) END-EXEC
   EXEC CICS READ UPDATE DATASET('X') RIDFLD(KEY2-FIELD) END-EXEC
   EXEC CICS REWRITE DATASET('X') END-EXEC
   Which record is actually rewritten, KEY1 or KEY2?

d) EXEC CICS READ UPDATE DATASET('X') RIDFLD(KEY1) END-EXEC
   EXEC CICS READNEXT DATASET('X')    RIDFLD(KEY1) END-EXEC
   EXEC CICS READNEXT DATASET('X')    RIDFLD(KEY1) END-EXEC

e) EXEC CICS READ DATASET('X')        RIDFLD(KSDS-KEY) END-EXEC
   EXEC CICS DELETE DATASET('X')      RIDFLD(KSDS-KEY) END-EXEC

f) EXEC CICS READ DATASET('X')        RIDFLD(KEY1) END-EXEC
   EXEC CICS WRITE DATASET('X')       RIDFLD(KEY2) END-EXEC
   EXEC CICS REWRITE DATASET('X') END-EXEC

g) EXEC CICS READ UPDATE DATASET('X') RIDFLD(KEY1) END-EXEC
   EXEC CICS WRITE DATASET('X')       RIDFLD(KEY2) END-EXEC
   EXEC CICS REWRITE DATASET('X') END-EXEC

h) EXEC CICS READ UPDATE DATASET('X') END-EXEC
   EXEC CICS REWRITE DATASET('X')     RIDFLD(KSDS-KEY) END-EXEC

i) EXEC CICS READ UPDATE DATASET('X') RIDFLD(KSDS-KEY) END-EXEC
   EXEC CICS DELETE DATASET('X') GENERIC NUMREC(REC-COUNT) END-EXEC

j) EXEC CICS STARTBR DATASET('X')  REQID(+0) END-EXEC
   EXEC CICS READNEXT DATASET('X') REQID(+0) END-EXEC
   EXEC CICS STARTBR DATASET('X')  REQID(+1) END-EXEC
   EXEC CICS READNEXT DATASET('X') REQID(+1) END-EXEC
   EXEC CICS READNEXT DATASET('X') END-EXEC (no REQID coded)

k) EXEC CICS STARTBR DATASET('X') END-EXEC
   EXEC CICS READNEXT DATASET('X') END-EXEC
   EXEC CICS READ UPDATE DATASET('X') END-EXEC
   EXEC CICS READ DATASET('X') END-EXEC
   EXEC CICS RESETBR DATASET('X') END-EXEC
```

Figure 16.17 Syntax and logic problems with CICS statements.

the others. Thus, assume that no additional CICS commands precede or intermix with the commands coded for each question. Identify specific CICS exceptional conditions that might result. With many commands, irrelevant parameters are not shown.

2. A deadly embrace occurs when one task needs a resource held by a second task. Explain how a potential deadly embrace situation involving two programs, each trying to update records in the same control intervals in two data sets, can be avoided by specifying appropriate coding standards, specific program logic or design, or some other approach. Can a deadly embrace involve just one control interval? If so, how? Can a single program cause a deadly embrace condition? If so, how? Can one data set cause a deadly embrace condition? If so, how? Can a deadly embrace occur with a

```
a)  EXEC CICS READ UPDATE DATASET('PRI') RIDFLD('150') END-EXEC
    EXEC CICS DELETE DATASET('PRI') END-EXEC
    EXEC CICS READ DATASET('ALT') RIDFLD('JONES') END-EXEC

b)  EXEC CICS DELETE DATASET('PRI') RIDFLD('2')
         NUMREC(REC-COUNT) GENERIC KEYLENGTH('1') END-EXEC

c)  EXEC CICS READ UPDATE DATASET('ALT') RIDFLD('JONES') END-EXE
    EXEC CICS DELETE DATASET('ALT') END-EXEC

d)  Move 125 to PRI, SMITH to ALT
    EXEC CICS WRITE DATASET('PRI')     RIDFLD('125') END-EXEC
    EXEC CICS WRITE DATASET('ALT') RIDFLD('SMITH') END-EXEC
    EXEC CICS STARTBR DATASET('ALT') RIDFLD('SMITH') END-EXEC
    EXEC CICS READNEXT DATASET('ALT') END-EXEC
    EXEC CICS READNEXT DATASET('ALT') END-EXEC
    EXEC CICS READNEXT DATASET('ALT') END-EXEC
    EXEC CICS READNEXT DATASET('ALT') END-EXEC
    EXEC CICS WRITE DATASET('ALT') RIDFLD('SMITH') END-EXEC

e)  EXEC CICS STARTBR DATASET('ALT') KEYLENGTH('2')
         RIDFLD('BB') GENERIC GTEQ END-EXEC
    EXEC CICS READNEXT DATASET('ALT') END-EXEC
    EXEC CICS READPREV DATASET('ALT') END-EXEC
    EXEC CICS READPREV DATASET('ALT') END-EXEC
    EXEC CICS READPREV DATASET('ALT') END-EXEC

f)  EXEC CICS READ UPDATE DATASET('PRI') RIDFLD('300') REQID(1)
         END-EXEC
    EXEC CICS READNEXT DATASET('ALT') REQID(1) END-EXEC
    EXEC CICS READNEXT DATASET('ALT') REQID(1) KEYLENGTH(3)
         RIDFLD END-EXEC

g)  EXEC CICS STARTBR DATASET('ALT') RIDFLD('QQQQQ')END-EXEC
    EXEC CICS READPREV DATASET('ALT') END-EXEC

h)  EXEC CICS STARTBR DATASET('PRI') REQID(1) RIDFLD('000')
         GTEQ END-EXEC
    EXEC CICS STARTBR DATASET('ALT') REQID(2) RIDFLD('AAAAA')
         GTEQ END-EXEC

i)  EXEC CICS STARTBR DATASET('ALT') RIDFLD('ZZZZZ') END-EXEC
    EXEC CICS READPREV DATASET('ALT') END-EXEC
```

Figure 16.18 Tracing CICS program execution with VSAM data sets.

TABLE 16.8 Key Fields for Exercise 4.

Record Number	Primary Key Value	Alternate Key Value
1	100	SMITH
2	150	JONES
3	200	SMITH
4	250	ALPHA
5	300	SMITH
6	350	JONES
7	400	JONES

VSAM data set that is not a KSDS? If so, how? How are deadly embrace situations affected when the data sets involved are recoverable?

3. Write the CICS commands and accompanying PL/I or pseudo-code in ascending order based on key value that are required to read all the records in a KSDS. Assume that 15 records can be displayed on a terminal screen at one time. Hence, the records should be read in groups of 15, and the bottom record on one screen becomes the top record on the next screen. How can this code be modified to read the same records in descending key order? Finally, read the records in ascending order based on an alternate key value. Duplicate alternate keys can exist. How can this code be modified to read the same records in descending key order?

4. A KSDS defined to CICS contains seven records. The primary and alternate key values for each record are listed in Table 16.8. Trace the results of performing each of the segments of code listed in Fig. 16.18. Numerous invalid situations occur. Specify the appropriate CICS conditions raised. The DATA-SET parameter will contain one of two values—'PRI' or 'ALT'—depending on whether processing is performed on the primary or secondary key. In this case, ALT identifies the path over the base cluster. Each set of commands is independent of the others and assumes the status shown in Table 16.8. Irrelevant parameters are not shown with many commands.

5. Much of the information used to process a VSAM data set provided in a batch application program cannot be included within a CICS application program. How are the following types of information concerning a VSAM data set supplied to CICS?:

- Data set name to identify the actual data set.
- DDname to identify the actual data set.
- Types of access permitted.
- Logical record size and record format.
- Access method.
- The length and location of the key field.

17

Optimizing VSAM's Performance

The material in this chapter is not concerned with explaining how to use VSAM, but rather how to use VSAM wisely. Wisely for the application programmer employing VSAM for specific processing and wisely for other, concurrent applications on the system competing for resources. A broad overview of the types of optimization features available with VSAM is included, followed by a detailed discussion of several of the most significant optimization features, including buffers and string numbers. Finally, the remaining optimization features are discussed.

Scope Of Optimization

A large number of optional programming choices can be made in order to increase the speed and efficiency with which VSAM performs I/O operations. The appropriate features to use are determined by two major factors: (1) The specific data set organization, and (2) the type of processing being done. Many of these optimization options can be selected with the DEFINE CLUSTER command when the data set is initially created.

These options are, for the most part, permanent, although a few of them can be modified with the ALTER command. Other options can be coded within an executing application program. Assembler allows the largest number of these, but some are permitted with COBOL and PL/I. Still others can be specified through JCL with the AMP or DISP parameters on a DD statement or the JOB-CAT/STEPCAT DD statements. Those specified through JCL or application code are, in effect, for a single job step. Finally, some can be assigned by a systems programmer, such as when VSAM is used with an on-line teleprocessing monitor such as CICS.

TABLE 17.1   VSAM Optimization Features.

Optimizing Feature	IDCAMS DEFINE CLUSTER	IDCAMS ALTER	Application Program	JCL AMP/DISP Others	System Tables
REPLICATE	X	X			
IMBED	X	X			
Data and index components on different volumes	X				
KEYRANGES	X	X			
Buffers and BUFFERSPACE	X	X	X	X	
Sharing buffers			X		X
CI size (Data and Index)	X				
Location of the keyfield in the logical record	X				
String numbers			X	X	
CI locking and deadly embrace			X		
Alternate indexes (update offline)	X	X	X		
Minimize CI splits	X	X	X		
Prohibit CA splits, i.e. No secondary allocations	X	X			
Skip sequential processing			X		
Catalog structure				X	
Catalog search	X			X	
Dynamic allocation and DISP=OLD or DISP=SHR	X			X	

With on-line programming, the speed of various I/O operations is especially crucial to system performance. Optimizing features and where they can be specified are shown in Table 17.1. An X identifies the one or more categories used to specify the option. By analyzing Table 17.1, it appears that buffers and strings are probably two of the most common and important factors in optimizing VSAM's performance because they can be specified in so many ways. Buffers are the only item that occurs in each of the categories. In addition, strings and buffers are interrelated. Ordinarily, the string number value is used to determine the total amount of buffer space for all data set users.

Buffers and Buffer Space

Buffers are the part of an application program's region used to hold data as it is read from, or written to, control intervals on disk. When batch sequential processing is performed, the blocking factor is often more important than the number of buffers. The more buffer space available, the more data set records that can be held concurrently in memory.

There are two advantages to having as many buffers as possible. Program execution will not need to be suspended to wait for an I/O operation to complete. The fewer actual I/O operations that must be performed, the faster a program executes. Unnecessary I/O operations should always be avoided.

Before an actual disk read operation is performed with a VSAM data set, the buffers will first be searched to see if one of them contains the desired CI. VSAM can perform several logical operations that add and change records in a control interval in a buffer before writing the modified control interval to disk. The programmer has some control over this. Hence, the greater the number of buffers, the fewer I/O operations that need to be performed. By default, a KSDS is assigned two data buffers and one index buffer. It is the role of the index buffer that is the most crucial in determining processing time with random processing.

Whenever a VSAM data set consists of one control area, the default single buffer is sufficient to hold the complete index component, which is a single control interval (record). With multiple control areas, there are at least two levels of index records. For simplicity, assume there are exactly two levels of index. If only one index buffer is available, two actual I/O operations involving the index must be performed for every random I/O operation. This is illustrated in Fig. 17.1.

The single index buffer is required to initially hold the high-level index CI. The sequence set must then be read into the same buffer. This process is repeated for each random retrieval. Hence, two buffers should minimally be assigned to the index when multiple control areas exist. This way, the high-level index control interval can always be kept in one buffer. With additional buffers, fewer read and write operations involving the sequence set control intervals need to be performed.

Generally, one buffer should be available for each level in the index structure. Recall that one, second-level index record can ordinarily monitor a very large number of sequence set control intervals. Hence, only an extremely large data set will contain three or more levels of indexes.

When performing random processing with a KSDS, each I/O operation frequently accesses a different data control interval. Unlike the case with index control intervals, the present contents of the data buffers are usually irrelevant when performing the next I/O operation. Hence, two buffers should be provided for data control intervals. The second buffer is needed whenever a control interval split occurs.

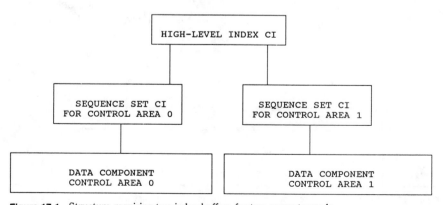

Figure 17.1 Structure requiring two index buffers for two separate reads.

TABLE 17.2   Buffers Required for a Single Application Program.

KSDS Component	Buffers Needed for Random Processing	Buffers Needed for Sequential Processing
Data Component	2 (1 for CI splits)	as many as possible often 5 or more
Index Component	minimally one for each index level and sequence set	1

Sequential processing with a KSDS is basically similar to sequentially processing an ESDS data set. For the data component, as many buffers as possible should be specified. This way, read ahead processing can be done and the program does not have to halt and wait for I/O to be performed. Five or more data control interval buffers are frequently used during sequential processing.

When sequentially processing a KSDS, one buffer is usually sufficient for the index component. There are two reasons for this. Ordinarily, there are many data control intervals associated with one sequence set record. Second, during sequential processing, the horizontal pointers in the sequence set records are used to locate the next sequence set record. It is unnecessary to examine any of the higher-level index records. This is further examined with skip sequential processing below. Table 17.2 summarizes the results covered in this section.

Skip Sequential Processing

The method used to perform sequential processing can also be used for direct processing with minor modifications by using the horizontal rather than the vertical pointers to locate the next sequence set or higher-level index record. This method is called skip sequential processing. Ordinarily, only one buffer is needed for the index. Note that in Fig. 17.2, the two sequence set records require the high-level index record only for the first record read. Remaining

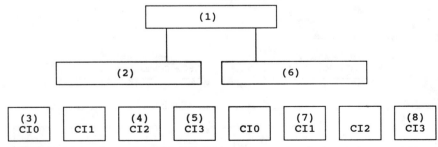

Figure 17.2   Order of record retrieval with skip sequential processing.

read operations begin with the sequence set record. In this case, the control intervals are retrieved in the numeric order shown in the Fig. 17.2.

Random processing requires that the records being accessed be in ascending order by key value in order to use skip sequential processing. This will ordinarily require all transactions to be batched and sorted before the I/O operations can be performed. This should be weighed against the overhead associated with true random processing, where every I/O operation always begins with the highest-level index record.

String Numbers

String numbers cannot be specified with the IDCAMS DEFINE CLUSTER command. A string is assigned to each primary user or program processing a VSAM data set. A string number is used to limit the number of users concurrently processing a VSAM data set. String numbers can prohibit too many jobs from trying to process the records in the data set. This is especially important in an on-line environment. A single, on-line user can tie up more than one string. In addition, Table 17.2 must now be modified to account for the number of buffers required by the N concurrent users that the string number permits. Suppose that a string number of N is specified. This permits up to N concurrent users, and the values for a single string in Table 17.2 are now modified to become the values shown in Table 17.3.

A string is not released until the program explicitly releases it or finishes executing. A batch program ordinarily holds only one string for each VSAM data set. An on-line program associated with a TP monitor or database management system can have two or more. They are released by rewriting or deleting records read for update, ending browses, or explicitly releasing the string. Often, the total string number value assigned to a VSAM data set is quite small.

Disk I/O Considerations

The time it takes to perform disk I/O operations is dependent on three factors:

1. The time it takes to move the read/write head or access arm (access arm movement).

TABLE 17.3   Buffer Requirements with N Strings.

KSDS Component	Buffers Needed for Random Processing	Buffers Needed for Sequential Processing
Data Component	N + 1	as many as possible often 5*N or more
Index Component	# of index levels - 1 + N	N

2. The time it takes the disk to rotate (rotational delay).

3. The amount of time required to actually read or write the data (rate of data transfer).

The first two of these factors are affected by the next optimization parameters. Only the index component is directly affected by IMBED and REPLICATE. The rate of data transfer is fixed for a given amount of data.

The IMBED parameter

The IMBED parameter is used to reduce the time required for access arm movement. In theory, placing the sequence set record in the same cylinder as its associated data control interval would require no access arm movement. There is no guarantee, however, that the sequence set record and data control interval will be read consecutively. It is quite possible that another I/O request to the same volume will occur between the two operations. When this happens, the benefits supposed to be associated with IMBED do not result. These hidden seeks can, of course, occur at any time. There is only one way to guarantee that this does not happen. The VSAM data set must be the only data set on the volume. With a very large or very important data set, this might be quite reasonable. When this is not the case, IMBED is of minimal benefit. With multiple concurrent accesses to a single data set, the effects of IMBED are lost. Remember that IMBED subtracts 1 track from the associated data control area.

The REPLICATE parameter

The REPLICATE parameter is used to reduce rotational delay. Like IMBED, this seems like a good idea when speed is an important issue. However, there are several disadvantages. The data in a single index control interval now occupies an entire track. With read only processing, this might not be significant, but suppose an index record must be changed. In this case, every copy of the control interval must be rewritten.

On a positive note, there is very little rotational delay during rewrite operations. In some cases, changing one index control interval causes changes in a second control interval. REPLICATE is an excellent choice for a data set whose index records will almost never be changed (e.g., a data set whose records are read only retrieved). One other point should be noted. Disk drive speeds continue to increase. Maximum rotational delay is not as significant as it was one or two decades ago.

CI and CA splits and the FREESPACE parameter

In order to increase processing efficiency, fewer I/O operations should be done. A control interval split requires a minimum of three I/O operations unless one or more of the control intervals involved are in buffers. Hence, a control interval split slows processing. How can control interval splits be minimized? Sufficient freespace should be provided to minimize the occurrance of a split. Examine a LISTCAT of the data set on a periodic basis to determine if control interval splits are occuring too frequently, or at all. When appropriate, recreate the data set with a larger space allocation and the same or larger freespace values.

Control area splits are far more time-consuming than control interval splits. During a control area split, a theoretical minimum of five data and index control intervals must be written or modified. At the worst, several hundred I/O operations must be performed. The average lies somewhere between these extremes. Because a control area split requires a secondary allocation, significant cluster information must also be modified. The same techniques used to minimize control interval splits can also be applied to avoid control area splits.

The second FREESPACE value should be carefully chosen. Output from the LISTCAT command should be monitored to determine if any control area splits have occurred. In addition, SHR(X 4) can be coded. This pair of values prohibits control area splits. It is important to note that a secondary allocation is not allowed when control area splits are prohibited. Conversely, if there is no secondary allocation, there can be no control area split.

When selecting values to code with the FREESPACE parameter, care must be taken not to specify extremely large percentages. This is wasteful of disk storage, both in the data and index component. In fact, in some data sets, it can result in an additional index level.

These factors must be balanced against the time required to read a LISTCAT and, if necessary, recreate the data set. It is surprising that VSAM does not contain any feature equivalent to the ISAM reorganization statistics. There is no easy way for an application program to inspect the cluster totals for control interval splits and control area splits and then make a dynamic decision on whether a reorganization is necessary.

Locking Out a User Application

An application program can request exclusive control of an entire data set, a control interval, or a single logical record. In all three circumstances, the exclusively controlled object cannot be processed by any other application program.

The SHAREOPTIONS parameter

Exclusive control of an entire data set must be coded with the SHAREOPTIONS parameter or by requesting a DISP value of OLD. This request can either be explicit, by coding DISP = OLD on a DD statement or implicit, by coding INDATASET or OUTDATASET with the REPRO and PRINT commands. When a record is read with the declared intent of updating it, the entire control interval containing the record is held in exclusive control until the update operation completes or is cancelled. This commonly occurs with CICS programs. A record can be held exclusively by coding SHR(1 x).

With exclusive control on both the control interval and record level, a deadly embrace situation can develop. Suppose CICS programs A and B are processing records in the same data set. Program A has read record X and intends to update it. However, it must read record Y for some information needed to do the update. Records X and Y are in different control intervals. Program B has read record Y and intends to update it. However, it must read record X for some information needed to do the update. Program A has exclusive control of the control interval containing record X, and program B has exclusive control of the control interval containing record Y. Neither program can process any records in the control interval held by the other program. A deadly embrace results. To end the deadly embrace, one of the two programs must be cancelled.

The ENQ macro

Another method to gain exclusive control of a VSAM resource is the ENQ macro, which is not restricted to just VSAM data sets. Once issued, no other program can use the resource until it is released by the DEQ macro. The resource can be one logical record, a control interval, or an entire data set.

Alternate indexes

Alternate indexes, which reduce the burden of work for an application programmer, are a very powerful and important component of VSAM. Many applications require the use of one or more alternate indexes and accompanying paths. However, if a change in a base cluster record causes a change in an alternate index, the amount of actual I/O approximately doubles. In an on-line environment where speed is essential, the alternate key modification is often postponed. Although the alternate indexes are still allowed, processing modifying the alternate index cannot be permitted while the on-line system is running. The NOUPGRADE parameter can be used for this.

When the on-line system is down, a batch program can then be run to reflect all the changes to the alternate indexes. This is done to avoid the delays caused by permitting on-line updating of alternate indexes. Clearly, for each additional alternate index, the delay becomes greater. Note that the ALTER command can be used to switch back and forth between UPGRADE and NOUPGRADE.

By prohibiting alternate index modification, one significant problem remains. Suppose a user has added a record to a data set using Social Security number as the primary key and last name as the alternate key. The add was successful. Soon after, the same user tries to retrieve the record using the last name. VSAM responds that the record does not exist (because the access is through the alternate index). This can cause the user to doubt that any part of the program can be trusted. Users must be told the alternate indexes are upgraded in a batch job when the on-line system is down. The record can always be retrieved using the primary key.

Placing Data and Index Components on Different Volumes

Under some circumstances when processing a KSDS, processing can be speeded up if the data and index components are placed on different disk volumes. When this is done, I/O operations can be simultaneously performed with both components. This type of processing should be contrasted with placing both components on the same volume. While a data record is processed, nothing can be done with the index component. Like IMBED, this feature is of questionable value when many other users are processing data sets concurrently on the same volume. Under idealized conditions, it is a relevant optimization factor. Recall that, when IMBED is coded, the sequence set record is placed on the same volume (cylinder) as the data component.

The KEYRANGES parameter

The KEYRANGES parameter, which specifies where a logical record is to be written from among several disk volumes, can only be coded with a KSDS. The range of key values associated with each disk volume are selected in the DEFINE CLUSTER command. Using KEYRANGES should be contrasted with creating a multivolume data set, because it gives the programmer more control over where records are to be placed and how roughly equivalent parts of the data set relative to their key values.

For example, if last name is used as the key, the data set can be placed on four disk volumes by coding VOLUME (WORK01 WORK01 WORK03 WORK04) and KEYRANGES ((A E),(F K),(L R),(S Z)). Every record whose key begins with a letter from A to E inclusive is placed on WORK01. Those records whose first key byte ranges from F to K inclusive are placed on WORK02, etc. The two keyrange values can be complete keys or generic values as these.

The ORDERED parameter is used with KEYRANGES when the preceding division of a data set is desired. Otherwise, volumes are used in the order in which they are listed in the DEFINE CLUSTER. Without coding KEYRANGES and ORDERED, the time at which a record is added to a multivolume data set is more important than its key value in determining which volume will hold the record. More syntax of both parameters is described with the DEFINE CLUSTER command in chapter 4.

Dynamic Allocation Control Interval Size

Control intervals are equivalent to non-VSAM physical records or blocks. The same criteria that are used to determine a 'good' or 'optimal' block size can also be used with control intervals in the data and index components. Small CIs result in more I/O being performed with sequential processing and a lower proportion of the disk being used to hold actual data. Large CIs result in a large amount of buffer space being required when processing the data set.

There is a drawback to small index CIs. Small index CIs can lead to processing inefficiencies or problems when they are not large enough to contain index entries for all the data CIs in a CA. This is never a problem with large index CIs. A fundamental point to consider is the number of CIs in the CA. This value, times the size of an average index entry, should be smaller than the index CI size—31.

There is some advantage to small data CIs when most of the processing is random. This is analogous to small blocks or unblocked ISAM data sets. There is a strong possibility that no other records in the CI will be processed. Hence, there is no advantage to reading a very large block which, exclusive of the present record, will not be used.

One other important point. Small CIs are much more likely to require CI splits if many records are randomly added to a data set. All factors being equal, the frequency of requiring a CI split is proportional to the size of the CI.

Catalog Structure and Catalog Search

How an installation creates its catalog structure can either optimize retrieval time for a data set or considerably lengthen it. On most systems, there is one master catalog that contains the two basic types of entries: important system data sets (SYS1.xxxxxxxx) and the names of aliases for user catalogs. Most data sets are thus actually cataloged in one of the many user catalogs that the system contains. Catalog structure and details of how the catalog is searched are an important consideration in processing VSAM data sets. All of chapter 12 is devoted to catalogs. The role of the JOBCAT and STEPCAT DD statements must also be considered.

Location of the key field

There are several processing advantages associated with having the key field for a KSDS as the first field within a record because the key field can be accessed more efficiently. For sorting operations, the key field(s) should always be the beginning field(s) in the record for maximum efficiency. Otherwise, duplicate copies are created at the beginning of the records. This is standard throughout MVS systems.

Shared buffers

Major applications should be permitted to share their buffers. If this is not done, major processing problems will almost certainly occur. This topic is discussed in the *VSAM Advanced Applications* manual.

Type of VSAM data set

Naturally, processing speed is affected by the type of data set selected for the processing. In general, an RRDS is superior to a KSDS for random processing.

| | Index Buffers | | Data Buffers | |
	On-line	Batch	On-line	Batch
Sequential Processing				
Random Processing				

Figure 17.3   Determining buffer requirements.

An ESDS can also be processed randomly through an alternate index and by specifying an RBA. The trade-offs among a KSDS, RRDS, and ESDS are discussed in detail in chapters 10 and 11.

Exercises

1. It is possible to dynamically reorganize an ISAM data set using the values in the three reorganization parameter fields that are available to an application programmer, the step return code, and the COND parameter or (IF-THEN-ELSE JCL logic). How can a comparable dynamic reorganization be performed with a VSAM KSDS? Where and what values must be examined to determine if such a reorganization is necessary, and where is this information located? Can these values be interrogated while a program is executing?

2. If possible, describe a situation where exactly five data and index CIs need to be processed during a CA split. Can a smaller number ever occur? Is five a possible number on a 3350 disk, a 3380 disk or a 3390 disk? Give the details in each case, including index CI size, data CI size, and the number of CIs in a CA. What is the minimum number of CIs that must be processed if there are three levels in the index structure.

3. Suppose you are in charge of maintaining an on-line system that processes a VSAM KSDS data set with a maximum of seven concurrent users. Hence, STRNO = 7. There are three levels in the index structure of the KSDS, the sequence set plus two others, as it is an extremely large data set. Supply the "optimal" number of buffers for both the data and index components when doing both sequential and random processing in Fig. 17.3. Along with each numeric value, briefly supply the reason why the specific value is required. Finally, if the data set is to be used for batch processing rather than on-line processing, what do the answers become?

4. A KSDS is to be updated in an on-line environment. The secondary key accompanying alternate index processing is not to be performed until the on-line system is brought down. Supply all of the details as to how the base cluster and AIX can subsequently be resynchronized to remove any data integrity problems.

5. Describe a set of circumstances for each of the following options a reason to reduce the amount of time required to perform an I/O operation: REPLI-

CATE, IMBED, KEYRANGE, separate volumes for DATA and INDEX components, where coding them will substantially

6. An index CI should be sufficiently large so that Index CI size = (average index entry)*(#CIs/CA) + 31. Verify that this formula is correct. Explain the role of 31.

Index